W9-DGM-644

THE YIGAEL YADIN MEMORIAL FUND
under the auspices of
THE HEBREW UNIVERSITY OF JERUSALEM • THE ISRAEL EXPLORATION SOCIETY

MASADA VI
The Yigael Yadin Excavations 1963–1965
Final Report

THE MASADA REPORTS

Editors
Joseph Aviram, Gideon Foerster, Ehud Netzer

Associate Editor
Alan Paris

Trustees of Yadin's literary legacy
N. Avigad , J. Aviram, A. Ben-Tor

MASADA VI

Yigael Yadin Excavations 1963–1965
Final Reports

HEBREW FRAGMENTS FROM MASADA

SHEMARYAHU TALMON

With Contributions by Carol Newsom and Yigael Yadin

THE BEN SIRA SCROLL FROM MASADA

YIGAEL YADIN

With Notes on the Reading by Elisha Qimron
and Bibliography by Florentino García Martínez

(pages 151–252)

DS
110
.M39Y122
v.6
seab, over

ISRAEL EXPLORATION SOCIETY
THE HEBREW UNIVERSITY OF JERUSALEM

JERUSALEM 1999

84847

Publication of this volume was made possible by a grant
from the Dorot Foundation, U.S.A.

© 1999 by the Israel Exploration Society
ISBN 965–221–034–x

All enquiries relating to the reproduction of any part of this book should be referred to
the Israel Exploration Society

Typeset and printed by Z. Ben-Zvi Hafakot Ltd., Jerusalem
Layout: A. Pladot; Plates by Old City Press Ltd., Jerusalem

Yigael Yadin
21.3.1917–28.6.1984

FOREWORD

Following a three year hiatus, we are pleased to present scholars and the interested public with the sixth volume in the Masada final excavation report series. The current volume includes the Hebrew written fragments from the Masada excavations, directed by the late Yigael Yadin from 1963–1965. Professor Yadin entrusted publication of the fragments reported in the first part of this volume to Professor Shemaryahu Talmon of the Hebrew University of Jerusalem.

The Ben Sira Scroll from Masada, presented in the second part of this volume, was first published by Yigael Yadin immediately following its discovery in 1965, in honor of the opening of the Shrine of the Book in Jerusalem. We are indebted to Professor Elisha Qimron, who has prepared notes reflecting developments in the study of the Ben Sira scroll from Masada since its initial publication over 33 years ago, presented at the end of this book. Despite the passage of time, Yadin's thorough and complete *editio princeps* remains largely unchanged and unchallenged. Its inclusion here was prompted by our desire that all of the Hebrew scroll fragments found at Masada be made available in a single volume. Several technical improvements made in the presentation of Yadin's material further justify, we believe, this re-presentation of the Ben Sira Scroll from Masada. These include a more convenient presentation of the restored Hebrew and English texts, new and improved photographs of the scroll, and a list of publications on Ben Sira that have appeared since Yadin completed his book in 1965. Sincere thanks go to Professor Florentino García Martínez who prepared this bibliography.

With completion of this volume, there still remain several topics from Yadin's Masada excavations which have not yet been brought to press. These include the pottery, weapons, and artifacts of glass, stone, iron, bone, bronze, leather, and wood as well as floral and faunal remains. This material is still being prepared for publication in future volumes that will also cover findings from the renewed Masada excavations, underway for several years.

The publication of Yadin's scholarly legacy began immediately following his death in 1984 and included final reports in three series:

— Masada final reports — Six volumes have been completed and a seventh is in preparation
— Hazor final reports — The text of *Hazor III–IV* and a combined volume of text and illustrations, *Hazor V*, have been published
— The Judean Desert Series final reports — Two volumes of documents from Naḥal Ḥever. One devoted to Greek documents, has been published. The second, dealing with the Hebrew, Aramaic and Nabataean documents is still in preparation.

Thus, the complicated project of publishing Yadin's scholarly legacy is nearing completion. We express sincere thanks to the many individuals who devoted themselves to the tasks that made this enterprise possible, and to the many private and institutional contributors without whose assistance the project could have never been undertaken.

These publications constitute a living memorial to Yigael Yadin and his unparalleled contribution to Israel archaeology. Through them, the results of Yadin's scholarship will be made readily accessible to future generations.

JOSEPH AVIRAM

HEBREW FRAGMENTS FROM MASADA

SHEMARYAHU TALMON

The Hebrew University of Jerusalem

With Contributions by Carol Newsom and Yigael Yadin

CONTENTS

[3]

List of Illustrations

[4]

List of Abbreviations

Ancient Sources

LXX   = Septuagint
MT   = Masoretic Text
OL   = Old Latin
PsJ   = Targum Pseudo Jonathan to the Pentateuch
Sam   = Samaritan Hebrew Version of the Pentateuch: A. Freiherr von Gall ed., *Der Pentateuch der Samaritaner* (Giessen: Töpelmann, 1914–1918).
SamTg = Samaritan Aramaic Targum
Sym   = Symmachus
Syr   = Peshitta
Targ   = Aramaic translations
TFr   = Fragment Targum to the Pentateuch
TJ   = Targum Jonathan to the Prophets
TJer   = Jerusalem Targum of the Pentateuch, Ms Neofiti
TO   = Targum Onkelos
V   = Vulgata
VSS   = Ancient Versions

Major Manuscripts of MT

A = Aleppo Codex
C = Cairo Codex of the Prophets
L = Ms Leningrad B19a
S = Ms Sassoon 1053

Hebrew Bible Editions

BH(S)   = Biblia Hebraica (Stuttgartensia)
Ginsburg = C.D. Ginsburg, תורה נביאים כתובים, מדויק היטב על פי המסורה ועל פי דפוסים ראשונים עם חלופים והגהות מן כתבי יד עתיקים ותרגומים ישנים (London: Bible Society, 1908–1926; repr. Jerusalem, 1970)
Snaith   = N.H. Snaith, ספר תורה נביאים וכתובים מדויק היטב על פי המסורה (London, 1958)

Abbreviations of Qumran Texts and Editions

1QapGen = Genesis Apocryphon
1QH = Thanksgiving Scroll
1QIsa[a] = First Isaiah Scroll
1QIsa[b] = Second Isaiah Scroll
1QM = Scroll of the War of the Sons of Light Against the Sons of Darkness
1QpHab = Pesher Habakkuk
1QS = Rule of the Community
11QTemp = The Temple Scroll
CD = Damascus Covenant

Discoveries in the Judaean Desert series (Oxford: Clarendon):

DJD I = D. Barthélemy and J.T. Milik, *Qumrân Cave 1* (1955)

DJD II = P. Benoit O.P., J.T. Milik, R. de-Vaux O.P., *Les Grottes de Murabbaʿat* (1961)

DJD III = M. Baillet, J.T. Milik, R. de Vaux O.P., *Les 'Petites Grottes' de Qumrân* (1962)

DJD IV = J.A. Sanders, *The Psalms Scroll of Qumrân Cave 11 (11QPsᵃ)* (1965)

DJD V = J.M. Allegro, *Qumrân Cave 4. I (4Q158–4Q186)* (1968)

DJD VII = M. Baillet, *Qumrân Grotte 4. III (4Q482–4Q520)* (1982)

DJD IX = P.W. Skehan, E. Ulrich and J.E. Sanderson, *Qumran Cave 4. IV Palaeo-Hebrew and Greek Biblical Manuscripts* (1992)

DJD X = E. Qimron and J. Strugnell, *Qumran Cave 4. V Miqṣat Maʿaśe Ha-Torah* (1994)

DJD XI = E. Eshel et al., *Qumran Cave 4. VI, Poetical and Liturgical Texts, Part 1* (1998)

DJD XII = E. Ulrich et al., *Qumran Cave 4. VII Genesis to Numbers* (1994)

DJD XIII = E. Tov and J.C. VanderKam ed., *Qumran Cave 4. VIII Parabiblical Texts, Part 1* (1994)

DJD XIV = E. Ulrich ed., *Qumran Cave 4. IX Deuteronomy, Joshua, Judges, Kings* (1995)

DJD XIX = M. Broshi et al., *Qumran Cave 4. XIV Parabiblical Texts, Part 2* (1995)

DJD XX = T. Elgvin et al., *Qumran Cave 4. XV Sapiential Texts, Part 1* (1995)

DJD XXII = G. Brooke et al., *Qumran Cave 4. XVII Parabiblical Texts, Part 3* (1996)

Freedman-Mathews, *Leviticus* = D.N. Freedman and K.A. Mathews, *The Paleo-Hebrew Leviticus Scroll (11QPaleoLev)* (Winona Lake, IN: Eisenbrauns, 1985)

Qimron, *CD* = E. Qimron, The Text of CD, in: M. Broshi ed., *The Damascus Document Reconsidered* (Jerusalem: IES/ The Shrine of the Book, 1992)

Rabin, *CD* = C. Rabin ed., *The Zadokite Documents. I. The Admonition. II. The Laws* (Oxford: Clarendon, 1954)

Text Editions of Apocrypha and Pseudepigrapha

Charles, *Little Genesis* = R.H. Charles, *The Book of Jubilees, or The Little Genesis* (Oxford: Clarendon, 1902)

Charles, Jubilees = The Book of Jubilees, in R.H. Charles ed., *The Apocrypha and Pseudepigrapha of the Old Testament in English* etc., vol. II (Oxford: Clarendon, 1913) 1–82

Milik-Black, *Enoch* = J.T. Milik and M. Black, *The Book of Enoch* (Oxford: Clarendon, 1976)

VanderKam, *Jubilees* = *The Book of Jubilees*, trans. J.C. VanderKam, *Corpus Christianorum Orientalium* 511 (Louvain: Peeters, 1989)

VanderKam, *Text* = J.C. VanderKam, *Textual and Historical Studies in the Book of Jubilees, Harvard Semitic Monographs* 14 (Missoula, MO: Scholars Press, 1977)

Greek and Roman Literature

Hist. nat. = Pliny, *Naturalis Historiae*

War = Josephus, *The Jewish War*

Rabbinic Literature

b. = Babylonian Talmud

j. = Jerusalem Talmud

m. = Mishnah

Massekhet Soferim = M. Higger ed., *Massekhet Soferim etc.* (New York: Bloch, 1937; repr. Jerusalem: Makor, 1970); *idem., Seven Minor Treatises* etc. (New York: Bloch, 1930); R. Kirchheim ed., *Septem Libri Talmudici parvi Hierosolymitani* (Francfurti a/M: Kaufmann, 1851)

MidHag = Midrash Hagadol

MidRab = Midrash Rabba

MidTan = Midrash Tanḥuma, ed. S. Buber (New York: Horowitz, repr. 1946)

t. = Tosefta, ed. Zuckermandel

tL = Tosefta, ed. Lieberman

YalShim = Yalkut Shimʿoni

Tractates in the Babylonian Talmud:

Shab. = Shabbat	*Meg.* = Megillah
Sanh. = Sanhedrin	*Men.* = Menaḥot

Periodicals and Serials

AB	Anchor Bible
BA	Biblical Archaeologist
BASOR	Bulletin of the American Schools for Oriental Research
BCH	Bulletin de Correspondance Hellénique
BIES	Bulletin of the Israel Exploration Society
BJPES	Bulletin of the Jewish Palestine Exploration Society
BJRL	Bulletin of the John Rylands Library, Manchester
BKAT	Biblischer Kommentar zum Alten Testament
BZAW	Beihefte zur Zeitschrift für die Alttestamentliche Wissenschaft
DJD	Discoveries in the Judaean Desert
DSD	Dead Sea Discoveries
EAE	Encyclopaedia of Archaeological Excavations in the Holy Land
EI	Eretz-Israel
HTR	Harvard Theological Revue
HUCA	Hebrew Union College Annual
IDB	The Interpreter's Dictionary of the Bible
IEJ	Israel Exploration Journal
JAOS	Journal of the American Oriental Society
JBL	Journal of Biblical Literature
JJS	Journal of Jewish Studies
JSJ	Journal for the Study of Judaism
JSOT	Journal for the Study of the Old Testament
JSS	Journal of Semitic Studies
NTS	New Testament Studies
OLP	Orientalia Lovaniensia Periodica
PSBA	Proceedings of the Society of Biblical Archaeology
RB	Revue Biblique
RQ	Revue de Qumrân
Shnaton	An Annual for Biblical and Ancient Near Eastern Studies
Textus	Annual of the Hebrew University Bible Project
VT	Vetus Testamentum
VTSup	Supplement to Vetus Testamentum
ZNTW	Zeitschrift für die Neutestamentliche Wissenschaft

Publications Frequently Cited

Aharoni, Expedition B = Y. Aharoni, Expedition B, *IEJ* 11 (1961) 11–24

Albright, Nash = W.F. Albright, A Biblical Fragment from the Maccabaean Age: The Nash Papyrus, *JBL* 56 (1937) 145–76

Avigad, Palaeography = N. Avigad, The Palaeography of the Dead Sea Scrolls and Related Documents, *Scripta Hierosolymitana* IV, ed. C. Rabin and Y. Yadin (Jerusalem: Magnes, 1958) 56–87

Bruneau, Délos = P. Bruneau, Les Israélites de Délos et la Juiverie Délienne, *BCH* 106 (1982) 467–79

Cross, Scripts = F.M. Cross, Jr., The Development of the Jewish Scripts, *The Bible and the Ancient Near East. Essays in Honor of W.F. Albright*, ed. G.E. Wright (Garden City, NY: Doubleday, 1961; repr. Winona Lake, IN: Eisenbrauns, 1979) 133–202

Deichgräber, Fragmente = R. Deichgräber, Fragmente einer Jubiläen-Handschrift aus Höhle 3 von Qumran, *RQ* 5 (1964–66) 415–22

Kippenberg, *Garizim* = H.G. Kippenberg, *Garizim und Synagoge* (Berlin: de Gruyter, 1971)

Lewis, *Papyrus* = N. Lewis, *Papyrus in Classical Antiquity* (Oxford: Clarendon, 1974)

Lieberman, *Hellenism* = S. Lieberman, *Hellenism in Jewish Palestine* (New York: JTS, 5711–1950)

Maori, Tradition = Y. Maori, The Tradition of Pisqaʾot in Ancient Hebrew MSS: The Isaiah Texts and Commentaries from Qumran, *Textus* 10 (1982) 1–50 (Hebrew)

Masada I = Y. Yadin and J. Naveh, *Masada I. The Aramaic and Hebrew Ostraca and Jar Inscriptions* (Jerusalem: IES/ Hebrew University, 1989)

Masada II = H.M. Cotton and J. Geiger, *Masada II. The Latin and Greek Documents* (Jerusalem: IES/ Hebrew University, 1989)

Masada III = E. Netzer, *Masada III. The Yigael Yadin Excavations 1963-1965. Final Reports* (Jerusalem: IES/ Hebrew University, 1991)

Naveh, *Alphabet* = J. Naveh, *Early History of the Alphabet* (Jerusalem: Magnes/ Leiden: Brill, 1982)

Nebe, Handschrift = G.W. Nebe, Die Masada Psalmen-Handschrift M1039-160 nach einem jüngst veröffentlichen Photo mit Text von Psalm 81,2–85,6, *RQ* 14 (1989) 89–97

Newsom, 4QApocryphon = C. Newsom, 4QApocryphon of Joshua[a–b] (4Q378–379), *DJD* XXII 241–88

Newsom, *Songs* = C. Newsom, *Songs of the Sabbath Sacrifice: A Critical Edition* (Atlanta, GA: Scholars Press, 1985), revised edition in *DJD* XI

Newsom-Yadin, Songs = C. Newsom and Y. Yadin, The Masada Fragment of the Qumran 'Songs of the Sabbath Sacrifice', *IEJ* 34 (1984) 77–88, reprinted in the present volume

Oesch, *PUS* = J.M. Oesch, *Petucha und Setuma, Orbis Biblicus et Orientalis* 27 (Fribourg/ Göttingen: Vandenhoeck & Ruprecht, 1979)

Perrot, Alinéas = Ch. Perrot, *Petuhot et Setumot:* Étude sur les Alinéas du Pentateuque, *RB* 76 (1969) 50–91

Perrot, *Lecture* = Ch. Perrot, *La Lecture de la Bible dans la synagogue: Les anciennes lectures palestiniennes du Shabbat et des fêtes* (Hildesheim: Olms, 1973)

Puech, Notes = E. Puech, Notes sur le manuscrit des Cantiques du Sacrifice du Sabbat trouvé à Masada, *RQ* 12 (1987) 575–83

Pummer, Criterion = R. Pummer, ΑΡΓΑΡΙΖΙΝ: A Criterion for Samaritan Provenance, *JSJ* 18 (1987) 18–25

Purvis, *Samaritan* = J.D. Purvis, *The Samaritan Pentateuch and the Origin of the Samaritan Sect, Harvard Semitic Monographs* 2 (Cambridge, MA: Harvard University Press, 1968)

Reynolds, *Scribes* = L.D. Reynolds, *Scribes and Scholars. A Guide to the Transmission of Greek and Latin Literature* (Oxford: Clarendon, 1968, 1974²)

Rofé, Fragments = A. Rofé, Fragments of Another Manuscript of the Book of Jubilees from Qumran Cave 3 (3QJub), *Tarbiz* 34 (1965) 333–36 (Hebrew)

Siegel, *Scribes* = J.P. Siegel, *The Scribes of Qumran. Studies in the Early History of Jewish Scribal Customs. With Special Reference to the Qumran Biblical Scrolls and to the Tannaitic Traditions of Massekhet Soferim.* Ph.D. Dissertation, Brandeis University 1972 (Ann Arbor, MI: University Microfilms, 1972)

Talmon, *KCC* = S. Talmon, *King, Cult and Calendar in Ancient Israel* (Jerusalem: Magnes, 1986)

Talmon, Renewed Covenant = S. Talmon, The Community of the Renewed Covenant: Between Judaism and Christianity, *The Community of the Renewed Covenant. The Notre Dame Symposium on the Dead Sea Scrolls*, ed. E. Ulrich and J.C. VanderKam (Notre Dame, IN: Notre Dame University Press, 1994) 3–24

Talmon, Textual Study = The Textual Study of the Bible — A New Outlook, *Qumran and the History of the Biblical Text*, ed. F.M. Cross and S. Talmon (Cambridge, MA: Harvard University Press, 1975) 321–400

Talmon, *WQW* = S. Talmon, *The World of Qumran from Within* (Jerusalem: Magnes, 1989)

Torczyner, *Lachish* = H. Torczyner et al., *Lachish I. The Lachish Letters* (Oxford: Clarendon, 1938)

Tov, Consonants = E. Tov, Interchanges of Consonants between the Masoretic Text and the *Vorlage* of the Septuagint, *Sha'arei Talmon. Studies in the Bible, Qumran and the Ancient Near East Presented to Shemaryahu Talmon*, M. Fishbane and E. Tov, ed. with the assistance of W.W. Fields (Winona Lake, IN: Eisenbrauns, 1992) 255–66

Tov, Manuscripts = E. Tov, Hebrew Biblical Manuscripts from the Judaean Desert: Their Contribution to Textual Criticism, *JJS* 39 (1988) 5–37

Tov, Orthography = E. Tov, The Orthography and Language of the Hebrew Scrolls found at Qumran and the Origin of the Scrolls, *Textus* 13 (1988) 31–57

Tov-Pfann, *Microfiche* = E. Tov with the collaboration of S.J. Pfann ed., *The Dead Sea Scrolls on Microfiche: Companion Volume* (Leiden: Brill, 1993)

Turner, *Papyri* = E.G. Turner, *Greek Papyri. An Introduction* (Princeton: Princeton University Press, 1968)

Tur-Sinai, מנצפ״ך = N.H. Tur-Sinai, מנצפ״ך צופים אמרום, *Halashon weHasefer. Volume Halashon* (Jerusalem: Kiryath Sefer, 1948) 10–31

Yadin, *Ben Sira* = Y. Yadin, *The Ben Sira Scroll from Masada* (Jerusalem: IES / Shrine of the Book, 1965), reprinted in the present volume

Yadin, *EAE* = Y. Yadin, Masada, *Encyclopaedia of Archaeological Excavations in the Holy Land*, ed. M. Avi-Yonah (Jerusalem: Masada, 1975) 793–816

Yadin, Expedition D = Y. Yadin, Expedition D, *IEJ* 11 (1961) 36–52

Yadin, *Fortress* = Y. Yadin, *Masada — Herod's Fortress and the Zealots' Last Stand* (London: Weidenfeld & Nicholson/ New York: Random House, 1966)

Yadin, *IEJ* 15 = Y. Yadin, *The Excavations of Masada 1963/64. Preliminary Report, IEJ* 15 (1965)

Yadin, Qumran (Hebrew) = Y. Yadin, Qumran and Masada, *BIES* 30 (1966) 117–27

Yadin, Zealot = Y. Yadin, Masada: A Zealot Fortress, *Archaeological Discoveries in the Holy Land. Compiled by The Archaeological Institute of America* (New York: Crowell, 1967) 169–74

Yalon, מנצפ״ך = H. Yalon, מנצפ״ך לפי מקורות חז״ל, *Studies in the Dead Sea Scrolls* (Jerusalem: Shrine of the Book/ Kiryath Sefer, 1967) 12–4

Technical Conventions

— A margin is always taken as part of the column to the right of it.

— Inter-line spaces are measured from the letter tops in one line to the letter tops in the next line.

— The first number in measurements pertains to the width of a given item, the second to the height of it.

[ ] — Reconstructed text

{ } — Superlinear letters

· — Partially preserved letter

° — Traces of a letter

PREFACE

The rich finds of artefacts and of written documents discovered in the excavations of Masada, conducted by the late Yigael Yadin in two seasons, 1963/4 and 1964/5, also included remains of fifteen manuscripts in the Hebrew language, fourteen of which are written on parchment in the Hebrew square alphabet, and one on papyrus in the Palaeo-Hebrew script. Yadin published in a critical edition the fragments of a scroll of the *Wisdom of Ben-Sira* (*Ecclesiasticus*) in the original Hebrew version, and, together with Carol Newsom, a fragment of a work entitled *Songs of the Sabbath Sacrifice*, of which larger parts had been found among the discoveries in the Qumran caves (both items are reprinted in the present volume), but commented only briefly on the other items. After his untimely death, their publication was entrusted to me by the editors of *The Masada Reports*, Joseph Aviram, Gideon Foerster and Ehud Netzer. I wish to thank them for including this volume in the series, and for assistance and advice at various stages of its preparation.

Early photographs of the fragments, taken by the late Mrs. H. Bieberkraut, were provided by the editors of the *Reports*, and by Magen Broshi, past Curator of the Shrine of the Book, in which the fragments were initially kept. More recent photographs, taken at my request, are published here courtesy of the Israel Antiquities Authority. Magen Broshi and his successor Adolfo Roitman, as well as Lena Liebman and the team of restaurators at the Rockefeller Museum where the fragments are now deposited, readily placed the originals at my disposal, whenever rechecking of particulars was called for.

I benefitted from information provided by Ehud Netzer concerning certain aspects of the excavation reports, and from discussing some of my readings with Ada Yardeni and Emanuel Tov, and especially with Joseph Naveh.

Carol Newsom kindly supplied for inclusion in the present volume an edited version of 'The Masada Fragment of the Qumran Songs of the Sabbath Sacrifice,' which she had co-authored with Yigael Yadin (*IEJ* 34 [1984] 77–88).

In the initial stages of work on the fragments, I was assisted in succession by Garth Gilman and Daliah Amarah. Shlomo Ketko and Sarah Collins copyedited my manuscript. Alan Paris was most helpful in seeing the manuscript through the press. Mr. Z. Ben-Zvi, director of Z. Ben-Zvi Hafakot Ltd., marshalled the resources of his publishing house for the production of this volume, and gave it his personal attention. I express thanks to all of them.

PREFACE

I wish to thank the chairpersons and the members of the Research Committee of the Faculty of Humanities of the Hebrew University of Jerusalem, as well as Joseph Aviram and the Israel Exploration Society, for granting financial assistance towards the completion of the project.

Very special thanks go to my assistant Jonathan Ben-Dov who never tired of checking readings, offered valuable comments, and proofread my text at various stages of its preparation and final production.

Introduction

The excavations of Masada, led by Yigael Yadin, yielded a considerable number of inscribed artefacts, among them remains of fourteen parchment documents written in Hebrew square characters, and one papyrus fragment penned in the ancient Hebrew alphabet.[1]

Most fragments were found in the second half of November 1963, the first year of the excavations, in locus 1039, the third casemate of the fortress wall, near the 'synagogue'.[2] However, the exact dates of the finds were not recorded in all instances.

Because of the importance of "the locus of the scrolls",[3] I quote in extenso relevant parts of E. Netzer's description of that locus in the definitive excavation report, and the circumstances of the discovery of the fragments (*Masada* III, 416–22):

> *Casemate 1039 — the "Casemate of the Scrolls"* (length 9.2–12.4 m, width 3.4–3.8 m). It was no easy task to prepare the report on this locus, one of the most important on Masada. Apart from the objective difficulty of explaining the position and condition of the significant finds discovered here, there are several subjective problems. First, the tapes of the discussions held during the period 13–22 November 1963, when some of the more important finds were made, have unfortunately been lost. Second, there exists no graphic log specifying the exact locations of the finds. Nevertheless, it would appear that the available data [logs recorded on other dates, photographs, basket lists, the locus card and the preliminary report (Yadin, *IEJ* 15, 79–83) provide a fairly accurate picture of the stratigraphic situation of the casemate ... There is no doubt that this casemate which ... had a single entrance was occupied by a Zealot family.

> *Discussion*
> We now consider the outstanding concentration of finds discovered on top of the accumulation of ballista stones. Both their varied nature, which is almost unique (the sole exception being the assemblage in Locus 1276), and the relative positions of some of the objects (such as the torn parchment scrolls)

---

1. In *EAE*, 812, Yadin stated that altogether "the remains of fourteen apocryphal, biblical, and sectarian scrolls were found" on Masada. He gave the same summary in the Hebrew edition of the encyclopaedia, ed. B. Mazar et al. (Jerusalem: Masada and IES, 1970) 388, as well as in the popular book on the Masada discoveries, *Fortress*, 189, possibly not including the very small fragment 1039–274. See below.
2. Yadin gave a concise description of the discovery of this locus in: The Synagogue at Masada, *Ancient Synagogues Revealed*, ed. L.I. Levine (Jerusalem: Israel Exploration Society, 1981) 19–23. See also G. Foerster, The Synagogues at Masada and Herodium, ibid. 24–29.
3. Yadin, *IEJ* 15, 79.

indicate that they were assembled here and may have been sifted through *repeatedly*. As to the identity of the persons who gathered them, the only two possibilities are the Zealots or the Roman military personnel (or stragglers from the Roman army). The conflagration layers discovered in many rooms on Masada and the finds they yielded indicate that the Zealots burned various objects deliberately. Perhaps, then, this was the original intention here, except that for some reason it was not carried out. The second scenario seems more plausible: Roman soldiers (or looters in their wake) collected the plundered objects after the destruction, choosing the corner of the casemate as a convenient (perhaps also somewhat hidden) location for this purpose. (It is quite probable that the original concentration was larger and these are only the remnants — the "leftovers" as it were.) Nevertheless, even if the actual assemblage was the work of the Zealots, who did not manage to set fire to the objects, the latter would certainly have been discovered by the soldiers who undoubtedly searched for loot everywhere and gathered what they could, as described above.

Illustration 1: Casemate 1039

In sum: Casemate 1039 yielded two concentrations of finds, in close proximity, both of which illustrate the drama which took place on Masada. One group, the ballista and the rolling stones, exemplifies the battle itself, and in particular the dismantling of the roofs to build the wooden wall; the other, by contrast, reflects the intensive looting which invariably occurred when a site was overrun after a battle or siege.

Loci and Dates of the Discovery of the Fragments in the Order of their Ensuing Presentation:[4]

a. Fragments of Biblical Scrolls:

1039–317 MasGen (Mas1) — Genesis 46:7–11 — found on November 29, 1963 in the southern part of the locus.[5]

1039–270 MasLev^a (Mas1a) Leviticus 4:3–9 — found on November 25, 1963 in the same vicinity.

92–480 MasLev^b (Mas1b) Leviticus 8:31–11:40 — found on November 11, 1964.

1043/a-d MasDeut (Mas1c) Deuteronomy 33:17–34:6 — found in the synagogue, just before the excavation closed down in 1965.[6]

1043–2220 MasEzek (Mas1d) Ezekiel 35:11–38:14 — also found in the synagogue at the same time.

1039–160 MasPs^a (Mas1e) Psalms 81:2–85:6^a — found on November 20, 1963 at the southwestern end of the locus, near the group of sheqels. On top of it and beside it were three coins of the revolt.

1103–1742 MasPs^b (Mas1f) Psalms 150:1–6 — found on December 12, 1964.

b. Fragments of Bible-Related Compositions:

1045–1350 + 1375 MasapocrGen (Mas1m) Genesis Apocryphon[7] — found on February 2, 1964.

---

4. The first two numbers in the siglum of an item designate the locus and its registration number in the excavation records, e.g. 1039–317, followed by its siglum in Tov-Pfann, *Microfiche*, e.g. MasGen (Mas 1i).

5. I retract my tentative suggestion offered in the preliminary Hebrew publication that the fragment may stem from a copy of the Book of Jubilees.

6. For a description of this locus and the circumstances of the discovery, see *Masada* III, 402–13 quoted below.

7. Yadin, *IEJ* 15, 105, surmised that it was "a kind of apocryphon on Esther." Accordingly this item was at first registered in Tov-Pfann, *Microfiche* as 'apEsther'.

1039–211 MasapocrJosh (Mas1l) Joshua Apocryphon[8] — found on November 22, 1963 in the southern part of the locus.

1276–1786 MasJub or MaspsJub (Mas1j) — found on January 31, 1965.

c.   Fragments of Extra-Biblical Works

1109–1357 Sir (Mas1h Sir) Ben Sira 39:37–44:20 — found on April 8, 1964 in a casemate of the eastern wall.

1039–200 Fragment of the Songs of the Sabbath Sacrifice (Mas1k ShirShabb) — found on November 21, 1963 in the southern corner of the room, within the semi-circular enclosure.

1063–1747 Unidentified Fragment (Mas1n Qumran type frg.) — found on March 23, 1964 in the debris of the cistern in the northwestern section of the casemate wall.

1039–274 Unidentified (Aramaic?) Fragment (Mas1p) — found on November 26, 1963 in the southern part of the locus.

1039–320 Text of Samaritan Origin (Mas1o) — found on November 29, 1963 in the southern part of the locus.[9]

Yadin published in full the fragments of the Ben Sira Scroll (Yadin, *Ben Sira*), and with C. Newsom, the fragments of the 'Songs of the Sabbath Sacrifice,' שירות עולת השבת (Newsom-Yadin, Songs), both reprinted below,[10] but described only briefly three of the

---

8.   Yadin, ibid., presumed that "possibly we have here an apocryphon on Samuel." See below. I use the term 'apocryphon' as the designation of an extra-biblical composition woven around a book of the Hebrew Bible or part of a book. The terms 'retold', 'rewritten', 'reworked', and 'parabiblical texts', which are now being applied in Qumran research to a variety of such extra-biblical works (see int. al. *DJD* XIII and XIX) stand in need of a clearer definition.

9.   I published three more Hebrew fragments without any identifying sigla, which turned up in Yadin's *Nachlass*, in *Tarbiz* 66 (1997) 113–21 (Hebrew). On one sliver, measuring 5.6×2.4 cm, a few letters of three partial lines are preserved. On another, almost rectangular piece of parchment, which measures 3.5×2 cm, legible parts of seven written lines are extant. The third item consists of one fragment measuring 5.4×5 cm, which contains the beginnings of three lines of Ps 18:26–29. On two additional slivers, remains of some letters are extant. These items do not seem to stem from Masada, but rather from Qumran. Yadin probably acquired them on the antiquities market. And indeed, E.J.C. Tigchelaar has now proposed to identify the item as part of 11QPs^c (publication pending). Equally, a parchment fragment containing Exod 13:11–16, which P. Wernberg-Møller published on the basis of a photograph in *The Times* (February 16, 1960) and the *Illustrated London News* (February 20, 1960, 293) as: The Exodus Fragment From Massada found in a Cave between Massada and Ein Gedi, *VT* 10 (1960) 229–30, is in fact one of two pieces of a phylactery of the Bar-Kokhba period. The erroneous identification was reiterated by F. Vattioni, Il Frammento Dell'Essodo Scoperto a Massada, *Revista Biblica* 8 (1960) 180. The other fragment contains the preceding text of Exod 13:2–10. See Aharoni, Expedition B, 22–3. The Bedouins from whom these items were acquired claimed that they were found at Naḥal Ṣeʾelim (Wadi Seiyal). They may, however, actually stem from Naḥal Ḥever.

10.   This work is known from more extensive finds in the Qumran Caves. See J. Strugnell, The Angelic Liturgy at Qumran — Serek Širot ʿOlat Haššabbatʾ, *VTSup* 7 (1960), 318–45; Newsom, *Songs*.

seven items which hail from scrolls of biblical books — Genesis, Leviticus[a] and Psalms[a], and three of the six small pieces of non-biblical compositions. Some of these can be identified with a measure of confidence, while others escape identification.[11]

For a preliminary publication of the biblical items see S. Talmon, Fragments of Two Scrolls of the Book of Leviticus From Masada, *EI* 24, *A. Malamat Volume*, ed. S. Aḥituv and B.A. Levine (1993) 99–110 (Hebrew); idem, Fragments of a Deuteronomy Scroll from Masada, *FS Cyrus Gordon* (in press); idem, Fragments of an Ezekiel Scroll from Masada, *OLP* 27 (1996) 29–49; idem, Fragments of a Psalms Scroll From Masada, MPs[b] (Masada 1103–1742), *Minḥah le-Naḥum. Biblical and Other Studies Presented to Nahum M. Sarna in Honour of his Seventieth Birthday*, ed. M. Brettler and M. Fishbane, *JSOTSup* 154 (Sheffield: JSOT Press, 1993) 318–27. For the non-biblical items see: idem, Masada 1045–1350 and 1375: Fragments of a Genesis Apocryphon, *IEJ* 46 (1997) 248–55; and Hebrew Written Fragments From Masada, *DSD* 3 (1996) 168–77, rev. translation of the Hebrew publication in *EI* 20, *Y. Yadin Volume*, ed. A. Ben-Tor, J.C. Greenfield, A. Malamat (1989) 278–86; idem, Fragments of an Apocryphal Book of Joshua from Masada, *JJS* 47 (1996) 129–39, rev. translation of the Hebrew publication in: *Hebrew Language Studies in Honor of C. Rabin at his 75th Birthday*, ed. M. Goshen-Gottstein, S. Morag, S. Kogut (Jerusalem: Akademon, 1991) 147–57.

Writing Materials[12]

The works of a literary nature from Masada in the Hebrew language and the square Hebrew alphabet are written on prepared hides of ritually 'pure' livestock — goats, sheep and cattle, as prescribed by rabbinic law: "one should write on the skins of pure domestic and wild animals" (*Sefer Torah* 1,1). The same pertains to similar items found at other sites in the Desert of Judah,[13] e.g. at Murabbaʿat,[14] Naḥal Ḥever and Naḥal Ṣeʾelim (Wadi Seiyal).[15] By contrast, all Greek, Latin and Nabatean non-literary Masada documents are inscribed on papyrus, as is the apparently literary Samaritan Hebrew text written in Palaeo-Hebrew.[16] The same applies to the majority of Greek and Latin items, and the Aramaic and Nabatean Babatha finds of the Bar-Kokhba Period from the Cave

---

11. Yadin, *IEJ* 15, 79–82; 103–5.
12. See also below, 'Excursus on the Use of Parchment and Papyrus.'
13. Presumably, some Qumran fragments stem from hides of game, such as ibex or deer.
14. See J.T. Milik, Textes Hébreux et Araméens, *DJD* II, 57–86, 181–205.
15. See A. Yardeni, '*Naḥal Ṣeʾelim*' Documents. *Judean Desert Studies* (Jerusalem: IES/Ben Gurion University, 1995). Scholars presume that many, if not most, fragments which Bedouins sold as finds from Naḥal Ṣeʾelim stem, in fact, from Naḥal Ḥever.
16. It is of interest to note that also the fourth century BCE Samaritan Hebrew documents from Wadi Daliyeh are inscribed on papyri. See F.M. Cross, Papyri of the Fourth Century B.C. from Daliyeh. A Preliminary Report on Their Significance, *New Directions in Biblical Archaeology*, ed. D.N. Freedman and J.C. Greenfield (New York: Doubleday, 1969) 41–62; idem, Aspects of Samaritan and Jewish History in Late Persian and Hellenistic Times, *HTR* 59 (1966) 201–11; idem, The Discovery of the Samaria Papyri, *BA* 26 (1963) 110–21.

of Letters in the Judaean Desert.[17] However, papyri with literary texts and parchments with non-literary texts were also found there.[18]

Physical Condition of the Finds

With the exception of the Palaeo-Hebrew papyrus and the fragment of 'Songs of the Sabbath Sacrifice', none of the Masada items is preserved in one piece. Even the smallest (MasPs[b] 1103–1742) consists of two slivers of parchment. All show signs of deterioration, particularly at the ragged margins, caused by climatic conditions and/or vermin, which also affected Latin, Greek and Nabatean papyrus and parchment finds at Masada, as well as manuscript finds at other sites in the Judaean Desert, especially at Qumran. In some instances however, the straight and smooth edges of some fragments seem to evince wilful tearing, as Yadin pointed out,[19] presumably by Roman soldiers who vented their rage on the sacred writings of the defenders after the conquest of Masada, as Josephus alleges. The colour of the diverse pieces ranges from paperwhite (MasPs[b]) to a very dark brown. In some instances the pitchy colour prevents the decipherment of the writing, as e.g. in parts of MasEzek.

Scripts

The fragments are written in the 'Jewish' square script. On the basis of a palaeographical comparison with documents from the last centuries BCE and the first century CE, inscribed in the same alphabet, particularly with the plethora of scroll fragments from Qumran, the Masada items can be dated to the Herodian period. Only the script of the Ben Sira scroll indicates that it stems from Hasmonean times.[20] It stands to reason that the Palaeo-Hebrew papyrus also comes from this time-span,[21] although specimens of the Palaeo-Hebrew script on pliable material, in distinction from stone and clay inscriptions,[22] especially of Samaritan provenance, are not readily available for a comparative analysis.[23]

17. Yadin, Expedition D, *IEJ* 12 (1962) 227–57; idem, *The Finds From the Bar-Kokhba Period in the Cave of the Letters. Judean Desert Studies I* (Jerusalem: IES/Hebrew University/Shrine of the Book, 1963); *The Documents From the Bar-Kokhba Period in the Cave of Letters. Greek Papyri*, ed. N. Lewis; *Aramaic and Nabatean Signatures and Subscriptions*, ed. Y. Yadin and J.C. Greenfield; *Judean Desert Studies* 2 (Jerusalem: IES/Hebrew University/Shrine of the Book, 1989).
18. See P. Benoit, O.P., Textes Grecs et Latin, *DJD* II, 209–77.
19. Yadin, *Fortress*, 172, and Newsom-Yadin, Songs (below, 118). See also (below) MasLev[a], n. 4.
20. Yadin, *Ben Sira*, 000–000; Cross, Scripts; Avigad, Palaeography, Tables.
21. Cf. *Masada* I, 6–7, and see below.
22. Such as some sherds, tags and bullae inscribed in Palaeo-Hebrew, which were found on Masada (See *Masada* I, 12–68).
23. See Purvis, *Samaritan*, Tables.

Scribal Customs

The scribes of the Masada biblical scrolls, and to a lesser degree also of the non-biblical manuscripts, followed rabbinic instructions for the writing of 'holy books',[24] laid down in several early and later sources,[25] int. al. *j. Meg.* 1.71d–72a; *b. Shab.* 103a–105a; *b. Men.* 29b–32b; Tractate *Soferim*, Tractate *Sefer Torah*, et al. In any given item, letters are uniformly executed, evincing the scribes' craftsmanship. However, occasionally some irregularity can be observed, e.g. in MasGen and the 'Sectarian (?) fragment' (1063–1747). As a rule, letters hang from horizontal dry rulings, as in most ancient Hebrew manuscripts (*j. Meg.* 1. 71d). Or else, the letter-tops form a straight line, with only the heads of *lamed* protruding above it, and the down-strokes of *qof*, final *kaf*, *nun*, *peh* and *ṣade* descending below the foot bars of the other letters. Most letters measure 3×3 mm. *Lamed*, *qof*, and final *kaf*, *nun*, *peh* and *ṣade* come to double that height (e.g. in MasPs^a col. I, ll. 24–25^a and II, l. 1).

Individual letters are clearly separated by a space of less than 1 mm, and words by a space of ca. 1 mm, in compliance with the rabbinic dictum: "One leaves (a space) between words so that they are separated, and (between) letters so that they do not entwine," מניחים בין שם לשם כדי שיהיו ניכרים ובאותיות כדי שלא יהיו מעורבין (*Sefer Torah* 2,1). Now and then, two or more letters will flow together ligature-like, as כה in הכהן (MasLev^a ll. 3–5); צב in ואצבעו (l. 4); עגל (MasLev^b col. I, 20); חטא (col. III, 18); לבם (MasPs^a col. I, 26^b); אכן (col. II, 10^b); נו in נועצו (col. II, 18^b). Occasionally words also coalesce when the scribe misjudged the amount of text which could be accommodated in a line, and so was forced to crowd the writing at the end of a hemistich, e.g. אלהיישענו (MasPs^a col. III, 28^b) and תאנפכנו (III, 29^a), or of a line, e.g. שפתההארץ (col. II, 11), כסיסרא (II, 22), שיתמוכגלגל (II, 26), תבעריער (II, 27). In some instances, the last word, or words, of a line or a hemistich will actually spill over into the inter-hemistich space or into the left margin, as in MasPs^a col. II, 15 (Ps 83:2^b–3^a): אל תחרש ואל תשקט אל כי הנה איביך יהמיון (cf. II, 18 and 19 = Ps 83:5^b–7^a), also when the column width is marked by vertical dry rulings for the guidance of the scribe.

The columns of a manuscript usually hold the same number of lines, give or take one. The numbers of lines do, however, vary from one manuscript to another, within the range of 25–26 in MasLev^b and 42 in MasEzek.

Top and bottom margins are 3–3.5 cm wide, in compliance with rabbinic tradition: "In a Torah scroll one leaves (a margin) of the breadth of the palm of a hand at the bottom, and of a third of the palm of a hand at the top; in (scrolls of) the prophets and of

---

24. For a comparison with scribal customs which prevail in Qumran manuscripts, see M. Martin, *The Scribal Character of the Dead Sea Scrolls* (Louvain: Publications Universitaires, 1958).

25. L. Blau, *Studien zum althebräischen Buchwesen und zur biblischen Literatur- und Textgeschichte* (Strassburg i/E: Trübner, 1902); S. Krauss, *Talmudische Archäologie*, vol. III (Leipzig: Fock, 1912, repr. Hildesheim: Olms, 1966) 131–98; E.L. Sukenik, *Megilloth Genuzot. First Report* (Jerusalem: Bialik, 1948) 11–13 (Hebrew).

single books of the Pentateuch, of a three-fingers-breadth at the bottom and a two fingers-breadth at the top. One may make them broader under the condition that their combined width (viz. of the top and bottom margins) does not exceed that of the (column) space taken up by the writing" (*Sefer Torah* 2,4; cf. *b. Men.* 30a). Inter-column margins come to "a thumb's breadth", viz. to ca. 2 cm. The width of a column depends on the length of the written line combined with the width of the right-hand margin; and the height of a scroll on the number of lines of text together with the widths of the top and bottom margins.

Blanks in the lines of the more extensively preserved biblical fragments — MasLev[b], MasEzek and MasPs[a] — indicate internal text divisions or sections, which mostly coincide with the section system, פרשות, of one of the major MT codices.[26] At the same time, the divisions in Masada biblical fragments reflect the fluidity which pertains to this matter in the masoretic tradition, particularly in books of the Prophets and the Writings.

The scribes' carefulness is evinced by the scarcity of scribal mistakes, which stands out in a comparison with the plentitude of such mistakes in biblical scrolls and scroll fragments from Qumran. A few cases of apparent *lapsus calami* were corrected by the scribe himself or by a corrector through entering omitted letters above the line. In several instances the emendations align the text with MT, as e.g. in MasLev[b] col. III, 20 (Lev 10:16) והנותר{י}ם; III, 21 (Lev 10:17) {הוא}; col. V, 14 (Lev 11:32) יט{מ}א; V, 19 (Lev 11:35) וכ{י}רים; MasEzek col. I, 4 (Ezek 35:13) על{י}; col. II, 18 (Ezek 36:25) ט{מ}אותיכם; II, 26 (Ezek 36:30) ותנ{ו}בת; col. III, 6 (Ezek 37:4) הנ{ב}א. One also notes the absence of cancellation dots, fairly often encountered in Qumran[26a] and MT manuscripts.[27] One would have expected such dots to be supplied e.g. in MasEzek col. III, 22 (Ezek 37:12) to correct a manifest case of dittography: כה אמר אמר.

Some remarks are in order concerning instances of an indiscriminate use of the medial and final forms of the letters *kaf, mem, nun, peh* and *ṣade* in several Masada documents, e.g. in MasEzek col. III, l. 12: עצמות (MT Ezek 37:7: עצמות), col. II, l. 7 עמ יהוה (MT 36:20: עם יהוה), and in Mas 1039–317 and 1063–1747. An anonymous sage of the 3rd century CE denoted the seemingly random employment of the medial and final forms of the letter *mem* a Jerusalem custom: Jerusalemites used to write ירושלים and ירושלימ(ה) indiscriminately" (*j. Meg.* 1.71d). Only in the early centuries CE did their

26. For the masoretic section system, especially in the Pentateuch, see Perrot, Alinéas; idem, *Lecture*; Oesch, *PUS*. The issue has again come under scrutiny in the light of the Qumran biblical manuscripts (see Maori, Tradition).

26a. E. Tov, Correction Procedures in the Texts From the Judean Desert, *Proceedings of the Provo, UT Conference July 1996* (forthcoming).

27. See S. Talmon, Prolegomenon, to R. Butin, *The Ten Nequdoth of the Torah and The Meaning and Purpose of the Extraordinary Points of the Pentateuch* (repr. New York: Ktav, 1969) I–XXVII; S. Lieberman, The Ten Dotted Places in the Torah, *Hellenism* 43–6.

differentiated employment become the rule, as can be deduced from a saying attributed to the Babylonian Amora Rab Hisda (3rd century CE): "People did not know which form comes in the middle of a word and which one comes at the end. And the 'watchmen'[28] came and ordained that the open forms should be in the middle of a word and the closed forms at the end" (b. Meg. 2b–3a).

The epicene use of the two forms of these letters can be observed in the Nash Papyrus (last but one line from the bottom),[29] and has also left traces in Qumran scrolls. E.g. 1QIsaᵃ 5:1, כרם היה לידידי ;5:2, וגם יקב ;39:2, ויראם ; 1QIsᵇ 38:11, עם יושבי חדל ;40:26, המוציא ; במספר צבאם לכולם בשם יקרא; and especially in 40:24 where a medial *mem* and a medial *peh* close two adjacent words: וגם נשף בהמה. More examples are found in non-biblical Qumran documents: עצם אל עצמו ופרק ואל פרקו (4Q385 2, 5);[30] גם (1QS VI, 1); להברכ (1QS VI, 6); להוסיף (לחֶפֶץ); lege לחפצ, vocalized לחֵפֶץ; להפצ (1QS VI, 11; mברכ (1QS VII, 1); ולברכ (1QS VI, 8); (1QS VI, 14); בקשי עורפ (1QS VI, 26) et al.[31] It would appear that in 1QS VIII, 26, the employment of a medial *mem* in a final position caused the contraction of two words into one. In a paragraph concerning the readmission of a member who had been expelled in punishment for transgressing community rules,[32] the text reads: אם תתם דרכו במושב, "if his ways become perfect in the session," instead of the evidently required reading: אם תתם דרכו בם ושב, "if his ways become perfect regarding them (viz. those rules) he may return."[33] A similar mis-contraction resulting from the employment of a medial instead of a final *mem* may be observed in the Greek translation of Jer 31:8: וקִבַּצְתִּים מִיַּרְכְּתֵי־אָרֶץ בָּם עִוֵּר וּפִסֵּחַ, "I will gather them in from the ends of the earth, among them blind and crippled." The LXX rendition (38:8): καὶ συνάξω αὐτοὺς ἀπ' ἐσχάτου τῆς γῆς ἐν ἑορτῇ φασεκ, "I will lead them from the end of the earth on the Passah festival," mirrors the altogether faulty reading במועד פסח, instead of בָּם עִוֵּר וּפִסֵּחַ, with the added inversio of וע for ע, and the substitution of *daleth* for *reš* — מועד עור (ב)מ.[34] We should further mention the well known occurrence of a final *mem* in a medial position in the first component of a honorific title given to the future ruler of Israel in MT Isa 9:6 למרבה המשרה.[35] An example of the opposite case is the employment of a medial *mem* in a final position in Neh 2:13: אשר המ פרוצים.

28. I.e. the 'sages' who decided in the matter. The designation 'watchmen' is presumably derived from a word-play based on a rearrangement of the letters concerned, and the division of the resulting compound מנצפך into two words, read as מִן צָפָך, 'from your watchmen'. See Tur-Sinai, מנצפ״ך; Yalon, מנצפ״ך; Lieberman, *Hellenism*, 23.
29. Albright, Nash, dated the papyrus to the second half of the 2nd century BCE.
30. It is, however, possible that the *waw* at the end of עצמו resulted from a dittography of the *waw* at the beginning of the next word ופרק.
31. A medial *peh* in final position is also documented in the word ואפ in 4Q397 frg. 1–2, 1; frg. 5, 3; frg. 14–21, 12 (*DJD* X, 25, 26, 27).
32. Cf. 1QS VIII, 22: אשר יעבר דבר מתורת משה ... ישלחהו מעצת היחד ולוא ישוב עוד.
33. See M. Kister, Notes on Some New Texts from Qumran, *JJS* 44 (1993) 280–90.
34. See E. Tov, On 'Pseudo-Variants' Reflected in the Septuagint, *JSS* 20 (1975) 172.
35. Cf. 4Q175, 5–6 (Testimonia, *DJD* V, 58): לאהםה, אחיהםה, אליהםה *et al.*

While this scribal phenomenon cannot be definitely dated, its manifestation in a variety of ancient sources of the late Second Temple period proves that it reflects a stage of development of scribal norms which cannot be later than the first century CE.[36] Thus it can serve as an auxiliary criterion for the dating of Masada fragments in which it occurs.[37]

Dating the Fragments

The fall of Masada in 73 CE[38] provides the definite *terminus a quo* for dating all the above finds. The actual dates are probably earlier since there is no reason for assuming that any one of the scrolls represented by these fragments was written on Masada, notwithstanding the fact that the presence of a tannery (*Masada* III, 634–5) gives evidence to the preparation of hides on the site, and some abecedaries evince scribal exercises (*Masada* I, 61–2). Rather, it can be postulated that all items were carried to the fortress by fugitives who fled there before the Roman army effectively cut it off from the *Hinterland*, or were brought there at an earlier date.

Languages and Linguistic Criteria

The non-biblical documents, like the biblical, are in Hebrew, with the possible exception of the small unidentified fragment 1039–274 which may be in Aramaic. The presence in some Masada items of typical Covenanters' terms and linguistic features — such as שר המשטמה, "prince of evil" (1276–1786), and the super-plene spelling הואה (1063–1747) — may reveal their Qumran provenance. This characterization applies most manifestly to the fragment of the 'Songs of the Sabbath Sacrifice' (1039–200), which exhibits characteristic Covenanters' idioms, e.g. "before they came into being," לפני היותם; "all everlasting testimonies," כול תעודות עולמים; "wondrous words," דברי פלא. The Proverbs of Ben Sira, a second century BCE composition, is naturally marked by intrinsic linguistic traits and structures of the period.

The Biblical Text

A synoptic view of the Masada biblical fragments with fragments of biblical books discovered at other sites in the Judaean Desert, above all with the plethora of the

36. For a discussion of the issue, see Siegel, *Scribes*.
37. Milik based the early dating of an Aramaic Qumran fragment of the Book of Enoch *int. al.* on the absence of final letter forms: "I would date 4Qenastrᵃ to the end of the third or else to the beginning of the second century B.C. The scribe never used final forms of letters, e.g. ימם, תרין, מנ, דנ." Milik-Black, *Enoch* 273.
38. Or possibly 74 CE, if Lucius Flavius Silva, the conqueror of Masada, left Rome only in 73 CE, as two Latin inscriptions from Italy seem to imply. This means that he would have needed several months to prepare the siege, before taking the fortress in the spring of next year at the time of Passover, as Josephus reports. See W. Eck, Die Eroberung von Masada, *ZNTW* 60 (1969) 282–9. For a recent review of this still debated question see H.M. Cotton and J. Geiger, Excursus on the Date of the Fall of Masada, *Masada* II, 21–3.

Qumran finds, contribute important information concerning the history of the textual transmission of the Hebrew Bible. The Masada biblical fragments exhibit uniformly the text of some books of the Hebrew Bible in the masoretic tradition (MT), with only a few 'true' variant readings and a larger number of minor differences, pertaining mostly to plene and defective spelling. The basic textual identity of the Masada biblical fragments is underscored by their concurrence with MT in almost every instance in which an ancient version exhibits a variant reading. The overall conformity with the masoretic tradition also characterizes the fragments of biblical texts in Hebrew found at other sites in the Judaean Desert, at Naḥal Ṣeʾelim (Wadi Seiyal),[39] and Wadi Murabbaʿat.[40] This identity contrasts sharply with the abundance of textual variants in biblical scrolls and fragments from the Qumran caves. The divergent readings in these manuscripts range from types of variants which emerge from a collation of MT with the Samaritan Hebrew Pentateuch and/or the ancient translational versions in Greek, Latin, Aramaic and Syriac, to textual traditions which deviate to such an extent from MT that scholars designate them 'Retold,' 'Reread,' 'Rewritten Bibles', or 'Parabiblical Texts'.[41] The exceedingly large scope of variation suggests that the 'Community of the Renewed Covenant,' יחד or עדת באי הברית החדשה / אשר באו בברית החדשה,[42] a dissident faction in Judaism of the late Second Temple period, did not propagate an exclusively binding text of the biblical books.[43] In contradistinction, the Masada biblical fragments give witness to the existence of a stabilized proto-masoretic textual tradition which had taken root in 'normative Judaism' of the time.[44] When readings from the Law (Pentateuch) and the Prophets, and the recitation of the Five Megilloth became a pivotal component of the synagogal service of the mainstream community,[45] at the latest in the 1st century CE, this text was recognized as the exclusively legitimate version of the biblical books, the definitive *textus receptus*. In contrast, the textual fluidity, which can be observed in the Qumran scrolls and fragments of biblical books and bible-related works, which stem from the last centuries BCE, proves that these manuscripts were not subjected to such a stabilizing process. Moreover, nothing in the Covenanters' literature gives reason for assuming that Bible-readings were ever included in their devotional service, which was

39. See Aharoni, Expedition B.
40. Milik, Textes Littéraires, *DJD* II, 75: "The biblical text, conserved in these fragments, is actually identical with the *textus receptus* established towards the end of the first century of our era."
41. See e.g. *DJD* XIII and XIX.
42. This designation, by which the author-members refer to their community, should be adopted in Qumran research, instead of 'Essenes', 'Qumran Essenes' et sim. See Talmon, Renewed Covenant.
43. S. Talmon, Aspects of the Textual Transmission of the Bible in Light of Qumran Manuscripts, *Textus* 4 (1964) 95–132, reprinted in idem, *WQW*, 71–116.
44. See G.F. Moore, *Judaism in the First Century of the Christian Era. The Age of the Tannaim* (Oxford: Clarendon, 1927) vol. I, 3.
45. Song of Songs on Passover, Ruth on Pentecost, Ecclesiastes on Tabernacles, Lamentations on the Ninth of Ab, and Esther on Purim.

evidently constituted of prayers only.[46] Therefore, the need for a unification and stabilization of the text of Scriptures did not arise in the 'Community of the Renewed Covenant.'

Excursus on the Use of Parchment and Papyrus

Fourteen Hebrew writings on parchment, both biblical and non-biblical, were found at Masada, as against a single non-biblical item on papyrus.[47] This ratio is paralleled by the scarce presence of papyri among the Qumran finds. Scholars presume that the scrolls and fragments found in the caves are the remains of ca. 800 scrolls which had been stored there originally. Of these, less than 100 are papyrus items, heavily outnumbered by the collection of over 700 parchment scrolls.

Scholars have dated the earliest parchment items from Qumran by various palaeographic and linguistic criteria, historical references and radio-carbon tests to the second or the third century BCE. The numerous scroll fragments found at Qumran, Masada and other sites in the Judaean Desert prove that parchment had evidently established itself as the preferred writing material in Palestine at the height of the Second Temple period,[48] at the latest from the beginning of the second cetury BCE.[49]

A quite different situation occurs in respect to papyrus. Scriptural references evince that in biblical times the papyrus plant, Hebrew גמ(ו)א, grew abundantly on river banks and in water-rich areas of Palestine (Isa 35:7), foremost in the Jordan Valley and the Ḥuleh swamps in northern Galilee (Job 8:11). Then, like today, גומא fibers were used for the production of various articles, such as baskets and mats, and even for building small boats (Exod 2:3; Isa 18:2).[50] But there is no mention in the biblical writings or in any other source that גומא fibers served for the manufacture of papyrus in Palestine as writing material. According to Lewis, "Papyrus could no doubt have served for manufacturing paper but there is no direct evidence that it ever was so employed."[51] Therefore, it had to be imported to Palestine either directly from Egypt, or from the northern coast of the Mediterranean, where Byblos served as a trading centre for transit goods such as

---

46. S. Talmon, The Emergence of Institutionalized Prayer in Israel in Light of Qumran Literature, *WQW* 200–43.

47. The statement by H.M. Cotton and J. Geiger, *Masada* II, 1, that "biblical scrolls and other Jewish sacred writings on both parchment and papyrus" were found on Masada, contradicts the facts and needs to be corrected.

48. This fact is tangibly illustrated by the recent discovery at Qumran of bales of animal hides in various stages of preparation, possibly for use as writing material.

49. In the classical world "it is not until the early centuries of the Christian era that parchment comes into common use for books". Reynolds, *Scribes*, 3.

50. See I. Loew, *Die Flora der Juden* 1–4 (Wien: Loewit, 1924–34) vol. 1, 559–71; A. Lucas, *Ancient Egyptian Materials and Industries*[4] (London: Arnold, 1962), 162–5.

51. Lewis, *Papyrus*, 8.

papyrus and linen, which were hauled there by boats from Egypt.[52] The 11th century BCE tale of Wen-Amon, the Egyptian emissary who was dispatched to Byblos to procure lumber, a local export staple, for the ceremonial barge of the deity Amon at Karnak, provides an illuminating illustration of this state of affairs. Wen-Amon reports that in exchange for the lumber which he received, he handed over to the local prince a variety of goods and "10 pieces of clothing in royal linen, 10 *kherd* of good Upper Egyptian linen; 500 rolls of finished papyrus."[53]

Egyptian manufacturers maintained a monopoly on the production of papyrus and ensured high prices for their products by restricting output to prevent 'dumping'. Experts tell us that "In Ptolemaic Egypt ... the manufacture of the best kinds of papyrus was subject to such a degree of royal control that the word 'monopoly' has (probably rather loosely) been applied to it."[54] And "as there was only one large source of supply the book trade was presumably exposed to fluctuations arising from war or a desire by the producers to exploit their virtual monopoly."[55] Again, "Papyrus was expensive (in Palestine, S.T.) especially in war-time."[56] According to "an oft-repeated story, attributed to if not originating with Varro ... parchment was invented in Pergamum when the Ptolemy of Egypt embargoed the shipment of papyrus to his Attalid rival."[57] An ostracon which refers to a gift or grant, recently discovered at Qumran and dated by palaeographic criteria to the first century CE, possibly provides an interesting illustration of such a situation.[58] Since it is "unique among the Qumran finds," and since one would expect "such documents to be written on papyrus," the authors consider it "not impossible that in the second year of the Revolt ... papyrus was in short supply" (ibid., p. 26). These mundane commercial considerations need to be taken into account in discussing the question of which writing materials were used on Masada and where they came from. Turner's general statement (ibid., 2) that "there was a connection between content and writing material" is well taken, but still does not answer the question satisfactorily.

It would appear that papyrus served predominantly for the writing of relatively short

---

52. The same pertains to the growth of the flax plant and the manufacture of linen which became locally produced commodities in Palestine only in Roman times. See S. Talmon, The Gezer Calendar and the Seasonal Cycle of Ancient Canaan, *JAOS* 83 (1963) 177–87 = idem, *KCC*, 91–100.
53. See J.B. Pritchard, ed., *Ancient Near Eastern Texts Relating to the Old Testament* (Princeton, NJ: Princeton University Press, 1950, 1955) 25–9; J.A. Wilson, *The Burden of Egypt* (Chicago: Chicago University Press, 1951) 289–92.
54. See *int. al.* Turner, *Papyri*, 2–3.
55. Reynolds, *Scribes*, 3.
56. Torczyner, *Lachish*, 16.
57. Lewis, *Papyrus*, 9.
58. See F.M. Cross and E. Eshel, Ostraca from Qumran, *IEJ* 47 (1997) 17–28.

letters, and for the recording of business dockets and family documents,[59] replacing pottery sherds which had served these purposes in the First Temple period. This is evinced *int. al.* by the already mentioned 4th century BCE Wadi Daliyeh papyri, and by papyrus fragments inscribed in Aramaic and Greek from Jericho. The excavators dated some of these to the second half of the fourth century, among them one which appears to be a record of loans and repayments, and some to the second and first centuries BCE.[60] Crisscross fiber impressions on clay bullae from the end of the First Temple period, which were discovered in a local archive in the City of David, show that originally these bullae had been affixed to papyrus documents, which are now lost through decomposition.[61] Similar impressions are recognizable on bullae from other Palestinian sites, e.g. from Lachish.[62] The oldest papyrus found in Palestine, a palimpsest from Murabbaʿat in the Judaean Desert, is dated by Milik on palaeographic and archaeological grounds to the 8th and by others to the 7th century BCE. It contains parts of a letter and a list of names written in Palaeo-Hebrew.[63] From Saqqarah in Egypt comes an Aramaic letter on papyrus, written ca. 600 BCE, in which a certain Adon, king of a Philistine or Phoenician city,[64] asks the Pharaoh for military aid against the invading Babylonians.[65] Also, the much later Wadi Murabbaʿat papyri (1st and 2nd century CE), some of which are connected with Bar-Kokhba, are invariably 'documents': marriage contracts, sales agreements, administrative dockets, deeds, letters *et sim.*[66] The same pertains to papyri discovered at other sites in the Judaean Desert: Naḥal Ḥever, Khirbet Mird et al.[67] In contrast, all 'literary texts' from Wadi Murabbaʿat, biblical — including a scroll of the Twelve Prophets —[68] and non-biblical, are written on parchment.[69]

59. An updated roster of such items from the Roman Near East may be found in: H.M. Cotton, W.E.H. Cockle and F.G.B. Millar, The Papyrology of the Roman Near East: A Survey, *Journal of Roman Studies* 85 (1995) 214–35. However, in this roster papyri are not separated from inscriptions on parchment. Rather, "as is normal, 'papyrology' is taken to include also any writing in ink on portable, and normally perishable, materials: parchment, wood and leather, as well as on fragments of pottery (ostraca)" (p. 214). I am indebted to Prof. Cotton for bringing this paper to my attention.

60. H. Eshel and H. Misgav, A Fourth Century B.C.E. Document From Ketef Yeriḥo, *IEJ* 38 (1988) 158–76; H. Eshel and B. Zissu, Ketef Jericho, 1993, *IEJ* 45 (1995) 293–8.

61. Impressions of the twine with which the rolled up papyrus was bound, are still visible. See Y. Shiloh, A Hoard of Hebrew Bullae From the City of David, *EI* 18. *Nahman Avigad Volume*, ed. B. Mazar and Y. Yadin (1985) 73–87 (Hebrew).

62. See Torczyner, *Lachish*, 106–9; Y. Aharoni, Trial Excavation in the Solar Shrine at Lachish, *IEJ* 18 (1968) 164–8; *Inscriptions Revealed, Israel Museum Catalogue 100* (Jerusalem, 1973) nos. 26–31.

63. See J.T. Milik, Textes Hébreux et Araméens. Papyrus, *DJD* II 93–100.

64. B. Porten, The Identity of King Adon, *BA* 44 (1981) 36–52.

65. Naveh, *Alphabet*, 82.

66. See *DJD* II, nos. 17–71, pp. 93–171.

67. See Tov-Pfann, *Microfiche*, 62–72.

68. *DJD* II, no. 88, pp. 181–205.

69. Ibid., nos. 1–6, pp. 75–86.

In sum: no papyrus scrolls or fragments have come to light to date, which contain an expansive literary composition. It appears that literary texts of an appreciable length, whether of a sacred or secular nature, in Hebrew, Aramaic or in a non-Semitic language, in Palaeo-Hebrew or the square alphabet, were routinely written on parchment, which was readily available locally, whereas, as said, at any time papyrus had to be imported at considerable cost from Egypt.[70] The writing is always on the outer side of the skin from which the hair had been shaven off: "One writes on the hairy side of the hide" (*j. Meg.* 1. 71d; *Sefer Torah* 1,4). The practice made for a better preservation of the writing since it allowed the ink to filter into the pores.

The sparse presence of papyri, and the wide use of parchment at the height of the Second Temple period as a pliable and easily transportable material for committing to writing literary, and to a lesser degree also non-literary texts, evinced by the discoveries in the Judaean Desert, cannot be explained by the claim that papyrus is more easily perishable than parchment. The preservation of papyrus next to parchment fragments at various sites in the Judaean Desert, over a span of two, almost three millennia, proves that under the propitious conditions of the dry desert climate, both materials have the same chance of survival. Turner says: "In Europe and most of the countries bordering on the Mediterranean, writing materials are unlikely to resist the onset of damp unless they are protected in libraries .... But in Egypt, parts of Palestine and Mesopotamia the climate is not hostile to long life. Away from the Delta and the coastal belt in Egypt rain does not fall in any appreciable quantity. Papyrus books, parchment books, wooden tablets all have an excellent chance of survival even in ordinary ground, provided that they are not too close to the surface and not so far down that they grow damp from water rising from below. If papyri can have the protection of a cave, a jar, or a ruined building there are many places where they can remain intact, outside as well as inside Egypt."[71] Therefore, the extremely scant remains, practically the non-existence of inscribed papyri and parchments from the First Temple period and the early part of the Second, raises again the moot question of which materials were used in ancient Judaism for committing literary texts to writing. The theory that already in the First Temple period papyrus was readily available for the purpose remains open to discussion.[72]

---

70. This conclusion is not put in doubt by a few papyrus fragments of literary composition from Qumran, nor by a solitary tiny papyrus fragment from Masada (no. 739) inscribed]ολουδομματα.[, whether one reads]ολου δ'όμματα.[or]ολ' ουδ' όμματα.[, as tentatively suggested by Cotton and Geiger. While "Ὄμματα is a 'poetic word, rare in prose'... the combination of the letters ολουδ with όμματα is apparently not attested anywhere in Greek literature" (*Masada* II, 81–2).
71. Turner, *Papyri*, 18.
72. See Torczyner, *Lachish*, 16; Naveh, *Alphabet*, 75; M. Haran, Book Scrolls at the Beginning of the Second Temple Period: the Transition from Papyrus to Skins, *HUCA* 54 (1983) 111–22.

A. Writings on Parchment in the Square Hebrew Script

1. Fragments of Biblical Scrolls

(a) Mas 1039–317; Mas 1; Genesis 46:7–11 (MasGen, final photo 302363, earlier 302374)

Yadin's description of this item runs as follows:

> This small fragment (5.5 × 4 cm) is also torn. It contains the ends of five lines from Genesis 46:7–11. The script resembles, on the whole, that of the Isaiah scroll A. Although the kaf of the word Hanokh resembles a median kaf, it seems that this particular form is somewhat later, i.e., from the beginning of the first century B.C.E. The fragmentary state of the scroll does not allow us to make any statement concerning the text; it seems, however, that it contains some variants, as in verse 8: הבאים מצרימה] את יעקוב [ובניו.[1]

The item was found on November 29, 1963 in the southern part of the third casemate to the south of the 'synagogue', locus 1039 (ibid., 79–82). It consists of one fragment and five scraps of parchment of a greyish-brown colour. Judging by the irregular edges, it appears that the smaller pieces became detached from the larger one through disintegration of the parchment, rather than through wilful tearing. They can still be rejoined on the basis of their contours and preserved parts of letters, so that one fragment can be reconstituted which measures 5.6×4.5 cm. It contains parts of two adjoining columns, separated by a 1.6 cm wide margin, which proves that they are indeed remains of a scroll.

0   1   2   3

Illustration 2: MasGen 1039–317

Transcription

[מצרים	1
מצרי]ם את יעקוב	2
ו[בנ]י ראובן חנוך	3
ימ[ו]אל וימין	4
[ובנ֗י לוי	5

1. Yadin, *IEJ* 15, 104–5.

Script

The script could be characterized "semi-cursive," רהוט במקצת, as Yadin proposed,[2] but it is doubtful whether it can appropriately be termed "elegant," מהודר.[3] Letters measure mostly 3×3 mm but are not uniformly executed. The irregularity becomes evident when one compares the three *alephs* at the beginning of ll. 2, 3, 4. The final *mem* of מצרים in l. 1 is appreciably larger, measuring more than 4×4 mm, and its execution differs from that of the final *mem* of that same word in l. 2. As usual, the width of the thin letters זיו amounts to somewhat less than 1 mm. Although there are no rulings, the tops of letters are perfectly aligned. Words are unequally separated by a blank of roughly the width of one letter. In l. 4 וימ[ו]אל and וימין actually seem to fuse. The inter-line space amounts to ca. 8 mm.

Text[4]

The preserved remains of text stem from the ends of five lines in the list of Jacob's sons who went down to Egypt with their father (Gen 46:7–11). There are some slight deviations from MT. Noteworthy is the plene spelling יעקוב (l. 2) which occurs only five times in MT (Lev 26:42; Jer 30:18;[5] 33:26; 46:27; 51:19), as against 345 occurrences of the defective spelling יעקב. On the strength of this instance it may be assumed that plene spelling was the rule in this Masada scroll.

The fragment twice contains the reading מצרים (ll. 1 and 2) as against MT's reading מצרימה (Gen 46:7, 8; cf. 46:3, 4, 6, 26, 27; Exod 1:1), which in both instances is supported by LXX: εἰς Αἴγυπτον, TO, TFr: למצרים, and by TJer: מצרימה (46:7); למצרים (46:8). The reading מצרים is further documented in MT Gen 43:15: ויקמו וירדו מצרים. However, a rabbinic tradition reports that the Torah scroll of the renowned sage and scribe Rabbi Meir, and the Torah scroll preserved in the Synagogue of Severus in Rome, which antedated the destruction of the Second Temple, also read מצרימה in these places.[6] Sam often differs from MT on the same point. The variant spellings מצרים/מצרימה/ירושלים/ ירושלימה probably emerged when the differently shaped form of the final *mem* was introduced in the square script, but was not accepted in all text traditions of the Bible.

2. Y. Yadin, מצדה — חפירות תשב״ד. סקירה ראשונה, *BIES* 29 (1965) 117.
3. It seemingly resembles the script of a fragment from Cave 1, which Milik ascribed to an apocryphal work about Noah. J.T. Milik, Livre de Noé, *DJD* I, 84–7, pl. XVI.
4. The passage under review is not extant in any Qumran fragment of the Book of Genesis. See *DJD* XII, 7–78.
5. Cf. the defective spelling in the parallel verse Ezek 39:25 עתה אשוב את שבות יעקב.
6. Ch. Albeck, ed., *Midraš Berešit Rabbati. Ex Libro Mosis Hadaršan* (Jerusalem: Meqize Nirdamim, 1940) 210, 5. The midrashist presents a list of variant readings in the Pentateuch found in the "Torah scroll which was taken into captivity from Jerusalem, was brought to Rome and deposited in the Severus Synagogue" (ibid., par. 45, 8, p. 209, 13–15 cf. 212, 2). Cf. further the talmudic report: "Rabbi Simon and Rabbi Naḥman say: Jerusalemites used to write [indiscriminately] ירושלים and ירושלימה" (*j. Meg.* 1.71d).

We may similarly explain the shape of the *kaf* at the end of חנוך (l. 3), which resembles a median rather than a final *kaf*, as Yadin correctly observed.[7]

The phrase את יעקוב (l. 2) deserves special attention. The particle את, which in this context means "with", is not transmitted in MT or the Samaritan Hebrew text of Gen 46:8, nor is it translated in the VSS (LXX,[8] Targ,[9] and Syr). The scribe of MasGen may have added the particle under the influence of similar phrases which recur in the context: בניו ובני בניו אתו ... וכל זרעו הביא בניו אתו (Gen 46:7), and יעקב וכל זרעו אתו (Gen 46:6), context: ואלה שמות בני ישראל הבאים מצרימה את יעקב especially in the parallel list, Exod 1:1:.

The fragmentary state of the scroll does not allow any definite pronouncement concerning its text. However, it is exceedingly probable that it contained the variant reading הבאים מצרים את יעקוב אביהם, which is preserved in the expanded version of this passage in the Book of Jubilees: "And these are the sons of Jacob who went into Egypt with Jacob their father, מסלה יעקוב אביהומו. Reuben, the first-born of Israel ..." (44:11–13).[10] This variant does not contain the awkward MT phrase: הבאים מצרימה יעקב ובניו בכר יעקב ובניו (Gen 46:8), in which יעקב ובניו seems to sever the continuity between the superscription ואלה שמות בני־ישראל הבאים מצרימה,[11] and the ensuing detailed enumeration of Jacob's sons, introduced by the statement בכר יעקב ראובן.

At the same time, MasGen exhibits an important agreement with MT. The first line of the fragment is not fully written out. It ends on the word מצרים, thus evidently marking a break before the roster of names of Jacob's sons. This break dovetails with the masoretic section-divider (*parašah*) after Gen 46:7. It is noteworthy that a Qumran fragment of Jubilees (3QJub5) also begins a new paragraph here.[12]

Taking into account the above divergences from MT, the extant line endings of MasGen make it possible to determine the number of letters and words in each line, and concomitantly also the width of the partly preserved column of the original manuscript.

---

7. On the emergence of the differentiation between medial and final letters see Introduction, pp. 20–22.
8. However, LXX[A]: + μετ αὐτοῦ.
9. R. Le Déaut, *Targum de Pentateuque. Traduction des Deux Recensions Palestiniennes Complètes* etc. (Paris: Cerf, 1978) 411, seemingly felt a need for smoothing the targumic rendition ואילין שמהת בני ישראל דעלו למצרים יעקב ובנוהי by adding a connecting link: "Voici les noms des fils d'Israel qui entrerent en Égypte, (à savoir) Jacob et ses fils."
10. The Hebrew fragments of Jubilees from Qumran occasionally exhibit a shorter text than the Ethiopic, Greek and Latin translations. See M. Baillet, Remarques sur le manuscrit du livre des Jubilés de la grotte 3 de Qumran, *RQ* 5 (1964–66) 423–33; Rofé, Fragments, 336; A.S. van der Woude, Fragmente des Buches Jubiläen aus Höhle XI (11QJub), in: G. Jeremias, H.W. Kuhn, H. Stegemann, ed., *Tradition und Glaube. Das frühe Christentum in seiner Umwelt. FS K.G. Kuhn*, (Göttingen: Vandenhoeck & Ruprecht, 1971) 140–6; VanderKam, *Jubilees*; J.T. Milik, A propos de 11QJub, *Biblica* 54 (1973) 77–8; M. Kister, Newly-Identified Fragments of the Book of Jubilees, *RQ* 12 (1987) 529–36.
11. The Masoretes recorded a half-sentence divider *'etnaḥ* after בניו.
12. Therefore, Rofé's proposal, ibid., 335–6, also weighed by Deichgräber, Fragmente, 420, to insert here the words אף הוא וילך is unwarranted.

L. 2 holds 33 letters and l. 3 32. Each one contains eight words and seven inter-word spaces, viz. altogether 40 and 39 spaces respectively. L. 4 contains 35 letters with seven words and six inter-word spaces, viz. 41 spaces in all, and l. 5 has 35 letters of eight words and seven inter-word spaces, viz. a total of 42 spaces. The larger number of letters and spaces in the latter two lines is set off by the fact that they contain each 16 thin letters, whereas ll. 2 and 3 hold only eight.[13] Thus all four lines were originally of approximately the same length. As stated, the blank at the end of l. 1 means that the text in this line is somewhat shorter. It contained presumably seven words with 29 letters and six inter-word spaces, viz. 35 spaces in all.

On the strength of these calculations and the supporting evidence of the Book of Jubilees, the text of the partly preserved lines of the Masada fragment can be reconstructed as follows:

1 ובנות בניו וכול זרעו הביא אתו] מצרים vac

2 ואלה שמות בני ישראל הבאים מצרי]ם את יעקוב

3 אביהם בכור יעקוב ראובן] ו[בנ]י ראובן חנוך

4 ופלוא וחצרון וכרמי ובני שמעון ימ]ו[אל וימין

5 ואוהד ויכין וצוחר ושאול בן הכנענית] ובני לוי

Comments

1 וכול. Plene, as in 4QJub[f].

2 יעקוב. On the basis of this reading, plene spelling was adopted throughout in the proposed restoration of the text. Thus, יעקוב (ll. 2,3), ואוהד and וצוחר (l. 5), as against MT: ואהד and וצחר (= Exod 6:15, MT and Sam).

2–3 את יעקוב appears to reflect the variant את יעקוב אביהם of Jubilees against MT: יעקב ובניו.

3 בכור יעקוב ראובן. In the parallel text Exod 6:14, MT reads: ראובן בכר ישראל.

5 The name ואו(ו)הד, also recorded in Exod 6:15 and Jub 44:11, is missing in the parallel lists in Num 26:12; 1 Chr 4:24. It is required here because of considerations of space. Thus, MasGen indirectly supports the MT of Genesis.

5 הכנענית. The readings of Jubilees ms. A: צפנאות and ms. B: פנצואתא reflect the variant: הצפתית, viz. "a woman from the city of Zephath". The author possibly intended to particularize the general definition הכנענית, by having recourse to the statement in Judg 1:17: "Judah ... attacked the Cananites in Zephath and destroyed them". The Sages, followed by medieval interpreters, took הכנענית to refer to Jacob's daughter Dinah who was given in marriage to Simeon, and "behaved like a Canaanite." Another tradition maintains that she was in fact a Canaanite, and begot with Simeon a son named

---

13.   In Rofé's reconstruction, a line in 3QJub5 holds 38–42 letters; in Deichgräber's 40–44.

Shelumiel ben Ṣurishaddai, who became the leader of the tribe.[14] The midrash identifies this son with Zimri ben Salu, another tribal leader who engaged in fornication with a Moabite woman in the Shittim incident (Num 25:1–15). Cf. TFr: "Saul is Zimri who engaged in Canaanite harlotry at Shittim."[15]

Measurements

In the above reconstruction, the extant letters and spaces in each of the last four lines comprise about 25–30 percent of the 39–41 spaces which a line contained. In ll. 3 and 4 the extant writing takes up ca. 3 cm. Therefore we can estimate the original width of the column at approximately 11–12 cm. Adding a right hand margin of 6–8 mm, the width of an average column in the scroll would have come to 11.5–12.5 cm.[16]

14. MidHag on Genesis, ed. M. Margolies, 3–6.
15. See also Exod 6:15, *b. Sanh.* 82b; MidRab Num 21.3; MidTan, 3, 20–1; YalShim I, 161.
16. Deichgräber, Fragmente, 415–22, assesses the width of a column in 3QJub5 at 11.5–12 cm, which in his opinion is the standard width of a column in Qumran manuscripts. But there are certainly also scrolls extant with broader or narrower columns.

(b)   Mas 1039–270; Mas 1a; Leviticus 4:3–9 (MasLev^a, final photo 5251)

Yadin described this find as follows:

> *Leviticus* (1039–270). This fragment (11×10 cm)[1] appears to have been deliber-
> ately torn. It contains the second halves of eight lines from Leviticus 4:3–9. The
> text agrees with the Massoretic both in contents and spelling. The script is
> Herodian and resembles that of the Thanksgiving Hymns.[2]

Description

MasLev^a was found on November 25, 1963 in the southern part of the third casemate to
the south of the 'synagogue' (Yadin, *IEJ* 15, 82). It consists of two pieces of very light
brown, almost white parchment.[3] The larger piece (a) measures 9.7×6.3 cm, the smaller
(b) 5.5×7.6 cm. The lower edge of (a) dovetails with the upper edge of (b). The top line of
(b) intertwines in fact with the bottom line of (a), so that elements of letters and even
words in one line complement fragmentary letters in the other, giving a consecutive text.
Conjoined, (a) and (b) constitute a fragment which measures 9.7×11.5 cm. On (a) the
end parts of six lines are extant, on (b) the beginnings of three, so that altogether the
remains of eight fragmentary lines are preserved. A lower margin, over 3 cm wide,
proves that these lines come from the bottom of the sheet.

A vertical string of needle holes on the left-hand side of (a) indicates that the partially
extant column was the last on this sheet, which had been stitched on to the next. Since
the last letters in (a) ll. 3 and 5 actually abut on the stitching marks, the column was set
apart from the next by the right-hand margin of the adjoining one. A tiny part of the
margin still protrudes beyond the stitching marks at l. 4.

The upper almost straight edge of (a) may indeed evince deliberate tearing, as Yadin
surmised,[4] but the disjunction of the two pieces of parchment appears to have resulted
from rupture of the material due to natural causes. Also the ragged left-hand edges of
both (a) and (b) do not seem to have resulted from wilful tearing. Rather, they seem to
have been caused by the deterioration of the leather, facilitated by the decay of the
thread with which that sheet had been stitched to the adjoining one.

---

1.   The measurements need to be emended slightly. See below.
2.   Yadin, *IEJ* 15, 104. See also his short remark in *EAE*, 812: "Leviticus: 1. A small fragment found in
     casemate 1039, containing half of eight lines of Leviticus 4:3–9. The text corresponds throughout to
     the Masoretic text."
3.   The colour has somewhat darkened.
4.   In his discussion of several items found on Masada, among them the fragment of the 'Songs of the
     Sabbath Sacrifice,' he refers to the report of Flavius Josephus that Roman soldiers maliciously tore
     up Torah scrolls to anger and debase the Jews. See Newsom-Yadin, Songs, below, 118.

Script

The scroll from which this fragment stems was penned in an early Herodian formal script comparable to that of the Hodayoth Scroll (1QH), as Yadin stated, and can be dated to the last quarter of the 1st century BCE.[5] The letters measure ca. 2×2 mm and are mostly uniformly executed. They are evenly spaced, with a fraction of a millimeter separating one from the other, but in some instances two or more letters flow together ligature-like, e.g. in לפני (l. 3), כה in הכהן (ll. 3, 4, 5); אצבעו in צב (l. 4), מן (ll. 4, 5), פתח (l. 6), and ממנו (l. 7). At the end of the bottom line the letters are appreciably smaller and somewhat crowded, for no apparent reason. There would have been ample room for accommodating the short word על, which follows ואת היתרת, in the now missing part of the line. A fault in the leather possibly forced the scribe to reduce the letter size. A large ink stain covers the word אל in line 2. Another stain is partly visible above the preceding word הפר, and a third in the inter-line space between ll. 3 and 4.

Inter-line spaces of 9 mm separate the upper four and the last two lines from one another. The middle lines are separated by a space of 8 mm. Although there are no discernible dry rulings for the guidance of the scribe the lines run parallel, except for the endings of ll. 6 and 7 which bend slightly downwards.

The extant partial lines contain an unequal number of letters. However, since the preserved text tallies with the MT, the original written lines can be fully restored. The restoration shows that a complete line originally held an average of 55–56 letters and 14–16 inter-word spaces. The shortest, line 4, would have contained 53, and the longest, line 5, which abuts on the stitching marks, 59. L. 1 has 15 words and 14 inter-word spaces; ll. 2–6 and 8 hold each 16 words and 15 inter-word spaces, and l. 7, 17 words and 16 inter-word spaces. The average total of letters and inter-word spaces amounts to 70. It follows that the lines of this manuscript were appreciably longer and the columns accordingly wider than in other biblical fragments from Masada.[6]

Restored Text

אם הכהן המשיח יחטא לאשמת העם וה]קריב על	1
חטאתו אשר חטא פר בן בקר תמים ליהוה לחטאת] והֹבֿיֿא את הפר אֹל פתח אהל מוֹעֿוֿד	2
לפני יהוה וסמך את ידו על ראש הפר] ושחט את הפר לפני יהוה ולקח הכהן המשיח	3
מדם הפר והביא אתו אל אהל מועד] וטֿבל הכהן את אצבעו בדם והזה מן הדם שבעֿ	4
פעמים לפני יהוה את פני פר]כֿת הקדש ונתן הכהן מן הדם על קרנות מזבח קטרת הסמים	5
לפני יהוה אשר באהל מועד ואת כ]ֹל דם הפר ישפוך אל יסוד מזֿבח העלה אשר פתח	6
אהל מועד ואת כל חלב פר החטאת ירים] ממנו את החלב המכסה על הקרב ואֹת כל החֹלב	7
אשר על הקרב ואת שתי הכלית ואת החלב אשֿ]וֿר עליהן אשר על הכסלים ואת היתרֹת על	8

---

5. See Cross, Scripts, 138, l. 4.
6. E.g. in MasLevᵇ, the figures fluctuate between 44 and 55 spaces (see below).

Illustration 3: MasLev^a 1039–270

Comments

As stated, the text of MasLev^a is identical with MT, except for the plene spelling ישפוך (l. 6) against MT: ישפך.[7] The persuasive identity of MasLev^a and MT becomes fully apparent in four instances of variants and pluses exhibited in an ancient version or versions, where the extant text of MasLev^a actually concurs with MT or a letter count requires the restoration of a concordant reading, as e.g. in l. 5 = Lev 4:6–7.[8]

Lev 4:4 MT	= MasLev^a l. 3: הפר[1]	LXX:		+ ἔναντι κυρίου
4:5	=	l. 3: המשיח	LXX, Sam:	+ אשר מלא את ידו
4:6	=	l. 5: פעמים	LXX^{BA}, Sam:	+ באצבעו
4:8	=	l. 7: על הקרב	LXX, Sam, TJ, TO^{mss}, Syr:	את הקרב[9]

7. Therefore, possibly also other words, such as אתו (Lev 4:5), were spelled plene in difference from the defective MT spelling.

8. The comparison with the only Qumran fragment of Leviticus which contains a few words from Lev 4:4–6 (4QLev^c frg. 2), shows that its reconstituted text is identical with that of MT and MasLev^a: ‏[ושחט את הפר] לפני יהוה ולקח הכ̇הן המשיח מדם הפר והביא אתו אל אהל מועד̇ וטבל הכ̇הן את אצבעו בדם והזה מן הדם ‏שבע פעמים לפני יהו[ה את פ̇נ̇י פרכת הקדש]. See: *DJD* XII, 190.

9. Also MT^{mss}. Possibly a harmonization of the text with Lev 3:3 et al. where MT and all versions read את הקרב ... על הקרב.

Measurements

We can calculate the actual width of the original column on the basis of l. 5. The extant 39 letters of eleven words and ten inter-word spaces cover approximately 9.4 cm. The restored text comprises 23 letters of seven words which, together with six inter-word spaces, take up another 3.8 cm. It follows that the fully written out line would have been ca. 13.2 cm long. With an expected right-hand margin of some 1.2 cm, the width of the column came to about 14.5 cm, and was appreciably wider than the average column of other biblical manuscripts from Masada (see below).

The comparatively large width suggests that the scroll was also of exceeding height. This assumption is supported by the width of its lower margin, which measures more than 3 cm. Its actual measurement cannot be ascertained though, because the upper part of the column is not preserved. Neither can we assess the amount of text which could be accommodated in one column. Therefore, we have no means for assessing the original length of MasLev^a.

(c)   Mas 92–480; Mas1b; Leviticus 8:31–11:40 (MasLev[b], photos 302359, 302360, 302368, 302369, 302370)

Yadin did not mention this item in his first report, but apparently referred to it in passing in a lecture presented at the twenty-second annual meeting of the Israel Archaeological Society in 1965,[1] and then described it in short:

> Large fragments of Leviticus found torn and crumpled in a corner of the square between the Northern Palace and the large bathhouse. It contains a large part of chapters 8–12,[2] and is identical with the Masoretic Text, with spaces between the chapters.[3]

Yadin had evidently begun working on this item, since among his papers a provisional restoration of the text was found. A revised version of this reconstruction serves as the basis for the ensuing discussion.

Description

MasLev[b] consists of over forty fragments, ranging from mere scraps of parchment to pieces of approximately the size of the palm of a hand, all of a very dark brown hue. About half are blank and come from the margins. Some contain only a few letters, whereas others display complete, or almost complete lines, at times even successive lines. A string of needle holes at the left edge proves that col. V was the last column of the sheet. The smoothness of the edge at the bottom of the sheet resulted from the break of the parchment along the stitching. There still remains some of the thread by which that sheet was joined to the next.

Script

The ink has faded, but the writing is still easily legible on infra-red photographs, and to a large extent even on the original. The scroll was penned by an expert scribe in a Herodian bookhand, and may be dated to the late last century BCE or the early 1st century CE.[4] Thus, it was written somewhat later than MasLev[a]. Recurring letters are executed uniformly. They measure mostly ca. 2.5×2.5 mm, and are separated by spaces measuring a fraction of a millimeter. Now and again two or more letters flow together, ligature-like, e.g. in עגל (col. I, l. 20); חטאת (col. III, l. 18); לכם (col. V, l. 23), and בגדיו (col. V, last line). Words are separated by a space of somewhat less than 1 mm.

---

1.   Yadin, Qumran (Hebrew) 16: "The fragments of the biblical scrolls, among them parts of Psalms, Leviticus, Genesis, Deuteronomy and Ezekiel ... were discovered in the destruction-level of Masada ... some of them sealed in the *genizah* under the floor of the synagogue."
2.   *Lege* 8–11, and see below.
3.   Yadin, *EAE*, 813–4.
4.   See Cross, *Scripts*, 138, ll. 3 and 4.

Illustration 4: MasLev^b 92–480

The lines are straight and run parallel, and line beginnings are justified, although neither horizontal nor vertical dry rulings can be discerned. In the middle of col. IV, ll. 14–18, the lines are somewhat slanted, probably due to a slight fault in the parchment. Inter-line spaces are 6 mm wide. In some instances, the scribe seems to have misjudged the amount of text which could be accommodated in a line. This resulted in excessively wide blanks at the end of the four bottom lines in col. V, since he avoided dividing words. In l. 9 of that column, the last word, הערב, spills over into the margin.

A top margin 1.8 cm wide is extant in col. II, and a bottom margin 2.7 cm wide in col. V. The width of the inter-column margins is not uniform. Between cols. I and II it comes to almost 3 cm, between cols. III and IV to 2 cm, and to only 1.7 cm between cols. IV and V.

Text

The two largest fragments can be conjoined comfortably because of their dovetailing edges. The combined piece measures 12×15.5 cm. It contains the virtually complete text of col. V, extending over 22 lines, and serves as the basis for the restoration of practically the entire text preserved in MasLev[b]. Since the text is essentially identical with MT, almost all remaining smaller fragments can be accommodated in four preceding columns.[5] The preserved run of text leads to the conclusion that MasLev[b] is indeed part of a scroll which contained a proto-MT text of the Book of Leviticus or possibly of the entire Pentateuch.

Restored Text

Column I

1 [הבשר פתח אהל מועד ושם תאכלו אתו ואת הלח]ם אשר

2 [בסל המלאים כאשר צויתי לאמר אהרן ובניו יא]כֹלֻהו

3 [והנותר בבשר ובלחם באש תשרפו ומפתח אהל מועד ל]א

4 [תצאו שבעת ימים עד יום מלאת ימי מלאיכם כי שבע]תֿ

5 [ימים ימלא את ידכם כאשר עשה ביום הזה צוה יהו]הֿ

6 [לעשת לכפר עליכם ופתח אהל מועד תשבו יומם ולילה]

7 [שבעת ימים ושמרתם את משמרת יהוה ולא תמותו כי כן]

8 [צויתי ויעש אהרן ובניו את כל הדברים אשר צוה יהוה]

9 [ביד משה   ויהי ביו]ֹם השֹֿמיני קרא משה לאהרן]

10 [ולבניו ולזקני ישר]אֿל ויאמר [אל אהרן קח לך עגל בן]

11 [בקר לחט]אֿת וֹאֿיל לעלֹה [תמי]ֹמם ו]הקרב לפני יהוה ואל]

12 [בני ישרא]ֹל תדבֹֻר] לאמֹר [קחו] שֿעיר עזים לֻ[חטאת]

13 [ועגל וכב]ֿש בני שֻֿנה תמי]ֿמֿם [לעל]ֿה ושור וֹאֿיל לשלמים]

---

5. Manuscript finds from Masada and Qumran suggest that five was the standard number of columns on a sheet of parchment.

Column I (Cont.)

14 [לזבח לפני י]הוה ו[מנחה] בֿלולֿהֿ בשמן כי היום יהוה [נראה]

15 אליכם ויקחו את אשר צוה משה] אֿלֿ פני אהל מֿוֿעד [ויקרבו]

16 [כל העדה ויעמדו לפני יהוה ויאמר מש]ה זה הד[בר אשר]

17 [צוה יהוה תעשו וירא אליכם כבוד יהוה ויאמר משה]

18 [אל אהרן קר]בֿ אֿלֿ המזבח ועשה את חטא[ת]ֿךֿ [ואת עלתך וכפר]

19 [בעדך ובעד] העם ועֿ[שֿ]ה את [קרבן] אֿת [העם וכֿפֿוֿר] בעדם

20 [כאשר צוה יהו]ה ויקרב אהרן אל המז[בֿ]חֿ וישֿחט את עגל

21 [החטאת אש]רֿ לו ויקרבו ב[נ]י אהרן את הדם אל[יו וי]טבֿ[ל] אצבעו

22 [בדם ויתן על קרנו]ת הֿ[מ]זֿבח ו[את הדם יצק אל יסוד המזבח]

23 [ואת החלב ואת הכ]לֿית [ואת היתרת מן הכבד מן החטאת ה]קטיר

24 [המזבחה כאשר צוה יהוה את משה ואת הבשר ואת העור]

25 [שרף באש מחוץ למחנה וישחט את העלה וימצאו בני]

Column II

1 אֿהֿרֿ[ן] [אליו א]תֿ ה[דם ויזרקהו על המזבח סביב ואת העלה]

2 [המצֿיֿ]או אליוֿ [לנתחיה ואת הראש ויקטר על המזבח וירחץ]

3 [את הקרב ואת הכרעים ויקטר על העלה המזבחה ויקרב]

4 [את קרבן העם ויקח את שעיר החטאת אשר לעם וישחטהו]

5 [ויחטאהו כראשון ויקרב את העלה ויעשה כמשפט ויקרב את]

6 [המנחה וימלא כפו ממנה ויקטר על המזבח מלבד עלת הבקר]

7 [וישחט את השור ואת האיל זבח השלמים אשר לעם וימצאו]

8 [בני אהרן את הדם אליו ויזרקהו על המזבח סביב ואת]

9 [החלבים מן השור ומן האיל האליה והמכסה והכלית ויתרת]

10 [הכבד וישימו את החלבים על החזות ויקטר החלבים המזבחה]

11 [ואת החזות ואת שוק הימין הניף אהרן תנופה לפני יהוה]

12 [כאשר צוה משה וישא אהרן את ידו אל העם ויברכם וירד]

13 [מע]שֿת הֿחֿ[ט]את והעלה והשלמים ויבא משה ואהרן אל]

14 [א]הֿל מועד ויצאֿוֿ ויברכו את העם וירא כבוד יהוה אל כל]

15 העם ותצא אש [מלפני יהוה ותאכל על המזבח את]

16 העלה ו[ו]אֿתֿ הֿ[ח]לבים וירא כל העם וירנו ויפלו על פניהם]

17 [ו]יֿקֿחו בני אהרן נדב ואביהוא איש מחתתו ויתנו בהן אש]

18 [וישימו עליה קטרת ויקרבו לפני יהוה אש זרה אשר לא]

19 [צוה אתם ותצא אש מלפני יהוה ותאכל אותם וימתו לפני]

20 [יהוה ויאמר משה אל אהרן הוא אשר דבר יהוה לאמר]

[43]

Column II (Cont.)

21 [בקרבי אקדש ועל פני כל העם אכבד וידם אהרן ויקרא]

22 [משה אל מישאל ואל אלצפן בני עזיאל דד אהרן ויאמר]

23 [אלהם קרבו שאו את אחיכם מאת פני הקדש אל מחוץ למחנה]

24 [ויקרבו וישאם בכתנתם אל מחוץ למחנה כאשר דבר משה]

25 [ויאמר משה אל אהרן ולאלעזר ולאיתמר בניו ראשיכם]

Column III

1 [אל תפרעו ובגדיכם לא תפרמו ולא תמתו ועל כל העדה]

2 [יקצף ואחיכם כל בית ישראל יבכו את השרפה אשר שרף]

3 [יהוה ומפתח אהל מועד לא תצאו פן תמותו כי שמן]

4 [משחת יהוה עליכם ויעשו כדבר משה]

5 [וידבר יהוה אל אהרן לאמר] יֹין ושכֹר אֹל תֹשת אתֹה וֹ[בנ]יֹך

6 [אתך בבאכם אל אהל מוע]ד ולא תמתו חקת עולם לדרתיכם

7 [ולהבדיל בין הק]דֹש ובין החל ובין הטמא ובין [הט]הֹוֹר

8 [ולהורת א]תֹ בנ[י] ישראל את כל החקים [אשר] דֹבֹֹר יהוה

9 [אליהם ביד מ]שֹֹה

10 [וידבר משה אל אהרן ואל אלעזר ו]אֹל איתמר בניו הֹ[נותרים]

11 [קחו את המנחה הנותרת מאשי יה]וֹה ואכלוֹהֹ מֹ[צות אצל]

12 [המזבח כי קדש קדשים הוא ואכ]לֹתם אתה ב[מקום קדוש כי]

13 [חקך וחק בניך הוא מאשי יהו]הֹ כי כן צֹוויתי ואת חזה]

14 [התנופה ואת שוק התרומה תאכלו במקום טהור אתה] וֹ[בניך]

15 [ובנתיך אתך כי חקך וחק בניך נתנו מזבחי שלמי] בני

16 [ישראל שוק התרומה וחזה] התֹנֹוֹ[פה] עֹ[ל] אֹשי החל[בֹ]ים

17 [יביאו להניף תנופה לפני יה]וֹה והֹיֹה לך ולבניך [אתך] לֹחק

18 [עולם כאשר צוה יהוה וא]ת שעיר החטאת דֹרֹש דרש משה

19 [והנה שרף ויקצף] על אלעזֹ[ר] וֹ[עֹ]ל איתמר בנֹי אהרן

20 [הנות]רים לֹאמר מדוע לא אכלתם אֹת החֹטֹאֹת בֹמֹקום ה[קדש כי]

21 [קד]ש קדשים הוֹא ואתה נתן לכם לשאֹת את עוֹ[ן העדה לכפר]

22 [עלי]הֹֹם לפני יהוה הן לֹֹא [הוב]א את דמה אל ה[קדש פנימה]

23 [אכו]ל [תאכלו אתה בקדש כאשר צוית]י וידבר אהֹרן אל משה

24 [הן היום ה]קֹרי[בו את חטאתם ואת עלתם לפנ]יֹ יהוה וֹתֹ[קראנה]

25 [אתי כאל]הֹ ואכלתֹ[י] חטאת היום הייטב בעינֹ[י] יהֹ[וה] ויֹ[שמע]

Column IV

1 ‏[משה וייטב בעיניו]‏

2 ‏[וידבר יהוה א]ל מ̇ש̇ה ואל אהרן לאמר אלהם דברו אל בני]‏

3 ‏[ישראל לאמר] זאת החיה א̇ו̇שר תאכלו מכל הבהמה אשר]‏

4 ‏על הא]רץ כל מפרסת] פרסה וש̇ו]סעת שסע פרסת מעלת]‏

5 ‏גרה בבהמה [אתה] ת̇ו]אכל̇ו אך את [זה לא תאכלו ממעלי]‏

6 ‏הגר]ה̇ וממפריס̇ו]י̇ הפ̇ר̇ו]סה] את [הגמל כי מעלה גרה הוא]‏

7 ‏ופרסה] איננו [מפרי]ס̇ טמא הוא לכם ואת השפן כי מעלה]‏

8 ‏גרה הו]א ופרסה̇ ל̇א [יפריס טמא הוא לכם ואת הארנבת]‏

9 ‏כי מעל̇ת גרה הוא ופ̇ו]רסה לא הפריסה טמאה הוא לכם]‏

10 ‏ואת] החזיר כי מפרי]ס פרסה הוא ושסע שסע פרסה]‏

11 ‏והוא] גרה לא יגר טמא הוא לכם̇ [מבשרם לא תאכלו ובנבלתם]‏

12 ‏לא] תג̇עו טמ̇אי]ם̇ הם לכם   [את זה תאכלו מכל אשר]‏

13 ‏במים כ]ל א̇שר לו] סנפיר וק̇ש̇ו]קשת במים בימים ובנחלים]‏

14 ‏א]ת̇ם ת̇ו]א̇כלו [וכל אשר אין לו סנפיר וקשקשת בימים ובנחלים]‏

15 ‏מכל [שרץ] המים [ומכל נפש החיה אשר במים שקץ הם]‏

16 ‏ל]כ̇ם̇ ושקץ יהיו [לכ]ם̇ מבשרם [לא תאכלו ואת נבלתם תשקצו]‏

17 ‏כ]ל̇ אשר אין לו סנפיר וקשקשת במים [שקץ הוא לכם]‏

18 ‏ואת א]ל̇ה̇ תשקצו [מן] ה̇ע̇ו]ף לא יאכלו שקץ הם את]‏

19 ‏ה̇ו]נשר ואת ה]פר]ס̇ ו̇את ה̇ו]עזניה ואת הדאה ואת האיה למינה]‏

20 ‏את] כ̇ל̇ ערב למינו ואת [בת היענה ואת התחמס ואת השחף]‏

21 ‏ואת הנץ למינ]ו̇ ואת הכ̇ו̇ו]ס ואת השלך ואת הינשוף̇]‏

22 ‏ואת התנשמת וא]ת̇ הקאת ואת ה̇ו]רחם ואת החסידה האנפה]‏

23 ‏למינה ואת הדוכיפת] וא̇ת̇ [העטלף כל שרץ העוף ההלך על]‏

24 ‏ארבע שקץ הוא] לכ̇ם̇   [אך את זה תאכלו מכל שרץ]‏

25 ‏העוף ההלך על] א̇ר̇ב̇ו]ע̇ אשר לא כרעים ממעל לרגליו לנתר]‏

Column V

1 ‏[בהן על הארץ את אלה מהם תאכלו את הארבה למינו ואת]‏

2 ‏[הסלעם למינהו ואת ה̇חרגל למינהו ואת החגב למינהו]‏

3 ‏[וכל שר]ץ̇ ה̇ו]עוף אשר לו ארבע רגלים שקץ הוא לכם ולאלה]‏

4 ‏תטמ̇א̇ו כל הנג̇ו]ע̇ בנבלתם יטמא] עד [הערב וכל הנשא מנבלתם]‏

5 ‏יכבס בגדיו וטמא עד הע̇ו]ר̇ב ל̇כל הב̇ו]המה אשר הוא מפרסת]‏

6 ‏פרסה וש̇ו]ס̇ו]ע̇ איננה שס]עת וג̇רה̇ אי̇ו]ננה מעלה טמאים הם]‏

7 ‏לכם כל ה̇ו]נגע בהם̇ יטמא וכל הול̇ו]ך̇ [על כפיו בכל החיה]‏

8 ‏ההלכת על] ארב̇ע̇ו]‏ טמאים הם לכם כל הנג̇ו]ע̇ בנ̇בלתם יט̇ו]מא]‏

Column V (Cont.)

9 ‏[עד הער]וֹב והנשא את נב[ל]תם יכב[ס בגדיו וטמא עֹד הערב

10 ‏[טמאי]םֹ הֹמה לכם   וזה לכֹם הטמא בשרץ

11 ‏[ה]שֹרץ [על] הארץ ה[ח]לֹד והעכ[ב]רֹ והצב למֹינהו והאנקֹה

12 ‏[וה]כֹח והלטאה והחמט והתנ[שמת] אלה הטמאים לכם ב[כל]

13 ‏הֹשרץ כל הנגע בהֹם במתֹם יטמא עֹ[ד] הערב [וכ]ל אשר יפֹל

14 ‏עליֹו מֹהֹם במתֹם יטֹ⌐מ⌐א מכל כלי עץ או בֹגֹד או [עֹור] או שֹק

15 ‏כל כלי אשר יֹעשה [מלא]כֹה בהם במים יובֹא וטמא עד

16 ‏הער[וב] וטהר וֹכֹלֹ [כל]יֹ חֹרֹשֹ אשר יפל מֹ[ה]ם אֹל תוכֹוֹ כֹל אֹשֹר

17 ‏בתוכֹו יטמא ואתו תשברו מכל האכלֹ אשר י[א]כֹל א[שר יבֹו]א

18 ‏[ע]לֹיֹו מים יטמא וכל משֹקה אשר ישתה בכל כלי יטמֹא

19 ‏וכֹלֹ אשר יפל מנ[וב]לֹתם עליו יטמא תנור וכֹ'רים יתֹץֹ [טמאי]םֹ

20 ‏[הם] וֹ[ט]מאֹיֹםֹ יהיו לכם אך מעין ובור מקוה מים יֹהיה טהור

21 ‏[ונגע] בֹנבלתֹ[ם] יטמא ו[כי יפל מנבלתם על כל זרע זרוע אשר יזרע

22 ‏טהור הֹ[וא וכי י]תֹן מים על זרע ונפל מנבלתם עליו טמא הוא

23 ‏[לכם]   וכי ימות מן הבהמה אשר היא לכם לאכלה

24 ‏[הנגע בנב]לֹ[תה] יטמא עד הערב והאכל מנבלתה יכבס בגדיו

25 ‏[וטמא עד הערב] והנשא את נבלתה יכבֹס בגדיו וטמא עד

1. The textual identity of MasLev[b] with MT is evinced by the meticulous preservation of the defective and plene spellings, both in readings which are actually extant in MasLev[b] and in instances in which considerations of space and a letter count make the proposed restoration of a missing text part a certainty. Thus, MasLev[b] exhibits the MT plene spelling of ‏הֹ[וקטיר (col. I, l. 23 = Lev 9:10), ‏המצֹיאו (col. II, l. 2 = Lev 9:13); ‏הֹקרינֹבו (col. III, l. 24 = Lev 10:19); ‏וממפריסֹי (col. IV, l. 6 = Lev 11:4, cf. 11:7)[6] *et sim.*

The agreement is particularly apparent in cases in which MasLev[b] exhibits the same inconsistency as MT in the employment of defective and plene spellings. E.g. ‏תמי[מם is twice spelled defectively (col. I, ll. 11, 13), as in Lev 9:2, 3,[7] and throughout Leviticus and Numbers. Similarly ‏ויַֹקֹרֹבו (col. I, l. 21 = Lev 9:9 in contrast to Lev 10:19: ‏הקריבו = col. III, l. 24: ‏הֹ[וקרינֹבו); ‏הכֹלית (col. I, l. 23 = Lev 9:10, and thus throughout Leviticus); ‏לדרתיכם (col. III, l. 6 = Lev 10:9). See especially ‏במתם (col. V, l. 14 = Lev 11:32) and ‏במתֹם (col. V, l. 13 = Lev 11:31), in contrast to the plene spelling of Sam, ‏במותם, which is also

6. Ginsburg adopts in his main text the defective spelling ‏וממפרסי from a minority of witnesses (Hilleli).
7. Neither Ginsburg nor BHS record here a plene spelling in any masoretic manuscript. Contrast the plene spelling of similar morphemes in both MT and MasLev[b], e.g. ‏הטמאים, טמאים (Lev 11:8, 31 cf. 11:17 = col. V, l. 8, 12).

the spelling of the Palaeo-Hebrew Leviticus Scroll from Qumran.[8] The tendency to preserve defective spellings clearly differentiates the scribal tradition of MasLev^b from that of Qumran biblical mss in which one observes a distinct preference for plene spelling.[9]

2. The identity of the text-tradition of MasLev^b with MT is highlighted by their concurrence in instances in which an ancient version, foremost LXX, exhibits a variant reading, especially when the variant contains a textual plus:

MasLev^b = MT	LXX
Lev 10:9 = III, 1. 6 אהל מוע[ד	+ ἤ προσπορευομένον πρὸς τὸ θυσιαστήριον
10:15 לך ולבניך = III, 1. 17	+ καὶ ταῖς θυγατράσιν σου (cf. v. 14)
11:4 וממפריסי הפרסה = IV, 1. 6	+ καὶ ὀνιχυστῆρας
11:12 כ[ל = IV, 1. 17	καὶ πάντα (= Sam: וכל)
11:26 וש[ס]וע איננה שס[עת = V, 1. 6	Sam: ושסעה איננה שסע
11:26 כל ה[נ]גע בהם = V, 1. 7	+ τῶν θνησιμαίον αυτῶν (cf. v. 10)
11:28 והנשא את נבו[לתם = V, 1. 9	Sam: מנבלתם (= v. 25)
11:28 המה = V, 1. 10	Sam: הם
11:35 יתץ = V, 1. 19	καθαιρεθήσοντο (= Sam: יתצו)
11:36 אך מעין = V, 1. 20	+ ὑδάτων (= Sam: + מים)
11:38 על זרע = V, 1. 22	ἐπί + πᾶν σπέρμα (cf. v. 37)
11:40 יכבס בגדיו = V, 1. 24	+ καὶ λούσεται ὕδατι (cf. Sam ad v. 25)
11:40 והנשא את נבלתה = V, 1. 25	ἀπο θνησιμαίων αυτῶν (cf. v. 25)

There are several additional instances of the interchange of את/מן in the biblical text tradition.[10]

Of interest is a variant in a Qumran fragment of Leviticus where MasLev^b again sides with MT:[11]

11:27 וכל הולך [ועל־כפיו = V, 1. 7   4Q365 17a–c, 2: כול ההולך א[ל

3. Three mistakes were subsequently corrected, apparently by the scribe himself. In col. III, 1. 21 an initially omitted הוא was inserted interlinearly above the words קדשים ואתה (Lev 10:17). Equally, an omitted מ was written over יטא in col. V, 1. 14 (Lev 11:32) to restore the reading יטמא. These two instances are evidently corrections of *lapsus calami*. But in the third instance, the scribe may have adjusted an originally defective spelling

8. Freedman-Mathews, *Leviticus*.
9. See Tov, Manuscripts; idem, Orthography, and pertinent publications adduced there.
10. Talmon, Textual Study, 349–50.
11. *DJD* XIII, 286.

וכרים to the MT plene reading וכירים (Lev 11:35) by entering a *yod* above the line (col. V, l. 19). Similarly, in col. III, l. 20: הנות[ר]ים, he may have harmonized the MT defective spelling הנותרם with the more regular plene spelling הנותרים like e.g. in MT Lev 10:12 = col. III, l. 10.

4. Attention must be drawn to one detail of definite divergence between MasLev[b] and MT, which, though, does not put in doubt their textual affinity. In col. V, ll. 9–10 the preserved text of the fragment agrees word for word and letter for letter with MT of Lev 11:28, including the marking of a section, with one exception: in the concluding phrase of the passage, the fragment undoubtedly displays a final *mem* in the word המם, instead of the expected medial form, as in MT, טמאים המה לכם. This anomaly may have arisen from an incomplete text correction. The scribe presumably wrote at first הם לכם, like in MT Lev 11:10, שקץ הם לכם where the final *mem* is appropriate, but subsequently adjusted his text to the MT reading המה לכם by appending a *he* to his הם, without replacing the final *mem* by the now required medial form.

However, an alternative and possibly preferable explanation can be offered: MasLev[b] may have been copied at a time in the transmission history of the biblical text when the differentiation between the medial and the final forms of the letters צ,פ,נ,מ,כ, viz. ץ,ף,ן,ם,ך, especially of ם/מ had not yet become stabilized.[12] While, as stated, this scribal phenomenon cannot be accurately dated, its manifestation in a variety of sources from the late Second Temple period, can serve as an auxiliary criterion for dating MasLev[b] to that particular timespan.

The Section System[13]

One other characteristic puts MasLev[b] squarely in the MT tradition. The scribe seems to have adhered throughout to the masoretic section system. This becomes evident when he left a blank in a line in which MT indicates a closed section, פרשה סתומה, viz. a mid-line caesura: col. IV between שקץ הוא לכם (Lev 11:12) at the end of l. 18 and ואת אלה תשקצו at the beginning of l. 19 (Lev 11:13);[14] col. V, l. 10 after הםה לכם (Lev 11:28);[15] col. V, l. 22–23 between הוא ולכם] and וכי ימות, viz. after Lev 11:38 where MT marks a closed section.[16] In addition, there are two instances in which the proposed restoration of the text on the basis of a letter count requires a blank in the line, which coincides with a closed section in the major MT witnesses: col. I, l. 9, after ביד משה at the end of ch. 8 (Lev 8:36); col. IV,

---

12. See above, Introduction, 200–22.
13. For the masoretic section system, especially in the Pentateuch, see: Perrot, Alinéas; idem, *Lecture*; Oesch, *PUS*. The issue has again come under review in the wake of the Qumran discoveries of fragments of biblical manuscripts. See Maori, Tradition.
14. Here L marks a section, but Ginsburg does not.
15. Listed in Maimonides' roster of *parashot*. See Oesch, *PUS*, T 2+, L and Ginsburg.
16. Oesch, *PUS*, T 2+, L, Ginsburg.

l. 24 after לכם (Lev 11:20). Further, an open ended or not fully written out line marking an open section is indicated in col. III, l. 9 after ביד מ[ש]ה (Lev 10:11). It is also required in the restored text of col. III, l. 4 after כדבר משה (Lev 10:7); col. IV, l. 1 after בעיניו, the last word of Lev 10; col. IV, l. 12, after ט[מ]אי[ם] הם לכם (Lev 11:8), where Ginsburg records a *parashah*, but L does not.

Measurements

The intact lower part of column V enables us to ascertain the length of the written line, and accordingly also the width of the written column at 9–10 cm. There are, on average, 39 letters in a line with 10 inter-word spaces, i.e. 49 spaces in all. The actual number fluctuates between a maximum of 44 letters and 11 inter-word spaces, viz. a total of 55 spaces, in col. V, l. 21, and a minimum of 34–35 letters and nine inter-word spaces, with a total of 43–44 spaces in lines 15 and 18 of the same column. The other four columns are somewhat narrower. Here the comparable figures can be derived from fully or partially preserved successive lines. In cols. I and III, the average number of letters per line comes to 36, with eight inter-word spaces, i.e a total of 44 spaces. In cols. II and IV, a line holds an average of 38 letters and 8 inter-word spaces, viz. a total of 46 spaces, the maximum being 40–42 letters and 9–10 inter-word spaces, with a total of 50–52 spaces (col. I, ll. 21, 23; col. III, ll. 10, 17, 24; col. IV, ll. 11, 14), and a minimum of 34 letters and 8 inter-word spaces, or 42 spaces in all (col. II, l. 15; col. III, l. 19). L. 9 of col. III and l. 1 of col. IV hold only 11 letters with 2 inter-word spaces. In these exceptionally short lines, a blank denoting a section division, which conforms with the masoretic פרשות system, accounts for the small number of spaces (see above).

Taken together these data make it possible to delineate the layout and the measurements of the sheet which contained the five columns:

The height of the scroll can be estimated by the following calculations. Each column holds 25 lines (col. II has possibly 26). Reckoning an average letter height of 2.5 mm, the written text would have taken up ca. 6 cm (25×2.5 mm). 24 inter-line spaces of 3 mm each amount to approximately 7 cm. Allowing for some fluctuation, it may be concluded that the written column reached a height of about 13 cm. Adding top and bottom margins with an assumed width of ca. 2.5 cm each, the scroll would have stood about 18 cm high.

As stated, the complete lines in col. V show the width of the written column to have been between 9 and 10 cm. The right hand margin is 1 to 2 cm wide, depending on the uneven length of the written lines. Accordingly, the average width of the written column with its blank margin can be estimated at 11 cm, and likewise the width of cols. I–III. Col. IV is somewhat narrower. Here the lettering with the right hand margin covered approximately 10 cm of a line. It follows that the five columns together covered ca. 54 cm of the width of the sheet.

On the basis of these calculations, the length of the complete scroll can be estimated.

The part of Leviticus preserved in the five reconstructed columns comprises a little less than one tenth of the text of the book, both by a verse and a page count: in BHS the Book of Leviticus takes up 43 pages, and the portion of the restored text in the five columns of MasLev[b] (8:31–11:40) about 4.5 pages. In the Snaith edition of the text without any critical apparatus, Leviticus occupies 48 pages, and the relevant portion preserved in MasLev[b] five pages. The Masoretes counted 859 verses in Leviticus, of which the text part 8:31–11:40 takes up 90 verses. We may, therefore, conclude that some 48–50 columns would have been required for accommodating the entire text of Leviticus in the Masada scroll. Since, as said, the width of the restored five columns comes to ca. 54 cm., the scroll would have measured about 5.4–5.6 m when fully rolled out, not taking into account the length of the handle sheet, if such a sheet had been attached to it.

(d) Mas 1043/a-d; Mas 1c; Deuteronomy 33:17–34:6 (MasDeut, photos 302367, 302372)

This item was discovered in the second excavation season. Yadin first referred to it in the published text of his "Qumran and Masada" lecture,[1] and later described it briefly as follows:[2]

> Deuteronomy. Fragments of this scroll were found hidden beneath the floor of the synagogue, next to the fragments of MasEzek.[3] The top of the last parchment with several verses from chapter 33 was mainly preserved. To the left of the text was a wide blank sheet, which was rolled up and sewn to the scroll to make it easier to unroll it.

Netzer provides a more detailed description of the location of the discovery:

> In a later phase, undoubtedly while the synagogue was still in use, two pits were dug in the floor of room 1043: one in the middle, near the western wall, and the other in the southern half. The first pit was circular (some 80 cm in diameter) and about 70 cm deep; the second was oval (ca. 2 m long and 1.4 m wide) and of similar depth. These pits also contained a mixture of gravel, sherds and organic material; more notably, they also yielded several parchment scroll fragments — among the most important and significant finds not only in the synagogue but in all of Masada. The circular pit contained fragments of Deuteronomy, and the oval pit — fragments of the book of Ezekiel ... The scrolls were found near the sides and bottoms of the pits, mainly near their eastern sides (*Masada* III, 410).

Description

MasDeut consists of four inscribed or partially inscribed fragments of parchment of unequal size: (a) measures 8×8 cm. The extant text contains the beginnings of seven lines of the last column of the sheet. A part of the top margin of this column is extant to the width of 3.4 cm. The largest fragment (b), 13.8×10 cm, consists primarily of a blank length of parchment, sewn on to the preceding written sheet, and a strip of the left-hand margin of the last column of that sheet, next to which the endings of seven lines are preserved, of which five continue those on (a). (c) is considerably smaller, 4×3.3 cm, and holds parts of four written lines. On the other small fragment (d), which measures 2×4.5 cm, letters from the middle parts of six lines are extant. (c) and (d) can be conjoined

---

1. Yadin, Qumran (Hebrew), 138.
2. Yadin, *EAE*, 813.
3. See below. Yadin considered these finds an added proof that the locus in which they were found was indeed a synagogue (Yadin, *Fortress*, 187–8).

on the strength of their contours and textual sequence, and will henceforth be designated (c). Similarly, (a) and (b) can be aligned. Since the extant text is identical with MT, all components of MasDeut can be appropriately placed with confidence in the proposed restoration of its text.

Illustration 5: Photo of Synagogue (casemate 1043)

The colour of the parchment is various shades of brown. The right-hand side of (a) is of a dark brown hue; its left-hand side is much lighter; (b) and (c) are of a light-brown colour. The upper right-hand part of (b) is flaked so that the writing has become illegible. The edges of all the fragments are ragged, and all, but especially (b), are perforated with holes of various sizes, which resulted from the deterioration of the material or from damage caused by vermin.

A blank stretch of parchment measuring 9.7×11 cm makes up most of (b). This is evidently the remainder of the handle sheet which served as a protective wrapper for the written columns, and was probably stitched to the scroll after the completion of the writing.[4] Needle holes with a slip of thread running through them are clearly visible where this piece was sewn to the last written sheet.[5] In this respect MasDeut differs from Qumran scrolls in which the blank handle piece is usually part and parcel of the last written sheet.[6]

The handle sheet is preserved to a much greater extent than the last written sheet which, like all preceding sheets, is mostly lost because of the deterioration of the material. This condition suggests that the scroll had been readied for reading by rolling it up from end to beginning. As a result, the handle sheet and the adjoining column constituted the innermost part of the roll, and therefore suffered less from the eroding impact of climate and/or vermin than the other sheets. These were increasingly exposed to the detrimental impact the closer they were to the beginning of the scroll. The progression of deterioration would have been reversed had the scroll been rolled up for storing, after having been fully read out. Then the handle sheet at its end would indeed have served as a protective outer wrapper for the written columns.

Script

The lettering on the darkish brown leather has faded, but on infrared photographs the text is legible. The scroll was evidently penned by an expert scribe in an early Herodian formal hand.[7] The size of the letters is mostly 3×3 mm, with some larger ones, like final *mem*, reaching a width of 4 mm, and the thin letters *waw, yod* and final *nun* of 1 mm. Letters are visibly separated by less than 1 mm, with a space of 2 mm separating one word from the next. Only in some instances are two letters contiguous, e.g. תך in בצאתך (a, l. 2), גד in לגד (a, l. 4) פו in ספון (a, l. 6) גו in גור (b, l. 7) or עב in תעבר (c, l. 6). Although there are no dry rulings, the scribe managed to keep his lines straight and parallel to each other, with an inter-line space of ca. 8 mm, measured from the letter tops in one line to those in the next. Also the line beginnings on (a) are perfectly adjusted.

4. I am indebted to Prof. H. Stegemann for the following observation: Judging by the lineaments of the deteriorated material, the leather of the handle sheet, and probably of the entire scroll, was about twice as thick as that of the Hodayoth Scroll from Qumran (1QH), and approximately 2.5 mm thicker than that of the Temple Scroll (11QTemp), and had been very tightly rolled.
5. In addition, there remain photographs of three small and two long blank strips of parchment, the originals of which could not be located. The smaller ones are 3.5, 2.2 and 1.6 cm long, and between 0.3 and 0.9 cm broad. The two larger ones measure 10.2×2.4 and 10.2×1.9 cm respectively. Judging by their contours, all these strips come from the left-hand edge of the handle sheet.
6. E.g. in the Pesher Habakkuk from Qumran (1QpHab) the blank piece is preceded by six columns of text recorded on the same sheet.
7. See Cross, Scripts, 136, fig. 2, ii; 3, 4.

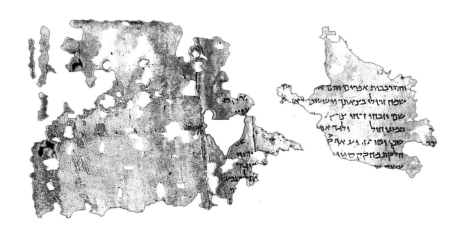

Transcription

Illustration 6: MasDeut 1043/a–d

(a)+(b)

והם רבבות אפרים והם אלֹופי מנ]שֹׁה	1
שמח זבולֹן בצאתך ויששכר באהֹלֹי]ךֹ [עמים] הֹר יקראֹו	2
שם יזבחו זבֹחי צדֹק כֹ]יֹן שֹׁ]פע ימים יינקו ו]שֹׁפֹנֹי	3
לשמֹ]ר טמוני חול ולגד אמרֹ]	4
]ֹדֹבר שכן וטרֹֹף זרֹוע אף קֹ]דקד] וי]רא ראֹ]שֹׁיֹתֹ לֹֹו [כי] שֹׁם	5
חלקת מחקק ספֹון [ויתא ראשי עם] צֹדֹקֹת יהוה	6
עשה וֹמֹ]שפטיו עם ישראל ולדן אמֹֹר דן גור	7
]פֹֹתליֹ] שבע	8
] ולאֹ]שֹׁר	9

(c)+(d)

ו]את כל נֹ]פֹתלי]ן	1
]ארץ יהודֹה]	2
]בֹקעתֹ]	3
יהו]הֹ אליו זאת]	4
לי]צֹחֹק וליעקֹ]בֹ] לאמֹֹר	5
ו]שֹׁמֹ]הֹ] לֹא תעבר וימת שם	6
יהו]הֹ ויקבר]	7
א]יֹשֹׁ]	8

[54]

Comments

The extant fragments contain parts of Deut 33–34, with (a) holding most of the preserved text. Opposite the endings of ll. 4 and 5 on (a), across the margin which separates this column from the one before it, a *reš* can still be discerned. This is the last letter of לשמור (Deut 32:46) at the end of the parallel line in the preceding column. Beneath it, the word דבר of the phrase כי לא־דבר (Deut 32:47) is legible. The preserved fragments are evidently remains of the last inscribed sheet which contained the closing part of Deuteronomy.[8]

The preserved text of MasDeut is identical to MT, with the exception of the defective spelling שפני at the end of (a)+(b), l. 3, as against the MT plene spelling שפוני (Deut 33:19).[9] Although the relevant letters are only partially extant, the reading is not in doubt. Remnants of not more than four letters can still be seen: the top of the first is patently the head of *sin/šin*; the second intact letter is a *peh*;[10] and the last one a *yod*. Only a fraction of the somewhat rounded top of the third letter remains. It resembles the top of *nun* in טמוני at the beginning of the next line, and differs from the pointed head of *waw* which precedes *nun* in that word. While *waw* could have been omitted in a defective spelling of שפוני, the *nun* is indispensable.

This slight divergence does not impair the overall textual agreement of MasDeut with MT which is underlined by its agreement with the masoretic section system. The Masada fragment exhibits a blank in (a+b), l. 4 after the word חול with which the blessing of Issachar ends (Deut 33:19). MT (A and L)[11] marks here a פרשה סתומה (cs). The evident concurrence suggests that MasDeut probably contained the MT sections throughout.[12] This supposition was taken into account in the proposed restoration of its text by positing blanks at pertinent junctures: (a+b), l. 7 — before the blessing of Dan (33:22, MT: cs), with the line containing 29 letters and seven inter-word spaces; (a+b), l. 9, before the blessing of Asher (33:24, MT: cs), with the line containing 32 letters and seven inter-word spaces;[13] and an especially large blank after תדרך, the last word of the eulogy

---

8. It follows that MasDeut differed significantly from a Deuteronomy scroll found in Qumran Cave IV (4QDeut[q]), which is represented by a fragment containing the ending of Deut 32. To the left of the written column there is an "extremely wide left margin, with no trace of stitching, after the ending of Deut. 32." This shows "with certainty that Deut. 33 and 34 were never intended to follow it in this copy, so that we are not dealing with parts of a complete scroll." P.W. Skehan, A Fragment of the 'Song of Moses' (Deut 32) from Qumran, *BASOR* 136 (1954) 12–15. See now *DJD* XIV, 137.

9. However, some printed editions exhibit the defective spelling שפני.

10. Cf. the letter *peh* in ספון (l. 6). Note that the word is spelled with a ס, as in MT, while in l. 3 it is spelled with a ש both in MT and in MasDeut.

11. See Oesch, *PUS*, T 2+. In A this word opens a new line, and is followed by a blank of eight spaces. The line ends on ולגד אמר.

12. But see below.

13. However, since the number of spaces in the line approximates to an average of 40, the scroll possibly did not contain here the *parashah* marked in MT.

which is adjoined to the blessings of the tribes (33:29, MT: cs). That line would have held only 22 letters.[14]

The textual similarity to MT provides a secure basis for the restoration of the exact layout of the last two columns of MasDeut.[15]

Column II   Column I

#	Column II	Column I
1	[ולזבולן אמר] והם רבבות אפרים והם אל[פי מנ]שֹה	[באזני העם הוא והושע בן נון ויכל משה לדבר]
2	[עמים] הר יקרא[ו] שמח זבולן בצאתך ויששכר באהל[י]ך	[את כל הדברים האלה אל כל ישראל ויאמר]
3	שם יזבחו זבחי צדק כֹי] ש[פע ימים יינקו ו]שֹפני	[אלהם שימו לבבכם לכל הדברים אשר אנכי]
4	[ברוך מרחיב גד כלביא] ולגד אמֹר טמוני חול	[מעיד בכם היום אשר תצום את בניכם לשמר]
5	[כי] שם שכן וטרֹף זרוע אף קֹ[דקד] ויֹרא רא[שֹיֹת לֹו	[לעשות את כל דברי התורה הזאת כי לא] דבר
6	צֹדֹקֹת יהוה [ויתא ראשי עם] חלקת מחקק ספון	[רק הוא מכם כי הוא חייכם ובדבר הזה תאריכו]
7	ולדן אמֹר דן גור עשה ומֹשפטיו עם ישראל	[ימים על האדמה אשר אתם עברים את הירדן]
8	[ולנפתלי אמר נ]פֹתל[י] שבע [אריה יזנק מן הבשן	[שמה לרשתה]
9	ולא[שר רצון ומלא ברכת יהוה ים ודרום ירשֹה	[וידבר יהוה אל משה בעצם היום הזה לאמר עלה]
10	[אמר ברוך מבנים אשר יהי רצוי אחיו וטבל בשמן]	[אל הר העברים הזה הר נבו אשר בארץ מואב]
11	[רגלו ברזל ונחשת מנעלך וכימיך דבאך אין כאל]	[אשר על פני ירחו וראה את ארץ כנען אשר אני]
12	[ישרון רכב שמים בעזרך ובגאותו שחקים מענה]	[נתן לבני ישראל לאחזה ומת בהר אשר אתה עלה]
13	[אלהי קדם ומתחת זרעת עולם ויגרש מפניך אויב]	[שמה והאסף אל עמיך כאשר מת אהרן אחיך בהר]
14	[ויאמר השמד וישכן ישראל בטח בדד עין יעקב]	[ההר ויאסף אל עמיו על אשר מעלתם בי בתוך בני]
15	[אל ארץ דגן ותירוש אף שמיו יערפו טל אשריך]	[ישראל במי מריבת קדש מדבר צן על אשר לא]
16	[ישראל מי כמוך עם נושע ביהוה מגן עזרך ואשר]	[קדשתם אותי בתוך בני ישראל כי מנגד תראה את]
17	[חרב גאותך ויכחשו איביך לך ואתה על במותימו]	[הארץ ושמה לא תבוא אל הארץ אשר אני נתן]
18	[תדרך ויעל משה מערבת מואב אל]	[לבני ישראל]
19	[הר נבו ראש הפסגה אשר על פני ירחו ויראהו]	[וזאת הברכה אשר ברך משה איש האלהים את בני]
20	[יהוה את כל הארץ את הגלעד עד דן ו]את כל נ[פתלי]	[ישראל לפני מותו ויאמר יהוה מסיני בא וזרח משעיר]
21	[ואת ארץ אפרים ומנשה ואת כל] ארץ יהוד[ה עד]	[למו הופיע מהר פארן ואתה מרבבת קדש מימינו]
22	[הים האחרון ואת הנגב ואת הככר ב]קעֹת [ירחו]	[אשדת למו אף חבב עמים כל קדשיו בידך והם]
23	[עיר התמרים עד צער ויאמר יהו]ֹה אליו זאת [הארץ]	[תכו לרגלך ישא מדברתיך תורה צוה לנו משה מורשה]
24	[אשר נשבעתי לאברהם לי]צֹחק ולי[עקֹב] לאמֹר לזרעך]	[קהלת יעקב ויהי בישרון מלך בהתאסף ראשי עם]
25	[אתננה הראיתיך בעיניך ו]שֹמֹ[ה] לא תעבר וימת שם [משה]	[יחד שבטי ישראל יחי ראובן ואל ימת ויהי מתיו]
26	[עבד יהוה בארץ מואב על פי יהו]ֹה ויקבר [אתו בגי]	[מספר וזאת ליהודה ויאמר שמע]
27	[בארץ מואב מול בית פעור ולא ידע א]יֹשֹ [את קברתו]	[יהוה קול יהודה ואל עמו תביאנו ידיו רב לו]
28	[עד היום הזה ומשה בן מאה ועשרים שנה במתו לא]	[ועזר מצריו תהיה וללוי אמר תמיך ואוריך]
29	[כהתה עינו ולא נס לחה ויבכו בני ישראל את משה]	[לאיש חסידך אשר נסיתו במסה תריבהו על]
30	[בערבת מואב שלשים יום ויתמו ימי בכי אבל משה]	[מי מריבה האמר לאביו ולאמו לא ראיתיו ואת]

14. All three cases are listed by Maimonides. See Oesch, *PUS* T 2+. In A the line opens with an indentation in which five letters could be accommodated.
15. I cannot offer any explanation of the wedge-like sign over the first letter of קדקד in (a+b), l. 5.

Column II (Cont.)	Column I (Cont.)

Column I (Cont.)

31 ‏[אחיו לא הכיר ואת בנו לא ידע כי שמרו אמרתך]

32 ‏[ובריתך ינצרו יורו משפטיך ליעקב ותורתך לישראל]

33 ‏[ישימו קטורה באפך וכליל על מזבחך ברך יהוה]

34 ‏[חילו ופעל ידיו תרצה מחץ מתנים קמיו ומשנאיו מן]

35 ‏[יקומון   לבנימן אמר ידיד יהוה ישכן לבטח]

36 ‏[עליו חפף עליו כל היום ובין כתפיו שכן   וליוסף]

37 ‏[אמר מברכת יהוה ארצו ממגד שמים מטל]

38 ‏[ומתהום רבצת תחת וממגד תבואת שמש וממגד]

39 ‏[גרש ירחים וממראש הררי קדם וממגד גבעות]

40 ‏[עולם וממגד ארץ ומלאה ורצון שכני סנה תבואתה]

41 ‏[לראש יוסף ולקדקד נזיר אחיו בכור שורו הדר לו]

42 ‏[וקרני ראם קרניו בהם עמים ינגח יחדו אפסי ארץ]

Column II (Cont.)

31 ‏[ויהושע בן נון מלא רוח חכמה כי סמך משה את ידיו עליו]

32 ‏[וישמעו אליו בני ישראל ויעשו כאשר צוה יהוה]

33 ‏[את משה ולא קם נביא עוד בישראל כמשה אשר ידעו]

34 ‏[יהוה פנים אל פנים לכל האתות והמופתים אשר שלחו]

35 ‏[יהוה לעשות בארץ מצרים לפרעה ולכל עבדיו ולכל ארצו]

36 ‏[ולכל היד החזקה ולכל המורא הגדול אשר עשה משה]

37 ‏[לעיני כל ישראל]

Measurements

The fully restored two columns give us a basis for calculating, with a high degree of probability, the height and the width of a column in the scroll, the number of columns it contained, and its overall length. The reconstruction shows that there were most probably 37 lines in the last column which was not fully written out, with a slight margin of error, and in the preceding one, which may be considered representative of the average column size, 42 lines.[16] Accordingly, the height of the scroll can be ascertained by the following computation: a written column contained 42 lines, with 41 inter-line spaces of 8 mm each, and one blank line at the bottom marking an os, like in MT and the end of Deut 32. Thus, the fully written out column was ca. 33 cm high (8 mm × 41). With the almost fully preserved top margin of 3.5 cm, and a bottom margin of presumably the same size, the scroll stood at a height of approximately 40 cm.[17]

The width of the standard column can be assessed by the following calculation: A line holds an average of 33 letters and seven inter-word spaces, i.e. forty spaces in all. Line 25 in the restored col. II contains the largest number — 37 letters and eight inter-word spaces; l. 18, in which we posit a substantial gap marking a cs, has the smallest number — 22 letters and six inter-word spaces. The average written line is 8.5 cm long. Together with the right-hand margin of ca. 1.0 cm col. II measures 9.5 cm in width. Being the last column it connects directly with the blank handle sheet. Therefore its margin is probably

---

16. A column in MasEzek (see below) held exactly the same number of lines.
17. The data are comparable with those of MasEzek (see below). These two scrolls were considerably larger than MasLev[b] (see above), MasPs[a] (see below) and most Qumran mss. E.g. the average height of a written column of 1QIsa[a] is 22 cm. With a top margin of 2 cm and a bottom margin of 3 cm, that scroll stood ca. 27 cm high. The comparable figures for 4QpalExod are: 24.7 + 2.7 + 4.3 = 31.7 cm; 1QapGen: 26 + 2.5 + 2.8 = 31.3 cm; 1QS: 19.8 + 1.5 + 2.7 = 24 cm.

somewhat narrower than that of the preceding column which comes to 1.2–1.4 cm at lines 4 and 5.

On the basis of these figures we can estimate the original length of MasDeut: the reconstructed two last columns contain Deut 32:44–34:12. This portion consitutes approximately a nineteenth part of the text of Deuteronomy. It follows that, when complete, the scroll would have held about 38 columns. The combined width of the last two columns comes to ca. 21 cm. We may therefore conclude that the rolled out scroll was ca. 4 m (19 × 21 cm) long.

One more point needs to be considered. As stated, MasDeut, like MasEzek, was discovered under the floor of the synagogue in a cavity which Yadin termed *genizah*.[18] In Jewish tradition, the term defines a chamber in a synagogue set aside for the storage of 'holy books', such as Torah scrolls, which had become unfit for public use, either because their text was found to be faulty to an excessive degree or because they were tattered beyond repair.[19] To prevent the desecration of such unusable, but still considered 'holy', scrolls and books they were deposited in such a storage room, and eventually buried in the grave of a rabbi or a community member of distinction. Now, if those pits under the floor of the synagogue served indeed as a *genizah*, this would imply that MasDeut had deteriorated to a considerable degree, and was therefore put away in that cavity.[20] This would suggest that the scroll had been in use for a considerable length of time prior to the fall of Masada in 73/74 CE, and support the dating of MasDeut by palaeographic criteria to not later than the beginning of the Herodian era.

---

18. The classical example is the famous 'Cairo Genizah', which was discovered towards the end of the last century in the Ben Ezra synagogue in Fustat (Old Cairo).
19. See: S.Z. Leiman, Withdrawal of Biblical Books, *The Canonization of Hebrew Scripture: The Talmudic and Midrashic Evidence* (Hamden, CO: Archon Books, 1976) 72–86; S. Talmon, Heiliges Schrifttum und kanonische Bücher aus jüdischer Sicht — Überlegungen zur Ausbildung der Grösse 'Die Schrift' im Judentum, in *Mitte der Schrift? Ein jüdisch-christliches Gespräch. Texte des Berner Symposiums vom 6.-12. Januar 1985* (Bern/Frankfurt a.M/New York/Paris: Lang, 1987) 74–9.
20. The same pertains to MasEzek (see below).

(e)   Mas 1043–2220; Mas 1d; Ezekiel 35:11–38:14, (MasEzek, photo 302367)

This item too was discovered in the second season. Yadin first referred to it in 1966, in the above mentioned public lecture,[1] and then described it briefly in *EAE*:[2]

> Fragments of this scroll were hidden beneath the floor of the synagogue.[3] Large portions of chapters 35–38 were preserved including chapter 37 (the vision of the dry bones). It was also identical with the Masoretic Text, apart from a few unimportant variants.

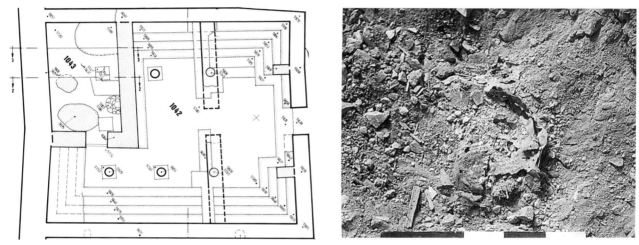

Illustration 7: Plan of Synagogue: Photo of scroll in oval pit

Description

MasEzek consists of more than fifty pieces of parchment[4] from four columns which together cover a sheet measuring 41×29.5 cm. The right-hand margin of the first, and the left-hand margin of the last column are missing. Therefore, it cannot be ascertained whether the four partially extant columns filled the entire sheet or whether that sheet contained an additional column or additional columns which preceded or succeeded the extant ones.

1.   Yadin, Qumran (Hebrew), 126.
2.   Yadin, *EAE*, 813.
3.   Actually in one of two "pits dug into the upper floor and then refilled with dirt and pebbles." In the other pit, fragments of the Book of Deuteronomy (MasDeut) were discovered. Yadin inclined to the hypothesis that these cavities served as a *genizah*. See Netzer's more detailed description of the circumstances of the discovery (above, MasDeut, p. 51).
4.   It cannot always be decided whether two adjoining pieces were originally parts of one fragment or were skilfully combined. Hence no exact count can be given.

One large fragment, measuring 13.5×6.5 cm, holds parts of the first six lines of cols. I and II, together with the incompletely preserved top and inter-column margins. Another fairly large fragment, measuring 9.5×8.2 cm, contains parts of 14 lines from the middle of cols. III and IV, and remains of the inter-column margin. On some tiny slivers of parchment only one or two letters can be read. Others are altogether blank, coming most probably from the partially preserved top margin or from the bottom margin which is no longer extant. On sectional photographs three more small fragments can be identified, some of which were joined to the reconstructed plate. It appears that these pieces were no longer available when the exhibit was mounted. One sliver holds small remains of text which can be integrated into col. II, ll. 31–35.[5]

The upper right hand part of the parchment is of a light brown colour, turning progressively darker towards the left, and becoming altogether black in the bottom left part. There the text is illegible on the original, but can be recovered with the help of infrared photographs.

Script

The scroll was evidently penned by an expert scribe in an "early Herodian bookhand" or "formal Herodian script," and can be dated to the second half of the last century BCE.[6] The script resembles that of MasLev[a,b] and is seemingly somewhat more developed than that of MasDeut.

Individual letters measure ca. 3×3 mm, with the exception of the very narrow letters ז,י,ו which are just 1 mm wide, and some larger letters, such as ם,מ,ל, which protrude above or below the line and reach a height of ca. 5 mm. A space of less than 1 mm separates one letter from another. However, in some instances two or more letters are contiguous, seemingly forming a ligature, e.g., ני of אני in col. I, l. 8 (Ezek 35:15), בכם of בקרבכם in col. II, l. 21 (Ezek 36:27), and נבאתי in col. III, l. 17 (Ezek 37:10).

Inter-word spaces measure somewhat less than 1 mm. At line endings, words are sometimes compressed and occasionally even run together, e.g. in col. I, l. 1: כאשראשפטך וידעת (Ezek 35:11–12); col. III, l. 11: כאשרצויתי (Ezek 37:7).

The number of letters and inter-word spaces in a line varies, and concomitantly the length of the written lines. The essentially complete lines in cols. I and II hold a maximum of 35 letters and a minimum of 27 letters, with 5–8 inter-word spaces. In col. III the comparable figures per line are 36 and 29, and in the restored col. IV, also 36 and 29, again with 5–6 inter-word spaces. It follows that in cols. I and II the average number of letters in a line amounts to 32, and in cols. III and IV to 33, with 5–8 inter-word spaces in both. Col. IV, l. 9 has only 13 letters; col. I, l. 9 contains only the

---

5. See below the proposed reconstruction of the recoverable text.
6. Cross, Scripts, 136, fig. 2, ii; 3, 4.

Tetragrammaton. Equally, the five letters of לעו[ולם in col. IV, l. 16 are followed by a *vacat* to the end of the line. In these cases, the blanks mark a section, פרשה (see below).

No horizontal or vertical dry rulings can be discerned. Nevertheless, the letter heads are practically rectilineal, with only the top strokes of ל protruding above an imaginary horizontal line. Where several consecutive line beginnings are preserved they are perfectly justified. Most are equally spaced 6 mm apart, measured from the letter tops in one line to those in the next, e.g., in col. II, ll. 8–13 and 27–30 (Ezek 36:21–23, 30–32); col. III, ll. 17–20 (Ezek 37:9–11); col. IV, ll. 15–22 and 26–28 (Ezek 37:28–38:4; 38:7–8). Line endings are rather uneven, as might be expected.

Measurements

In col. I, the maximal length of a line is 8.2 cm, in col. II 9.2 cm, in col. III 8.8 cm, and in (the restored) col. IV an estimated 8.6 cm. With a left-hand inter-column margin of ca. 1.5 cm, col. I is 9.9. cm wide, col. II 10.7 cm, and col. III 10.3 cm. Accordingly, the four preserved columns together took up approximately 41 cm of the width of the sheet.[7]

These data can serve as a fairly secure basis for estimating the original length of MasEzek. A page count in an edition without apparatus shows that the text portion, preserved or restored, viz. Ezek 35:11–38:14, constitutes approximately one fifteenth of the entire book. For example, it takes up 5.5 pages out of a total of 79 in the Snaith edition of the text without apparatus. Similar results are achieved by a verse count. The Masoretes counted 1273 verses in the book of Ezekiel. Of these 85, i.e. a fifteenth part, are contained in the four columns of MasEzek. It follows that ca. 60 columns would have been required for accommodating in the scroll the entire text of Ezekiel. As said, the four restored columns with their margins measure ca. 41 cm in width. Multiplied by 14 or 15, the length of the fully rolled out scroll may have come to between 5.74 and 6.15 m, or to about 6–6.4 m, if a handle sheet of ca. 25 cm was attached to the written columns.

7.   The width of col. IV cannot be assessed on the basis of the extant marginal fragment, but we may assume that it more or less equalled those of cols. I and III. The proposed placing of a tiny sliver of parchment on which the letters שי of the word לבשי (Ezek 38:4) can be read, at the very end of col. IV, l. 21 (see reconstruction), implies that this line contained 36 letters and 7 inter-word spaces. Its width would have come to ca. 10 cm.

Illustration 8: MasEzek 1043–2220

Restored Text

Column I

1	מְ[שַׂנאתיך בם ונ]וד[עתי בם כ]אֹשֶׁר אשפטך וידעֹתָ
2	[כי] אנִ֗י יהוה שָׁ[מעתי א]תֹ כל נ[אֹצוֹתיך א]ֹשר אמֹרֹת
3	[ע]ל[הרי֯]ישׂרֹאֹל לאמר שָׁ[מֹמֹה] לנֹו נתנו לֹאֹכֹלה]
4	ותֹ[גדי]לֹו עלי בפיכם והֹעתֹ[רֹת]ֹם עֹל֗ דבר[ֹכֹם [אני]
5	שָׁ[מ]עֹתי [כה אמֹ֗ר אדני [יהוה] כֹשמחֹֹת] כל
6	הארֹץ֗ שֹׁממה אֹ[עשה לך] כֹשמחתך לנֹחֹלֹֹת בית
7	ישׂר[אֹל] עֹל אֹשֹׁר שָׁ[ממה כֹן אעשֹׂה֗ לך שֹׁממה]
8	תֹהֹיה הֹֹר שעי[ר] וכל אֹדום כלה וידעו כי אני
9	[יהוה]
10	[ואתה בן אדם הנבא א]ל[הרי י]שׂרֹ֗אל ואֹמרֹת הרֹי
11	ישׂר[אֹל] שמעו דבר יהוה כֹה] אֹמר אדני יהוה
12	יֹען [אמר האויב עליכם האח ובמ]וֹת עולֹם֗ למֹֹוֹרשֹׁ[ה]
13	[היתֹ]הֹ לנו לכן הֹ[נ]בא ואמרת כה אמר] אֹֹדֹנֹ֗י יהוה
14	[יען ביעֹן] שֹׁמֹֹוֹת ושאף אתכם מסביב להֹיותכם]
15	מֹ[וֹ]רשה לשארית הגוים ותעלו על שפת לשוֹן]
16	וֹדֹ[בת עם לכן הרי ישראל שמעו דבר אדני יהוה]
17	[כה אמר אדני יהוה להרים ולגבעות לאפיקים]
18	ולֹ[גאיות ולחרבות השממות ולערים הנעזבות]
19	אשֹׁר הֹ[יו לבז וללעג לשארית הגוים אשר]
20	מֹסֹביב לכן כה אֹמר אדני יהוה אם לא באש]
21	קנֹ[א]תֹי֗ דֹברתי עֹ[ל שארית הגוים ועל אדום כלא]
22	א[ֹשֹׁר נתנ]וֹ את אֹרֹצי להם למורשה בשמחת]
23	[כל לבב בשאט נ[פֹש [למען מגרשה ל]ֹבֹז [ל]ֹכֹן
24	[הנבא על אדמת ישראל ואמרת להרי֗ם ולגבעֹ֗ות]
25	[לאפיקים ולגאיות כה אמר אדני יהוה הנני]
26	בקנֹ[אתי ובחמ]תֹי דֹברתֹ֗י יען כלמת גוים נשאתם לכן]
27	כֹ[ה] אמֹ֗ר אֹדני יהוה אֹ[ני נשאתי את ידי אם לא]
28	[הגוים] אֹשר לכֹם מסֹבֹ֗[יב המה כלמתם]
29	[ישאו ואת]ֹם֗ הרֹי֗ ישֹ[ראל ענפכם תתנו ופריכם]
30	[תשאו לעמי] ישראל כֹ֗י קרבו לבוא כי הנני אליכם]
31	[ופניתי אליכם ונֹ[עֹב]ֹדתם ונזרעתם והרביתי]
32	[עליכם אדם כל בית ישראל כלה ונשבו הערים]
33	ו[הֹחרבות תבנינה והרביתי עליכם אדם ובהמה]
34	[ורבו ופרו והושבתי אתכם כקדמותיכם והטבתי]

[63]

Column I (Cont.)

35 [מראשתיכם וידעתם כי אני יהוה והולכתי עליכם]

36 [אדם את עמי ישראל וירשוך והיית להם לנחלה]

37 [ולא תוסף עוד לשכלם   כה אמר אדני יהוה]

38 [יען א]מר[י]ם לכם אכלת אדם אתי ומשכלת גויך היית]

39 [לכן אד]ם לא תאכלי עוד וגויך לא תכשלי עוד נאם]

40 [אדני יהוה ולא אשמיע אליך עוד כלמת הגוים וחרפת]

41 [עמים לא תשאי עוד וגויך לא תכשלי עוד נאם]

42 [אדני יהוה   ויהי דבר יהוה אלי לאמר בן]

Column II

1 אד[ם] בית ישרא[א]ל ישבים ע[ל א]דמתם ויטמאו

2 אתה בדרכם ובֹ[עלי]לותם [כ]טמאת הנדה [היתה]

3 ד[ר]כם לפנֹי ואשפך חֹ[מ]תי עליה[ם] על הדם א[שר]

4 שפכו עֹל הארץ] ובגילוֹלֹיֹהֹ[ם] טֹמאוה ואֹפיץ אתם]

5 בֹגוֹים [ויזרו בארֹ]צות [כ]דרכם וֹכעלילוֹתֹם [שפטתים]

6 [ויבו]אֹ אל [הגוים א]שר באו שם ויחֹלֹלו את שם]

7 קֹדֹשֹי באמֹ[ר] להם עם יהוה אלֹה וֹמארצֹ[ו] יצאו

8 ואחמל עֹל שם קדשי אשר חללהו בית ישראל

9 בגוים אשר באֹו שם

10 לכן אמר לבֹי[ת] יֹ[ש]רֹ[א]ל כֹה אמר אדֹנֹ[י יהוה] לֹ[א]

11 למ[ען]כֹם אני עשֹה [בי]ת ישֹראֹ[ל כי אם] לֹ[שם קד]שֹי

12 אשר חללתם בגוים בֹית אשר בֹאתם [שם וקדשתי]

13 את שֹמֹי הגדול הֹ[מחל]ל בֹגֹוֹיֹ[ם א]שֹר חֹלֹלֹתֹ[ם]

14 [בתו]כֹם וידעֹו הגוים כי א[נֹ]י יהוה נֹאֹם אֹדֹני יהוֹה

15 בֹ[הקדשי] בכֹם לעיֹניהם ולקחתי אֹתֹכֹם מֹן הֹגוים

16 [וקבצתי אתכם מכל הארצוֹ]ת והֹבֹאתֹי [אתכם אל]

17 אֹד[מ]תכם [וזרקתי עליכם מֹי]ם טהורֹי[ם] וֹטֹ[ה]רֹתם

18 מכל טֻמאותיֹכֹם ומכל גלולֹיֹכם אטֹ[הר] אֹתכֹם ונֹתתי

19 לכם לב חדש ורוח חֹ[ד]שה אֹתֹן בקרֹ[ב]כֹם והֹסרותֹי

20 א[ת] לב האבן מבשרכֹם ונתתי לֹכֹם לב [בש]רֹ ואת

21 [רוחי] אֹתֹן בקרבכם ועשיֹתֹ[י] את אשֹר [בחקֹי] תלכו

22 [ומשפטֹ]טֹי תשֹמֹרֹו ועשיתם וֹיֹשֹ[ב]תֹם בֹארֹץ אֹשֹֹֹר

23 [נתתי ל]אֹ[בֹתֹו]יֹכֹם והייתם לי לעֹם [ואנכי אהיה לכם]

24 לאֹלהים והֹוֹשעֹתֹיֹ אתכם מ[כל טמ]אותיכם וקראתֹי

25 אֹל הדגן והרביתי אֹ[תֹ]וֹ ולֹאֹ [אתן עליכם רעב]

Column II (Cont.)

26 ו[ה]רביתי את פרי העץ ותנ[ו]בת ה[שדה למען]

27 אשר לא תקחֹו [עוד] חר[פ]ת רעֹב ב[ג]ו[י]ם וזכרתם

28 את דרכיכֹם הרֹעֹים ו[מ]עליכם] אשֹר [לא טובים]

29 ונקטתם בפני[כם על עונתיכם ועל תועבותיכם]

30 לא למענכם אנֹי עשה נאם אדני יהוה יודע לכם

31 בֹושֹו והכל[מו] מדרכי[כ]ם בי[ת ישראל כה אמר אדני]

32 יהוה ביום טהר[י] אתכם מ[כל עונתיכם והושבתי]

33 [את הערים ונבנו ה]חרבות והארץ הנשמה תעבד

34 [תחת] אשר היתֹ[ה] שממה לעיני כל עובר ואמרו

35 [הארץ ה]לזו הנ[ש]מה היתה כגן עדן והערים]

36 [החרבות והנשמו]תֹ [והנהרסות בצורות ישבו וידעו]

37 [הגוים אשר ישארו סביבותיכם כי אני יהוה בניתי]

38 [הנהרסות נטעתי הנשמה אני יהוה דברתי ועשיתי]

39 [כה אמר אדני יהוה עוד זאת אדרש לבית ישראל]

40 [לעשות להם ארבה אתם כצאן אדם כצאן קדשים]

41 [כצאן ירושלם במועדיה כן תהיינה הערים החרבות]

42 [מלאות צאן אדם וידעו כי אני יהוה]

Column III

1 היתה [עלי יד] יֹהֹוֹה ויוצֹ[אני ברוח יהוה ויניחני]

2 בֹתֹו[ך הבק]עה והי[אֹ מל]אֹה עצמות והע[ב]יֹרֹנֹי

3 עֹלֹיהם [ס]ביב סבֹ[י]ב והנה רבות מאד על פני הבקעה]

4 והֹנֹה יבשות [מאד ויאמר] אֹלֹי [בן אדם התחיינה]

5 [העצמות] הֹאלה וֹאמר אדֹ[ני יהוה אתה ידעֹתֹ

6 ויאמר אֹ[לֹי הנ]בֹא עֹ[ל העצמות האלה ואמר]ת

7 אֹליהם הֹעצֹמות היב[שות שמעו דבר יהוה] כֹהֹ

8 [א]מֹר אדֹנֹי יהוה לעצמות [האל]הֹ [ה]נֹה אני מב[יא]

9 [בכ]ם רוח וחֹ[י]יֹתֹם ונתֹתֹי עליֹכֹם גידיֹם והֹעלי[תֹי]

10 [ע]עֹליכם בשֹ[ר וקרמתי עליכם] עור וֹ[נ]תֹתֹי בכם רוח

11 [וחי]יֹתֹם [וידעתם כי אני] יהוֹה ונבאתי כֹאשר צויתי

12 [ויה]יֹ קולֹ [כהנבאי והנה] רֹעש תקרבו [ה]עֹצֹמות

13 עֹצֹםֹ אל עֹ[צמו וראית]יֹ וֹהֹנֹה עליהם גֹדים ובשר

14 עֹ[לה וי]קֹרֹם [עליהם עו]רֹ מלמעלה ורוח אין בהם

15 ו[י]אֹמֹר אלֹי הנבא אל הרוח] הֹנֹבא בן אדם ואמרֹת

16 אֹל [הרוח כה א]מֹר אֹדֹנֹי יֹהֹוֹה מארבע רוחות בא[י]

Column III (Cont.)

17 הרוח ופחי בהרוגים [ה]אֵלה ויחֿיו והנבאתי כאשר

18 צוני ותבא בהם הרוח ו[יחי]וֹ ויע[מ]דו על רגליהם

19 חיל גֿדול מאד מאד ויאמֿר אלֿי בֿ[ן] אדם העצמות

20 האלה כל בֵית ישרֿאֿל [המֵ]הֿ הנה אמרים יבשו

21 עצמותינו ואבדה] תקֿוֹתֿנֿוֹ [נגזר]נו לנו לכן הנבא

22 ואמרתֿ [אליהם כה א]מֿר אמר אדני יהוה הֿ[נה אני]

23 פֿתח את [קברותיכם] והֿעליתי אֿתכם מק[ברותיכם]

24 עמי והבאתֿיֿ אתכם [א]לֿ [אדמת יש]רֿאל וידעֿתֿםֿ

25 כֿיֿ [אני י]הֿוה בפתחֿ[י את] קֿברותיכם ובהעלותֿיֿ

26 [את]כֿםֿ מק[ברותיכם עמ]יֿ ונתתי רוחי בכם וחייתֿ[ם]

27 [והנחתי א]תֿכם על אדמתכם וידעֿתֿ[ם כי] אני [יהוה]

28 [דברתי וע]שֿ[י]תי נאם יהוה]

29 [ויהי דבר יהוה אלי לאמר ואתה ב]ן אדם קח לך

30 [עץ אחד וכתב עליו ליהודה ולבֿ]נֿֿי ישראל חב[רו]

31 [ולקח עץ אחד וכתוב עליו ליוס]ףֿ עֿץ אֿפֿר[ים]

32 [וכל בית ישראל חברו וקרב אתם אחד אל אחד לך]

33 [לעץ אחד והיו לאחדים בידך וכאשר יאמרו אליך]

34 [בני עמך לאמר הלוא תגיד לנו מה אלה לך דבר]

35 [אלהם כה אמר אדני יהוה הנה אני לקח את עץ]

36 [יוסף אשר ביד אפרים ושבטי ישראל חברו ונתתי]

37 [אותם עליו את עץ יהודה ועשיתם לעץ אחד והיו]

38 [אחד בידי והיו העצים אשר תכתב עליהם בידך]

39 [לעיניהם ודבר אליהם כה אמר אדני יהוה הנה]

40 [אני לקח את בני ישראל מבין הגוים אשר הלכו]

41 [שם וקבצתי אתם מסביב והבאתי אותם אל אדמתם]

42 [ועשיתי אתם לגוי אחד בארץ בהרי ישראל ומלך]

Column IV

1 [אחד יהיה לכלם למלך ולא יהיה עוד לשני גוים]

2 [ולא יחצו עוד לשתי ממלכות עוד ולא יטמאו]

3 [עוד בגלוליהם ובשקוציהם ובכל פשעיהם]

4 [והושעתי אתם מכל מושבתיהם] אשֿר חטֿאֿו בהם

5 [וטהרתי אותם והיו לי לעם ואני א]הֿיֿהֿ לה[ם]

6 [לאלהים ועבדי דוד מלך עליהם ורועה אחד יהיה]

7 [לכלם ובמשפטי ילכו וחקתי ישמרו ועשו אותם]

Column IV (Cont.)

8   [וישבו על הארץ אשר נתתי לעבדי ליעקב אשר]

9   [ישבו בה אבותיכם וישבו עליה המה ובניהם]

10   [ובני בניהם עד עולם ודוד עבדי נשיא להם]

11   [לעולם וכרתי להם ברית שלום ברית עולם יהיה]

12   [אותם ונתתים והרביתי אותם ונתתי את מקדשי]

13   [בתוכם לעולם והיה משכני עליהם והייתי להם]

14   [לאלהים והמה יהיו לי לעם וידעו הגוים כי]

15   אֹ[ני יהוה מקדש את ישראל בהיות מקדשי בתוכם]

16   לעֹ[ולם]

17   ויהי דֹ[בר יהוה אלי לאמר בן אדם שים פניך אל]

18   גוג אֹ[רץ המגוג נשיא ראש משך ותבל והנבא עליו]

19   ואמֹ[רת כה אמר אדני יהוה הנני אליך גוג נשיא]

20   רא[ש משך ותבל ושובבתיך ונתתי חחים בלחייך]

21   והֹ[וצאתי אותך ואת כל חילך סוסים ופרשים לב]שי

22   מכֹ[לול כלם קהל רב צנה ומגן תפשי חרבות כלם]

23   [פרס כוש ופוט אתם כלם מגן וכובע גמר וכל אגפיה]

24   [בית תוגרמה ירכתי צפון ואת כל אגפיו עמים רבים]

25   [אתך] הכן והכן [לך אתה וכל קהלך הנקהלים עליך]

26   והיית להם לֹ[משמר מימים רבים תפקד באחרית]

27   השנים [תבוא אל ארץ משובבת מחרב מקבצת]

28   מעֹמֹ[י]ם רבים על הרי ישראל אשר היו לחרבה]

29   [תמיד והיא מעמים הוצאה וישבו לבטח כלם]

30   [ועלית כשאה תבוא כענן לכסות הארץ תהיה אתה]

31   [וכל אגפיך ועמים רבים אותך   כה]

32   [אמר אדני יהוה והיה ביום ההוא יעלו דברים]

33   [על לבבך וחשבת מחשבת רעה ואמרת אעלה על ארץ]

34   [פרזות אבוא השקטים ישבי לבטח כלם ישבים באין]

35   [חומה ובריח ודלתים אין להם לשלל שלל ולבז בז]

36   [להשיב ידך על חרבות נושבת ואל עם מאסף מגוים]

37   [עשה מקנה וקנין ישבי על טבור הארץ שבא ודדן]

38   [וסחרי תרשיש וכל כפריה יאמרו לך הלשלל שלל]

39   [אתה בא הלבז בז הקהלת קהלך לשאת כסף וזהב]

40   [לקחת מקנה וקנין לשלל שלל גדול   לכן]

41   [הנבא בן אדם ואמרת לגוג כה אמר אדני יהוה]

42   [הלוא ביום ההוא בשבת עמי ישראל לבטח תדע]

[67]

Text

The extant text of MasEzek accords with MT, with the exception of some minor deviations:

1. Several supralinear emendations of scribal mistakes, presumably by the scribe himself, bring the text in line with MT:

Col. I, l. 4: the scribe inserted a *yod* above על{י} and דבר{י}כם (Ezek 35:13).

Col. II, l. 18: an omitted *mem* is written above the first two letters of ט{מ}אותיכם (Ezek 36:25 — טמאותיכם).

Col. II, l. 26: an omitted *waw* was inserted in the space above the third and fourth letters of ותנ{ו}בת (Ezek 36:30: ותנובת).

Col. III, l. 6: a *beth* is supplied above הנ{ב}א (Ezek 37:4 — הנבא).

2. It appears that in two instances the scribe did not emend a patently faulty text:

Col. III, l. 12: והנה] רעש תקרבו. A *waw* is evidently required before the verb, as in Ezek 37:7: ותקרבו.[8]

Col. III, l. 22: כה א[מר אמר (Ezek 37:12: כה־אמר), probably a dittography.

3. In several cases small letters or parts of letters can still be discerned between lines, but their meaning and purpose cannot be established for certain.

Col. II, l. 12: Three such small letters, apparently ב–י–ת, are written above the words בגוים אשר which are part of the locution כי אם־לשם־קדשי אשר חללתם בגוים אשר־באתם שם (Ezek 36:22). The proposed reading בית prompts the conjecture that the scribe began to insert the expression בית ישראל at the end of the verse or before the word בגוים, under the influence of שם קדשי אשר חללוהו בית ישראל בגוים אשר באו־שמה in the preceding verse (Ezek 36:21), either due to a *lapus calami* (vertical dittography) or on the strength of his *Vorlage* which differed from MT and the VSS.

Col. III, l. 20: At the beginning of the line, a tiny part of a letter can be seen above the *aleph* of האלה (Ezek 37:11).

4. The following two instances suggest that the alternative use of medial and final *mem* had not yet stabilized when MasEzek was penned:[9]

Col. III, l. 12: a final *mem* turns up in a medial position in ה[עצמות (Ezek 37:7). Less certain is the possible occurrence of a medial *mem* in a final position in col. II, l. 7, in the construct עם יהוה (Ezek 36:20: עם־יהוה). The relevant letter resembles the medial *mem* in ומארצו in the same line, rather than the final *mem* in the preceding word להם.

5. In several instances MasEzek differs from MT in the employment of *matres lectionis*:

8. Sebirin: ויקרבו; LXX: καὶ προσήγαγε; cf. PseudoEzekiel 4Q385 frg. 2, 5: ו[ו[ו.
9. See Introduction, 20–22, and MasLev[b] (92–480) col. V, l. 10 = Lev 11:10 (above, 44).

[68]

Defective versus plene spelling:

Col. II, l. 2: אתה	Ezek 36:17: אותה
II, l. 8: חללהו	36:21: חללוהו[10]
II, l. 26: ותנבת[11]	36:30: ותנובת
III, l. 18: ותבא	37:10: ותבוא

Plene versus defective spelling:

I, l. 3: לֹאוֹכֹלה	35:12: לאכלה
II, l. 4: ובגיליהֹם[12]	36:18: ובגלוליהם
II, l. 19: והסרותי	36:26: והסרתי
III, l. 9: גידים והעליֹותי	37:6: גדים והעלתי[13]

However, against the background of the apparent inconsistency in the employment of *matres lectionis* in MT, these differences do not amount to 'textual variants'.

6.   Also the following deviation of MasEzek from MT cannot be deemed a textual variant:

In col. II, l. 9 MasEzek reads אשר באו שם, followed by a blank which marks a section. Ezek 36:21 reads here שמה, followed by a פרשה סתומה.[14] The variation שמה/שם is often found in a comparison of MT with other traditions of the biblical text, such as the Samaritan Pentateuch and Qumran scrolls, and also in the collation of masoretic manuscripts.[15] In the present instance, the scribe wittingly or unwittingly harmonized the text with אשר באתם שם in Ezek 36:22 = col. II, l. 12 (cf. 37:21, אשר הלכו־שם, not extant in MasEzek). In all three cases, TJ renders לתמן, which seems to reflect שמה rather than שם.

7.   More weight is attached to two deviations of MasEzek from MT, which possibly evince variants that may also underlie LXX:

Col III, l. 12: on the face of it, the reading תקרבו עצמות equals MT 37:7: ותקרבו עצמות, except for the lack of the conjunctive *waw*. However, in MasEzek the two words are separated by an unusually large space, actually a *lacuna*, which suggests that a letter is missing. LXX renders the noun עצמות with the definite article: καὶ προσήγαγε τὰ ὀστᾶ, as in its preceding mentions, both in MT and LXX (37:4–5). In Ezek 37:3, 4, 11 the same noun is further defined by the demonstrative pronoun העצמות האלה, LXX: τὰ ὀστᾶ ταῦτα,

10.   Snaith: חללהו.
11.   See above.
12.   In col. II, l. 18: גלולוֹיכם, MT 36:25: גלוליכם, the crucial part of the word is not preserved.
13.   Ed. Snaith: גידים. Col. III, l. 13: גדים, like MT 37:8: גדים.
14.   See below the discussion of the Section System.
15.   Cf. the discussion of the interchange of הם with המה, with a final *mem* in medial position in the Introduction (above, 20–22), and MasLev[b] col. V, ll. 9–10, Lev 11:28 (above, p. 44).

[69]

and in 37:11 by a possessive pronoun: עצמותינו, LXX: τὰ ὀστᾶ ἡμῶν.[16] This stylistic usage, preponderant in this context, suggests that in MasEzek III, 12 a ה was lost in the *lacuna*, and that the text originally read העצמות, like LXX and possibly its Hebrew *Vorlage*.[17]

Again, in col. I, l. 5 a vestige of a lost letter can be discerned between the first two words of the phrase כשמֹחַ כל־הארץ (Ezek 35:14). This tiny remnant is possibly part of the lower bar of a *beth*. However, it is more likely to be the very end of the left downward stroke of a *taw*, which suggests the restoration כשמחת כל הארץ, with a noun rather than with the infinitive, as in MT. This reading would thus concur with כשמחתך in the ensuing verse, Ezek 35:15, which is very similar linguistically. LXX has here a considerably shorter text than MT. The two verses Ezek 35:14–15 are rendered as one, possibly as a result of *homoioarkton* on the translational level or in the translator's Hebrew *Vorlage*: τάδε λέγει κύριος Ἐν τῇ εὐφροσύνῃ πάσης τῆς γῆς ἔρημον ποιήσω σε ἔρημον ἔσῃ, ὄρος Σηιρ, καὶ πᾶσα ἡ Ιδουμαία ἐξαναλωθήσεται[18] καὶ γνώσῃ ὅτι ἐγὼ εἰμι κύριος ὁ θεὸς αὐτῶν. The scribe or the translator seemingly skipped from שממה אעשה־לך in v. 14 to the practically identical phrase שממה כן אעשה לך in v. 15, thereby eliminating the text portion between them:

שממה אעשה־לך   כשמח כל הארץ

כשמחתך לנחלת בית־ישראל על אשר־שממה כן אעשה לך

שממה תהיה הר־שעיר וכל־אדום כֻּלָּה

Such an omission could more easily occur in a text which read כשמחת כל הארץ in v. 14 as well, especially since in both instances the letter sequence כשמח(ת) is followed by the letters כ–ל: כשמחת בל ישראל and כשמחת כל הארץ. The conjecturally restored reading כשמחת כל of MasEzek would constitute a mediating link between MT and LXX, and help in explaining the development of the Greek variant.

8. In sum, the above differences do not obfuscate the basic textual identity of MasEzek with MT. The persuasive agreement is highlighted by their concurrence wherever an ancient version, foremost LXX, exhibits a variant reading. The accordance is best illustrated by pluses or minuses in LXX versus MT,[19] which have no parallel in MasEzek.[20]

a. *Pluses*

Col. II, l. 8: ואחמל על שם קדשי   = 36:21   LXX: καὶ ἐφεισάμην αὐτῶν
                                                        διὰ τὸ ὄνομά μου τὸ ἅγιον

16. In Ezek 37:1: והיא מלאה עצמות, LXX again supplies a defining addition: ὀστέων ἀνθρωπίνων. See below.
17. W. Zimmerli, *Ezechiel 25–48*, BKAT XIII, 2 (Neukirchen-Vluyn: Neukirchener Verlag, 1979) 887, suspects that the ו at the end of the word may in fact stand for a ה.
18. The translator probably read כָּלָה Instead of MT: כֻּלָּה.
19. In most instances the variant reading is found in either G[B] or G[A]. Where preserved, the Hexaplaric tradition is adjusted to MT.
20. The same holds true for MasLev[a,b], MasDeut, and MasPs[a].

III, l. 2: עצמות   = 37:1   LXX: ὀστέων ἀνθρωπίνων
                                                 = TJ: גרמי אנשא

b. *Minuses*

Col. I, l. 3: עַ[ל וְהַר]ֵי ישראל[21]   = 35:12   LXX: om. על

      I, l. 4: ו[העתרו]ת[ם על דבר]כם   = 35:13   LXX: om.

      I, l. 27: כ[ה] אמר אדני יהוה   = 36:7   LXX: om.

      I, l. 29f: [וענפכם תתנו ופריכם תשאו לעמי] ישראל   = 36:8   LXX: τὴν σταφυλὴν καὶ τὸν καρπὸν ὑμῶν καταφάγεται ὁ λαός μου, om. תתנו and ישראל.

      II, l. 3f: על הדם.....טמאוה   = 36:18   LXX: om.

      III, l. 12: ויהי קול [כהנבא]י   = 37:7   LXX: καὶ ἐγένετο ἐν τῷ ἐμὲ προφητεῦσαι, om. קול

      III, l. 16f: בא[וי] הרוח ופחי   = 37:9   LXX: ἐλθὲ καὶ ἐμφύσησον, om. הרוח

      III, l. 20: המ[ה] הנה אמרים   = 37:11   LXX: καὶ αὐτοὶ λέγουσιν, om. הנה

      III, l. 24: עמי   = 37:12   LXX: om. (=Syr)

      III, l. 29: ואתה ב[ן] אדם   = 37:16   LXX: Υἱὲ ἀνθρώπου,[22] om. ואתה

Special mention should be made of a recurring minus in LXX versus MT. The Greek often renders the divine epithet אדני יהוה (probably a *qere/ketib* conflation) by κύριος. MasEzek preserves the MT reading consistently (col. I, l. 5 = Ezek 35:14; I, l. 25 = Ezek 36:6; II, l. 10 = 36:22; III, l. 8 = 37:5; III, l. 16 = 37:9; III, l. 22 = 37:12), and thus gives witness to its antiquity.[23]

9. Equally important for gauging the concurrence of MasEzek with MT are two Greek variants which either derive from a divergent Hebrew *Vorlage*, or evince the translator's deviation, unintentional or intentional, from the text underlying the masoretic tradition:

Col. I, l. 2: שו[מ]עתי א[ת] כל נאצותיך = 35:12   LXX: ἤκουσα τῆς φωνῆς = קול, voice .

      I, l.3: לנו נתנו לאוכלה = 35:12   LXX^A: ἡμῖν δέδοται εἰς κατάσχεσιν = נחלה, inheritance

21. The restoration of the text is required by considerations of space and the partially preserved letter *lamed*.

22. In several instances Hebrew words, which are not translated in LXX, must be restored in passages not preserved in MasEzek because of considerations of space and a letter count, otherwise the lines would be too short, e.g.: col. I, l. 3 = 35:12; I, l. 16 = 36:4; I, l. 29 = 36:8; I, l. 40 = 36:14; I, l. 41 = 36:15; III, l. 5 = 37:3.

23. The double epithet must be restored in passages not extant in MasEzek on the strength of space considerations and a letter count: col. I, l. 20 = 36:5; I, l. 37 = 36:13; II, l. 30 = 36:32; II, l. 39 = 36:37.

10. In the following instances of a syntactical inversion in LXX, MasEzek again agrees with MT:

Col. I, l. 28: ‏36:7 = הגוים] אשר לכ]ם מס]בויב‎   LXX: τὰ περικύκλῳ ὑμῶν

III, l. 15f: ‏ויאמר אל]י הנבא אל הרוח] הנבא‎

‏37:9 = בן אדם ואמרת אל]הרוח‎   LXX: καὶ εἶπεν πρός με Προφήτευσον υἱε ἀνθρώπου προφήτευσον ἐπὶ τὸ πνεῦμα καὶ εἶπον τῷ πνεύματι

MasEzek sides with MT against LXX in several other cases of textual discrepancy:

Col. I, l. 1: ‏משנאתיך‎ = 35:11 (pl.)   LXX: κατὰ τὴν ἔχθραν σου (sing.)

I, l. 4: ‏ות]ג]די]לו עלי‎ = 35:13 (pl.)   LXX: καὶ ἐμεγαλορημόνησας (sing.)

I, l. 8: ‏וידעו‎ = 35:15 (pl.)   LXX: καὶ γνώσῃ (sing.)

I, l. 10f: ‏ואמרת הרי ישר]אל‎ = 36:1   LXX: τοῖς ὄρεσιν

III, l. 9: ‏רוח וחז]יי]תם‎ = 37:5   LXX: πνεῦμα ζωῆς

III, l. 11: ‏כאשר צֻוֵּיתי‎ = 37:7   LXX: καθὼς ἐνετείλατό μοι[24]

One variant seems to be of greater import:

Col. I, l. 1: ‏משנאתיך בם ונ]וד]עתי בם‎ = 35:11   LXX: καὶ γνωσθήσομαί σοι...σε

The translator possibly harmonized the 3rd person plural pronoun, with the 2nd person singular pronouns at the beginning of the verse, ‏כאפך ... וכקנאתך ... עשיתה‎ ... ‏משנאתיך‎, or else an amply documented interchange of *kaph* and *mem*, ‏בכ/בם‎, is involved,[25] which may already have occurred in the translator's *Vorlage*.[26]

---

24. Possibly a harmonization with ‏כאשר צֻוִּני‎ in 37:10 = col. III, l. 17–8.

25. The interchange of graphically similar consonants in biblical texts, including variants between MT and LXX, has been extensively discussed. See int. al.: F. Delitzsch, *Die Lese- und Schreibfehler im Alten Testament* etc. (Berlin/Leipzig: Vereinigung Wissenschaftlicher Verleger, 1920); J. Kennedy, *An Aid to the Textual Amendment of the Old Testament* (Edinburgh: Clark, 1928); F. Perles, *Analekten zur Textkritik des Alten Testaments* (Munich: Ackermann, 1895) 52–3; Neue Folge (Leipzig: Engel, 1922) 3–31. Tov, Consonants, presented the phenomenon in statistical tables.

26. Cf. e.g. 1 Kgs 4:10 MT: ‏לו שכה וכל ארץ חפר‎; LXX: Λουσαμηνχα etc. The translator evidently conjoined the possessive pronoun ‏לו‎ with the town name ‏שכה‎, at the same time misreading *kaf* as *mem*. The graphic interchange of ‏כ‎ and ‏מ‎ is occasionally at the root of text variants in parallel passages in MT: Josh 19:30: ‏ועמה ואפק ורחב‎, Judg 1:31: ‏ואת־אפיק ואת־רחב ... את־ישבי עכו‎; 1 Chr 16:18–19: ‏לך אתן ארץ כנען‎ ...; ‏בהיותכם מתי מספר‎, Ps 105:11: ‏בהיותם‎. LXX and V render ‏בהיותם‎ in 1 Chr as well as in Ps, whereas the renditions of Targ and Syr reflect ‏בהיותכם‎. It appears that in both parallels haplography of ‏מ‎ after ‏כ‎ in ‏לכם‎ at the beginning of the verse resulted in the reading ‏לך‎. Similarly the omission of ‏כ‎ before ‏מ‎ in ‏בהיותכם‎ (Ps 105:12) produced ‏בהיותם‎. The interchange of ‏כ‎ and ‏מ‎ is occasionally at the root of variations between *qere* and *ketib*, or between MT and other Hebrew witnesses: 1 Kgs 1:47, *ketib*: ‏ייטב אלהיך‎; *qere*: ‏אלהים‎ (=mss, LXX, V); Isa 40:17 MT: ‏מאפס ותהו‎, 1QIsaᵃ: ‏וכאפס‎; Isa 58:13 MT: ‏אם תשיב‎, 1QIsaᵃ: ‏כמכה‎; Isa 66:3 MT: ‏שוחט השור מכה איש‎, 1QIsaᵃ: ‏משבת רגלך מעשות‎, 1QIsaᵃ: ‏משבת רגלך עשות חפציך ביום קדשי איש‎. It cannot be determined whether in the above instances we are concerned with a haplography in MT or a dittography in 1QIsaᵃ. Cf. also: 1 Sam 2:29: ‏להבריאכם מראשית כל‎, TJ: ‏לאוכלותהון‎; 1 Sam 15:18: ‏עד כלותם אתם‎, LXX, TJ, Syr: ‏עד כלותך אתם‎; 2 Kings 22:4: ‏ויתם את הכסף‎, possibly to be read: ‏ויתך‎ (cf. 22:9 ‏התיכו עבדיך‎).

[72]

11. Like the diversity which characterizes the masoretic פרשות tradition, the sections marked in MasEzek do not fully dovetail with the system of any major manuscript of MT. In some instances, the scroll is aligned with L, in others with the section roster transmitted by Maimonides, and best represented by A. Of special interest are section markings in MasEzek which have no parallel in either A or L, and others which are marked in those manuscripts but not in MasEzek. However, the broad conformity, even though not complete, may still be considered proof for the basic accord of MasEzek with MT.

The Section System

It will suffice to compare the findings of MasEzek with the section system of four major MT codices: A, C, L and S.

Table[27]

Ezek	MasEzek	(L)	(S)	(C)	(A)	MasEzek
35:14	I, l. 5	cs	cs	cs	cs	cs
36:1	I, l. 10	os	cs	os	os	os
36:5	I, l. 20	cs	cs	cs	—	—
36:13	I, l. 37	cs	cs	os	cs	?
36:16	I, l. 42	cs	os	os	os	?
36:22	II, l. 10	cs	os	os	os	os
36:33	II, l. 31	cs	cs	cs	cs	—
36:37	II, l. 39	cs	cs	cs	cs	?
37:1	II–III	cs	os	os	os	?
37:9	III, l. 16	—	—	—	cs p.b.p.	—
37:11	III, l. 19	cs	—	—	—	—
37:13	III, l. 24	cs	—	—	—	—
37:15	III, l. 29	os	os	os	os	os
38:1	IV, l. 17	cs	os	cs	os	os

Generally speaking, the findings in the scroll match those of the major manuscripts of MT. A section indicated in MasEzek, or one which can be restored with some confidence on the strength of space calculations, whether os or cs, always coincides with a section in the masoretic tradition. While in some instances MasEzek does not exhibit a

27. The table is based upon a list prepared for the Bible Project of the Hebrew University. A פרשה פתוחה will be marked os = open section, a פרשה סתומה cs = closed section, a פסקה באמצע פסוק pbp = mid-verse section.

section recorded in those manuscripts, there is not one section marked in it which is not present in one of them. An especially consistent affinity exists between MasEzek and A, C, S.

a. In several cases, MasEzek exhibits an os or a cs in accordance with all four manuscripts:

Col. I, l. 5: A blank of some seven to eight letters separates אני [שומ]עתי from the ensuing phrase [כה אמר אדני (Ezek 35:13–14) marking a cs, as in A, L, C and S.

Col. III, ll. 27–29: Between אני (l. 27) and בן אדם (l. 29) 53–55 letters and inter-word spaces can be accommodated. But the relevant text portion of Ezek 37:14–16, not extant in MasEzek, amounts to only 45 letters and spaces. It follows that in the scroll nearly half of l. 28 was left blank to mark an os, as in all four MT manuscripts.

Col. I, l. 9: The line contains only the Tetragrammaton, followed by a blank which dovetails with the os in A, C and L, with S alone exhibiting a cs.

Col. I, l. 37: The text restored between ו[ה]חרבות (l. 33) and אמרים (l. 38) suggests that the line 33 held only 29 letters. Therefore, it is reasonable to conclude that a cs was marked before כה אמר, as in A, S and L. Only C marks an os.

b. In the following instances, MasEzek concurs with A, C and S in marking an os, against a cs in L:

Col. II, l. 9: The opening locution of l. 10, לכן אמר (36:22) leads to the conclusion that the preceding line contained only the words בגוים אשר באו שם. The resulting blank between these phrases marks an os, while L has a cs.

Col. IV, l. 16: This line held only the word [לע]ולם, as can be deduced from the consecution of א[ני] at the beginning of l. 15 and ויהי at the beginning of l. 17. Therefore, we conclude that like A and S, MasEzek contained here an os which is not indicated in L and C.

Cols. II-III: Equally, the restored text between והנשמות (col. II, l. 36) and היתה (col. III, l. 1) shows that col. II, l. 42 (the last line in the column) held only 25 letters. The resulting blank of eight to nine letters in the line marks an os as in A, C and S, while L has a cs.

c. Agreements of MasEzek with L.

Col. I, l. 42: The restored text between [לכן אדם (col. I, l. 39) and אד[ם] (col. II, l. 1) implies that l. 42 in col. I contained a cs, five to six spaces long, which concurs with a cs in L before ויהי דבר יהוה אלי לאמר (37:15), whereas A, C and S exhibit an os.

d. In the following cases, MasEzek does not exhibit a section marked in one or more of the above MSS.

Col. II, l. 31: The restored text does not leave room for a cs which is recorded in all four manuscripts before Ezek 36:33.

Col. II, l. 39: The same applies to the cs marked in all four MSS before Ezek 36:37.
Col. I, l. 20: A cs is marked in L, C and S before Ezek 36:5. In contrast, in MasEzek vv. 4 and 5 follow upon one another with no break between them, as in A.

    e. In col. III, l. 16, MasEzek does not exhibit a cs marked only in A as a mid-sentence pbp after הרוח in Ezek 37:9.

    f. Two cs sections marked only in L are not indicated in MasEzek: Col. III, l. 19 before Ezek 37:11, and col, III, l. 24 before Ezek 37:14.

The striking concurrence, documented above, proves that the extant or restorable sections of MasEzek were basically identical with the MT sections.

(f)   Mas 1039–160; Mas1e; Psalms 81:2ᵇ–85:6ᵃ; (MasPsᵃ, final photo 5255)

The item was found "on 20th November 1963 at the southwestern end of the room (casemate 1039, S.T), near the group of sheqels.[1] On top of it and beside it were three coins of the Revolt .... The room was covered with a big heap of debris, including many large stones ... numerous fragments of the roof ... had fallen and covered many of the finds, including the scrolls," which were found in the same vicinity, namely MasGen (1039–317) and MasLevᵃ (1039–270), the Joshua Apocryphon (1039–211), a small unclassified fragment (1039–274) and MasSam (1039–320), together with fragments of the 'Songs of the Sabbath Sacrifice' (1039–200).[2] The circumstances of the discovery and the objects found there gave "the impression that articles from various rooms were thrown in disorder into this one, and heaped up there" (Yadin, *IEJ* 15, 80).

It appears that Yadin gave more attention to these fragments than to other written items found in that locus,[3] since he described it in some detail, and also published a partial photograph of the first lines of Ps 82:1–4:[4]

> This is part of a scroll of the Book of Psalms, 25.5 cm in height. The scroll is in a
> bad state of preservation, and parts of it could be read only with the help of

---

1.   Yadin, *IEJ* 15, 81–2, pl. 19 F–G.
2.   Cf. Yadin's lively description of the important discovery in Yadin, *Fortress*, 171–2: "About three feet away from the shekels the first scroll was found. All the details of this discovery are sharp in my mind. In the early hours of the afternoon, while I was in one of the northern storerooms, Shmaryahu Guttman came running to me, followed by some of the volunteers working with him, and flourished before me a piece of parchment. It was so black and creased that only with difficulty could one make anything out. But a quick examination on the spot showed us immediately that here was a fragment from the *Book of Psalms*, and we could even identify the chapters: the section ran Psalm 81 to Psalm 85... This discovery is of extraordinary importance for scroll research. It is not only that this is the first time that a parchment scroll has been found not in a cave, and in circumstances where it was possible to date it without the slightest doubt. It could not possibly be later than the year 73 AD, the year Masada fell. As a matter of fact, this scroll was written much before — perhaps twenty or thirty years earlier; and it is interesting that this section from the *Book of Psalms*, like the other biblical scrolls which we found later, is almost exactly identical (except for a few very minor changes here and there) to the text of the biblical books which we use today. Even the division into chapters and psalms is identical with the traditional division. This not only testifies to the strength and faithfulness of the Jewish tradition, but it enables us to learn many things about the development of the biblical text, particularly in the light of the fact that many of the scrolls of biblical books which were discovered in Qumran and in the caves north of Masada, contained significant textual changes from the accepted traditional text."
3.   With the exception of the fragment of the 'Songs of the Sabbath Sacrifice.'
4.   Yadin, *IEJ* 15, 103–104, and pl. 19 A. In Yadin, *EAE*, 811–2, he gave a shorter summary of MasPsᵃ with a photograph of Ps 82:1–4, which was used by J.C. Trever in his discussion of the late Herodian Script: 1QDanᵃ, the Latest of the Qumran Manuscripts, *RQ* 7 (1970) 277–86. A reduced photograph (ca. 4 to 1) was published by J.K. McDonald, Treasures of the Holy Land: Ancient Art from the Israel Museum, *BA* 49 (1986) 163. J.A. Sanders recorded MasPsᵃ in *The Dead Sea Psalms Scroll* (Ithaca, NY: Cornell University Press, 1967) Appendix II, 147; III, 152.

infra-red photography. The fragment has been torn both on the right and the left, and from the shape of the tears it seems that they were made deliberately. The writing is what is now termed the late Herodian formal style (Cross, Scripts, 133, fig. 2; Avigad, Palaeography, 75), and can be dated to the first half of the first century C.E.[5]

The psalms are written in two columns, each containing a hemistice (lege: 'hemistich', S.T). One can observe horizontal lines, marked with a sharp instrument before the writing. The letters are written below the above mentioned lines, as is usual in scrolls and ancient books of the Bible. The vertical line which bounds from the right, and from which the scribe began to write is also clearly visible. The height of the average letter is 4 mm; the *lamed* 8 mm high. The widths of the margins are: above — 30 mm (i.e. 'two fingers-breadths,' cf. *b. Men.* 30a);[6] below — 37 mm, and an average of 20 mm on the sides (i.e. 'a thumb's breadth').

If we take into account fragments of verses to the right and left, the scroll (lege 'fragment', S.T.) contains chapters 81:3 to 85:10.[7] The order of chapters is absolutely identical with that of the masoretic text. The chapter headings are as follows: chapter 82 — "A Psalm of Asaph" — the heading written above both columns, chapter 83 — "A Song, a Psalm of Asaph" — the heading constitutes the whole line of the right column, the first verse starting with the left column in the same line; chapter 84 — "To the Chief Musician upon Gittith, A Psalm for the Sons of Korah" — the heading written in the right column, the first verse starting with the next line of the right column.

A "line's" breadth divides the psalms. The text corresponds to the Masoretic text, in both contents and spelling, except for an interesting variant in chapter 83:7. Here the scroll reads אלהי אדום instead of אהלי אדום.

Description

MasPs[a] consists of two fragments of parchment, light brown at the right side, and darkening progressively towards the left.[8] The two pieces can be conjoined on the basis of the extant or restorable text portions of three columns, and the edge contours. A spur at the top of the lower fragment (b) projects almost perfectly into a concave indentation in the bottom edge of the upper one (a). At the join, parts of four lines of text were lost in a fairly large lacuna which extends from about the middle of the fragment, i.e. the

5. In *Fortress,* Yadin dated the writing more precisely to 20–30 years before the fall of Masada.
6. Cf. Y. Yadin, *The Scroll of the War of the Sons of Light against the Sons of Darkness,* translated by B. and C. Rabin (Oxford: Clarendon, 1962) 116, note 6.
7. Actually 81:2[b]–85:6[a]. See below.
8. A blank sliver of parchment, shown in varying positions on different photographs, is probably not part of 1039–160.

second column, to its left end. The raggedness of the edges, especially noticeable at the right side of (a), seems to evince deterioration of the parchment rather than wilful tearing, as Yadin assumed.

Fragment (a) measures 18×14.7 cm, and fragment (b) 20.2×13.5 cm. (a) and (b) combined stand 25.5 cm high.[9] The height of the written column is 20 cm. The completely extant bottom margin measures 3.4 cm, and the top margin 2.1 cm.[10]

MasPs[a] encompasses the text of Ps 81:2b-85:6a in one complete and two partial columns of hemistichs.

The middle column (col. II) is the best preserved. It contains the text of Ps 81:16b-83:17a in 27 lines, with the superscription of Psalm 82 written in an added half-line. There are two blanks in the column: one, 2.1 cm wide, separates Psalm 81 from Psalm 82, except for the latter's superscription, מזמור] לאסף, which is kept apart from אשביעך, the last word of Psalm 81, by a somewhat broader than usual inter-line space. The other, between Pss 82 and 83, comes to 2.2 cm below the empty half-line in the left half-column (Ps 82:8[a]), and to 1.5 cm below the right half-column with the concluding hemistich of the psalm (v. 8[b]).[11] Thus, col. II holds 27 fully written lines, one half line, and two blanks. The combined width of the blanks equals roughly the widths of five written lines. It follows that 32 lines could be accommodated in the column.

The left-hand part of col. III is lost, but in the right-hand part all first hemistichs of Ps 83:17b-85:6a are fully preserved, again in 27 lines. A blank of 1.2 cm separates Psalm 83 from Psalm 84, and a slightly larger one keeps Psalm 84 apart from Psalm 85. Also these blanks take up the space of ca. five written lines, so that this column too held 27 written and five empty lines, viz. 32 lines altogether.

Only the lower half of the left-hand part of col. I with the second hemistichs of Ps 81:2b-16a written in 16 lines is extant. We may presume that like cols. II and III, col. I also held 32 lines. The lost portion contained for certain the superscription of Psalm 81 in one line, an empty line between the Psalms 81 and 80, and the text of approximately the second half of the quite long Psalm 80 in 14 lines, with its first part written in the preceding column.

It follows that the average column of MasPs[a] held 27–29 written and four-five empty lines.

---

9. The apparent loss of some 2.7 cm (14.7 + 13.5 = 28.2 cm) results from the ingress of the spur at the top of (b) into the concavity at the bottom of (a).
10. These figures are somewhat smaller than those given by Yadin. They are based on photographs, and are subject to some margin of error.
11. A similar separation of two consecutive psalms by a blank line, can be observed in a fragment from Naḥal Ḥever which holds the end of Ps 15 and the superscription of Ps 16. See Yadin, Expedition D, 40 (Pl. 20).

Script

I would classify the script as "formal Herodian" (Cross, Scripts, 138, l. 4), and accordingly date it to the end of the last century BCE. The regular lettering evinces the hand of a trained scribe. Most letters measure 3×3 mm. As is the rule, the head of the *lamed* protrudes above the lines to double the height of the other letters (e.g. in col. II, l. 1), and the lower strokes of *qof* and the final forms of *kaf, mem, nun, peh* and *ṣade* descend below the line. Like the *lamed*, these letters are 5–6 mm high (e.g. in col. I, ll. 24–25ᵃ).

Letters are clearly separated, and so are words. But now and then two or more letters will flow together ligature-like, e.g. in לבם (col. I, 1, 26ᵇ), אכן (col. II, l. 10ᵇ) נו in נועצו (col. II, l. 18ᵇ). Also words will sometimes coalesce when a larger than usual length of text forced the scribe to crowd the writing or slightly reduce the size of letters, foremost at the end of a hemistich, such as אלהיישענו (col. III, l. 28ᵃ) and תאנפבנו (col. III, l. 29ᵃ), or at the end of a line, e.g. שפטה הארץ (col. II, l. 11), כסיסרא (II, l. 22), שיתמוכגלגל (col. II, l. 26), תבעריער (col. II, l. 27). In some instances, the last word or words of the first hemistich actually spill over into the inter-stich margin, almost joining with the first word of the second hemistich, e.g. אל תחרש ואל תשקט אל כיא הנה אויביך יהמיון (col. II, l. 15 = Ps 83:2ᵇ–3ᵃ; cf. col. II, ll. 18 and 19 = Ps 83:5ᵇ–7ᵃ).

The written lines are mostly kept straight, but swerve slightly upwards at the top and bottom of col. III. The letters hang from horizontal dry rulings impressed with a stylus. The width of inter-line spaces amounts to 7–8 mm. The beginnings of lines in cols. II and III are 'justified'. Vertical dry rulings are still visible in the upper part of col. II. The length of a full line fluctuates between 8.1 (l. 23) and 9.3 cm (l. 25), the length of a hemistich between 3.3 (col. II, l. 14ᵇ) and 4.7 cm (col. II, l. 25ᵇ), and the width of the inter-column margins between 1 and 2.3 cm.

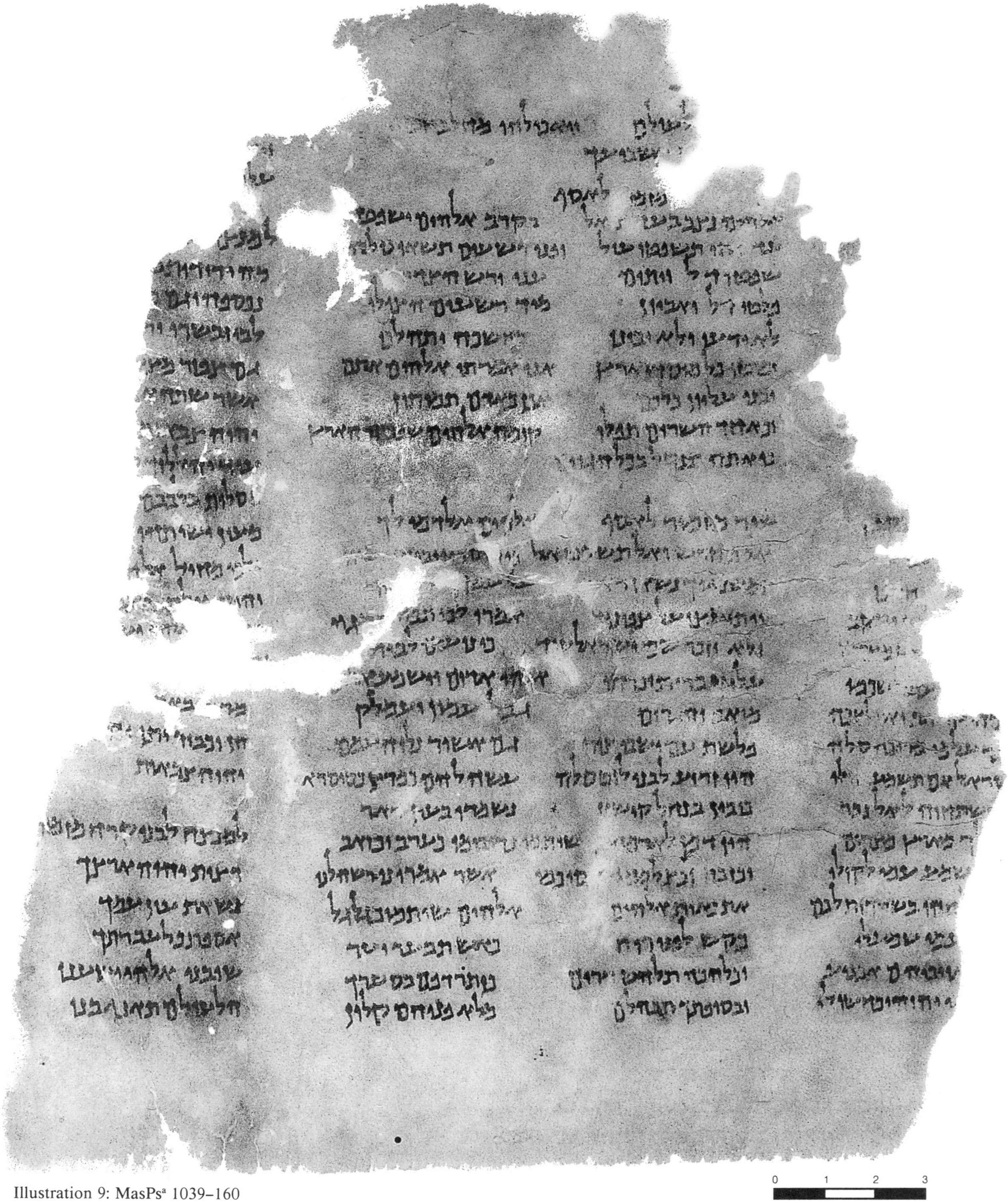

Illustration 9: MasPs[a] 1039–160

Transcription[12]

Column I

13 [למנצח על הגתית לאסף]

14 [הרנינו לאלהים עוזנו]   הריעו לאלהי י]עֹקֹב

15 [שאו זמרה ותנו תף]   כנור נעים] עֹם [נֹ]בֹֹל

16 [תקעו בחדש שופר]   בכסה ליום] חֹגֹנֹוֹ

17 [כי חק לישראל הוא]   משפט לא]לֹֹהֹי יעקב

18 [עדות ביהוסף שמו]   בצאתו על א]רֹץ מצרֹֹים

19 [שפת לא ידעתי אשמע]   הסירותי] מסבֹל שכמו

20 [כפיו מדוד תעברנה]   בצ]רה ק[ר]את וא[ח]לֹצכה

21 [אענך בסתר רעם]   אבח]נֹך על מי מריבה סלה

22 [שמע עמי ואעידה בך]   י]שֹראל אם תשמע קֹולֹי

23 [לא יהיה בך אל זר]   ולא] תֹשתחוה לֹאל נכר

24 [אנכי יהוה אלהיך]   המע]לֹך מארץ מצרים

25 [הרחב פיך ואמלאהו]   ולא] שמע עמי לקולי

26 [וישראל לא אבה לי]   ואש]לֹחהו בשררות לבם

27 [וילכו במועצותיהם]   לו] עמי שמע לי

28 [ישראל בדרכי יהלכו]   כמעט] אֹויביהם אכניע

29 [ועל צריהם אשיב ידי]   משנא]י יהוה יכחשו לו

Column II

1 [ויהי עתם] לעולם   ויאכילהו מחלב חֹטֹה

2 [ומצור דב]שֹ אֹשביעך

3 מזמֹו]ר] לאסף

4 אלהים נצב בעדת אל   בקרב אלהים ישפט

5 עד מתי תשפטו עול   ופני רשעים תשאו סלה

6 שפטו דל ויתום   עני ורש הצדי[קו]

7 פלטו דל ואביון   מיד רשעים הצילו

8 לא ידעו ולא יבינו   בֹחשכה יתהלכו

9 ימוטו כל מוסדי ארץ   אני אמרתי אלהים אתם

10 ובני עליון כלכם   אכן כאדם תמותון

11 וכֹאחד השרים תפלו   קומה אלהים שפטה הארץ

12. A transcription and a discussion of the restored text was published by Nebe, Handschrift, on the basis of a photograph.

Column II (Cont.)

12	כי אתה תנחֹל בכל הגוי֗ם
13	
שיר מזמור לאסף	אלהים אל דמי לך
אל תחרש ואל תשקֹט אל	כיֹא הֹנֹה אויביך֗ יֹהֹמֹי֗וֹן
ומשנֹאיך נשאֹו ראֹשֹ	על עמך֗ יע[ר]ימו ס[ו]דֹ
ויתיעצו על צפוניך֗	אמרו לכו ונכח[י]דֹ[ם] מֹגוי
ולא יזכר שם ישראל עוד	כי נועצו לב יח[ד]ו
עלי֗ך֗ ברית יכרתו	אלֹהי אדום וישמעאלֹ[י]ֹם
מוֹאב והגרים	גבל עמון ועמלק
פלשת עם ישבי צור	גם אשור נלוה עמם
היו זרוע לבני לוט סלה	עשה להם כמדין כסיסרא
כיבין בנחל קישוֹן	נשמדו בעין דֹאר
היו דמן לאדמה שיתמו	נדיבמו כערב וכזאב
וכזבח וכצלמנֹעֹ [כ]לֹ [נ]סיכמו	אשר אמרו נירשה לנו
את נאות אלהים	אלהים שיתמו כגלגל
כקש לפני רוח	כאש תבער יער
וכלהבה תלהט הֹרים	כן תרדפם בסערך
ובסופתך תבהלם	מלא פניהם קלון

(line numbers: 14–29 for the above text rows)

Column III

1	[ויבקשו שמך יהוה	יבשו ויבהלו עדי עד]
2	ויֹחֹ[פרו ויאבדו וידעו	כי אתה שמך יהוה לבדך]
3	עלי֗[ון על כל הארץ]
4	
5	למנצחֹ [על הגתית לבני קרח מזמור]
מה ידידות מֹ[ו]שכנותיך	יהוה צבאות]
נכספה וגם כ[ל]תה נפשי	לחצרות יהוה]
לבי ובשרי יר[נ]נו	אל אל חי]
גם צפור מצאֹ[ה] בית	ודרור קן לה]
אשר שתה א[פרחיה	את מזבחותיך]
יהוה צבאות [מלכי ואלהי	אשרי יושבי ביתך]
עוד יהללוך סֹ[ל]ה	אשרי אדם עוז לו בך]
מֹסלות בלבבם	[עברי בעמק הבכא]
מעין ישיתהו	[גם ברכות יעטה מורה]
ילכו מחיל אל חֹיל	יראה אל אלהים בציון]

(line numbers: 6–15 for the above text rows)

Column III (Cont.)

16   יהוה אֹלֹהֹיֹם צב[אות]   שמעה תפלתי[

17   הֹ[אזינה] אלהי יע[קב סלה   מגננו ראה אלהים]

18   וֹהֹ[ב]ט פני משיחך   כי טוב יום בחצריך]

19   [מאלף בחרתי   הסתופף בבית אלהי[

20   מד[ו]רֹ באהֹלי רשע   כי שמש ומגן יהוה אלהים]

21   חן וכבוד יתן יה[וה   לא ימנע טוב להלכים בתמים]

22   יהוה צבאות   [אשרי אדם בטח בך]

23

24   למנצח לבני קרח מזמ[ור]

25   רצית יהוה ארצך   [שבת שבות יעקב]

26   נשאת עון עמך   [כסית כל חטאתם סלה]

27   אספת כל עברתך   [השיבות מחרון אפך]

28   שובנו אלהי ישענו   [והפר כעסך עמנו]

29   הלעולם תאנף בנו   [תמשך אפך לדר ודר]

Stichometry[13]

Lines are invariably divided into hemistichs, forming two half-columns separated by a margin of between 1–2.3 cm, depending on the amount of text which the scribe accommodated in the first half-line. Whereas the beginnings of lines, viz. of the first stichs, are justified, the beginnings of the second half-lines are irregular. A hemistich contains between 2–5 words, contingent on the length of words and the sense unit: e.g. בחשכה יתהלכו (col. II, l. 8ᵇ); גבל עמון ועמלק (l. 20ᵇ); פלשת עם ישבי צור (l. 21ᵃ); היו זרע לבני לוט סלה (l. 22ᵃ). The shortest fully preserved hemistich, מואב והגרים (col. II, 20ᵃ), contains ten letters and one inter-word space, viz. 11 spaces altogether; the longest, וכזבח וכצלמנע [נ]סיכמו [וכ]ל (col. II, l. 25ᵃ), 20 letters and three spaces, viz. 23 spaces in all. The shortest line, כקש לפני רוח כאש תבער יער (col. II, l. 27), has 20 letters and four inter-word spaces, i.e. a total of 24 spaces; the longest, וכזבח וכצלמנע [וכ]ל [נ]סיכמו אשר אמרו נירשה לנו (col. II, l. 25), 35 letters and seven inter-word spaces, viz. 42 spaces in all.

In the masoretic tradition this system of half-lines, termed אריח על גבי אריח, 'half-brick on top of half-brick',[14] is essentially based on verses composed of sense units in

---

13. The oldest example of the stichic arrangement of a poetic text is found in an Aramaic funeral inscription of unknown provenance from the 5th or 4th century BCE. See H. Donner — W. Röllig, *Kanaanäische und Aramäische Inschriften* (Wiesbaden: Harrassowitz, 1966–1969) nr. 269; J.C.L. Gibson, *Textbook of Syrian Semitic Inscriptions*, vol. II: *Aramaic Inscriptions* (Oxford: Clarendon, 1975) nr. 24.

14. For a different system, cf. MasPsᵇ below.

parallelismus membrorum. The first hemistich is closed by the half-sentence divider *'etnaḥ*, equalling a comma or a semicolon, and the second by a *paseq*, equalling a full stop. But the bi-section of lines in MasPs[a] does not always dovetail with the system of the major masoretic manuscripts. Moreover, in Psalms 81–85 as in many other psalms, some verses do not lend themselves to the hemistich structure, but rather consist of three stichs. In such instances, the scribe of MasPs[a] adhered strictly to the half-columns arrangement, often disregarding the parallelism of a sense unit. In Psalm 81, e.g., most verses (vv. 2–5, 7, 9–10, 12–17) confirm to *parallelismus membrorum*.[15] But vv. 6, 8, 11 hold three stichs each, and thus clash with the hemistich system. In some printed editions of the Bible, e.g. BH(S) based on L, the first two stichs will be recorded in one line ending on an *'etnaḥ*, the third in another half-line ending on a *paseq*, with the second half of the line left blank (82:5):

לא ידעו ולא יבינו   בחשכה יתהלכו

ימוטו כל־מוסדי ארץ

In others, like in ed. Ginsburg, the two half-columns arrangement is dropped

לא ידעו ולא יבינו

בחשכה יתהלכו

ימוטו כל־מוסדי ארץ

In the Aleppo Codex (A) the hemistich structure is similarly disregarded and the internal verse division is indicated by a *vacat* after each half-verse. Here the bisection of the line is much less significant than in the hemistich structure. A poetic unit may stretch over the second half of one line and the first of the next, without impairing the sense cohesion of the verse. In verses composed of three stichs, there is no concordance of the poetic division, marked by *'etnaḥ* and *paseq*, with the line bisection, e.g. in Ps 82:5:

מיד רשעים הצילו   לא ידעו ולא יבינו

בחשכה יתהלכו   ימוטו כל־מוסדי ארץ

In distinction, the scribe of MasPs[a] preserved the two half-columns structure throughout,[16] altogether disregarding the resulting loss of content parallelism of hemistichs in a line. In a verse with three stichs, such as in Ps 82:5, one line contains the first two stichs, ending where MT marks an *'etnaḥ*, while the third stich, which in MT ends on a *paseq*, is written in the next line, together with the first stich of the following verse, which in MT again ends on an *'etnaḥ*:

Col. II, 8: בחשכה יתהלכו   לא ידעו ולא יבינו (82:5[a,b])

II, 9: אני אמרתי אלהים אתם   ימוטו כל מוסדי ארץ (82:5[c]–6[a])

---

15. With the exception of the superscription למנצח על הגתית לאסף (v. 1).

16. Psalms, which in MT exhibit a stichic structure, are often written in Qumran manuscripts as running texts, e.g. Psalm 91 in 11QPsAp[a] V 3–13. See E. Puech, Les deux derniers psaumes davidique du rituel d'exorcisme, *The Dead Sea Scrolls. Forty Years of Research*, ed. D. Dimant and U. Rappaport (Leiden: Brill/Jerusalem: Magnes, The Hebrew University, Yad Ben-Zvi, 1992) 75–8.

The following example of line division illustrates the disregard for concordance with the sense content of a passage:

Col. II, 22^a–b: עשה להם כמדין כסיסרא	היו זרוע לבני לוט סלה (83:9^b–10^a)
II, 23^a–b: נשמדו בעין דאר	כיבין בנחל קישון (83:10^b–11^a)
II, 24^a:	היו דמן לאדמה (83:11^b)

In MT the end of v. 9 is indicated by a *paseq* under the closing formula *selah*. The end of the next half-verse (10^a) is signalled by marking the last word, כמדין, with an *'etnaḥ*,[17] and the following hemistich (10^b) opens with the evident logical combination כסיסרא כיבין. In contrast, the scribe of MasPs^a closed the preceding line with כסיסרא, illogically linking the name of the commander of the Canaanite king's Yabin forces (Jdgs 4–5) with the totally distinct Midian episode (Jdgs 6–7), which is continued in ll. 24^b–25^a with the mention of the Midianite princes, *ze'eb* and *'oreb, zebaḥ* and *ṣalmuna'* (Jdgs 7:25–8:21).[18] It may further be surmised that in the concluding verses of Ps 83 the scribe arranged the hemistichs somewhat differently from MT. To avoid overloading the second stich in col. III, l. 2, he possibly entered the verb *weyed'u* at the end of the first:[19]

| Ps 83:18: ויחפרו ויאבדו | יבשו ויבהלו עדי־עד |
| 83:19: עליון על־כל־הארץ | וידעו כי אתה שמך יהוה לבדך |

Col. III, 1^b: [יבושו ויבהלו עדי עד]	
III, 2^a–b: [כי אתה שמך יהוה לבדך]	ויח[פרו ויאבדו וידעו
III, 3^a:	עלי[ון על כל הארץ]

Superscriptions

Superscriptions are recorded in MasPs^a in several ways. In Psalm 85 the superscription [למנצח לבני קרח מזמור] fills the first half of a line (which in MT ends on a *paseq*) with the second half left blank. The main text begins on the next line with the first stich, רצית יהוה ארצך. The proposed restoration is based on the assumption that at least up to v. 8 the psalm was written in two half-columns. The same pertains to Psalm 81. Here the extant second half-column of hemistichs prompts the restoration of the superscription [למנצח על הגתית לאסף] as a half-line followed by a blank half-line, or as straddling the two half-columns of the main text, as in Psalm 82. The heading of Psalm 84 can be either restored as one exceptionally long stich, [למנצח על הגתית לבני קרח מזמור], or as two hemistichs above the first two half-lines of the main text, [על הגתית   לבני קרח מזמור] למנצח. In distinction, the heading of Psalm 83, שיר מזמור לאסף, marked with a *paseq* in MT, forms the first stich

---

17. See Nebe, Handschrift, 92.
18. This peculiar arrangement may, however, reflect a textual variant. See below.
19. Comparing לבדך אלהים (4QPs^e 86:10), אתה הוא יהוה לבדך (Neh 9:6) and אתה אלהים לבדך (Ps 86:10), Nebe, Handschrift, 91–2, suggests that in difference from all witnesses, the text of MasPs^a did possibly not contain the word שמך (Ps 83:19^a).

of v. 1, completed by a second stich, אלהים אל דמי לך, which is actually part of the main text, and in MT ends with the half-sentence divider 'etnaḥ. Only the heading of Psalm 82 מזמור] לאסף occupies the middle of a line, written partly above the inter-stich margin of the first line of the main text.

Further, the blanks between the last line of Psalm 81 (v. 7[b]) and the superscription of Psalm 82, as well as between the superscription and the first line of Psalm 82, are appreciably narrower than the blanks which separate one psalm from another. In distinction, the width of the blank between the last line of Psalm 81 and the first line of Psalm 82, without taking the superscription into account, equals the widths of the regular blanks between two psalms. These facts induce the supposition that the scribe entered the superscription of Psalm 82 after he had already written the first line of text, and was therefore forced to reduce the width of the empty space between them.

Text

As Yadin stated, the text of MasPs[a] corresponds to all intents and purposes to MT. However, in addition to the one interesting variant, אלהי אדום (col. II, l. 19b) vs אהלי אדום (Ps 83:7) which he pointed out, and to which I shall yet give attention, some more textual differences should be noted:

Plene vs defective spelling:

Col. I, 20[b]: ואו‏[ח]‏לצכה   81:8: ואחלצך

II, 15[b]: כי‏ˈ הנה אויביך   83:3: כי הנה אויביך.[20]

Next to the *yod* of כי, and before a lacuna after which a part of the first *hē* in הנה can be seen, a faint trace of one more letter remains, possibly the top of the right-hand stroke of an *'aleph*, suggesting the reading כיא̊. This plene spelling, like that of the second person singular with an added *hē* as in ואו‏[ח]‏לˈצכה (col. I, l. 20[b]),[21] which is amply documented in Qumran manuscripts, is also found in other Masada fragments.

II, 24[b]: נדיבימו[22]   83:12: נדיבמו

Defective versus plene spelling

Col. I, 26[b]: בשררות   81:13: בשרירות

Col. III, 14[a]: ישיתהו, 84:7: ישיתוהו, mss: ישיתֵהו. Defective spelling is possibly reflected in the Greek rendition of the verb in the singular, ὃν ἔθετο, instead of the plural, which seems to be required by the plural form in the preceding phrase עֹבְרֵי בעמק הבכא.

20. In his apparatus Ginsburg records editions which exhibit the defective spelling איביך.
21. This reading is preserved in 11Q8 Ps[d], frg. 10, 5: ואא‏[ח]‏לצכה. See F. García Martínez — E.J.C. Tigchelaar, Psalms Manuscripts From Qumran Cave 11: A Preliminary Edition, *Hommage à Józef T. Milik*, ed. F. Garcia Martinez and E. Puech, *RQ* 17 (1996) 94.
22. Again plene. In contrast, נסיכמו is written defectively, like in MT.

More weight is attached to the following textual variants in an increasing measure of significance:

Col. II, 26ᵇ: אלהים שיתמו כגלגל, 83:14: אלהי. While LXX (82:14): ὁ θεός μου reflects אלהי of MT, the "most frequent address to God" in psalms,[23] Syr: אלהא sides with MasPsª, possibly harmonizing the reading with אלהים at the end of the preceding verse (col. II, 26ª, 83:13). The two variants are combined in Ps 43:4 MT: אלהים אלהי.

Col. I, 22ᵇ: אם תשמע קוֹלי, 81:9: אם תשמע לי = LXX 80:9: ἐὰν ἀκούσῃς μου. A close inspection of the original and of photographs reveals the foot of ק and the head of ו before לי.[24] MasPsª probably harmonizes here the text with the reading ולא שמע עמי לקולי in v. 12 (=LXX), and MT with the phrase לו עמי שמע לי in v. 14 (=LXX).

Col. II, 20ᵇ: גבל עמון ועמלק, 83:8: גְבָל ועמון ועמלק. MT is supported by LXX: Γεβαλ καὶ Αμμον καὶ Αμαληκ, and Tg: גובלאי ועמונא. But Syr does not render the connective *waw*, and evidently reads גְבֻל instead of גְבָל: "the territory of Ammon". This rendition probably reflects a true variant which may also underlie MasPsª, and possibly echoes the geopolitical term גבול בני עמון (Num 21:24; Deut 3:16; Josh 12:2, 13:10). It should be noted that the reference to the people of northern Transjordan and their territory by עמון is a *hapax legomenon* in biblical literature, in which invariably the designation בני עמון is employed (100 times).[25] Further, while the ethnic-national entities listed in the psalmist's 'historical summary' are considered Israel's traditional enemies,[26] this is not the case with the city of Gebal.[27] The name occurs only once more in the context of an oracle against Tyre (Ezek 27:9), viz. in a non-Israelite setting. There is also one mention of the territory ארץ הגבלי which the Israelites could not conquer in the days of Joshua (Josh 13:5), and a reference to its inhabitants, הגבלים (1 Kgs 5:32), in a manifestly favourable context.

Col. II, 19ᵇ: אלהי אדום,[28] the gods of Edom , 83:7: אהלי אדום, the tents of Edom .

MT is backed by the VSS. LXX: τὰ σκηνώματα τῶν Ιδουμαίων; Tg: משכני אדומאי.[29] The MasPsª reading אלהי could have resulted from an inversion of letters, a frequent scribal

23. See E.M. Schuller, 4Q380 and 4Q381: Non-Canonical Psalms from Qumran, in: *The Dead Sea Scrolls* (above, n. 16), 97.

24. Nebe's assumption, Handschrift, 92, that before לי one letter had possibly been erased does not stand up to scrutiny.

25. Ammonites are repeatedly referred to by the nom. gent. עמונית, עמוני, עמונים, עמוניות.

26. Cf. e.g. Num 24:17–23; Jer 25:15–26; Ps 60:10–11 = 108:10–11, and the various clusters of 'Oracles Against Foreign Nations' (Isa 13–21; Jer 46–51; Ezek 25–32; Am 1:2–2:3).

27. בני לוט, the descendants of Lot, are another exception.

28. A close investigation of the fragment and of photographs proves Nebe's tentative suggestion that a ל was inserted between ה and י (Nebe, Handschrift, 92) to be untenable.

29. אהלי אדום appears to parallel גבל עמון (col. II, 20ᵇ), possibly read גְבֻל עמון, territory of Ammon. As stated, this meaning may be reflected in the Syr rendition of Ps 83:8 MT: גְבָל ועמון, 'Gebal and Ammon,' by 'territory of Ammon.'

mistake,[30] which in this instance was possibly facilitated by the scribe remembering the phrase כי דרשו את אלהי אדום (2 Chr 25:20).

But we must also consider the possibility that the readings אהלי אדום/אלהי אדום are true variants. The very same difference distinguishes between MT: גוים ואלהיו, peoples and their gods,' (2 Sam 7:23 = Tg, Syr: עמא דאנת אלהה), and LXX (= OL): ἔθνη καὶ σκηνώματα, 'peoples and tents'. The Greek rendition is supported by the apocopated reading in a Qumran fragment: ואהלים without גוים (4QSam^a).[31] McCarter defined the 4QSam^a variant "an obvious error shared by LXX".[32] In contrast, A. Geiger maintained that the Greek σκηνώματα αὐτῶν evinces an intentional avoidance of the divine ·name.[33] He further opined that this tendency brought about the present MT texts of the episodes of Sheba ben Bichri's and Jeroboam ben Nebat's calls for rebellion against David and Rechobam respectively. He considered the readings איש לאהליו ישראל, 'Everyone (away) to his tents (home), O Israel' (2 Sam 20:1), and לאהליך ישראל ... וילך ישראל לאהליו, Away *to your tents* (homes), O Israel ... And Israel went *to their tents* (1 Kgs 12:16 = 2 Chr 10:16), to be emendations of לאלהיו and לאלהיך, 'everyone back to *his or your gods*' (ibid., 289–92).[34] A very similar inversion of the letter sequence אהל is present in a quotation of Am 5:27: והגליתי אתכם מהלאה לדמשק, "I shall exile you beyond Damascus", in the Damascus Document as: מאהלי דמשק, "from my tent (?) to Damascus" (CD VII, 14–15).[35]

Col. II, 22: כסיסרא at the end of the line seems to be out of place. As said, the conjunction כמדין כסיסרא is patently illogical, whereas MT's pairing of Sisera with Yabin, כסיסרא כיבין, is exceedingly appropriate. Moreover, כסיסרא is penned in somewhat different letter forms, and the writing in l. 22 penetrates notably into the column margin. The scribe neither crowded the protruding letters nor did he slightly reduce them in size, as he does in similar instances. This gives rise to the surmise that his original text read erroneously: עשה להם כמדין כיבין בנחל קישון, "deal with them as with Midian and Yabin at the Kishon river," and that he himself or a second hand entered כסיסרא as a corrective substitution. However, due to a scribal mistake or because of insufficient space, כסיסרא

---

30. A few examples will illustrate this textual phenomenon: Prov 11:2: ואת צנועים חכמה, "wisdom is with the humble"; 13:10: ואת נועצים חכמה, "with those who take counsel." Jer 12:4: לא יראה את אחריתנו, "he (God) will not see what we plan" (literally 'what our ends/aims are'); LXX: ὁδοὺς ἡμῶν, "our ways," = אֹרְחֹתֵינוּ. 1 Sam 15:9: מיטב הצאן והבקר והמשנים, "the best of the sheep and the cattle and the young" (lit. 'seconds'); Tg and Syr: וד)שמניא(, "the fat ones" (LXX: καὶ τῶν ἐδεσμάτων).

31. In the parallel verse 1 Chr 17:21, MT preserves the equally apocopated reading גוים without ואלהיו.

32. P.K. McCarter, Jr., *II Samuel. AB* 9 (Garden City, NY: Doubleday, 1984) 235.

33. A. Geiger, *Urschrift und Übersetzungen der Bibel in ihrer Abhängigkeit von der Entwicklung des Judenthums* (Breslau: Hainauer, 1887) 289: "Eine Umwandlung die eine absichtliche ist und die man in alter Zeit zur Verwischung des Gottesnamens ... auch sonst noch gebrauchte."

34. More speculative is his suggestion that MT: ותרגנו באהליכם (Deut 1:27) and וירגנו באהליהם (Ps 106:25), 'you/they murmured in *your/their tents*', read originally באלהיכם/באלהיהם, 'you/they murmured against *your/their God*.'

35. Pace Rabin, *CD*, 29, n. 15, 2, this "appears to be a genuine variant."

was not inserted in its proper position at the beginning of l. 23 before כיבין, but was misplaced at the end of l. 22.

Col. II, 24: The word שיתמו was secondarily entered in the interstich margin in somewhat smaller letters, possibly as a correction of an initial omission due to homoioteleuton, שיתמו נדיבימו (Ps 83:12).[36] MasPsᵃ supports MT שיתמו with the pronominal suffix מו, against LXX, Aquila and Origenes who render only the naked verbal form שית: θοῦ.[37] It could, however, be argued that the basic text of MasPsᵃ did not contain the word שיתמו, which was erroneously introduced in v. 12 from v. 14, and therefore that it preserved perfectly the pristine *parallelismus membrorum* of the verse: נדיבימו כערב וכזאב//וכזבח וכצלמנע כ[ו]ל [נ]סיכמו.[38]

The persuasive concordance of MasPsᵃ with MT is highlighted by their textual agreement against variants in ancient versions, foremost LXX:

Ps 81:5 = I, 14ᵇ: יַעֲקֹב	11Q8 Psᵈ frg. 10, 5: יעקוב[39]	
81:13 = I, 26ᵇ: ואש[ל]חהו	LXX, Sym: καὶ ἐξαπέστειλα αὐτούς = ואשלחם	
81:17 = II, 2ᵃ: אשביער	LXX: ἐχόρτασεν αὐτούς = אשביעם (plural)	
82:3 = II, 6ᵃ: שפטו דל ויתום	LXX: ὀρφανὸν καὶ πτωχόν (inversion)	
83:6 = II, 19ᵃ: עליך ברית יכרתו	Tg, Syr: ואמטולתך (+ copula)	
83:8 = II, 21ᵃ: פלשת עם ישבי צור	LXX: καὶ ἀλλόφυλοι (+ copula)	
83:12 = II, 24ᵇ: שיתמו נדיבימו	LXX: θοῦ τοὺς ἄρχοντας αὐτῶν; Tg + copula	
83:13 = II, 26ᵃ: את נאות אלהים	LXX: τὸ ἁγιαστήριον (singular) = Tg, Syr	
83:14 = II, 27ᵃ: כקש	Tg: והיך קשא (+ copula) = Syr, V	
84:3 = III, 7ᵃ: נכספה וגם כלתה	LXX: ἐπιποθεῖ καὶ ἐκλείπει om. גם = Syr	
84:5 = III, 12ᵃ: עוד יהללוך סולה	LXX: εἰς τοὺς αἰῶνας τῶν αἰώνων = לעדי עד	
84:6 = III, 13ᵃ: מסלות בלבבם	LXX: ἀναβάσεις ἐν τῇ καρδίᾳ αὐτοῦ = מעלות?	
84:7 = III, 14ᵃ: מעין ישית(ו)הו	LXX: εἰς τόπον ὃν ἔθετο = מעון/מקום?	
85:3 = III, 26ᵃ: נשאת עון עמך	LXX: ἀφῆκας τάς ἀνομίας (pl.) τῷ λαῷ σοῦ	
85:5 = III, 28ᵃ: שובנו אלהי ישענו	LXX: ἐπίστρεψον ἧμας = השיבנו.[40]	

In conclusion: it cannot go unnoticed that, with the exception of the superscription מזמור לאסף (Ps 82:1), the variants between MT and MasPsᵃ are concentrated in the textually rather uneven passage Ps 83:7–12 = col. II, 19–25. The *Vorlage* of MasPsᵃ may not have contained those difficulties, or else the scribe at first eliminated them from his text, but subsequently revised it toward MT.

36. Cf. Nebe, Handschrift, 92.
37. Cf. M. Dahood, *Psalms II. AB* 17 (Garden City, NY: Doubleday, 1968).
38. Tg reflects MT, but ameliorates the apparent textual difficulty by prefixing a conjunctive *waw* to נדיבימו, thus creating three instead of two objects which depend on the verb שית שית יתהון ורבניהון היך, עורב והיך זאב והיך זבח צלמונע והיך כל מלכיהון, "Make *them* and *their princes* like Oreb and Zeeb, and like Zebah and Zalmuna all *their kings*."
39. See García-Tigchelaar (above, n. 21) 100.
40. It is noteworthy that not one textual emendation proposed by modern exegetes is backed by MasPsᵃ.

A synoptic view of MT and MasPs[a] suggests the following tentative reconstruction of the original wording of Ps 83:7–11:

Ps 83:7	=	col. III, 19[b]–20[a]:	אהלי (אלהי) אדום וישמעאלים//מואב והגרים
83:8	=	III, 20[b]–21[a]:	גבל (ו)עמון ועמלק//פלשת עם ישבי צור
83:9	=	III, 21[b]–22[a]:	גם אשור נלוה עמם//היו זרע לבני לוט סלה
83:10	=	III, 22[b]–23[a]:	עשה להם כסיסרא//כיבין בנחל קישון
83:11	=	III, 23[b]–24[a]:	[41]כמדין נשמדו בעין דאר//היו דמן לאדמה
83:12	=	III, 24[b]–25[a]:	נדיב(י)מו כערב וכזאב//וכזבח וכצלמנע כל נסיכמו

41. The nom. loc. עין דאר remains a problem. Modern interpreters suggest reading עין חרד (LXX[A]: Αγαδ). Medieval exegetes were baffled. Rashi (Shelomo Jitzhaki): "I do not know which battle took place at Ein Dor, whether the one (fought) by Gideon or the one by Barak"; Ibn Ezra: "The place Ein Dor at which they (the enemy) fell was possibly named so, because Gideon came from there."

(g) Mas 1103–1742; Mas 1f; Psalms 150:1–6 (MasPs^b, final photo 302361; earlier 302364)

Yadin first referred to this fragment of a Psalms scroll in a paper read at the annual meeting of the Israel Exploration Society in 1966,[1] and related explicitly to it in *EAE*:

> A small fragment discovered in casemate 1103, north of the Snake Path Gate. The scroll (lege: fragment, S.T.) contains nearly the entire Psalm 150, and is also identical with the Masoretic Text. The blank space to the left of the text shows that it was the last Psalm on the parchment, corresponding to the Masoretic Text unlike the Septuagint and Psalms Scroll from Qumran.[2]

In a popular account of the Masada excavations, Yadin gave a vivid description of the discovery of this fragment:

> This was not the only casemate in which scrolls were found. We discovered other fragments, for example, in one of the chambers in the eastern sector, just north of the 'snake path'. The excavation work in this sector was very difficult because large sections of the outside wall had collapsed and they needed to be strengthened and supported before we could start digging.
> What we discovered was a piece of white leather which contained the last chapter of the *Book of Psalms*, namely, Psalm 150, 'Praise ye the Lord... Praise Him with the sound of the trumpet'. The writing on it was so faded and the colour of the parchment so light that it almost escaped our notice, and indeed when it was being cleaned one of the volunteers thought that what she was holding in her hand was a piece of newspaper.[3]

Description

MasPs^b consists of two small pieces of parchment, which can be comfortably fitted together, although at the join one line is seemingly missing.

Each piece contains four almost fully preserved lines of text. With the blank space at the top, frg. (a) measures 4.8×2.4 cm, and frg. (b) 7.5×2.1 cm. Taking into account the missing first line, which presumably held only the superscription הללויה, Ps 150 would have taken up ca. 5 cm of the height of the last column of the scroll.

The ragged contours of (a) all around, as well as of the top, bottom and right-hand edges of (b), were evidently caused by decomposition of the material. In contrast, the straight upper left-hand rim of (b) appears to have resulted from breakage of the dry parchment or possibly from wilful tearing.[4] The evenness of the left-hand edge of (b)

1. Yadin, Qumran (Hebrew), 126: "Fragments of Psalms".
2. Yadin, *EAE*, 811–2. The reference is evidently to 11QPs^a, *DJD* IV.
3. Yadin, *Fortress*, 174–5.
4. A comparable situation pertains to the unclassified frg. 1063–1747 (see below) and several others.

suggests that here the leather possibly broke along a string of still faintly discernible needle holes, where originally another length of parchment, which served as the handle sheet, had been stitched to the last written sheet. The 2 cm broad blank stretch of leather at the left of the fragment, which is about twice as broad as the inter-column margin, and is fully preserved to the width of 0.9–1.1 cm, was probably an additional part of that wrapper.[5] The assumption is borne out by the fact that horizontal dry rulings, 4 mm apart, run from the right hand inter-column margin, through the written column, but are discontinued at the left, before that blank stretch of leather. There are no vertical dry rulings.

Script

The expertly executed, regular lettering evinces the hand of a trained scribe. The letters are consistently about 1.5 mm high and equally broad, with the exception of the taller ל, and the thin letters י, ז, ו, which measure somewhat less than 1 mm. All letters hang from below the line, as was the custom, with only the heads of ל protruding above it. The written lines are 3.8–4 cm long. The inter-line space, measured from the tops of the letters in one line to the tops of those in the next, amounts to ca. 4 mm.

The width of the written column comes to 3.8–4 cm, as indicated by the length of the fully extant line 8 which holds 21 letters and 3 inter-word spaces, and the practically complete preceding line with 18 letters and 3 inter-word spaces. In the restoration proposed below, line 5 has 16 letters and 3 inter-word spaces, viz. 19 spaces in all. This line is the shortest in the column if the word וכנור was written in the presumably missing line 6 at the joint of (a) and (b), as suggested. But if וכנור was the last word in line 5, this line would have been the longest, holding 21 letters and 4 inter-word spaces, viz. a total of 25 spaces.

The script of MasPs[b] can be defined as "late Hasmonaean or early Herodian" (ca. 50–25 BCE), foremost on the strength of the letters ש, ק, צ, פ, ל, ג. But also its identification as an "early Herodian formal script" (ca. 30–1 BCE) cannot be ruled out.[6] We thus conclude that MasPs[b] was written in the last half-century BCE.

Text

As stated, the conjoined fragments (a) and (b) contain practically the entire text of Psalm 150. In addition, beyond the right-hand margin at lines 8 and 9, the letters חו and קיו of the corresponding line endings in the preceding column are still visible, evidently the remains of the words רו[חו and ח]קיו in Ps 147:18 and 19.[7]

---

5. Cf. above MasDeut 1043/1–4.
6. See Cross, Scripts, 133–202; 138, l. 3 and l. 4. Cf. the script of 1QIsa[a] and 4QSam[a].
7. As will yet be shown, these two line-endings enable us to restore conjecturally the preceding column, which presumably held Psalms 147 and 148. In consequence, the upper section of the partly preserved last column contained Psalm 149.

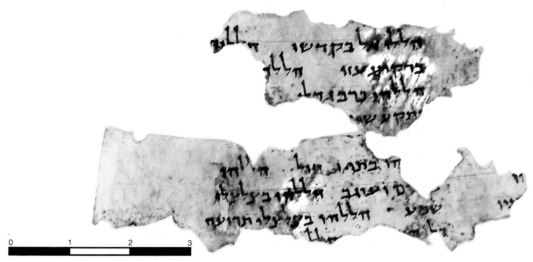

Illustration 10: MasPs^b 1103–1742

[הללויה]	1
הללו אל בקדשו הלֹלֹוֹהו]	2
ברקיע עזו הללהו] בגברתיו]	3
הללהו כרב גדלֹו [הללהו]	4
בֿתקע שפֿרֿ [הללהו בנבל]	5
[וכנור]	6
[הלל]הו בתף ו[מ]חול הללהו	7
ב[מ]נֿים ועוגב הללהו בצלצלי	8
שמע הללהו בצלצלי תרועה	9
כֹל הֹ[נ]שמה ת[הֹ]לֹלֹ יה הללויה]	10

[רו]חו	(against line 8)
ח[ק]יו	(against line 9)

The preserved text of Ps 150 is identical with MT with the exception of the defective reading שפֿרֿ (l. 5) against MT: שופר, and one recurrent variant: MT (both L and A) consistently uses the plene spelling הללוהו,[8] like 11QPs^a.[9] By contrast MasPs^b has the defective spelling הללהו. Only in l. 2 the barely discernible head of a ו, between ל and ה, evinces the reading הללוהו.[10] On the other hand, MasPs^b has the plene spelling עוגב (l. 8), like 11QPs^a (DJD IV, pl. XVI), herein concurring with a branch of the masoretic tradition represented by L, whereas another branch, represented by A, preserves the defective spelling עגב.[11]

8. Ginsburg does not register any variants.
9. See 11QPs^a, pl. XVI, DJD IV, 47.
10. It cannot be decided whether in the first line and at the end of l. 10 הללויה or הלליה should be restored. In the suggested restoration of the text I preferred here the plene spelling.
11. Ginsburg reads עגב in his text, but collates a manuscript which has the plene spelling: ס״א ועוגב מלא.

[93]

More importantly, MasPs[b] agrees with MT and the ancient VSS against two variant readings in 11QPs[a]. Ps 150:3 MT: בְּתֵקַע שׁוֹפָר = MasPs[b] l. 5 and VSS (LXX: ἐν ἤχῳ σάλπιγγος), 11QPs[a] XVI, 5: בתקוע; Ps 150:6 MT: כל הנשמה = MasPs[b] l. 10: כל הֹנשמה. The restoration is suggested by the ensuing sing. verb form תְּהֹלֵּל, and VSS (LXX: πᾶσα πνοή), 11QPs[a] XVI, 7: כל הנשמות (pl.). These readings underscore the close textual affinity of the Masada scroll with MT and concomitantly its divergence from the practically contemporaneous Psalms scroll from Qumran.

Text Division

MT accentuates the poetic structure of Psalm 150 by arranging the text in a column structure of hemistichs, which the masoretes termed אריח על גבי אריח, 'one half-brick atop another:' The first stich ends on a mid-sentence divider, *'etnaḥ*, the second on the sentence divider *paseq*, as reproduced in BH(S) from L. This structure is even more pronounced in A, although there remains only an extremely narrow blank space between the hemistichs of v. 5 because of the especially large number of letters which had to be accommodated in the line.

In contrast, the scribe of MasPs[b] wrote the text continuously, although he still called attention to the poetic structure by leaving a blank of two or three letters where MT marks an *'etnaḥ* or a *paseq*. Thus, like MasPs[a] and some Qumran biblical fragments, MasPs[b] attests to the antiquity of the masoretic punctuation and cantillation tradition, showing its roots to reach down into the Second Temple period.

The mostly blank line at the join of frgs. (a) and (b), between lines 6 and 7 (Ps 150:3 and 4) which, as stated, presumably contained only the word וכנור, effectively divides the psalm into two strophes. The exceptionally large blank appears to equal an os, a *parašah petuḥah* in the masoretic section system.[12] However, no such subdivision of Ps 150 is preserved in any of the main masoretic codices.[13]

Restoring the last two columns of MasPs[b]

In view of the textual identity of MasPs[b] with MT in Ps 150, it may be presumed that

---

12. Oesch, *PUS*, 290; 321ff.
13. In this context it should be pointed out that 11QPs[a] does not exhibit the strophic division of MsPs[b] nor the poetic arrangement of hemistichs, which is even more accentuated in the masoretic column structure. Similarly, Psalm 136 is written in 11QPs[a] as a running text, whereas L and A present it in the columnar arrangement. It is possible that such poetic structures were applied only in copies of books of the Bible. Their absence from 11QPs[a] may, therefore, buttress the proposition that this scroll is not a copy of the biblical book of Psalms, as proposed by its editor (J.A. Sanders, *DJD* IV) and others. Rather, it is a manuscript of an extra-biblical compilation of a variety of liturgical songs which the Covenanters used in their prayer service, as suggested by M.H. Goshen-Gottstein, The Psalms Scroll (11QPs[a]) — A Problem of Canon and Text, *Textus* 5 (1966) 22–33, and S. Talmon, Pisqah Be'emṣaᶜ Pasuq and 11QPs[a], ibid. 11–21 = idem, Extra-Canonical Hebrew Psalms from Qumran — Psalm 151, *WQW*, 244–72.

this identity characterized the Masada scroll throughout. The above mentioned end-letters of two lines, legible beyond the right-hand margin of the last column which contains Psalm 150, provide therefore the basis for proposing a tentative reconstruction of the layout of the last two columns of the scroll.

Column II		Column I	
[הללויה]	1	[הללויה]	1
[שירו ליהוה שיר חדש תהלתו בקהל]	2	[כי טוב זמרה אלהינו כי נעים נאוה]	2
[חסידים ישמח ישראל בעשיו]	3	[תהלה בונה ירושלם יהוה נדחי]	3
[בני ציון יגילו במלכם יהללו שמו]	4	[ישראל יכנס הרפא לשבורי לב ומחבש]	4
[במחול בתף וכנור יזמרו לו כי]	5	[לעצבותם מונה מספר לכוכבים לכלם]	5
[רוצה יהוה בעמו יפאר ענוים]	6	[שמות יקרא גדול אדונינו ורב כח]	6
[בישועה יעלזו חסידים בכבוד]	7	[לתבונתו אין מספר מעודד ענוים יהוה]	7
[ירננו על משכבותם רוממות אל]	8	[משפיל רשעים עדי ארץ ענו ליהוה]	8
[בגרונם וחרב פיפיות בידם לעשות]	9	[בתודה זמרו לאלהינו בכנור המכסה]	9
[נקמה בגוים תוכחת בלאמים]	10	[שמים בעבים המכין לארץ מטר]	10
[לאסר מלכיהם בזקים ונכבדיהם]	11	[המצמיח הרים חציר נתן לבהמה לחמה]	11
[בכבלי ברזל לעשות בהם]	12	[לבני ערב אשר יקראו לא בגבורת]	12
[משפט כתוב הדר הוא לכל]	13	[הסוס יחפץ לא בשוקי האיש ירצה]	13
[חסידיו הללויה]	14	[רוצה יהוה את יראיו את המיחלים]	14
[הללויה]	15	[לחסדו שבחי ירושלם את יהוה]	15
הללו אל בקדשו הללוֹהו	16	[הללי אלהיך ציון כי חזק בריחי]	16
ברקיע עזו הללוהו בגבורתיו	17	[שעריך ברך בניך בקרבך השם גבולך]	17
הללוהו כרב גדלו [הללהו]	18	[שלום חלב חטים ישביעך השלח]	18
בתקע שפֹר [הללהו בנבל]	19	[אמרתו ארץ עד מהרה ירוץ דברו הנתן]	19
[וכנור]	20	[שלג כצמר כפור כאפר יפזר משליך]	20
[הלל]הו בתף ומ[חול הללהו]	21	[קרחו כפתים לפני קרתו מי יעמד]	21
ב[מנ]ים ועוגב הללהו בצלצלי	22	[ישלח דברו וימסם ישב רו]חו	22
שמע הללהו בצלצלי תרועה	23	[יזלו מים מגיד דברו ליעקב ח]קיו	23
כל ה[נ]שמה ת[הלל] [יה הללויה]	24	[ומשפטיו לישראל לא עשה כן לכל]	24
		[גוי ומשפטים בל ידעום הללויה]	25
		[הללויה]	26
		[הללו את יהוה מן השמים הללהו]	27
		[במרומים הללהו כל מלאכיו]	28
		[הללהו כל צבאו הללהו שמש וירח]	29
		[הללהו כל כוכבי אור הללוהו]	30
		[שמי השמים והמים אשר מעל השמים]	31
		[יהללו את שם יהוה כי הוא צוה]	32
		[ונבראו ויעמידם לעד לעולם חק נתן]	33
		[ולא יעבור הללו את יהוה מן הארץ]	34

Column I (Cont.)

35	‏[תנינים וכל תהמות אש וברד שלג]
36	‏[וקיטור רוח סערה עשה דברו ההרים]
37	‏[וכל גבעות עץ פרי וכל ארזים החיה]
38	‏[וכל בהמה רמש וצפור כנף מלכי ארץ]
39	‏[וכל לאמים שרים וכל שפטי ארץ]
40	‏[בחורים וגם בתולות זקנים עם נערים]
41	‏[יהללו את שם יהוה כי נשגב שמו]
42	‏[לבדו הודו על ארץ ושמים וירם קרן]
43	‏[לעמו תהלה לכל חסידיו לבני]
44	‏[ישראל עם קרבו הללויה]

Between the words ‏רו[ח]‏ו and ‏ח[ק]יו, restored beyond the margin opposite lines 8 and 9 of our fragment, the segment of text ‏יזלו מים מגיד דברו ליעקב (Ps 147:18–19) needs to be inserted. It follows that the line in the penultimate column, which ended with ‏ח[ק]יו, contained twenty-four letters and five inter-word spaces, viz. twenty-nine spaces in all. The three end letters of ‏חקיו, viz. ‏קיו, protrude into the margin beyond ‏רו of ‏רוחו, the last word in the preceding line. That line was probably one or two spaces shorter. In any case, we cannot go wrong in assuming that a line in the penultimate column, in which Psalms 147 and 148 must be accommodated, contained on average 27–28 spaces, allowing for a vacillation between 25 to 30 spaces. It follows that the lines in this column, as presumably in all preceding ones, were a fraction longer than the lines in the last column. The difference was probably caused by the blanks of the hemistich structure, which forced the scribe to shorten somewhat the written lines of Psalm 150.

In the proposed conjectural reconstruction of the last two columns of MasPs[b], lines 8 and 9 of Psalm 150 correspond to lines 22 and 23 of Psalm 147, while line 24, the penultimate line of Psalm 147, corresponds to the closing line of Psalm 150. The bottom part of the last column was evidently left blank, a clear indication that the text of the scroll indeed ended here, ruling out the possibility that another psalm (Psalm 151) was yet to follow as in LXX and 11QPs[a].

The passage of Psalm 147 which preceded the short run of text demarcated by the words ‏רו[ח]ו and ‏ח[ק]יו (vv. 18–19) took up 22 lines in the upper part of the penultimate column. Together with the final clause of v. 19, ‏ומשפטיו לישראל, and v. 20 of Psalm 147, this section extended over four lines. These calculations lead to the conclusion that the lower part of the column contained Psalm 148, which presumably filled 20 lines. It follows that the penultimate column of MasPs[b] held 44 lines altogether, unless a blank line separated one psalm from the other, as in MasPs[a]. If that were the case, the column held 45 lines, probably the standard column format of the scroll, with the exception of the shorter final column.

The upper part of the last column contained 14 lines of text of Psalm 149, above the 10 lines of Psalm 150. Therefore Psalms 149 and 150 combined took up 24 lines. This number equals exactly the total of 24 lines of Psalm 147 in the upper part of the preceding column, with the last line written opposite the very top of the blank portion of the final column.

The height of the scroll can be established by the following calculation: the ten lines of text of Psalm 150 cover approximately 4.5 cm. Accordingly, 44 (or 45) lines of a fully written column would cover ca. 22–23 cm. It follows, that with the added top and bottom margins of about 1.5 cm each, MasPs[b] stood ca. 25–26 cm high.[14]

14. This was presumably a standard measure of a scroll. MasPs[a] (1039–160) stands 25.5 cm high, and the height of several Qumran scrolls is in that very same range.

2. Fragments of Bible-Related Compositions

(a) Mas 1045–1350 & 1375; Mas 1m; Genesis Apocryphon (MasapocrGen, final photo 302362)

In his preliminary report on the Masada excavations, Yadin described this item as follows:

> A few fragments were found of a scroll written in the advanced Herodian style. We have not been able thus far to identify the text. Judging by the combinations חן בעיניו and תלו את it seems to be a kind of apocryphon on Esther, but the other phrases do not allow to draw any clear conclusions on this matter.[1]

Illustration 11: Casemate 1045

1. Yadin, *IEJ* 15, 105.

The light-brown colour of the parchment, the form of the letters which are mostly legible, and their apparent similarity led Yadin to conclude that the fifteen fragments found in locus 1045, to the north of the 'synagogue', stem from one and the same scroll. Yadin pictured that locus as follows (ibid., 76):

> The whole of casemate 1045 was covered by a thick layer of ashes, especially in its southern third, where the ash layer reached a height of 2 m(!). Among the remains of the huge conflagration, traces of which could also be observed on the wall plaster, were found many pieces of burnt furniture, metal vessels and strips of embroidered cloth. There can be no doubt that furniture and utensils were collected from this vicinity (from locus 1042) and brought to this room to be deliberately incinerated.

The same holds true for another small piece measuring 3×3 cm, although it was given a different serial number (1045–1375). Three scraps which bear no traces of writing whatsoever (1350/2[c.d]; 1350/3[b]) are evidently parts of the top, the bottom, or possibly of an inter-column margin. On four other snippets of parchment only parts of letters or

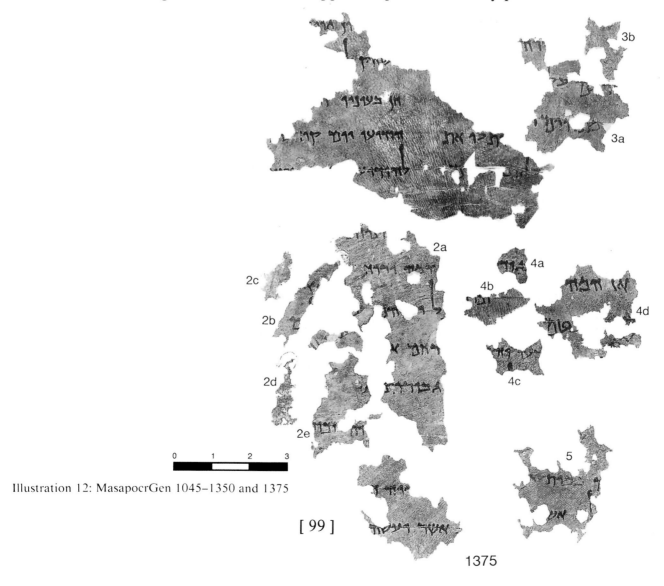

Illustration 12: MasapocrGen 1045–1350 and 1375

[99]

1375

blobs of ink can be discerned (1350/2[b]; 1350/4[b,c]). On the remaining eight fragments the preserved letters form complete words or partial words which, in some instances, can be completed. Truncated as they are, these bits of text nevertheless allow tentative suggestions concerning the content and character of the work from which they stem.

The fragments are kept under glass covers arranged in six subgroups, presumably at the instruction of Yadin who was possibly guided by the similarity of edge contours.

Transcription

Frg. 1350/1 measures 7.7×5.7 cm. It contains the last words of two lines of one column, and the beginning of five lines of the adjacent column.

Col. II	Col. I	
]ון גדול		1
]שחק לֹ		2
]חן בעיניו הֹ		3
]הודיעו יום קודשֹו	ותלו את	4
]להודיע - - - -	]להֹם ֹם ם	5

Frg. 1350/2[a] measures 2.9×6.5 cm. Below the middle sections of five lines, the bottom margin is partly preserved to a width of 1.1 cm, proving that this piece comes from the lower end of a column.

]וֹ נֹ רהֹ	1
]המה ורוֹח	2
]ל יןֹ]הנ[ ]עֹ[	3
]רחם א[	4
]גבורות[	5

Frg. 1350/2[b] is a small strip of parchment measuring 0.7×2.5 cm on which only a final *mem* is preserved, and before it the very top of a *lamed*.

On frg. 1350/2[c] (2.2×3 cm) the letter group הֹ[ ]הֹכוֹר[can be made out, with tiny remains of two letters in the line above it.

The irregularly shaped frg. 1350/3[a] measures 3×3.4 cm. It contains a few letters of three lines:

]ו /י רה[	1
]צ[ ]ים על[	2
]מֹ־ים ־[	3

On frg. 1350/4[d] (3×2.7 cm) some letters of two lines are preserved:

]אֹ המה[	1
]טמ[ ]ֹ[	2

The tiny frg. 1350/4[a] contains the letter combination גוד. On frg. 1350/4[b] יכו can be read, and on 1350/4[c] בֹּעֵד יהו[, under which the very top of a *lamed* of the next line can be seen, all written in smaller letters.

Frg. 1350/5 measures 2.5×3.1 cm with remnants of two lines of writing:

1]ֹם בֹּמות אֹ[

2]לֹ[ ]אשׁ[ ]יֹ[

Frg. 1375 (3×3 cm) also holds parts of two written lines with one complete phrase:

1]הֹוה הֹ[

2]אשר יעֹשֹה[

Script

The text was penned by a trained scribe in a late Hasmonean or early Herodian book hand, similar to that of 1QIsa[b], and can be dated to between 50 and 25 BCE.[2] The similarity is especially noticeable in the letter *ṭet*, executed with a pronounced loop at its top right-hand corner, e.g. in]טמֹ[(1350/4[d]); *taw*, whose left hand down-stroke ends in a perfect right angle, as in]וֹתלו את (1350/1, I, l. 4); final *mem*, as in יום (ibid. II, l. 4) and in]רחם (1350/2[a] l. 4). Most letters measure 3×3 mm, with the exception of the very thin letters *waw*, *yod* and final *nun*, and the slightly larger final *mem*. The letters hang from dry rulings, above which only the tops of *lamed* protrude, in keeping with the prevalent scribal custom. Recurring letters are identically executed. An exception is the rather large *ṭet* (1350/4[d]), and the somewhat irregular lettering on frg. 1350/3, e.g. in the execution of *ʿayyin*. On this fragment no dry rulings can be discerned. The letters are visibly spaced by less than 1 mm. Words are separated by a space of ca. 2 mm. The width of the inter-line space amounts to 0.9–1 cm.

Columns are bound by vertical dry rulings. Traces of both vertical and horizontal rulings are clearly discernible on frg. 1350/1 in the inter-column margin which measures 1–1.2 cm. The width of the partly preserved bottom margin of frgs. 1350/1 and 1350/2[a] comes to ca. 1.2 cm. It may be assumed that it was originally ca. 1.5 cm wide, and that the top margin, no longer extant, was of the same width.

Text

1, l. 4: The plene spelling קודשׁו in יום קודשׁו, which occurs also in the term ברוֹית קודשׁ of the fragment 1063–1747 (see below), brings to mind the prevalent plene spelling in Qumran documents, and induces the suggestion that the Masada fragments under review are remains of a composition which originated with the 'Community of the Renewed Covenant.'

Yadin's qualified assumption that frgs. 1045–1350, 1375 stem from "a kind of apocryphon" is well taken. However, his tentative surmise that the collocations חן בעיניו (1350/1, col. II, l. 3) and ויתלו/ותלו את (col. I, l. 4) link that apocryphon with the Book of

2. Cross, *Scripts*, 138, l. 4.

Esther, the former presumably referring to Queen Esther (Esth 5:8; 7:3; 8:5), the latter to Haman (ibid. 7:10; 8:7), is open to question.[3] I propose that in frg. 1350/3ᵃ, l. 2 the extant letters וֹצֹ[יֹם are possibly the final letters of מצרים, 'Egypt', which would underpin the suggestion that we are concerned with an apocryphal work based on the Joseph novel. While the phrases חן בעיניו, '(found) favour in his eyes', and וֹיתלו את or ותלו את, 'they hanged (him)', do indeed evoke a reminiscence of the Book of Esther, the use there of these collocations is easily explained by the well documented fact that the Esther story is saturated with expressions, motifs and descriptions of actions and circumstances which parallel particulars of the Joseph tale. As ancient and modern commentators have realized, the author of Esther manifestly borrowed suitable expressions and narrative details from the pentateuchal Joseph tradition and imported them into his own work.[4]

This evident dependence induces the conclusion that the Masada fragments are indeed remains of an apocryphal paraphrase woven on the Joseph novel, or possibly on the entire Book of Genesis, in the vein of the Book of Jubilees or Pseudo-Jubilees. Unfortunately, only a few letters of the passages pertinent to our investigation are preserved in the Qumran fragments of Jubilees and Pseudo-Jubilees, insufficient for bearing on the issue under review.[5] The collocation מצֹא] חן בעיניו echoes the biblical phrases וימצא יוסף חן בעיניו, "Joseph found favour in his (master's) eyes" (Gen 39:4), and ויתן חנו בעיני שר בית הסהר, "he (God) gave him favour in the eyes of the prison governor" (Gen 39:21). VanderKam and Milik restore the phrase נתן חן in the partly preserved report in a Qumran fragment of Joseph's introduction to Pharaoh: ויֹתן אלוהֹים ליוסף חן וחסדֹ] לפני פרעוֹה (4Q223-224 2 V, 27). A midrash based on the term וִיחֻנֶּךָ (Num 6:25), defines also the attitude of the Babylonian courtiers to Daniel by נתן/מצא חן, and applies the idiom to a trio of Israelite exiles who rose to prominence at the courts of foreign kings — Joseph, Daniel and Nehemiah. In quoting Dan 1:9, ויתן האלהים את דניאל לחסד ולרחמים לפני שר הסריסים, "God made Daniel find kindness and goodwill with the chief eunuch," the midrashist adds the term לחן, which is lacking in MT: ויתן אלהים את דניאל לחן ולחסד ולרחמים.[6] It is of interest that the author of Jubilees infuses that very same phraseology into his version of the Joseph tale, possibly under the influence of the Book of Daniel. Going beyond the biblical text, he uses the locution ויתן אלהים ליוסף חן וחסד לפני

---

3. The proposition becomes even more tenuous in view of the fact that, as stated, the fragments appear to be remains of a work which originated with the Covenanters' community, since Esther is the only biblical book that is absent from the Qumran discoveries of biblical manuscripts. However, the often propagated claim that not one quotation from Esther can be identified in a typical Covenanters' composition stands in need of revision. See S. Talmon, Was the Book of Esther Known at Qumran?, *DSD* 2,3 (1995) 249–67.

4. See S. Talmon, Wisdom in the Book of Esther, *VT* 13 (1963) 419–55 = idem, *Literary Studies in the Hebrew Bible. Form and Content* (Jerusalem: Magnes, 1993) 255–90, and earlier publications mentioned there.

5. See J. VanderKam and J.T. Milik, *DJD* XIII, 95–140, especially 4Q223–224 and 4QpapJubilees^h, unit 2 col. V; Vanderkam, *Jubilees*.

6. *Sipre*, ed. M. Ish-Shalom (Vienna: n. p., 1924; repr. New York: OM, 1948) I, 12, par. 41.

פרעה, to define the Pharaoh's appreciation of Joseph: "God made Joseph find favor and goodwill in the Pharaoh's eyes" (Jub 40:5).

Further, the collocation ו(ו)תלו את or ותלו את (1350/1 col. I, l. 4), which precedes חן בעיניו on the same fragment (col. II, l. 3), brings to mind the expressions ותלה אותך על עץ, "he (Pharaoh) will hang you on the gallows" (Gen 40:19), and ואת שר האופים תלה, "he hanged the chief baker" (Gen 40:22).

Also noteworthy is the use of the *hif'il* of ידע in the phrases הודיעו יום קודשו, 'he announced to him his holy day' (1350/1, col. II, l. 4), and להודיע, 'to inform (him)' or 'to reveal (to him)' (l. 5), in close proximity to the above mentioned idioms. Whereas the *hif'il* of ידע is never used in the Book of Esther in reference to either Esther or Haman,[7] it does occur at a critical juncture in the Joseph tale: ויאמר פרעה אל יוסף אחרי הודיע אלהים אותך, "Pharaoh said to Joseph, since God has all this made known to you ... you shall be in charge of my household" (Gen 41:39–40).[8] It is of significance that the double employment of הודיע in our fragment has a parallel in the Jubilees version of the Joseph tale where its Ethiopic cognate *'aydeʿo* turns up twice in that context: *'esma 'aydeʿo za-yekawwen wa-'i-tazakkara kama yāydeʿ lafar-ʿon* (Jub 39:18).[9] According to Vander-Kam — Milik, "The presence of two forms of *'aydeʿa* arouses suspicion, especially as the Latin (translation) *cum indicasset illi quaecumque uenisset ei et non fuit memor ut interueniret rex farao* is very different where the second instance is located: both versions have purpose clauses but Ethiopic *yāydeʿ* does not match Latin's *interrueniret*."[10] It would now appear that Mas 1045–1350, possibly a fragment of Jubilees, Pseudo-Jubilees or a related Genesis apocryphon, lends credence to an Ethiopic reading which on the surface "arouses suspicion," but may actually reflect a Hebrew *Vorlage*.

In frg. 1350/1, col. II, l. 2 the letter sequence]שחק ל is clearly legible just above the phrase חן בעיניו in the next line. Again, while שחק never turns up in the Book of Esther, the verb is used twice at significant turning points in the Joseph tale in the alternative spelling צחק.[11]]שחק ל may well echo the sham complaint of the wife of Joseph's master

---

7. The root ידע appears eight times in the book, but always in other conjugations (1:13 twice; 2:11, 22; 4:1, 5, 11, 14).

8. In addition, twelve other derivates of ידע are found in the Joseph story (Gen 39:6; 41:21, 31; 42:23, 33, 34; 43:7, 22; 44: 15, 27; 45:1; 47:6).

9. M. Goldmann, The Book of Jubilees, in: A. Kahana, ed., ספרים חיצונים vol. I (Tel Aviv: Masadah, 1956) 297, correctly retroverted the Ethiopic expressions כי הודיעו and ולא זכר להודיע.

10. VanderKam and Milik, *DJD* XIII, 127, 133. I am indebted to Prof. VanderKam for helpful comments in this matter.

11. The interchange of ש/צ in צחק/שחק is amply attested in biblical Hebrew in a variety of vocables. Besides the prevalent spelling of the name of the patriarch Isaac — יצחק (108 occurrences), also the variant ישחק is documented (Jer 33:26; Am 7:9, 16; Ps 105:9), which appears to be the preferred spelling in Qumran writings, especially in works connected with the Book of Jubilees. It occurs in fragments of Pseudo-Jubilees[a] (4Q225 2 I, 9–11; II, 2–12), next to יסחק (I, 9), and in Pseudo-Jubilees[b] (4Q226 7, 5): אברהם ישחק ויעקב, as well as in a "Reworked Pentateuch", 4Q364 8 I: אברהם וישחק ויהיו ימי and ישחק מאת שנה (*DJD* XIII, 145–9, 165, 214).

Potiphar:[12] הביא לנו איש עברי לצחק בנו בא אלי לשכב עמי, "he (viz. my husband) brought us a Hebrew to play around with us; he came in to me to lie with me" (Gen 39:14); and בא־אלי העבד העברי אשר הבאת־לנו לצחק בי, "the Hebrew slave whom you have brought us came to me to play around with me" (Gen 39:17).

The conjectural reading of מצרים on frg. 1350/3ᵃ, l. 2, followed by על, alludes conceivably to the sentence ויאמר פרעה אל־יוסף ראה נתתי אתך על כל־ארץ מצרים, "Pharaoh said to Joseph 'I put you in charge over all the land of Egypt'" (Gen 41:41).

We come now to consider the phrase אשר יעשה on frg. 1375, l. 2, possibly preceded by the restored Tetragrammaton in l. 1: יֹהוֹ. This word cluster is reminiscent of the biblical locutions ויאמר יוסף אל־פרעה ... את אשר אלהים עשה הגיד לפרעה ... וממהר אלהים לעשתו, "Joseph said to Pharaoh ... God has told Pharaoh what he is going to do ... and will very soon put it in effect" (Gen 41:25, 32), with the substitution of the Tetragrammaton for אלהים.

The implied references to events in the Joseph story, which are reflected in the above word combinations, induce the proposition that frg. 1350/3ᵃ should be placed after frg. 1350/1, viz. to the left of it, with frg. 1375 located between them. Thus the following sequence of events is achieved: the accusation of Potiphar's wife, לוֹשחק לֹנו (1350/1, II, l. 2), followed by the mention of Joseph's finding favour with the Pharaoh, מצאן חן בעיניו (ibid. l. 3), leads to his revealing God's intentions to the Pharaoh, להודיע, הודיעו (ibid. ll. 4–5), which God will soon put in effect אשר יעשה (frg. 1375, ll. 1–2), and results in the Pharaoh's putting Joseph in charge of Egypt, על מצרים (1350/3ᵃ, ll. 2–3).

There remains, however, a problem which must be clearly stated: the presumed reference to the hanging of the Pharaoh's chief baker (frg. 1350/1 col. I, l. 4) in the proposed rearrangement of the fragments precedes the allusion to the false accusation of Potiphar's wife (ibid. col. II, l. 2). This reversed sequence of events reported in the biblical Joseph tradition, could only be explained by the assumption that the Masada apocryphon reflects an extra-biblical version of the Joseph tale in which the crucial circumstances unfolded in a different order.

Notwithstanding this difficulty, we may still conclude that the examination of various facets of the fragmentary Masada text viewed synoptically, lends credibility to the proposition that frgs. 1045–1350 and 1375 are remains of an apocryphal composition based upon the Joseph story or on the entire Book of Genesis, of the same or similar literary genre as Jubilees or the Qumran Genesis Apocryphon[13], and the Masada Joshua Apocryphon (see below). This work was presumably carried to Masada by a member of the Covenanters' community, who fled to the wilderness fortress when the Romans overran their settlement at Qumran.

---

12. The added phrase לשכב עמי (37:14) explicates the sexual signification which attaches to לצחק בנו, and by implication also to לצחק בי (37:17). Cf. וירא... והנה יצחק מצחק את רבקה אשתו (26:8), and possibly also ותרא שרה את בן הגר המצרית ... מצחק (21:9).

13. N. Avigad and Y. Yadin, *A Genesis Apocryphon. A Scroll From the Wilderness of Judaea* (Jerusalem: Magnes/Shrine of the Book, 1956).

(b) Mas 1039–211; Mas1l; Joshua Apocryphon (MasapocrJosh, final photo 5254).

I

Yadin described the item as follows:

> The fragment measures 9.5×6 cm. It consists of the lower left part of a column with eight fragmentary lines. The script is 'Round' semiformal, of the early Herodian type. The text praises the man who fought 'for his people against their enemies' and succeeded 'because God was with them'. Possibly we have here an apocryphon on Samuel, because the text continues '(and all that) he spoke about them came upon them and nothing fell to the ground' (cf. 1 Sam. 3:19). This scroll needs further investigation. The spelling מאודה for מאוד is interesting; it resembles that in the 'War of the Sons of Light' ציון שמחי מאודה (19:5).[1]

The fragment was discovered on November 22, 1963 in the southern part of the third casemate to the south of the 'synagogue,' where several more inscribed pieces of parchment were found. A detailed examination of this item invites precisions regarding the interpretation of its contents, and reveals possible links with the Qumran discoveries.

Mas 1039–211 is of a light brown colour turning dark at the lower left side. It consists of one main fragment (a) which measures 9.5×5.8 cm with a large hole in its lower part, and a 3.3×2.5 scrap of parchment (b) with a small hole in it. The holes in the parchment and the ragged edges point to deterioration of the material due to natural causes rather than to deliberate tearing by Roman soldiers after their conquest of the fortress, as seems to be the case with some other scrolls, such as MasLev[a] (1039–270).[2]

On a photograph found among Yadin's papers, (b) is placed to the left of (a) so that the writing preserved on it seemingly continues the text in the upper lines of (a).[3] Technical and textual data suggest a different arrangement of the two pieces: Above the first line of (b) a blank of 8 mm is preserved, which is about twice as wide as the inter-line spaces on both (a) and (b). This blank is most probably part of the top margin, which originally may have equalled the bottom margin of (a), now partly extant to the width of 1.2 cm. Intact it may have measured approximately 1.5 cm. Since no trace of a top margin is preserved on (a), it is reasonable to assume that (b) should be placed above (a) rather than to the left of it, with the lower tip of its right-hand edge linking up with the

1. Yadin, *IEJ* 15, 79–83.
2. Yadin, *IEJ* 15, 83, 104.
3. It cannot be decided whether this arrangement is accidental, or whether it reflects Yadin's tentative proposal of reading and partly reconstructing the text.

top of right-hand edge of (a). This assumption is confirmed by the contours of the two pieces.

Script

The restored composite fragment holds parts of ten inscribed lines. Most letters measure 3 mm in width and height, with the exception of the very thin letters *waw* and *yod*, and the slightly larger final *mem*. The scribe took pains to space letters by less than 1 mm, and words by 2–3 mm. Although no dry rulings can be discerned, the lines had originally been kept straight. The present curvature seems to have resulted from the said deterioration of the material. The inter-line spaces are 6–7 mm wide. The ink is very well preserved, so that, with the exception of a few letters, the extant text is legible without difficulty. The script can be defined as 'Early Herodian', and may be dated to the end of the last century BCE, or the beginning of the first century CE.[4]

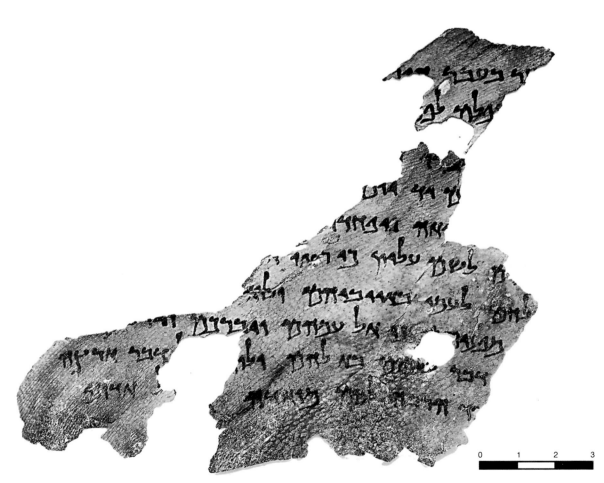

Illustration 13: MasapocrJosh 1039–211

4. Cross, Scripts, 138, ll. 3 and 4.

Transcription

(b) Upper margin

‏]שׁר בעבר הׄיׄרׄדׄ[‏	1
‏]וֹפלם לפנׄ[‏	2
‏]פׄנׄיו ׄ[‏	1 (a)
‏]ם יד יונׄי[‏	2
‏]וׄאה ויפחדוׄ[‏	3
‏]־ם לשם עליון כי ראׄוׄ אׄ[‏	4
‏]־לחם לעמו באויביהם ולוֹאׄ[‏	5
‏]מפניהׄםׄ כי אל עמהם ויברכם ויוׄ־־עׄ־[‏	6
‏]דבר עׄלׄיׄהׄם בא להם ולוׄ־[‏ ‏]־ׄל דבר ארצה‏	7
‏]ם הרבה להם מואדה‏ ‏־ׄל אדוני‏	8

Bottom margin

Notes on Readings

(b) l. 1: The remnant of a letter at the beginning of the line before the fully preserved *reš* is the head of the left stroke of a ‏שׁ‎. The tiny blob of ink after the last partly extant letters ‏הׄיׄרׄ‎ is the remnant of the upper right-hand corner of a *daleth*.

l. 2: It seems most likely to restore *waw* or *yod* at the beginning of the line, although it is also possible to read *nun*. The traces of a letter at the end of the line after ‏לפ‎ are evidently remains of the head and the foot of *nun*.

(a) l. 1: At the beginning of the line, the basestrokes of *peh* and *nun* seem to coalesce. At the end, there remains a tiny remnant of the first letter of a new word.

l. 2: A comparison with ‏וי‎ at the beginning of ‏ויפחדו‎ in l. 3 suggests that the last word in l. 2 opens with the letters ‏יוֹ‎, seemingly followed by ‏ני‎ written as a ligature. The reading of these letter traces as a final *mem* is ruled out by the fact that the resulting word combination ‏יד יום‎ does not make any sense.[5]

l. 3: The remnant of a letter at the beginning of the line could be a part of *waw, yod, peh* et sim.

l. 4: A tiny trace of a letter can be discerned before the basestroke of the final *mem* at the beginning of the line.

l. 5: The first *lamed* in the line is preceded by a trace of a letter top.

l. 6: The line ends with an *ʿayin*, possibly followed by a minute remnant of the base of another letter.

5. I doubt that these traces are the remains of a ‏ס‎, as was suggested to me by E. Tov, who tentatively proposed to read ‏ם[יד יוסֹף‎. In the Herodian hand the base of that letter is much narrower, and its upright stroke tends toward the left whereas in the present case it is perpendicular. But see below, p. 111.

l. 7: The trace of a letter after ולו appears to be the lower right hand end of the slanted stroke of an *aleph*, most of which is lost in a lacuna, in which there would be room for one inter-word space and two letters before the partly preserved *lamed*.

l. 8: The blank after מואדה, which is larger than the usual inter-word space, is probably a *vacat* which marks the ending of a paragraph. At the left side of the blank a *lamed* can be seen which closes a word, preceded by a minute remnant of the base of another letter.

Measurements

In the positioning of the two pieces of parchment proposed here, the dimensions of the resulting composite fragment are slightly larger than those given by Yadin. If the lines of (b) directly preceded the uppermost line of (a), the written column with the partly preserved top margin would have attained a height of 9.2 cm. Adding about 3 mm of the missing part of the top, and 1.5 cm of the entirely missing bottom margin, the scroll of which the fragment survived stood about 11 cm high.

The width of the page can be determined by the following calculations. The practically certain restoration of (a) ll. 6 and 7 indicates that the average written line was 9 cm long. The 23 preserved letters in l. 6, out of a restored total of 31, with six inter-word spaces[6] take up about 75 per cent of the length of the line. In l. 7, 23 extant letters out of a total of 31, and seven out of eight inter-word spaces, occupy about 87.5 per cent of the length of the line. In l. 6, the preserved letters cover 6.9 cm; and in l. 7, 7–7.6 cm. It follows that when fully written out, l. 6 was 9.2 cm long, and l. 7 about 8.7 cm. This calculation is substantiated by the bottom line of (a) in which, as mentioned, a *vacat* in its middle presumably indicates the end of a paragraph. The few letters to the left of the *vacat* take up 1 cm, and those to its right 4.3 cm. The text in this line, including the *vacat*, would have covered 9 cm. It follows, that with a right-hand margin of 6 mm added, the width of the column came originally to ca. 9.5 cm.

Spelling

The plene writing ולוא dovetails with characteristic scribal practices which prevailed in the Covenanters' community,[7] and even more so the peculiar spelling מואדה,[8] as Yadin correctly pointed out.

The partly preserved lines on our fragment give us a handle for determining the character of the work from which it stems. Yadin, as stated, ascribed it to an apocryphon on the book of Samuel, resting his assumption primarily on the similarity of the restored

6. There are no additional inter-word spaces in the restored text.
7. See Tov, Orthography, 31–57, and relevant publications adduced there.
8. Cf. 1QM XIX, 5: ציון שמחי מאודה, and 11QTemp LXII, 12: הרחוקות ממכה מאודה. Further 11QTemp LVI, 19: לוא ירבה לו מואדה, 4Q504 25, 3.

1 Sam) ויגדל שמואל ויהוה היה עמו ולא הפיל מכל דבריו ארצה with (a, l. 7) ולוא ‹נפ›ל דבר ארצה phrase 3:19). However, several textual details put this identification in question. The author does not praise 'a man who saved Israel from its enemies,' as Yadin surmised. Rather, he glorifies the God of Israel: '[Adonai] fought for his people against their enemies ... God was with them (Israel) and blessed them and saved them, and whatever he had promised them[9] came upon them, not one word was in vain,'[10] נ]לחם לעמו באויביהם כי אל עמהם אדוני ... The latter part of this sentence is evidently ויברכם ...[ואשר] דבר עליהם בא להם ולו‹א נפל] דבר ארצה a paraphrase of Josh 21:45: לא־נפל דבר מכל הדבר הטוב אשר־דבר יהוה אל בית־ישראל הכל בא, 'Not a word went unfulfilled of all the good things God had promised the house of Israel, all came true', and 23:14: כי לא נפל דבר אחד מכל הדברים הטובים אשר דבר יהוה אלהיכם עליכם הכל באו לכם לא נפל ממונו דבר אחד, 'Not one word went unfulfilled of all the good things that YHWH your God had promised you, all came true for you, none went unfulfilled'. The text of the fragment is appreciably closer to these passages than to the Samuel passage on which Yadin based his argument, and leads to the conclusion that it stems from a Joshua apocryphon. It appears that the writer inserted in his paraphrastic quotation of the Joshua text the word ארצה, '(fell) to the ground,' which he presumably took from 1 Sam 3:19. Authors of such apocryphal works did not necessarily quote a biblical text verbatim, but were wont to cite it paraphrastically or allude to it, slightly changing the wording, as the occasion required. Illustrations of this phenomenon abound in the ancient Versions of the Hebrew Bible and in Old Testament Apocrypha, in the Covenanters' literature,[11] especially in Pesharim, Florilegia[12] and similar compositions,[13] as well as in rabbinic literature. In some such instances a quotation may reflect a variant in the writer's *Vorlage*, which is occasionally still preserved in an ancient version

---

9. Or: had pronounced concerning them.
10. Literally: fell to the ground.
11. The subject has been discussed in many publications. See int. al.: M.H. Goshen-Gottstein, Bible Quotations in the Sectarian Dead Sea Scrolls, *VT* 3 (1953) 79–82; J. Carmignac, Les citations de l'Ancien Testament, et spécialement des poèmes du Serviteur, dans les Hymnes de Qumrân, *RQ* 2 (1959–60) 357–94; idem, Les citations de l'Ancien Testament dans la 'Guerre des Fils de Lumière contre les Fils de Ténèbres', *RB* 63 (1956) 234–60; J.A. Fitzmyer, The Use of Explicit Old Testament Quotations in Qumran Literature and in the New Testament, *NTS* 7 (1960–61) 297–333; J.M. Baumgarten, A 'Scriptural' Citation in 4Q Fragments of the Damascus Document, *JJS* 43,1 (1992) 95–8; D. Dimant, The Hebrew Bible in the Dead Sea Scrolls: Torah Quotations in the Damascus Document, *Shaʿarei Talmon, Studies in the Bible, Qumran and the Ancient Near East Presented to Shemaryahu Talmon*, ed. E. Tov and M. Fishbane with the assistance of W.W. Fields (Winona Lake: Eisenbrauns, 1992) 113*–22* (Hebrew); E.L. Greenstein, Misquotations of Scripture in the Dead Sea Scrolls, *The Frank Talmage Memorial Volume*, ed. B. Walfish (Haifa: University Press, 1993) 71–83; G. Brin, Explicit Quotations from the Torah and the Writings, *Issues in the Bible and the Dead Sea Scrolls* (Tel Aviv: Hakibbutz Hameuchad, 1994) 137–45 (Hebrew); M.J. Bernstein, Introductory Formulas for Citation and Re-citation of Biblical Verses in the Qumran Pesharim, *DSD* I (1994) 30–70, etc.
12. Characteristic examples may be found in Florilegium (4Q174), *DJD* V, 53–7; Testimonia (4Q175), ibid. 57–60.
13. See Newsom's remarks in Newsom, 4QApocryphon (4Q378 II), which I shall address shortly.

of the Bible, the Samaritan Hebrew Pentateuch or a midrashic extrapolation.[14] In the instance under review, the author quoted a phrase from the Book of Joshua rather accurately, and enriched his quotation with the added word ארצה which, as said, he borrowed from the similar text in 1 Sam 3:19.[15]

The dependence of the Masada apocryphon on the Book of Joshua is substantiated by additional considerations which highlight their close relation, and at the same time undermine the presumed connection of the apocryphon with the Book of Samuel. The Book of Joshua deals with the conquest of Canaan. Therefore, it is not surprising that it contains twenty mentions of the topographical term עבר הירדן (Josh 1:14–15; 2:10; 5:1; 7:7; 9:1, 10; 12:1, 7; 13:8, 27, 32; 14:3; 17:5; 18:7; 20:8; 22:4, 7; 24:8), which appears prominently in the first line of our fragment [(b), l. 1]. In contrast, there is only one solitary mention of עבר הירדן in the Book of Samuel, in the report of Israel's defeat at the hand of the Philistines at Mt. Gilboa (1 Sam 31:7), viz. in reference to an event which is diametrically opposed to a victory of Israel over their enemies, of which the Masada fragment manifestly speaks.

We can be even more precise in determining the link between Joshua and the Masada apocryphon. The sequence of circumstances to which the apocryphon alludes follows the succession of events described in the last chapters of the biblical book. The distinct parallelism prompts the tentative restoration of several missing words in the composite fragment, and concomitantly supports the proposition made at the outset that the small piece (b) should be placed above, that is to say before the larger one (a):

Restored Text

א[ש]ר בעבר הירד[ן]	1 (b)
נ[ו]פלם לפנ[י]הם	2
ל[פ]ניו י[	1 (a)
]ם יד יונ[י]הם	2
]ראה ויפחדו[	3
מהללים ומודי[ם לשם עליון כי רא]ו א[שר אדוני עמהם	4
ואלוהים נ[לחם לעמו באויביהם ולוא [ערצו ולוא חתו	5
ולוא יראו] מפניה[ם כי אל עמהם ויברכם ויו[שי]ע[ם	6
וכול אשר] דבר ע[לי]הם בא להם ולוא] נפ[ל] דבר ארצה	7
ואת זרע[ם הרבה להם מואדה י־ל אדוני	8

---

14. Cases in point are the "double *pesher*" on Hab 1:11 and 2:15 in 1QpHab; the reading בוניך in 1QIsaᵃ (Isa 54:13) which may be the basis of the midrash: "Do not read בניך but בוניך." See S. Talmon, *Aspects of the Textual Transmission of the Bible in the Light of Qumran Manuscripts, Textus* 4 (1964) 95–132.

15. The crucial phrase לא־נפל דבר ... מכל הדבר ... אשר דבר echoes e.g. in Ahasuerus' words to Haman: אל תפיל דבר מכל אשר דברת (Esth 6:10), and in the blessing which concludes Solomon's prayer: ברוך יהוה אשר נתן מנוחה לעמו ישראל ככל אשר דבר לא־נפל דבר אחד מכל דברו הטוב אשר דבר ביד משה עבדו (1 Kgs 8:56).

Comments

(b), l. 2: I completed לפנויהם on the basis of Josh 21:44 and 23:9. However, it is equally possible to read לפנויו, לפנוי [cf. (a), l.1] or לפנויכם.

(a), l. 1: Reading ל[פניו seems to be certain. After this word a remnant of the first letter of the next word can still be seen.

l. 2: I propose to restore יד יונים. For the term יונים = oppressors, cf. Isa 49:26 and Ps 74:8. Further Jer 25:38; 46:16; 50:16, and possibly Zeph 3:1.

ll. 3–5: (ואלוהיהם נ[לחם) ויפחדו ... כי ראו א[שר .... ואלוהים נ[לחם לעמו (read possibly: ואלוהיהם נ[לחם). Cf. Josh 10:14: ויהי פחד אלהים על כל ממלכות הארצות בשמעם כי; further 2 Chr 20:29: כי יהוה נלחם לישראל; נלחם יהוה עם אויבי ישראל. See also Exod 14:13–14 and Deut 3:22.

l. 3: ויפחדו. A suitable restoration would be ויפחדו]אויבי ישראל or אויביהם. Cf. Josh 21:44: ויהי כשמע אדני־צדק ... וייראו מאד 16; 10:1–2: ולא עמד איש בפניהם מכל־איביהם את כל־איביהם נתן יהוה בידם (cf. also Josh 2:9; Deut 2:25; Esth 9:2).

ll. 4–5: Another possible restoration of the text would be: כי ראו א[שר אדוני אלהי אבותיהם נ[לחם לעמו.

l. 4: I propose to read מודי[ם in accord with the subject matter (cf. Ps 140:14: אך צדיקים יודו לשמך), but we could also read מהללי[ם or מזמרי[ם. In any case, considerations of space require the restoration of two words, as suggested. The expression מהללים ומודים is paralleled in an explicit reference to Joshua in a fragment from Qumran Cave 4: בעת אשר כלה ישוע להלל ולהודות בתהלותיהו ויאמר... (4Q175, 21).17

Eighteen of thirty-four mentions of עליון as a divine epithet are found in the Book of Psalms. The verb זמר is repeatedly coupled in Psalms with שם and/or עליון: ואזמרה שם־יהוה עליון (18:50 = 2 Sam 22:50); ולשמך אזמרה (92:2); ולזמר לשמך עליון (9:3); אזמרה שמך עליון (Ps 7:18); זמרו לשמו (Ps 135:3).

At the end of the line, I propose to restore א[שר אדוני. The same divine epithet turns up in (a), l. 8.

ll. 5–6: The speculative restoration ולוא]ערצו ולוא חתו ולוא יראו is in keeping with Josh 1:9; 8:1; 10:8, 25, and seems to be required by considerations of space. Cf. Deut 1:29; 7:21; 20:3; 31:6; and also 2:25: ורגזו וחלו מפניך.

l. 6: כי אל עמהם. The use of the divine epithet אל, and presumably also of אדוני, spelled plene [(a), l. 4, cf. l. 8], instead of the Tetragrammaton, is possibly another characteristic which the Masada fragment shares with the Covenanters' literature. The reading of ויו[שי]עם at the end of the line is suggested by letter remains and by subject matter.

ll. 7–8: Similar ideas find expression in The 'Psalms of Joshua' (4Q378 III, 2–3): 18כי יהוה]אלהיכ[מה מ[־]... ה[עמיד דבריו אשר דבר הנשבע לאברהם לתת [לו ארץ] טובה ורחבה

l. 7: Cf. Josh 21:45: הדבר הטוב אשר־דבר יהוה אל־בית ישראל הכל בא; further Deut 9:1–5.

16. Read probably וירא מאד.
17. Testimonia, *DJD* V, 58.
18. Newsom, 4QApocryphon, 251.

[111]

l. 8: I restored this reading on the basis of Josh 24:3: וָאַרְבֶּ את זרעו.[19]

The *lamed* before אדוני at the end of the line is preceded by a tiny remnant of another letter which cannot be identified.

Translation

(b), l. 1	]which (is, or who are) on the other side of the Jordan[
l. 2	](when they) were falling before them[
(a), l. 1	]before him[
l. 2	]hand of their oppres[sors
l. 3	]they were afraid[
l. 4	were praising and giving thanks] to the name of the Most High because they saw that [the Lord was with them
l. 5	and God] fought for his people against their enemies and they were not fearful or dismayed
l. 6	nor were they afraid] of them because God (was) with them and blessed them and saved them
l. 7	everything he had] promised them came to them[20] and not one word fell to the ground[21]
l. 8	and their offspring he multiplied for them exceedingly *vacat* the Lord

The dependence of the Masada fragment on the latter part of the Book of Joshua is emphasized by the juxtaposition of significant phrases in both texts:

Comparative Table of Texts

Joshua 23–24		Masada 1039–211	
22:4	אשר נתן להם ... בעבר הירדן	b, 1	אשר בעבר הירדן
21:44	(23:9 =) לא עמד איש בפניכ/הם	b, 2	נ[ו]פלם לפנ[י]הם
23:3	ואתם ראיתם את כל אשר עשה	a, 4	כי ראו א[שר אדני
	יהוה אלהיכם לכל הגוים האלה מפניכם		
	כי יהוה אלהיכם הוא הנלחם לכם	a, 5	נ[לחם לעמו באויביהם
23:9:	ויורש יהוה מפניכם גוים גדולים	a, 5–6	ולא [ערצו ולא יראו] מפניהם
	ועצומים ... לא עמד איש בפניכם עד		כי אל עמהם ויברכם
	היום הזה		ויו[שי]ע[ם
23:14	כי לא נפל דבר אחד מכל הדברים		
	הטובים אשר דבר יהוה אלהיכם עליכם	a, 7	וכל אשר] דבר עליהם
	הכל באו לכם לא נפל ממנו דבר אחד		בא להם ולוא [נפ]ל דבר ארצה
24:3	ואקח את אביכם את אברהם ...		
	וארב את זרעו	a, 8	וזרע[ם הרבה להם מואדה

19. *Qere*: וארבה. This is the only mention in the Book of Joshua of a word derived from √רבה.
20. Viz. came true.
21. Viz. went unfulfilled.

Notes

If the proposed reading ם[יד יוֹסֹף in (a), l. 2 can be upheld (see above, n. 5), the final *mem* could possibly be the last letter of the verb ותרﬦ. The phrase ותרם יד יוסף, "the hand of Joseph was raised high,"[22] meaning 'Joseph had the upper hand (over his enemies)',[23] could possibly echo the clause ותכבד יד בית יוסף, "the House of Joseph brought increasing pressure (on the Amorites)" (Jdgs 1:35), which points to the one 'success' episode[24] in a roster of tribal 'non-conquest' notations (1:27–35ᵃ). The prominence accorded to the tribe of Joseph in that roster, like in the more comprehensive 'preface' to the exploits of the 'Saviors' related in the Book of Judges (Jdgs 1:1–2:10), which culminates in an iterated report of Joshua's death and Israel's ensuing failings (Jdgs 2:6–10, cf. Josh 24:29–31),[25] dovetails perfectly with the position of excellence maintained by Joshua the Ephraimite in the Book of Joshua, and by implication also in the Masada Apocryphon. These facts may have facilitated the inclusion of particulars drawn from the Book of Judges in the Joshua Apocryphon.

In conclusion, the evidence presented above buttresses the thesis that the Masada fragment 1039–211 is indeed a remainder of an apocryphon woven on the Book of Joshua and that it reflects, more precisely, vestiges of the report of the last episodes in Joshua's life: the summary of the conquest (Josh 21:43–45),[26] and Joshua's final address to the people (Josh 23) at the meeting in Shechem (Josh 24), in which he surveys major events in the history of Israel.

II

Since we are dealing with an apocryphon woven on the Book of Joshua, and since there are signs which point to a possible connection of that composition with the Covenanters' literature, it is appropriate to call attention to some resemblance of the Masada item with fragments of the apocryphal composition from Qumran cave 4, entitled by its editor Carol Newsom '4QApocryphon of Joshua' (4Q378; 4Q379). Newsom proposes that the author conceived his work as 'the last words of Joshua' and

---

22. Joshua is a prominent representative of the 'House of Joseph'.
23. Cf. Mic 5:8(9): תְּרֹם יָדְךָ עַל צָרֶיךָ, "Your hand shall be raised high over your foes."
24. Cf. Jdgs 1:22–26.
25. In this way, the episodes reported in the 'preface' of the Book of Judges are actually retrojected into the days of Joshua, and the record of the 'conquest period' in Jdgs 1 becomes a largely 'negative' foil of the 'positive' account in the Book of Joshua. See S. Talmon, In Those Days There Was No מלך In Israel — Judges 18–21, in Talmon, *KCC* 39–52; idem, Judges Chapter 1, in *Studies in the Book of Judges. Publications of the Israel Society for Biblical Research* (Jerusalem: Kiryat Sepher, 1966) 14–29 (Hebrew).
26. In the preserved text, there is no allusion to the erection of an altar in Trans-Jordan by the tribes of Reuben, Gad, and Manasseh (Josh 22).

that he patterned it after the Book of Deuteronomy.[27] The extant remains of text appear to stem from the beginning of the work. We find there a recognizable reference to the death of Moses (4Q378 14), and a verbatim quotation of the words of encouragement which Moses addressed to his servant and successor Joshua: חזק ואומץ אל תערץ] ואל תחת (4Q378 3 II = Josh 1:9). Newsom assumes that another phrase, תפלה על חטאתינו (4Q378 6 I), possibly hints at the Achan episode (Josh 7:10 ff.).[28] Mentions of the covenant which God established with Abraham, אשר כורת] יהוה עם אברהם (4Q378 22 I), and of his promise 'to make his words come true', לה]עמיד דבריו אשר דבר (4Q378 11), bring to mind phrases in the Masada apocryphon: וכול אשר] דבר עליהם בא להם ולוא [נפ]ל דבר ארצה [ואת זרע]ם הרבה להם מואדה (a), ll. 7–8.

Other fragments of the Qumran Apocryphon of Joshua refer to the crossing of the Jordan (4Q379 12, cf. Josh 3–4) and present a partial roster of the sons of Jacob, who are 'the twel[ve] tribes of Israel', שנים] עשר מטות [וישראל (4Q379 1). This passage pertains, possibly, to the erection at Gilgal of a memorial monument made of twelve stones taken from the Jordan River, as reported in Josh 4:20. At the end of the composition, the author speaks of a prayer, ברוך יהוה אלהי י]שראל, which he apparently attributes to Joshua (4Q379 22 II),[29] and which brings to mind the restored allusion in the Masada fragment (a), l. 4 to a prayer of thanks offered by the entire nation: מודי]ם לשם עליון.

The dissimilar scripts leave no doubt that the 'Joshua Apocryphon' from Masada, woven on the latter part of the biblical book, and the fragments of the '4QApocryphon of Joshua', which pertain to its earlier parts, are remains of different scrolls, notwithstanding the persuasive resemblance of contents and language. However, the linguistic and literary analogies buttress the proposition, proposed above, that the Masada fragment stems from a work of the Covenanters' school. If this was the case, the question arises why would the Community of the Renewed Covenant have preserved several extra-biblical compositions woven on the Book of Joshua,[30] whereas in the assemblage

---

27. See Newsom, 4QApocryphon.
28. Ibid. 247.
29. Newsom, 4QApocryphon, 278–81. Here follows an interesting variant reading of Joshua's 'Curse upon Jericho' which, however, does not touch on the matter at hand. That text was known from a fragment published by J.M. Allegro, Further Messianic References in Qumran Literature, *JBL* 75 (1956) 174–87. See now L. Mazor, The Origin and Evolution of the Curse Upon the Rebuilder of Jericho. A Contribution of Textual Criticism to Biblical Historiography, *Textus* 14 (1988) 1–25; H. Eshel, The Historical Background of the Pesher Interpreting Joshua's Curse on the Rebuilder of Jericho, *RQ* 15 (1992) 413–9; T.H. Lim, The 'Psalms of Joshua' (4Q379 fr. 22 col. 2): A Reconsideration of its Text, *JJS* 44 (1993) 309–12.
30. In addition to the items already mentioned, see E. Qimron, Concerning Joshua Cycles From Qumran, *Tarbiz* 63,4 (1994) 503–8 (Hebrew). Qimron argues convincingly that a piece which E. Puech connected with David and Solomon, La pierre de Sion et l'autel des holocaustes d'après un manuscrit hébreu de la grotte 4 (4Q522), *RB* 99 (1992) 676–96, actually relates to Joshua. See further 5Q9, *DJD* III, 179–80 which contains remnants of a list of place names in the land together with a mention of ישוע, the typical Second Temple version of the biblical name יהושע. E. Tov, The Rewritten Book of Joshua Found at Qumran and Masada (in press), "cautiously suggests" that four,

of scrolls and fragments from the Qumran caves no remains of similar apocryphal works woven on other biblical historiographies were found. Compositions of the apocryphal genre, as well as of the *pesher* type, are based on prophetic books and on Psalms. These components of the Hebrew Bible do not usually reflect identifiable, specific historical events. Therefore, they lend themselves more readily to an interpretation which plays on the existential experiences of the authors and their readers.

The exceptional subjection of the 'historiographical' Book of Joshua to such an exposition by *yaḥad* authors can possibly be explained by the Covenanters' predilection for traditions pertaining to the Israelites' conquest of Canaan and the period of the settlement, which are the warp and woof of the biblical book. The members of the 'Community of the Renewed Covenant' conceived of themselves as the first generation of returned exiles to the land after the destruction of the temple in 586 BCE, and of their community as the reconstituted biblical Israel with whom God had renewed his covenant with his people:[31]

> And now, hearken all ye that know righteousness and consider the works of God; for He has a controversy with all flesh, and He will execute judgment upon all that despise Him. For when they sinned in that they forsook Him, He hid His face from Israel, and from His sanctuary and gave them to the sword. But when He remembered the covenant of the forefathers, He caused a remnant to remain of Israel and gave them not up to be consumed. And in the epoch of wrath,[32] three hundred and ninety years after He had given them into the hand of Nebuchadnezzar, king of Babylon, He visited them; and He caused to grow forth from Israel and Aaron a root of cultivation to possess his land and to wax fat in the goodness of His soil (CD I, 1–8).

Therefore, they viewed those traditions as foreshadowing their fervent hope of regaining the land in their own days, reenacting the conquest of Joshua's time. The former generations had captured the land from the Canaanites in a series of military encounters. The Covenanters expected to win it from their Jewish adversaries, the 'Wicked Priest' and his party, in a future apocalyptic battle, described in the War Scroll (1QM). This interpretation underpins the thesis that both the 'Joshua Apocryphon'

five or six fragmentary manuscripts from Qumran and Masada which are based on the Book of Joshua, viz. 4Q378–79 (4QapocrJosh^a,b) 4Q522 (4QapocrJosh^c), 4Qpaleo ParaJosh (4Qpaleo apocr-Josh^d?), 5Q9 (5QapocrJosh?) and Mas 1039–211 (Mas apocrJosh?), are in fact remnants of different copies of one and the same 'Apocryphon of Joshua'.

31. Concerning this conceptual facet, see Talmon, Renewed Covenant, 15–22; and idem, Between the Bible and the Mishna, *WQW*, 21–52.

32. The Hebrew term ובקץ חרון should possibly be read ובקץ אחרון, meaning 'at the appointed (or preordained) period.'

from Masada and the Qumran 'Apocryphon of Joshua', are specific *yaḥad* works, rather than components of the general Jewish literary heritage of the time.

It stands to reason that the Joshua Apocryphon was neither composed nor copied on Masada. Rather, the scroll was brought there by a member of the *yaḥad*, like other items of presumed Qumran origin which were presumably carried to the fortress by refugees who fled the Qumran settlement when it was overrun by the Romans. Note especially the fragment of שירות עולת השבת (MasShirShabb, 1039–200), the several pieces of a Genesis Apocryphon (Mas1m, 1045–1350 & 1375), and a little fragment (Mas 1276–1786) on which שר המשטמה is mentioned, which may stem from a copy of the Book of Jubilees or Pseudo-Jubilees (see below).

3. Fragments of Extra-Biblical Works

(a) Mas 1276–1786; Mas1j; Jubilees or Pseudo-Jubilees (MasJub or MaspsJub, final photo 302358; earlier ones 302365; 302371)

Yadin did not mention this item in his initial report, but referred to it briefly in Yadin, Zealot, 174:

> One fragment was a part of the long-lost Hebrew original of the Book of Jubilees, which had been preserved only in Ethiopic, Greek and Latin manuscripts. Similar fragments were found at Qumran,

and again in Yadin, *EAE*, 814:

> BOOK OF JUBILEES. A tiny fragment found in a garbage heap in a tannery tower, beside the Western Palace, where it had been thrown by the Roman garrison stationed at the site after Masada's fall. It contains several lines in Hebrew of the ancient text of the book.

The fragment measures 5.8×5 cm and is of a light-brown colour. The lower left edge of the parchment is slightly flaked. It stems, most probably, from a scroll, since remnants of the lower parts of two columns are extant, separated by an inter-column margin of 2 cm. In the right-hand column (col. I) the last words of six lines are preserved and traces of three or four letters in the line above them; in the left-hand column (col. II) remain complete or partial words from the beginnings of five lines. A blank below the written lines, 7 mm wide, is evidently a portion of the truncated bottom margin.

Script
The early Herodian formal script bespeaks the hand of an expert scribe. There are no dry rulings discernible, but the letter heads are nevertheless perfectly aligned. Only the top strokes of the *lamed* protrude above the heads of the other letters (col. I, ll. 4, 7; col. II, l. 5), and the down strokes of final *kaf* (col. II, l. 7), final *nun* (l. 4) and *qof* (col. I, ll. 3, 4) descend below them, as was the custom. Most letters measure approximately 3×3 mm, with the exception of the thin letters *waw, yod* and final *nun*. The scribe took pains to separate letters by a space of less than 1 mm. But in some instances two letters will flow together ligature-like: נה (col. I, l. 6); כה (col. I, l. 7; col. II, l. 5); כר (II, l. 6).

Words are mostly kept apart by a space of ca. 2 mm. The lines are generally of equal length, and are separated by inter-line spaces of ca. 7–8 mm, measured from the heads of letters in one line to those in the next. The beginnings of the five lines of col. II are 'justified'. Also the line endings in col. I are almost vertically aligned. However, in l. 5 the text exceeds the length of the line. Here, the scribe had erred in assessing the amount of text which could be accommodated in the line. Evidently wishing to refrain from writing part of a word in one line and the rest in the next, he crowded the last letters. As a result, the words וֹשר המשטמה at the end of the line almost fuse, and the last three letters טמה spill over into the inter-column margin.

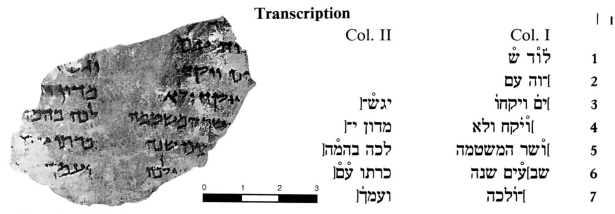

Transcription

Col. II	Col. I	
	לׄוד שׄ	1
	]דוה עם	2
יגשׄ]	]יׄם ויקחוֹ	3
מדון י]	]וׄיקח ולא	4
לכה בהמֹה]	]וׄשר המשטמה	5
כרתו עׄמֹ]	שב]עׄים שנה	6
ועמדׄ]	]וׄלכה	7

Illustration 14: MasJub or MaspsJub 1276–1786

Comments

Col. I, l. 1: The partly visible *lamed* is followed by either a *waw* or a *yod*, and a *daleth*, which appears to be the last letter of a word. The next word begins with a *šin* of which only the triangular confluence of the downward strokes remains.

ll. 3–4: Because of the graphic resemblance of *waw* and *yod*, which can be observed in other Masada finds, as well as in Qumran scrolls, one can read here either ויקחוֹ or יוקחוֹ, 'they took', or 'they shall be taken'.

l. 6: Apparent traces of the top and the foot stroke of ע suggest the tentative restoration of שב]עׄים, 'seventy'.

Col. II, l. 3: It is again debatable whether at the beginning of the line יגשׄ or וגשׄ should be read, followed by one more letter, viz. 'he shall approach', or 'and approach' (plural).

l. 4: Instead of מדון, 'strife', as suggested, one could read מדין.[1]

l. 6: After כרתו at the beginning of the line, traces of the heads of the letters עם are faintly visible, suggesting the conjectural restoration: כרתו עם [ברית], 'they established [a pact] with'.

---

1. Cp. 2 Sam 21:20 *ketib*: מָדְיָן, *qere*: מָדוֹן. Deichgräber, Fragmente, 416–7, weighed the restoration of מדין in a Qumran fragment of Jubilees 23:12–13 (3QJub5). Ultimately he preferred the reading מהו]מה, "turmoil." Rofé, Fragments, 323, restores there מ]כאוב. It should be noted that the nom. propr. מדין is not documented in published Qumran documents. The plural of the noun מדון occurs in the Hodayoth Scroll: ושקוי לבעל מדנים (1QH V, 35), and in a fragment of Mysteries (4QMyst[b] 2 II, 3): יעזוב קנאת מדנים. See L. Schiffman, Mysteries, *DJD* XX, 104.

The significant collocation שר המשטמה, 'prince of evil', (col. I, l. 5) is not extant in biblical Hebrew.[2] The naked noun משטמה appears twice in Hos 9:7–8. However, the textual remains in the Masada fragment do not give reason for linking it in any way with the Hosea passage.[3] By contrast, שר המשטמה is found in the Book of Jubilees,[4] which the 'Community of the Renewed Covenant' held in high esteem. In matters pertaining to festivals and the ritual calendar the 'Book of the Divisions of Times into their Jubilees and Weeks (of Years),' ספר מחלקות העתים ליובליהם ובשבועותיהם, ranked in authority with the 'Law of Moses', תורת משה (CD XVI, 2–4). In the Covenanters' vocabulary, a great religious-ideational import is attached to the noun משטמה (see e.g. 1QM XIII, 4; 1QS III, 23; 4QBer 10a II, 2; 6QHym 9 (*DJD* III, pl. XXVII); CD XVI, 5; cf. 1QM XIV, 9). The significant term שר המשטמה turns up twice in a Qumran fragment of Pseudo-Jubilees (4Q225 2 I, 9–10): ויבוא שר המ̇ש̇]ט̇מה [אל אל]והים וישטים את אברהם, 'and the prince of evil came before God and accused Abraham', and: ושר המשטמה (col. II, 13, 14),[5] next to the synonymous expressions שר המשטמות (4Q390 I, 11); מלאך המשטמה (CD XVI, 5) or מלאכי (ה)משטמה (1QM XIII, 11; 4Q225 2 II, 6; 4Q390 2 I). Therefore Yadin s suggestion that frg. 1276–1786 stems from a copy of Jubilees, or possibly Pseudo-Jubilees of Qumran vintage has exceeding merit. The further supposition that it was presumably brought to Masada by a *yaḥad* member, is supported by the elongated forms לכה (col. I, 7; II, 5) and בהמה (II, 5) which are characteristically qumranic.

2. The presence of this term favours reading מדון, 'quarrel, violence', in the preceding line rather than מדין. In biblical literature מדון is used in Jer 15:10; Hab 1:3 (coupled with ריב), and frequently in Prov (16:28, 17:14, 22:10, 26:20, 28:25). In Prov 15:18 it turns up together with איש חמה, and in 29:22 with the synonymous expression איש אף. In 3QJub5 the terms שמועה רעה, מכה, צרה, and אין שלום are employed in a similar context.
3. I am indebted to Jonathan Ben-Dov for the observation that the collocation 'they established [a covenant] with,' [ברית] כרתו עם̊, next to 'prince of evil,' שר המשטמה, and 'strife,' מדון, evokes a possible connection of our fragment with Isa 28:15: כרתנו ברית עם מות ועם שאול עשינו חוזה, 'We have made a treaty with Death and signed a pact with Sheol.'
4. Exclusively in passages pertaining to Abraham and the Exodus. See: Charles, *Little Genesis*, 80.
5. See: Jubilees, *DJD* XIII, 147–55. Since this fragment was not known to J. Licht, *The Rule Scroll* (Jerusalem: Bialik, 1965), 92, n. 23 (Hebrew), he maintained that the collocation שר המשטמה is altogether absent from the Qumran finds.

(b)   Mas 1039–200; Mas 1K; Songs of the Sabbath Sacrifice (MasShirShabb, photos 5280, 5280A)

The Masada Fragment of the Qumran Songs of the Sabbath Sacrifice

Carol Newsom   Yigael Yadin

One of the most important of the scroll fragments found at Masada is a copy of the "Songs of the Sabbath Sacrifice," a composition also known from copies found in Qumran Caves 4 and 11. The Masada fragment 1039–200 was discovered in the south-eastern corner of Room 1039 in the casemate wall,[1] a room which also yielded fragments from the books of Psalms and Leviticus and numerous silver and bronze coins struck during the revolt against Rome. Historically, the discovery of this fragment is significant because it suggests the participation of members of the Qumran community, almost certainly to be identified with the Essenes, in the revolt against Rome.[2]

The Masada fragment of the Sabbath Shirot contains portions of two columns of text. The left-hand edge of the fragment seems to have been deliberately cut or torn away. The height of the fragment as preserved is 21 cm, with a top margin of about 2 cm and a preserved bottom margin of 1.6 cm. Each column originally contained 26 lines of text. The space between the visible horizontal dry lines is 7 mm and the average height of the letters is 3 mm. Vertical dry lines are faintly visible and the space between the columns averages 18 mm. The original width of each of the two columns can be calculated at about 32 letter spaces counting *waw*, *yod*, *zayin*, final *nun* and the spaces between words as half-letters.

Palaeographically, the hand of the Masada fragment is a developed Herodian formal hand, comparable to Fig. 2:6 (4QDan[b]) in Cross's typology or to Col. XIII (1QH, first hand) in Avigad's schema.[3]

The Sabbath Shirot originally contained individual compositions for each of the first thirteen Sabbaths of the year. MasShirShabb preserves material from the conclusion of

---

1.   For details of the discovery, see Yadin, *Fortress*, 172–173. Previous discussion: Yadin, *IEJ* 15, 105–108, Pl. 20:B; Newsom-Yadin, Songs, 78–88, Pl. 9; Newsom, *Songs*, 167–184, Pl. XVI; Puech, Notes, 575–83.

2.   The participation of Essenes in the revolt is attested by Josephus in *War* II, 20, 4; III, 2, 1. Newsom now believes that the Sabbath Shirot may have originated as a non-sectarian or pre-sectarian text which was adopted by the Qumran sectarian community and which influenced sectarian works composed by the community. See C. Newsom, 'Sectually Explicit' Literature from Qumran, *The Bible and Its Interpreters*, ed. W. Propp and B. Halpern (Winona Lake, IN: Eisenbrauns, 1990) 167–187.

3.   Cross, Scripts, 177; Avigad, Palaeography, 75.

Illustration 15: MasShirShabb 1039–200

[121]

the song for the fifth Sabbath (Col. I, l. 1–6) and from the first half of the sixth Sabbath song. Substantial overlaps between the Masada fragment and fragments from Qumran Cave 4 allow for important mutual supplementation and the reconstruction of a significant amount of continuous text. The two most extensive overlaps occur between MasShirShabb I, 1–6 and 4Q402 (ShirShabb^c) 4 11–16, and between MasShirShabb II, 7–26 and 4Q403 (ShirShabb^d) 1 I, 1–11. Smaller overlaps occur with 4Q404 (ShirShabb^e) 1 and 4Q405 (ShirShabb^f) 3 I.

Transcription of Col. 1*

חדשות פלא כול אלה]עֹשֹׁהֹ פלֹא בֹמֹזמֹת חֹסֹדוכל	1
[ ]. כול דֹבֹרֹיֹ דֹּעת נהיו כ]ו]ל הוי עד ומדעתו	2
[ומזמו]תֹיֹוֹ היו כול תעודות עולמֹים עֹוֹשה ראישונות	3
[לעתו]תֹיהם ואחֹרונות למועדיהם ואין בידעים נגלי	4
[פלא]להֹבין לפני עשותו ובעשותו לא ישכילו כול	5
[אלוהי]םֹ מה יזום כיא ממעשי כבודו הם לפני היותם	6
[ממחשב]תֹו	7
[למשכיל] שֹׁיֹרֹ עולת השבת הששית בתשעה לחודש	8
[השני הללו א]לֹ[וה]יֹ אלים יושבי מרומי רומים	9
ק]וֹדש קדשים ורוממו כבודו	10
ד]עת אלי עולמים	11
קֹרואיֹ רֹום רומים	12
בֹ]כֹל קודש	13
[	14
[	15
[	16
יֹ].[ ]יו	17
ל]ֹ	18
[	19
תֹ]	20
[°	21

*   Material preserved in 4Q402 4 underlined.

Notes on the Transcription of Col. I

There is only one non-orthographic divergence between the present text and 4Q402: where MasShirShabb I, 2 reads כול דברי דעת, the corresponding portion of 4Q402 4 12 reads כיא מאלוהי דעת. One might suspect simple textual variants, but the discrepancy could also be accounted for by assuming that the Masada text is haplographic, becoming simply כול דברי דעת when the scribe's eye slipped from one occurrence of דעת to the next. The syntax and parallelism of the text favour כיא מאלוהי דעת as the better reading here:

c	b	a
כול הוי עד	נהיו	כיא מאלוהי דעת
c'	b'	a'
כול תעודות עולמים	היו	ומדעתו]ומזמו[תיו

The phrases כיא מאלוהי דעת, preserved in 4Q402 4, completes the parallel structure. The phrase כול דברי דעת from Masada I, 2 does not. Thus the phrase כיא מאלוהי דעת should be restored after כול דברי דעת in the Masada fragment.

Notes on the Readings of Col. I

L.1: בֿמֿזֿמֿתֿ חֿסֿדובל. This reading, proposed by E. Puech,[4] fits the traces well. The first trace preserves the lower corner of *beth*. Following *beth* the left upstroke of *mem* is well preserved. *Zayin* is certain (cf. יזום in l. 6). The outline of the following *mem* is clear. *Taw* is badly damaged, but the remaining trace is consistent with the left foot of *taw*. The traces of the following letter are consistent with *ḥet* (cf. החמישי in II, 12). *Samekh* is faint but clear. *Daleth* is certain. The scribe left no space between *waw* and the following letters, *beth* and *lamed*.

L.2: כול דֿבֿרֿיֿ .]. The trace of the letter before כול might be that of *he, yod,* or *waw*. The left portion of the head and the downstroke of *dalet* are clear. The corner of the base of the following letter is better for *beth* than for *kaf*. The traces of the two following damaged letters fit *reš* and *yod*. So also Puech.[5]

L.6: אלוהיֿ ֿם. Following the suggestion of Qimron and Puech, the first trace should be read as final *mem* rather than *qof*.[6] Context requires the restoration of an angelic designation, e.g., אלוהים or קדושים.

L.8: שֿיֿר. The traces are very fragmentary, and the line is restored according to parallels from Cave 4 fragments.

---

4. Puech, Notes, 576.
5. Ibid., 577.
6. E. Qimron, A Review Article of *Songs of the Sabbath Sacrifices: A Critical Edition*, by Carol Newsom, *HTR* 97 (1986), 362; Puech, Notes, 580.

L.9: ‫אלⁱ[ו]הי הללו‬ ‫והשני‬. The restoration originally proposed, ‫והשני הללו א[ל]והⁱי‬, is, as Puech correctly observes,[7] too short to fill the space available. In default of a better hypothesis, one may assume a small *vacat* between ‫השני‬ and the imperative to praise, or perhaps a double imperative, ‫הללו הללו‬.

Translation of Col. I

1   [...wondrous new (works). All this] He has done wondrously according to His gracious plan, not

2   [...]all the words of knowledge. «For from the God of knowledge» came into being everything that exists forever. And from His knowledge

3   [and] His [purposes] have come into existence all things that were eternally appointed. He makes the former things

4   [in] their [seasons] and the latter things at their appointed times. And there are none among those who have knowledge

5   who can discern [(His) wondrous] revelations before He acts. And when He acts no [godlike bei]ngs can comprehend that

6   which He purposes. For they *are* part of His glorious works; before even they existed

7   [*they were part of*] His [*pla*]n.

8   [For the instructor.] Song of the whole-offering of the sixth Sabbath on the ninth of the [second] month.

9   [Praise the G]o[d] of gods, O inhabitants of the highest of heights!

10 [...]most holy. And exalt His glory

11 [... k]nowledge *of* the eternal gods

12 [...] the dignitaries of the height of heights

13 [...] with all holiness

14–16

17 [...]*Y.*[ ]*YW*

18 [...]*L*[

19

20 [...].*T*

21 [...].

Comments to Col. I

L.1: ‫חדשות פלא‬. Note below in lines 3–4 the pair ‫ראישונות‬ and ‫אחרונות‬. All three terms are drawn from Deutero-Isaiah. For ‫חדשות‬, see Isa 42:9 (‫הראשנות הנה־באו וחדשות אני מגיד‬) and 48:6 (‫השמעתיך חדשות מעתה ונצרות ולא ידעתם‬).

7.   Ibid., 580.

Ibid.: כול אלה] עשה פלא. In view of the clear Isaianic language which appears elsewhere in this passage, this phrase probably derives from Isa 45:7, אני יהוה עשה כל־אלה. See also Isa. 66:2.

Ll.1–2: במזמת חסדו[בל | | | כול דברי דעת. The lacuna at the beginning of line 2 is approximately 2 cm wide, sufficient for 9–11 letters. Puech[8] suggests restoring בל וישכילו אל]ה, "these do not understand all the words of knowledge." Alternatively, one might achieve better parallelism by taking במזמת חסדו as a parallel to כול דברי דעת and assuming that the verb governing במזמת חסדו, as well as the verb governing כול דברי דעת, has been lost in the lacuna. Thus, schematically, במזמת חסדו בל ו]יבינו ולא ידעו] כול דברי דעת, "they do not discern His gracious plan nor understand all the words of knoweldge." 'They' would presumably be the angelic beings engaged in the eschatological war referred to in the preceeding lines (4Q402 4 7–10). Qimron's discussion of these difficult lines,[9] is based on an assumption that 4Q402 3 and 4Q402 4 are from the same column of text, a conclusion not accepted here.

Ll.2–7: The translation and interpretation of these lines is aided by the fairly regular parallelism of the text:

	d	c	b	a
	כו]ל הוי עד	נהיו	מאלוהי דעת«	»כיא

	d'	c'	b'	
	כול תעודות עולמים	היו	ומדעתו]ומזממו[תיו	

g	f	e	
]לעתו]תיהם	ראישונות	עושה	

g'	f'	
למועדיהם	ואחרונות	

k	j	i	h
לפני עשותו	להבין	נגלי [פלא]	ואין בידעים

i'	h'	j'	k'
מה יזום	כול]אלוהי[ם	לא ישכילו	ובעשותו

b'''	c'''	c''	b''	a'
]ממחשב[תו	לפני היותם	הם	ממעשי כבודו	כיא

8. Ibid., 578.
9. E. Qimron, Review Article (above, n. 6), 362–363.

The strong predestinarian element in these lines finds its closest parallels in the following passages from Qumran literature:

ופרוש קציהם לכל הוי עולמים ונהיות עד מה יבוא בקציהם לכל שני עולם

(CD II, 9–10)

מאל דעות כול הווה ונהייה ולפני היותם הכין כול מחשבתם

(1QS III, 15)

ובחכמת דעתכה הכ[י]נותה תעו[ד]תם בטרם היותם ועל פי ‏[‏.‏ ‏]יה כול ומבלעדיך לא יעשה

(1QH I, 19–20)

כי הראיתם את אשר לא ‏[‏]שר קדם ולברוא חדשות להפר קימי קדם ול[הק]ים נהיות עולם

(1QH XIII, 11–12)

L.3: תי[. The evident parallelism in lines 2–3 suggests that the lacuna be restored with some synonym for מדעתו, perhaps ומזמותיו. The occurrence of the phrase מזמת כבודו elsewhere in the text of the fifth Sabbath song (4Q402 3 II, 13) makes this suggestion plausible as a schematic restoration. See also מה יזום in line 6 below.

Ibid.: כול תעודות עולמים. The traditional derivation of תעודה from the root עוד and its translation as 'witness, attestation' has proved untenable for many of the occurrences of תעודות in Qumran literature (cf. 1QS I, 19; III, 10; 1QM II, 8; XIV, 13, etc.) and it has been recognized that in some instances תעודה and מועד are virtually synonymous; cf. line 4 below.[10]

Ll.3–4: עושה ראישונות ולעתו[תי]הם. The use of the plural suffix יהם- to refer to a feminine antecedent is well attested in Qumran literature. ולעתו[תי]הם is supplied here as a parallel to מועדיהם in the following phrase.

Ibid.: ראישונות.....אחרונות. This pair of words distinctly recalls the language of Deutero-Isaiah; see Isa 44:6, אני ראשון ואני אחרון (also Isa 48:12) and the contrast between ראשון and אחרונים in Isa 41:4. In Deutero-Isaiah the context in which these terms occur is often that of God's predetermination of events and God's revelation of future events through the prophets (e.g. Isa 46:10, מגיד מראשית אחרית). The idea of divine predetermination of history is frequent at Qumran (see, e.g., 1QpHab VII, 14, 18; 1QS III, 15–16), although the pair of terms ראישונות.....אחרונות is not otherwise attested in Qumran literature.

L.4–5: ואין בידעים נגלי [פלא] להבין לפני עשותו. The word order of this clause is somewhat awkward, apparently in order to achieve chiastic parallelism with the following stich.

Ll.5–6: עושה ... לפני עשותו [ ] ם מה יזום [ ] ובעשותו לא ישכילו כול. Note the sequence עושה ... לפני עשותו ... בעשותו. The text affirms not only that God is the author of all events but also that the wise cannot find out the divine secrets through their own wisdom. Moreover, even with the aid of divine revelation the full dimensions of God's intentions remain hidden from the

10. See also Y. Yadin, *The Scroll of the War of the Sons of Light against the Sons of Darkness* (Oxford: Clarendon, 1962), 330, notes to 1QM XV, 1. M. Baillet has recently commented on occurrences of תעודות as a parallel to עתים (1QM XIV, 13) and to קץ (4Q510 1 6–7): *DJD* VII, 26.

wise. The 'agnosticism' of this passage should not be contrasted with such passages as 1QS XI, 3; 1QH I, 21; VII, 26–27; XII, 11–13, where the Qumran community alludes to divine mysteries which have been revealed to them. The present passage is merely a highly rhetorical expression of the vast gulf between divine knowledge and creaturely knowledge, however exalted; cf. 1QH I, 2–3.

Ll.6–7: [תו. כיא ממעשי כבודו הם לפני היותם]. Judging from the reconstruction of line 8 below, only about 5–6 spaces are missing before [תו. One expects some reference to the predetermination of events by God and thus may perhaps restore ממחשב[ותו as a parallel to ממעשי כבודו; cf. 1QS III, 15 (מאל דעות כול הווה ונהייה ולפני היותם הכין כול מחשבתם). The pronoun הם and the suffix of היותם probably refer to the predetermined events of lines 2–5 rather than to the ידעים.

Ll.8–9:

[למשכיל] שיר עולת השבת הששית בתשעה לחודש

[השני הללו   א]ל[וה]י אלים יושבי מרומי רומים

The reconstructions of ll. 8 and 9 are based on the standard introductory headings preserved for the Sabbath songs in the fragments from Cave 4:

למשכיל שיר עולת השב[ת הראישונה לחודש הראישון הללו]

(4Q400 1 I, 1)

למשכיל שיר עולת השבת השביעית בשש עשר לחודש הללו אלוהי מרומים הרמים בכול אלי דעת

(4Q403 1 I, 30–31)

See also 4Q400 3 II, 8; 401 1 1–2; 403 1 II, 18.

למשכיל. The phrase למשכיל, which introduces each of the Sabbath songs, is both lexically and syntactically ambiguous. In some instances משכיל in Qumran literature seems to identify a particular office in the community; see, e.g., 1QS III, 13 and 1QS[b], where the משכיל has the responsibility for teaching esoteric doctrine to 'all the children of light' and for blessing the community, the priests, the high priest and the prince of the congregation. These actions seem more appropriately to belong to a specific office holder than to an ordinary member of the community. If such is the sense of משכיל here, then the phrase might be translated 'for/by the Instructor' or the like. On the other hand, one cannot rule out the generic sense of משכיל and the translation 'for the wise.' In superscriptions to biblical psalms למשכיל is a musical term which means "Song", or possibly "Singer".[11] Thus as a liturgical rubric למשכיל might here mean "for the Singer".

L.10: ורוממו כבודו. In the introductory portions of the Sabbath songs the initial call to praise (הללו) is usually followed by at least one more imperative sentence of praise and often by a series of such calls to praise. Compare Pss 29:1–2; 66:1–4; 81:2–4; 96:1–3; 105:1–3; 148:1–5; etc.

L.11: אלי עולמים. Angelic epithets of this pattern are common in the Sabbath Shirot (cf.

---

11. S. Talmon and E. Eshel, "והמשכיל בעת ההיא ידם (Amos 5:13)", *Shnaton* 10 (1990), 115–22.

(אלי רום, אלי הוד, אלי אור, אלי דעת). The use of אלים for the angels in other Qumran literature is well attested.[12]

L.12: [קרואי רום רומים. The term קרואי undoubtedly derives from Num 1:16, אלה קריאי [qere קרואי] העדה נשיאי מטות אבותם ראשי אלפי ישראל הם (see also Num 16:2; 26:9). The words parallel to קרואי in Numbers, נשיאי and ראשי, are the pair of terms frequently used in the Sabbath Shirot to designate the highest angels. רום רומים is, of course, an epithet for heaven (cf. Prov 25:3, שמים לרום וארץ לעמק).

Transcription of Col. II*

1		לו֗ [...]
2		ל[..
3		דֹ֗בֹרֹי[ן
4		אמת ו֗[
5		כול אֹלו֗[
6	השלישי לנשיאי	גדול[ן
7		רו֗ש[
8		רומ֗[ו֗]ם לאלוהי מלאכי רום שבעה בשבעה דברי רומי[
9		פלא[ן תהלת שבח בלשון הרביעי לגבור על כול[
10		אלהים[ן בשבע גבורות פלאה ושבח לאלוהי גבורות[
11		שבעה בֹ[ו]שבעה דברי תשבוחות פלא תהלת הודות[
12		בלשון החמישי ל[ו֗]מֹלך הכבוד בשבעה הודות פלאיה[
13		יודו לאל הכבוד שבעֹ[ה בשבעה דברי הדות פלא[
14		[תה֗]לת רנן בלשון הששי ל[ו֗]אל הטוב בשבעה רנות[
15		[פלאיה ורננ] למלך הטוב שבעֹה בשבעה דברי רנות[
16		פֹ[ו֗]לא תה֗]לת זמר בלשון השבֹ[ו֗]יעי לנשיאי רוש[
17		זמר עוז לאלוהי קודש בשבעֹ[ה זמרי נפלאותיה[
18		וזמר למלך הקודש שבעה בשֹ[ו]בעה דברי זמרי[
19		פלא שבע תהלי ברכותיו שבע תֹ[ו]הלי גדל צדקו[
20		שבע תהלֹי רום מלכותו שבע תהלֹי תֹ[ו]שבחות כבודו[
21		שבע תהלֹי הודות נפלאותיו שבע תהֹ[ו]לי רנות עוזו[
22		[שבֹ]עֹ תהלי זמירו[ו]ת קודשו תולדות רֹא֗ושי רום[
23		[יברכו שֹ[ו]בֹעֹה בשֹ[ו]עה דברי פלא֗ דבֹ[ו]רי רום הראישון[
24		[לנשיאי רוש יברו֗ך֗ בשם כבוד אלוהים לכֹ[ו]ול
25		בשבעה ד[ו]בֹרי פלא לברך כול סודי֗[ו]הם במקדש[ ]
26		[קודשו בשבעה דברי פלא וב]ֹם לידעֹי עולמים֗[

* Material preserved in 4Q403 1 I underlined.

Notes on the Readings of Col. II

L.3: דֹבֹרֹי. The first trace is the downstroke of either *dalet* or *reš*. The base of *beth* is certain.

L.4: אמת וֹ. The traces after *mem* are quite ambiguous but seem to belong to two different letters.

L.7: רוֹש. Only a small trace of the right edge of *waw* is visible. 4Q403 confirms the reading.

L.8: רומֹם. Medial *mem* is probable. 4Q403 confirms the reading.

L.11: שבעה בֹ. The base of *beth* is good.

L.16: פֹלא. For the base of *peh*, see פלא in line 19 below.

L.19: שבע תֹ. The two final traces belong to *taw* and not to two separate letters, e.g., *daleth, beth*. The reading שבע דבורי would not be good, since the base line of *beth* is usually slanted and breaks through the downstroke. Moreover, such a reading is excluded by the context.

L.21: תהלי and תהֹלי. The head of *he* is broken but certain in both cases.

L.22: זמירוֹות. The plural is favoured by the closely parallel text of 4Q400 3 II, 1, which reads זמירות קודשו.

L.22: רֹאֹשׁי. The first trace is compatible with *daleth* or *reš*. The Second is compatible either with *'aleph* (e.g. for ראשי) or with *beth* (e.g. for דברי). The restoration is based on the context, which introduces the blessings of the seven chief princes.

L.23: פֹלאֹ. The left and right arms of *aleph* are visible, as well as the right leg. The left leg has been obscured by abrasion of the leather. The outlines of the damage are clear on the photograph. A spot in the interlinear space further obscures the reading.

L.26: מֹֹ. The trace favours final *mem* rather than final *kaf*, which one would expect from the context (יברך), as the regular pattern of the blessings of the seven chief princes in 4Q403 1 I, 10–29 indicates.[13] The same reading (ובם) is attested, however, in the overlapping text of 4Q405 3 II, 1. It is possible that both texts derive from a corrupt archetype in which ligatured *reš* and *kaf* were misread as final *mem*.[14] Puech[15] suggests an alternate restoration for ll. 25–26: ובמקדש (26) [בשבעה דברי פלא וברך בם לידעי עולמים]השני. Although this proposal fits the space of MasŠirŠabb II, 25–26 and nicely solves the syntactical problems posed by בם, the reconstruction במקדש בשבעה is too short to fill the lacuna in the parallel text of 4Q401 1 I, 11, a problem that Puech himself acknowledges. He suggests that the text of 4Q403 1 I, 11 and MasŠirŠabb II, 25–26 diverged, with 4Q403 1 II, 11 reading במקדשוֹים] or [אל] במקדש or the like. But that is only to substitute one problem for another. A fully convincing solution has yet to be found.

---

12. For discussion of the term and a list of occurrences see Yadin (above, n. 10), 230.
13. See the discussion in Newsom, *Songs*, 178–180.
14. On this matter see p. 70, n. 26.
15. Puech, "Notes" 581.

Translation of Col. II

1 ....
2 ....
3 words of [...]
4 truth and [...]
5 all the god[s...]
6 great [... the third of the]
7 chief [princes ...]
8 will exal[t the God of exalted angels seven times with seven words of]
9 wondrous [exaltations. Psalm of praise by the tongue of the fourth to the Warrior who is above all the]
10 godlike beings [with its seven wondrous powers; and he will praise the God of powers]
11 seven times with [seven words of wondrous praise. Psalm of thanksgiving]
12 by the tongue of the fifth to [the King of glory with its seven wondrous thanks-givings;]
13 they will give thanks to the God of glory seve[n times with seven words of wondrous thanksgivings.]
14 [Ps]alm of rejoicing by the tongue of the sixth to [the God of goodness with its seven wondrous songs of joy;]
15 [and he will cry joyously] to the King of goodness seven [times with seven words of] won[drous rejoicings.]
16 [Ps]alm of praisesong by the tongue of the sev[enth of the chief princes,]
17 a mighty praisesong to the God of holiness with [its] seve[n wondrous praisesongs;]
18 and he will sing praise to the King of holiness seven times with s[even words of] wondrous [praisesong.]
19 Seven psalms of His blessings; seven p[salms of the magnification of His righteousness;]
20 seven psalms of the exaltation of His kingship; seven psalms of the p[raise of His glory;]
21 seven psalms of thanksgiving for His wonders; seven psa[lms of rejoicing in His strength;]
22 [sev]en psalms of praise of His holiness. The generations of the [exalted] chi[efs]
23 [will bless s]even times with seven wondrous words, wor[ds of exaltation. *The first*]
24 [of the chief princes will bles]s in the name of the glory of God a[ll the...]
25 [... with seven] wondrous [wor]ds; he will bless all [their] councils [in the sanctuary of]
26 [His holiness with seven wondrous words and *with*] *them* (he will bless) those who have knowledge of eternal things [...]

[130]

Comments to Col. II

The overlap of Col. II, 7–26 with 4Q403 1 I, 1–11 allows the line length of Col. II of the Masada fragment to be calculated at 32 spaces. The content of the beginning of the sixth Sabbath song after the introductory call to praise cannot be reconstructed. Beginning, however, with the last line of Col. I and continuing for the rest of the Sabbath song there were two highly formulaic sections of text. Col. I, 26 — Col. II, 23 contained a description of psalms spoken by each of the seven chief princes together with a summary listing of the seven types of psalms. In ll. 24–26 there began a formulaic account of the blessings uttered by each of the seven chief princes. While only a small part of the text of this section is preserved in the Masada fragment, it is well preserved in 4Q403 1 I.[16]

Ll.6–7: רוש לנשיאי]ן השלישי. The text of 4Q403 1 I, 1 reads רומם לו[מ]ולאֹכֹיֹ רוש לנשיאי השלישי רום, which would initially suggest an overlap between 4Q403 1 I, 1 and MasŠirŠabb II, 7–8. However, the formulaic nature of the account of the psalms of the chief princes indicates that the text of 4Q403 1 I, 1 is haplographic. The words רוש לנשיאי השלישי overlap MasŠirŠabb II, 6–7. The words רום לו[מ]ולאֹכֹיֹ רומם overlap MasŠirŠabb II, 8. The material that was lost by haplography in 4Q403 1 I, 1 and lost in the lacuna in MasŠirŠabb II, 7 can only be restored with some uncertainty, but following the formulaic pattern of the psalms, ll. 6–8 may be reconstructed schematically as follows: השלישי לנשיאי]ן רוש[רומם אמתו למלך מלאכים בשבעה רומי פלאה] רומ[ם לאלוהי מלאכי רום. See Newsom, *Songs*, 178–181 for further discussion.

Ll.8–9: רומ[ם לאלוהי מלאכי רום שבעה בשבעה דברי רומי] פלא. Though formally ambiguous, רומם is probably to be taken as a finite verb rather than a noun. Cf. יודו in line 13 below, which occurs in a parallel statement. The expression שבעה בשבעה דברי רומי פלא is difficult. One might take שבעה בשבעה as a construction similar to biblical יום ביום (cf. בד בבד in 1QS IV, 16) and translate with a distributive sense, 'with each of seven words...'. Alternatively, one could take the first occurrence of שבעה as a multiplicative ('seven times with seven words...'). Although the multiplicative in biblical Hebrew is expressed by the form of שבע, apparent errors in the use of masculine and feminine forms of numerals in 4Q403 (e.g., שבעה רנות) suggest that the form שבעה may simply be a phonetic spelling of שבע, reflecting the weakening of the guttural *ʿayin*. In the present instance the spelling is doubtless also influenced by the proximity of שבעה, the historically correct form of the numeral in the phrase בשבעה דברי רומי פלא. Finally, רומי is difficult. Biblical and Mishnaic Hebrew attest רום, 'height, loftiness, haughtiness', but that nuance is not appropriate here. In the descriptions of the psalms of the other chief princes the words corresponding to רומי are תשבוחות (line 11), הדות (line 13), רנות (line 15), and זמרי (line 18). Accordingly, one should probably see in רומי a word for a type of praise, e.g., 'exaltations'.

---

16. See Newsom, *Songs*, 187–189.

Ll.9–10: ‏ותהלת שבח בלשון הרביעי לגבור על כול] אלהים. The noun שבח is not found in biblical Hebrew and is rare in Qumran literature. It occurs in Ben Sira 44:1 and is well attested in Mishnaic Hebrew. ‏בלשון הרביעי is elliptical for 'by the tongue of the fourth chief prince'; see line 16, ‏בלשון השבו]עי לנשיאי רוש. For גבור as a divine title see Ps 24:8 ‏יהוה גבור. Exod 15:3 MT: ‏יהוה איש מלחמה, reflected in 1QM XII, 8 ‏וגבור מלחמה, parallel to ‏מלך הכבוד. Sam: ‏גבור מלחמה.

L.10: ‏בשבע גבורות פלאה. The feminine suffix of פלאה apparently refers to לשון or, perhaps less likely, to תהלת. See also פלאיה in line 15.

L.13: ‏יודה לאל הנכבד. 4Q403 1 I, 4 reads ‏יודו לאל הכבוד שבעה בשבעה דברי הדות פלא. One does not expect a plural verb here. Cf. the corresponding forms רומם (line 8), ושבח (line 10), ורנן (line 15), וזמר (line 18).

Ll.14–15: ‏ותה]לת רנן בלשון הששי לואל הטוב בשבעה רנות פלאיה. In biblical and Mishnaic Hebrew only the feminine רנה is attested, not the masculine רנן. The Sabbath songs show a strong tendency, however, to prefer masculine noun forms to feminine ones. Such forms attested elsewhere in the Sabbath songs include בין for biblical Hebrew בינה; ברך for ברכה; זמר for זמרה; מפלג for מפלגה.

L.17: ‏זמר עוז לאלוהי קודש בשבעה זמרי נפלאותיה. The phrase זמר עוז is perhaps derived from Exod 15:2 (‏עזי וזמרת יה). The substitution of נפלאותיה for the form פלאה, which occurs in the other psalms, may be intended to give a slightly climactic effect to the psalm of the seventh chief prince.

Ll.19–22: These lines recapitulate the psalms of the seven chief princes, employing the characteristic theme word of each, ‏זמרות, רנות, הודות, תשבחות, רום, גדל, ברכות.

Ll.22–23: ‏תולדות ראושי רום יברכו ש]בעה. The transition to the account of the blessings of the Seven Chief princes begins here. The damaged condition of the text makes the restoration somewhat speculative (see the notes on the readings). Since the end of the blessing section of the song concludes with all of the princes blessing together (4Q403 1 I, 26–29), their collective blessing here at the beginning forms an inclusio.

L.25: ‏לברך. The infinitive should probably be taken as a substitute for the finite form ‏יברך, which is regularly found in this position in the formulaic blessings preserved in 4Q403 1 I, 10–29.

Ibid.: ‏כול סודי]הם במקדש קודשו. The angelic councils are similarly referred to in 4Q403 1 II, 22 (‏מקדש פלא לשבעת סודי קודש), where they appear to be associated with seven angelic priesthoods.

L.26: ‏וב.[ם. One expects ‏יברך here. See notes on the readings.

(c) Mas 1063–1747; Mas1n; Unidentified Qumran-Type Fragment (photos 5500 5621)

Yadin's description of this item runs as follows:

> This is a tiny fragment written in a semi-formal script. It might have been part of a sectarian scroll. The combination ‏ת קודשו‎[is very interesting, as it appears frequently in the Dead Sea scrolls (‏שבתות קדשו, עצת קדשו‎, etc.). The spelling ‏הואה‎ (or ‏היאה‎)[1] should also be noted.[2]

The brownish piece of parchment measures 3.3×7.5 cm. The fairly straight right-hand and left-hand edges evince wilfull tearing, most probably by a Roman soldier,[3] so that the written lines are truncated on both sides. Several small holes in the parchment resulted from adverse climatic conditions or were made by insects.

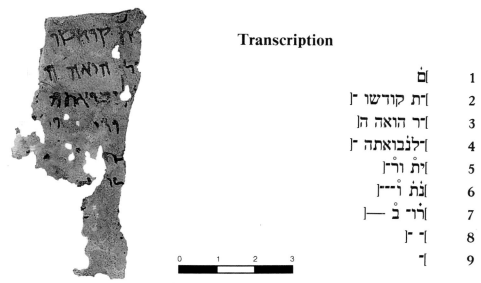

Transcription

‏ם‎[	1
‏]ת קודשו ‎[	2
‏]ר הואה ה‎[	3
‏]לנבואתה ‎[	4
‏]ית ור‎[	5
‏]נֹת וֹ‎[	6
‏]רוֹ בֹ —‎[	7
‏] ‎[	8
‏]‎	9

Illustration 16: Mas Unidentified Qumran-Type Fragment 1063–1747

Script

The fragment comprises remnants of nine lines. In ll. 2, 3 and 4 a few complete words can still be read, in ll. 1, 5 and 7 only single letters. Ink blots at the ends of ll. 3 and 4 are possibly remains of lost letters. In l. 6 traces of letters remain, and in ll. 8–9 (possibly also in a tenth line) flimsy traces of writing. The comparatively large letters hang from dry rulings impressed on the sheet. They average 4×4 mm in size. Some are broader (e.g.

1. Presumably due to a printing mistake, the word ‏היאה‎ was omitted from Yadin's text.
2. Yadin, *IEJ* 15, 105.
3. As is the case with other items found at Masada.

ש of קודשו in l. 2; א of לנבואתה in l. 4), and some higher. Letters are visibly spaced, except that in לנבואתה (l. 4) the *aleph* abuts on the *taw*. Words are separated by a space of 4–5 mm. Inter-line spaces amount to 7–8 mm. The bottom margin is partially preserved on the right-hand side of the fragment to the width of 1.8 cm.

It is doubtful whether the script can indeed be defined 'semi-formal,' as Yadin would have it, following the classification proposed by Cross. Rather, the writing seems to evince an untrained hand: the forms of letters appear to be shaky, and recurring letters are not executed uniformly (cf. e.g. *aleph* in l. 3 and l. 4; and *taw* in ll. 2, 4, 5). The upwards pointing cringle of *reš* (ll. 3 and 7) makes this letter come closest to the *reš* in what Cross defines "An Archaic or early Hasmonaean semiformal script of ca. 175–125 B.C."[4] This date is supported by the execution of *taw*, which is not closed on the left side by the usual straight downstroke, but rather by a sort of loop (ll. 2 and 5).[5] This special form brings to mind the *taw* in the Nash papyrus,[6] which Albright dated to the second half of the second century BCE.[7] These are possibly specimens of a final form of *taw*, occasionally also found in a medial position. Unlike the final forms of *kaf, mem, nun, peh* and *ṣade*, the final *taw* has not survived in the Jewish scribal tradition.[8] But, if what we have here is indeed a final *taw*, it remains an open question whether the apparently emended last letter in l. 4 belongs with the preceding word לנבואת or whether it opens the ensuing word.[9]

Spelling

The spelling הואה (or היאה), abundantly known from Qumran manuscripts, suggests that the fragment stems from a Covenanters work. This assumption is supported by the plene spelling of ת קודשו[(l. 2), as part of a restored phrase עצ[ת קודשו, שב(תו)]ת קודשו, ברי[ת קודשו, 'his holy covenant/ his holy sabbath(s)/ his holy congregation,' or a similar expression, which, as Yadin rightly noted, occur often in Covenanters writings. In biblical Hebrew,

---

4. Cross, *Scripts*, 137, l. 7.
5. It resembles the *taw* on ossuary inscriptions "which are thought to predate the end of Jewish settlement in Jerusalem in 70 A.D. and are generally dated to the Herodian period (37 B.C.–70 A.D.)". *Inscriptions Revealed, Israel Museum Catalogue* no. 100 (Jerusalem, 1973), apud Naveh, *Alphabet*, 164, fig. 149.
6. See S.A. Cooke, A Pre-Massoretic Biblical Papyrus, *PSBA* 25 (1903) 34–56. For a reproduction of the papyrus see *int. al.* J. Trever, *Annual Report, Smithonian Institution* (Washington, 1953), pl. 7 (opposite p. 430); Naveh, *Alphabet*, 163, fig. 147.
7. See Albright, *Nash*.
8. Tur-Sinai, מנצפ״ך; Yalon, מנצפ״ך; Siegel, *Scribes*, 223–54, and pertinent literature recorded there. Milik–Black, *Enoch*, 273, adduce the absence of final letters as an indicator of the early date of a Qumran fragment of the Book of Enoch.
9. It cannot be decided whether the scribe corrected a *he* to a *waw*, or whether he wrote a *he* over another letter.

the noun קֹדֶשׁ, with or without a possessive suffix, is invariably written defectively, whereas in Qumran mss the plene spelling קודש predominates, although the defective spelling קדש is also found.[10] In Masada items the term is spelled either plene or defectively. For example קודש קדשים in the fragment of the 'Songs of the Sabbath Sacrifice': זמירוות (l. 18) למלך הקודש (col. II, l. 17); לאלוהי קודש (col. I, l. 10, 13);]בכול קודש קודשו (l. 22),[11] and יום קודשו in frg. 1045–1350.[12] The inscription קודש on a store jar was completed with two added cursive letters to read לקודשא.[13] In contrast, two ostraca (1042–302; 1054–908/1–3) are inscribed כשרוין לטהרת הקדש (*Masada* I, 34, no. 452).

10. See: *Graphic Concordance to the Dead Sea Scrolls*, ed. J.H. Charlesworth et al. (Tübingen: J.C.B. Mohr (Siebeck)/Louisville: Westminster-John Knox Press, 1991) 474–7.
11. Newsom-Yadin, above, pp. 120, 126.
12. Above, p. 97.
13. Yadin, *IEJ* 15, 111–4.

(d) Mas 1039–274; Mas 1p; Unclassified (Aramaic?) Fragment (final photograph 302373; 302363)

This item was not mentioned at all in Yadin's report. It consists of a piece of dark-brown parchment measuring 3×2.8 cm, and a tiny scrap measuring 1.5×0.7 cm, which should be placed above or below the larger fragment so that the line beginnings of both are justified. The width of the partly preserved right-hand margin amounts to 1.4 cm. At its edge traces of stitching can be discerned.

Transcription

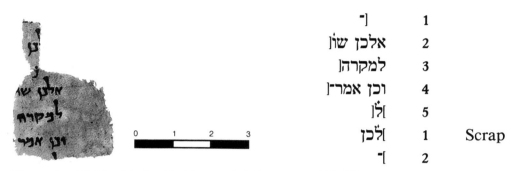

‎ַ]ׁ	1	
אלכן שׁוֹ]	2	
למקרה]	3	
וכן אמר־]	4	
לֹ]ן	5	
אׄלכן]	1	Scrap
‎]ַׁ	2	

Illustration 17: Mas Unclassified (Aramaic?) Fragment 1039–274

Script

The text was penned by a trained scribe in an early formal Herodian script, and can therefore be dated to the second half of the last century BCE. The letters are somewhat larger than 2×2 mm, and are clearly separated from each other. Recurrent letters are executed identically. Words are kept apart by a space of 1–2 mm, and the inter-line spaces amount to ca. 7 mm. Faint traces of dry rulings, from which the letters hang in accord with the prevailing scribal custom, can still be discerned in the margin. The 1.4 cm wide right-hand margin makes it likely that the fragment stems from the first column of a scroll or from the second of two adjacent columns.

Comments

The preserved words and letters are easily read. But the truncated lines do not constitute a meaningful text.

L. 1: The small remnant of a letter could be the foot of a final *nun*, which almost touches the head of the *lamed* in the next line. Before it, there is room for two (or possibly three) more letters. I would tentatively restore here the word אלכן or ולכן, '(and) therefore.'

L. 2: The letter after *šin* could be *waw* or *yod*.

L. 4: The tiny trace of a letter after *reš* is probably the head of *waw*.

L. 5: The *lamed* in the position of the second letter in the line, makes it reasonable to restore אלכן.

[136]

Scrap: The *lamed* does not come up to the very beginning of the line. It was probably preceded by an *aleph*, א[לכן.

L. 2: The tip of a letter beneath the *kaf* in the previous line, suggests also here the restoration of אל[כֹ]ן.

The apparently Aramaic vocable אלכן does not occur in the Hebrew Bible. But the collocation וכן אמר is extant three times in the Aramaic part of Daniel (2:24, 25; 4:11) and once in the plural וכן אמרין (6:7). The use of Aramaic (?) אלכן alongside the Hebrew noun מקרה (l. 3) suggests that the composition from which this fragment stems was possibly written in a combination of both languages. The recurring formula-like term אלכן reverberates in the opening of l. 4: וכן אמר. Altogether we seem to have here an enumeration of several 'cases,' or 'incidents,' למקרה (l. 3), of an undefined nature, each of which apparently triggers a specific, although unidentified reaction, אלכן, therefore.

B.   A Papyrus Fragment Inscribed
in Palaeo-Hebrew Script

Mas 1039–320; Mas 1o; A Text of Samaritan Origin (final photo 5252; others 302374, 302363)

Yadin provided only a brief description of this item, which was found in the casemate to the south of the 'Synagogue' (locus 1039), along with the fragments of Genesis (1039–317), one of the Leviticus (1039–270) and one of the Psalms scrolls (1039–160), the Joshua Apocryphon (1039–211), a scrap of an unclassified Hebrew composition (1039–274), a fragment of the 'Songs of the Sabbath Sacrifice' (1039–200), Latin and Greek papyri, and some ostraca.[1]

A small fragment, measuring 4×3.5 cm, written on both sides (in reverse directions) in the Paleo-Hebrew script, which resembles that of the coins. Each side is written by a different hand, in a different style of writing. The contents of this fragment is difficult to understand, because only a few letters have been preserved. The word לרננה is repeated at least twice. Points divide the words.[2]

Description

The light-brown papyrus fragment is slightly broader, and measures actually 4×3.8 cm. Its ragged contours, two small holes and a large one in its middle, in which two letters were lost, probably resulted from deterioration of the material or were caused by vermin. Mas 1039–320 is the only Hebrew written papyrus fragment found on Masada,[3] and the only one inscribed in Palaeo-Hebrew.[4]

Script

On both surfaces parts of five written lines are extant, and tiny remnants of letters of a sixth line above or below them respectively, since for writing on the reverse the fragment had been turned upside down. The somewhat different ductus leads to the conclusion that the texts on the obverse (A) and the reverse (B) were penned by different hands. The uniform execution of recurring letters, and the equally uniform inter-line spacing give evidence that both were written by expert scribes. The bolder and better preserved

1. Yadin, *IEJ* 15, 79–82.
2. Yadin, *IEJ* 15, 109.
3. In contrast, the Latin and Greek inscriptions are as a rule on papyrus. Only very few pieces are on parchment. See *Masada* II, 1–2.
4. Short inscriptions on ostraca and tags are generally in the Aramaic or Hebrew language, and in the square alphabet. However some bear single letters in Palaeo-Hebrew. See *Masada* I, 6–7.

writing makes the letters on the reverse appear to be somewhat larger than those on the obverse. Here the ink seems to have faded, possibly because this side had been more exposed to sunlight, or else because the text on the reverse was penned later than that on the obverse, suggesting re-use of the papyrus.

On the obverse, large letters, such as *he* and *lamed*, measure ca. 5×5 mm, smaller ones, like *gimel, nun* and *reš*, ca. 3×3 mm. On the reverse, large letters, like *he, yod* and *mem* measure approximately 6×6 mm, smaller ones, like *beth, reš* and *taw*, ca. 4×4 mm. Letters are clearly separated by a space of ca. 1–2 mm. Inter-word spaces amount to 3–6 mm. They are partly filled by triangular shaped separator dots, which show up most clearly in (B), ll. 3 and 4, and in (A), l. 2. The system of word-separators, known from lapidary inscriptions and inscriptions on potsherds of the First Temple period, was subsequently also applied in Palaeo-Hebrew writings on pliable materials, parchment and papyrus, but not in the square alphabet. It remains an open question why this important means of basic text-division, which helps minimizing misinterpretations and textual corruptions, was discontinued when the square alphabet progressively replaced the Palaeo-Hebrew script. To some degree, the loss was made up by the introduction of discrete forms of medial and final letters, of which, though, only צ–ץ; פ–ף; נ–ן; מ–ם; כ–ך have remained in use.[5] Inter-line spaces are 6–8 mm wide on the obverse, and 8 mm to 1 cm on the reverse.

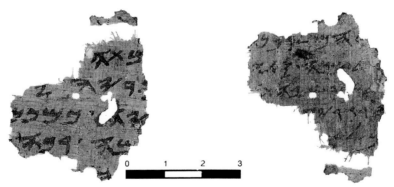

Illustration 18: Text of Samaritan Origin 1039–320 obverse + reverse

Transcription

Reverse (B)	*Obverse* (A)	
‏ןל‏ֺ‏‏]	‏]‏[‏‏	1
‏]מתה*‏‏	‏]‏ֺלהמ*לרננ‏ֺה‏‏	2
‏]‏ֺצריה*‏ֺצ‏‏[	‏]‏ֺלרננה*צל‏ֺו‏‏[	3
‏]‏ֺהוה*כמכמ‏‏[	‏]לכבד*אבה‏ֺות‏‏[‏	4
‏]מה*רבה*‏‏[	‏]‏ֺהרגריז‏ֺימ‏‏[	5
‏]‏ֺי*‏‏[	‏]מ‏ֺילא‏‏[	6
	‏]‏ֺ ‏ֺ ‏ֺ‏‏[	7

5. See Introduction, 20–22.

Notes on Readings[6]

A, l.2: The first word in the line ends with המ, followed by a separator dot. [N] proposes to take the fraction of a letter before המ as part of ע. I tend to view it as the curvature of the base stroke of ל, although the stroke bends slightly downwards, rather than upwards as in ll. 3, 4, 6. As a result I read the first word in the line להם (so also [EY]). The restoration of the second word as לרננה, like in the next line, is beyond doubt.

A, l.3: After לרננה and the separator dot, I propose to read צלו,[7] either as a word by itself or as the first letters of Aramaic צלותא = prayer . The *ṣade* is executed standing upright, in contrast to its usual horizontal position. An intermediate form of the letter shows e.g. on a coin from the Second Revolt dated 'year four and a half.'[8] A, l.4: I concur with [N] in reading the first word as לכבד, and read the next one, after the partially preserved separator, אבהות,[9] probaby a variant form of אבות. The phrase לכבד אבהות, 'to honour (the) forefathers,' may refer to the patriarchs in a devotional context.

A, l.5: I first proposed the reading הרגריזים, written as one word, on the basis of a photograph, in a paper delivered at a meeting commemorating the first anniversary of Yadin's death.[10] The proposition became a certainty when I later examined the original together with Prof. Naveh. After we removed the papyrus from the glass covers between which it was kept, allowing a tiny fold at its lower left end to be straightened out, the second *yod*, of which only the very tip had previously been visible, was fully revealed.

A, l.6: I tend to take the partially preserved first letter as the left-hand stroke of a *mem*. After it the middle and the left perpendicular strokes of a typical Palaeo-Hebrew *yod* can be discerned, abutting on a clearly visible *lamed*, followed by a less obvious *aleph*. The right down-stroke of the *yod* may have been lost in a slight crack in the papyrus. However, the resulting reading מילא, as a complete or a partial word, remains enigmatic. [N] reads נחלא, [EY] מלא.

B, l.1: If the ink speck above *mem* in the next line is the remnant of a letter, the space of ca. 2 mm between l. 1 and l. 2 would be appreciably narrower than the usual interlinear space.

B, l.2: Reading ומתה is certain. The tiny particle of ink after the hole in the papyrus could be part of a separator dot or of the first letter of the next word.

---

6. I wish to express thanks to Prof. J. Naveh for his comments on the decipherment of the text. While the ultimate responsibility for the transcription lies with me, I record under the siglum [N] Naveh's proposals where they differ from mine. Readings proposed by H. Eshel with the assistance of A. Yardeni in H. Eshel, תפילת יוסף מקומראן, פפירוס ממצדה והמקדש השומרוני בהר גריזים, *Zion* 56 (1991), 134–5, are recorded under [EY].
7. [N] reads ואת, [EY] סוב.
8. See S. Birnbaum, *The Hebrew Scripts* (London: Palaeographia, 1962), obverse of item 12; *apud* Purvis, *Samaritan*, plate V, l. 14.
9. [N] proposes אבהת, [EY] יבהת.
10. Jerusalem, January 9, 1986.

B, l.3: The reading of ריה followed by the remnant of a separator dot is beyond doubt. Before this group of letters I tend to restore a partially preserved *ṣade* and to read צְריה. [N] reads הְֿריה, [EY] פריה. I further suggest that the partial letter after the separator dot is also the remnant of a *ṣade*. This suggestion seems to be borne out by a comparison with the remains of the letter *ṣade* in צלו (A, l. 3). [N] and [EY] restore here a *yod*.

B, l.4: [N] and [EY] read ריה] at the beginning of the line. However, it would appear that the *he* is preceded by a *yod* or a *waw*, before which the partial head of another *he* can still be discerned. This suggests the restoration of the Tetragrammaton, יֿהֿוֿה, followed by a dot before the next word: כמכֿמ.

B, l.5: Two words separated by a word divider are legible, מה and רבה, if מה indeed constitutes a complete word rather than the ending of a longer one. [N] proposes to read רכה, because of the similarity of the middle letter with the two *kaf*s in כמכמ in l. 4. However, the reading of a *beth* can be defended on the assumption that the scribe inadvertently fully inked the head of the letter, thus giving it the rectangular shape of the head of *kaf* rather than the triangular shape of *beth*, as in אבהות (A, l.4). Whereas the phrase מה רבה, 'how great is...', could be part of an expression of praise or of a prayer, and would concur with the assumed religious nature of the text, the phrase מה רכה, 'how soft is ...' does not make sense in the context.

Notes on the Text

The devotional term לרננה (A, ll. 2 and 3), derived from רנן, is employed in the Hebrew Bible 91 times in a cultic setting in various noun and verb formations, well over half of them in the Book of Psalms, e.g. (לכו) נְרַנְּנָה (Ps 20:6, 90:14, 95:1), and in psalm-like compositions, combined with terms of invocation, such as תפלה (1 Kgs 8:28 = 2 Chr 6:19; Jer 7:16; 11:14; Ps 17:1), תהלה (2 Chr 20:22) or תודה (Ps 42:5), and most significantly, with רִנָּה (e.g. 1 Kgs 8:28; Isa 49:13; Jer 7:6, 11:14; Ps 17:1; 2 Chr 20:22). The masculine noun form רנן, which is not attested in biblical or mishnaic Hebrew, is found recurrently in the Qumran fragment of the Sabbath Songs (e.g MasShirShab II, 14: ותהֹלת רנן], which "show a strong tendency ... to prefer masculine noun forms to feminine ones,"[11] next to רנה/רנות, preserved also in other Qumran works, e.g in 1QS X, 1, 10; XI, 5, 14, 26; 1QM IV, 4; XII, 15; XIX, 7; 4Q401 14 II, 3; 4Q403 1 I, 5, 9). In our fragment לרננה occcurs once, as suggested, in combination with צלו or צלֹותא], an Aramaic equivalent of the above mentioned Hebrew terms for 'prayer.'[12] The formula-like recurrence brings to mind similar strings of devotional terms in biblical psalmody — such as הללויה or הללו(הו) (Ps 150), הודו (Ps 136:1–3, 26) יודו ליהוה חסדו (Ps 107:8, 15, 21, 31,

---

11. Newsom-Yadin, above, 130.
12. It should, however, be noted that in the (later?) Samaritan vocabulary the stem רנן equals לנן לון, לין, and signifies 'to complain.' Z. Ben Hayyim, המליץ. מילון עברי — ערבי — ארמי (שומרוני), in: *The Literary and Oral Tradition of Hebrew and Aramaic Amongst the Samaritans*, vol. II (Jerusalem: Bialik/The Academy of the Hebrew Language, 1957) 437–622; index, *s.v.* רנן.

cf. v. 1). In apocryphal literature we find, for example, in the Prayer of Azariah vv. 28–29 the formula ברכו את יהוה ... הללוהו, and in Qumran liturgical compositions collocations like הלל וברך in 4Q409 1 I, 1–11. The similarity makes it likely that the Obverse and possibly also the Reverse of the Masada papyrus contained a Samaritan prayer or hymn of adoration directed to holy Mount Garizim,[13] or to the deity whose sanctuary stood on that mountain.[14]

The presumed cultic character of the text meshes well with the mention in A, l. 5 of הרגריזֹים in *scriptio continua*. The custom of combining the noun הר with the name גריזים in one word is a prominent although not an exclusive feature of the Samaritan tradition.[15] In the Samaritan Hebrew version of the Pentateuch, הרגריזים is always recorded as one word,[16] whereas in MT הר is invariably separated from the *nomen proprium* גריזים.[17] Equally, the Samaritikon, the Samaritan Greek translation of the Pentateuch, of which only fragments are extant,[18] and the Samaritan Aramaic[19] and Arabic renditions read הרגריזים as one word.[20] Again, in Samaritan liturgical and other compositions — such as *Sefer Asatir, Tolidah* and *Memar Marqah* — הרגריזים is routinely

13. Cf. below the Delos inscriptions.
14. Eshel (above n. 6) 11, theorizes that the fragmentary Masada text stems from a "Jewish psalm which praises the destruction of the Samaritan temple and the city built around it, and is possibly connected with the observation of the Day of Mount Garizim on the 21st of Kislev." This unconvincing supposition seems to echo a suggestion that a Qumran document contained a prayer against the Samaritans and their temple on Mount Garizim. See E. Schuller, 4Q372:I. A Text about Joseph, *RQ* 14 (1990) 349–76.
15. Pummer, Criterion, adduces instances from non-Samaritan sources of הרגריזים written as one word — some of which may be, though, *lapsus calami*, and in contrast occurrences in Samaritan sources of the name written in two words. J. Strugnell, Quelques inscriptions samaritaines, *RB* 74 (1967) 562, published a Samaritan inscription, which he dates to the 5th or 6th century CE, in which הר is separated by a dot from גרזים. The genuineness of this item is, however, in doubt.
16. See Z. Ben-Ḥayyim, גרזים, הר גרזים, *Encyclopaedia Biblica*, vol. II (Jerusalem: Bialik, 1954) 557. In his eclectic edition of the Samaritan Pentateuch, von Gall adopted, without justification, the reading of הר גרזים in two words (Deut 5:18ᵇ; 11:29; 27:4, 12) on the evidence of a minority of manuscripts. See: A. Freiherr von Gall, *Der Pentateuch der Samaritaner* (Giessen: Töpelmann, 1914–1918). So also B. Blayney, ed., *Pentateuchus Hebraeo Samaritanus Charactere Hebraeo-Chaldaico* (Oxford: Clarendon, 1790). In the more recent comparative edition of Sam with MT by the Samaritan authors A. and R. Zedaka, *The Pentateuch, Jewish Version and Samaritan Version* (Tel Aviv: private publication, 1962), הרגריזים is always given as one word.
17. The name of the mountain is likewise written in two words in the Copper Scroll from Qumran (3Q15 XII, 4): בהר גריזין תחת המעלהא של השית העליונה.
18. See E. Tov, Pap. Giessen 13, 19, 22, 26: A Revision of the LXX, *RB* 78 (1971) 355–83, and below, n. 31.
19. See A. Tal, *The Samaritan Targum of the Pentateuch. A Critical Edition, vol. II. Texts and Studies in the Hebrew Language and Related Subjects* 6 (Tel Aviv: Tel Aviv University Press, 1983).
20. E.g. the Barberini Triglot of the 13th century, and Ms. Or. 7562 (13th–14th century) of the British Museum.

written as one word,[21] sometimes spelled *plene*, הרגריזים, sometimes defectively הרגרזים or הרגריזם.[22] The same applies to the Samaritan lapidary tradition, especially to Decalogue inscriptions.[23] For example the last two lines on the Jabneh Decalogue Inscription read אנכי•מ[צוה]•אתכם•הי[ום]•בהרגרם•קומה•יהוה•[*]. The separator dots leave no doubt that •בהרגרם•[*], spelled defectively, was incised in the stone as one word.[24] The custom can also be observed in the last line of the Beit al-Maʾ inscription (3rd or 4th century CE): א[שר•אנכי•מצוה•אתכם•הי]ום•יב[הרגריזים,[25] and in the broken Sychar Decalogue Inscription in which the name occurs as one word spelled plene: ו[רההרגריזים.[26]

It is of significance that the conjunction of הר with the name of a mountain applies in the Samaritan tradition only to Mount Garizim. In all other instances the noun הר is kept separate from the proper name of the mountain in question,[27] most importantly in reference to Mount Ebal, the twin peak of Mount Garizim (Deut 11:29; 27;4). In the Madaba Map the names are once given as ΓΑΡΙΖΕΙΝ and ΓΕΒΑΛ, and once as ΤΟΥΡΓΑΡΙΖΙΝ and ΤΟΥΡΓΟΒΗΛ, with Aramaic טור prefixed to the name of the mountain, instead of Hebrew הר.[28]

This traditional Samaritan practice shows up clearly in a dedication stele, dated palaeographically to 250–175 BCE, which was erected near a synagogue (evidently a Samaritan כינשא) on the Aegean island of Delos, by the Israelites ... who offer to holy Argarizim in honour of their benefactor, Serapion the son of Iason.'[29]

---

21. See *int. al.* Z. Ben-Ḥayyim, Sefer Asatir, *Tarbiz* 14–15 (1943/4) 13, 29 (Hebrew): דלית אשתה קרבה ליד הרגריזים; J. MacDonald, *Memar Marqah, BZAW* 84 (Berlin: de Gruyter, 1963); idem, *The Samaritan Chronicle* II, *BZAW* 107 (Berlin: de Gruyter: 1969) 36f; S. Lowy, *The Principles of Samaritan Bible Exegesis* (Leiden: Brill, 1977), Index: *s.v.* 'hargerizim.'

22. Because of the break at the end of A, l. 5 it cannot be established for certain whether in the Masada fragment the name is spelled הרגריז[ום], as suggested, or הרגריזם.

23. See F. Dexinger, Das Garizimgebot im Dekalog der Samaritaner, in *Studien zum Pentateuch*, ed. G. Braulik (Wien: Herder, 1977).

24. The mason inadvertently omitted the letter *zayin*. See J. Kaplan, An Inscription From a Samaritan Synagogue in Jabneh, *BIES* 8,1 (1941) 165–6, with comments by J. Ben Zvi, ibid. 166–7 (Hebrew); J. Ben Zvi, *The Book of the Samaritans*, rev. edition, ed. S. Talmon (Jerusalem: Yad Ben-Zvi, 1970) 186–9 (Hebrew); F. Hüttenmeister–G. Reeg, *Die antiken Synagogen in Israel. Beihefte zum Tübinger Atlas des Vorderen Orients*. Reihe B Nr. 12 (Wiesbaden: Reichert, 1977) 565.

25. J. Ben-Zvi, New Finds at Shechem, *BJPES* 3 (1935) 1–6, repr. in *BIES Reader* 1 (1965) 222–7 (Hebrew), and in *The Book* (above n. 24), 173–6, plate 11, transcribed erroneously בהר•גריזם; J.D. Purvis, An Early Samaritan Decalogue Inscription, *Israel Museum News* 11 (1976) 88–90; R. Pummer, *The Samaritans* (Leiden: Brill, 1987), pl. IIa; Hüttenmeister-Reeg, *Synagogen* (above, n. 24) 565–7.

26. See J. Bowman–S. Talmon, Samaritan Decalogue Inscriptions, *BJRL* 33, 2 (1951) 213.

27. Cf. הר סיני (Exod 19:11, 20, 23; 20:16; 31:8; 34:2, 4), הר חרמון (Deut 3:8 cf. 4:48), הר נבו (Deut 32:44; 34:1), הר שפר (Num 33:23, 24), הר פארן (Deut 33:2) et al.

28. See M. Avi-Yonah, *The Madaba Mosaic Map* (Jerusalem: IES, 1954) 47 and pl. 6.

29. Bruneau, *Délos*; A.T. Kraabel, New Evidence of the Samaritan Diaspora has been Found on Delos, *BA* 47 (1984) 44–6; L.M. White, The Delos Synagogue Revisited. Recent Fieldwork in the Graeco-Roman Diaspora, *HTR* 80 (1987) 133–60, esp. 141–7.

Illustration 19: Delos Samaritan Inscsription I (© EFA, Ph. Fraisse).

Transcription

Ὅι ἐν Δήλῳ Ἰσραελεῖται οἱ 'α
παρχόμενοι εἰς ἱερὸν Ἀργα
ριζεὶν[31] στεφανοῦσιν χρυσῷ
στεφάνῳ Σαραπίωνα Ἰάσο
νος Κνώσιον εὐεργεσίας
ἕνεκεν τῆς εἰς ἑαυτούς

Translation

The Israelites of Delos who
offer to holy[30] *Arga*
rizein crown with a golden
diadem Serapion son of *Jaso*
nos of Knossos for his good services
on their behalf

The absence from the text of the noun ὄρος, the Greek equivalent of הר, and the transliteration of הר by Ἀρ, prove that the Hebrew term was not understood as a general noun, but as a constitutive part of the name of the mountain.[32] In addition, the division of Ἀργαριζεὶν after the second syllable Ἀργα at the end of l. 2, and the transfer of the rest

30. Pummer, Criterion, n. 7, considers it "more likely that ἱερον means temple here."

31. The transcription ἀργαριζιμ turns up in the Samaritikon (Deut 27:4, 12). See P. Glaue–A. Rahlfs, *Fragmente einer griechischen Übersetzung des samaritanischen Pentateuchs, Nachrichten von der Königlichen Gesellschaft der Wissenschaften zu Göttingen. Philologisch-historische Klasse*, 1911, 167–200 = *Mitteilungen des Septuaginta-Unternehmens* I, 2 (Berlin, 1909–1915) 31–64; E. Tov, Giessen (above, n. 18).

32. The same may apply to the name of the 'mythical place called in Hebrew Armageddon,' or Harmaged(d)on = Ἀρμαγεδών (Revelation 16:16; see Tov, Giessen (above, n. 18) 374, n. 20), if the transliteration indeed reflects a Hebrew original (הר מגידו) or possibly עיר, עיר or ארע מגידו, 'the town' or 'the land' of Megiddo. For a concise summary of this issue see J.W. Bowman, Armageddon, *IDB*, vol. I (New York/Nashville: Abingdon, 1962) 226–7.

of the word, ριζεὶν, to the beginning of l. 3, clearly shows that the vocable was meant to be written as one word.[33]

This method of writing the name of Mount Garizim is also reflected in another stele (dated to 150–50 BCE) found at the same site, in which the sanctity of Ἀργαριζεὶν is again emphasized.[34]

Illustration 20: Delos Samaritan Inscription II (© EFA, Ph. Fraise).

Transcription	Translation
[Οἱ ἐν Δήλῳ]	The Israelites
Ἰσραελεῖται οἱ ἀπαρχόμενοι εἰς ἱερον Ἀρ	of Delos who offer to holy *Ar*
γαριζεὶν ᾽ετίμησαν *vacat* Μένιππον	*garizin* honour *vacat* Menippos
Ἀρτεμιδώρου	son of Artemidoros
Ἡρακλειον αὐτὸν καὶ τοὺς ἐγγόνους αὐτοῦ	of Heraklion and his offspring

The evidence of the Delos stelae dovetails with that of other sources which attest to the Samaritan practice of writing הרגרזים in *scriptio continua*.[35]

Sefer Abišaᶜ:[36] הרגרזים (Deut 11:29; 27:12–13 MT: הר גריזים; OL: Garzin).

33. Cf. the separation of ἁ at the end of l. 1, the first letter of ἀπαρχόμενοι, from the rest of the word, παρχόμενοι, continued at the beginning of l. 2, and the disjunction of the first two syllables of the nom. propr. Ἰάσο at the end of l. 4 from the third syllable νος at the beginning of l. 5.
34. Bruneau, Delos, 471–5.
35. Kippenberg, *Garizim*, 54–5.
36. F. Pérez Castro, *Séfer Abišaᶜ, Edicion Del Fragmento Antiguo Del Rollo Sagrado Del Pentateuco Hebreo-Samaritano De Nablus. Estudio, Transcripcion, Aparato Critico Y Facsimiles. Textos Y Studios Del Seminario Filologico Cardenal Cisneros* (Madrid: C.S.I.C, 1959).

SamTg: הרגריזים, in contrast to טור עיבל.[37] Unlike TO: טורה דגריזין, SamTg does not render הר separately with Aramaic טור(א) in references to Mount Garizim.

Samaritikon: Ἀργαρ(ι)ζιμ; but LXX: ὄρος Γαριζίν/Γαριζείν.

2 Maccabees 5:23; 6:2 (Latin translation): Argarisin.[38]

Josephus, *War* I, 63: Ἀργαριζιν,[39] but ibid. III, 307: Γαρίζειν ὄρος.

Pliny, *Hist. nat.* V, xiv, 68: mons Argaris (combining the transliteration of הר as *Ar* with its Latin equivalent *mons*).[40]

Pseudo Eupolemos:[41] Ἀργαριζείν.

Damascius: πρὸς ὄρει Ἀργαριζω[42] (cf. above: mons Argaris).

Itinerarium Burdigalense: Agazaren (miswritten for Argarazen).

Ioannes Malalas: Ἀρπαριζιν (miswritten for Ἀργαριζιν); Γαργαζι.[43]

The above quotations from diverse sources prove that in the Samaritan tradition the noun הר was generally regarded an integral part of the toponym גריזים.[44] Therefore, the occurrence of הרגריזים in the Masada papyrus in an evidently cultic context points up its Samaritan provenance.

One would have liked to argue for the Samaritan origin of the Masada fragment inscribed in Palaeo-Hebrew on palaeographic ground. However, for several reasons, such an attempt is beset by great difficulties. The date *a quo* of the fragment is 73/74 CE, the year in which Masada fell to the Romans. The work from which it stems was most probably not written on the site, but rather was brought there by a Samaritan who sought refuge on the mountain fortress to escape the Roman army which by that time had already occupied most of Palestine. Therefore it is reasonable to assume that the work was penned at least several decades before 73/74, perhaps even before the common era. However, for the period in question no Samaritan writing on pliable material like papyrus is extant. What is available are stone inscriptions, 'incised' not 'written', which

---

37. But cf. above the Madaba Map reference: ΤΟΥΡΓΑΡΙΖΙΝ and ΤΟΥΡΓΟΒΗΛ.
38. D. de Bruyne, Notes de philologie biblique II. Argarizim (2 Mac 5, 23; 6, 2), *RB* 30 (1921) 405–7.
39. Kippenberg, Garizim, suggests that Josephus possibly relied here on a Samaritan source.
40. M. Stern, *Greek and Latin Authors on Jews and Judaism*, vol. I (Jerusalem: Israel Academy of Sciences, 1974) 468–73.
41. Possibly Eupolemos son of John, a member of the priestly family of Haqoṣ, who was sent by Judas Maccabeus on a mission to Rome in 161 BCE (1 Macc 8:17; 2 Macc 4:11). See Milik–Black, *Enoch* 8–9. Or else, a Samaritan Hellenist. See: B.Z. Wacholder, 'Pseudo-Eupolemos': Two Greek Fragments on the Life of Abraham, *HUCA* 34 (1963) 85–7; idem, *Eupolemos: A Study of Judaeo-Greek Literature* (Cincinnati: Hebrew Union College, 1974). Further: J. Freudenthal, *Hellenistische Studien, Hefte 1 und 2: Alexander Polyhistor und die von ihm erhaltenen Reste jüdischer und samaritanischer Geschichtswerke* (Breslau: Skutsch, 1875) 82–103; 207–8; 223–5.
42. Quoted from Marinus of Flavia Neapolis.
43. Cf. further the above mentioned inscriptions from Beit al-Ma (בהרגריזים) and Jabneh (בהרגרם). For additional pertinent literature see Pummer, Criterion, above, n. 15, 20–21.
44. To quote Kippenberg, *Garizim*, 55, n. 121: "wo die samar. Form begegnet, kann mit einer samar. Quelle, einem samar. Verfasser oder einer samar. Tradition gerechnet werden".

require quite different techniques and modes of execution, and thus are not ready objects for comparison.[45]

The Samaritan papyri from Wadi Daliyeh are better suited to the purpose. However, these documents stem from the 4th century BCE,[46] which means that we are faced with a time-gap of close to three centuries, making the comparison most precarious. Some Palaeo-Hebrew Qumran documents of the last centuries BCE and the first century CE could be adduced in comparison,[47] but there is no tangible proof that the Samaritan Palaeo-Hebrew script differed appreciably from the Jewish script at that time. For example, "the shape of the letters on the 'Imwas insription," dated mostly to the 1st century CE or the last century BCE, "is very close to that of the Jewish coins with palaeo-Hebrew legends."[48] It would moreover "seem that the results of Samaritan epigraphy are not as assured as they might hitherto have seemed to be."[49] Therefore, a comparison with the contemporary Jewish Palaeo-Hebrew script cannot produce decisive results either. It follows that the identification of the Masada papyrus as a Samaritan document can be based only on the persuasive combination of scribal customs, cultic overtones, and linguistic criteria.

45. In this context, special mention should be made of fragmentary stone inscriptions in Palaeo-Hebrew, which in part are of a cultic nature, discovered in the last decade by Y. Magen on Mount Garizim, next to inscriptions in the square Hebrew alphabet. See: Y. Magen, Mount Garizim — A Temple City, *Qadmoniot* 23 (1990) 78–82 (Hebrew).

46. See Cross, Papyri; idem, Aspects; idem, Discovery (above, p. 17, n. 16).

47. See Freedman–Mathews, *Leviticus*, especially ch. II: Palaeography, 15–23; J.E. Sanderson, *An Exodus Scroll from Qumran: 4QpaleoExod^m and the Samaritan Tradition* (Atlanta: Scholars Press, 1986); *DJD* IX, 17–157; R.S. Hanson, Paleo-Hebrew Scripts in the Hasmonean Age, *BASOR* 175 (1964) 26–42; M.D. McLean, *The Use and Development of Paleo-Hebrew in the Hellenistic and Roman Periods* (Ph.D. Dissertation, Harvard, 1982); Naveh, *Alphabet*, ch. IV: The West Semitic Scripts, 53–112; and the tables offered by Purvis, *Samaritan*. See also E. Tov, Scribal Practices Reflected in the Palaeo-Hebrew Texts From the Judean Desert, *Scripta Classica Israelica* 15 (1996). *Studies in Memory of A. Wasserstein*, vol. 1, 268–73.

48. R. Pummer, Inscriptions, in: *The Samaritans*, ed. A.D. Crown (Tübingen: Mohr (Siebeck), 1989) 192.

49. A.D. Crown, Problems in Epigraphy and Palaeography: The Nature of the Evidence in Samaritan Sources, *BJRL* 62 (1979–80) 37.

Postscript

The Samaritan papyrus was discovered in the casemate near the 'synagogue' (locus 1039) together with several more items, among them fragments of the 'Songs of the Sabbath Sacrifice,' the 'Joshua Apocryphon' and others, that is of works which are manifestly or most probably connected with the dissident 'Community of the Renewed Covenant', known from the collection of manuscripts found in the Qumran caves. The very appearance of these writings sheds light on the heterogenous composition of the population on Masada: next to Zealots and fighters of Second Temple mainstream Judaism, also dissenters — Samaritans and *yaḥad* members — found refuge in the desert fortress.[1] Stopping short of C. Roth's identification of the 'Qumranites' with the Sicarii-Zealots,[2] Yadin construed the presence on Masada of a fragment of the 'Songs of the Sabbath Sacrifice' as "proof that many if not all Essenes," with whom he identified the Qumran community, "joined in the great revolt against the Romans."[3] Also Vermes weighs this possibility,[4] but at the same time offers another interpretation of the circumstances: "the discovery of a Qumran writing at Masada, ... does not *ipso facto* equate the inhabitants of the Dead Sea establishment with the garrison of Masada. It is more likely to mean, either that some of the Qumran sectaries made common cause with the revolution during the last stage of the Community's history and brought their manuscripts to Masada with them, or that the Masada rebels considered the Qumran Community politically unreliable and seized its settlement as the Romans advanced towards the Dead Sea."[5]

The presence on Masada of the earliest extra-biblical evidence of the Samaritan custom of writing the mountain name הרגר(י)(י)זי(י)ם as one word, next to finds of apparent Qumran vintage, and works of the mainstream community, suggests a more inclusive

---

1. For an overview of the state of art of Masada research, see L.H. Feldman, Masada: A Critique of Recent Scholarsip, in: *Christianity, Judaism and Other Greco-Roman Cults. Studies for Morton Smith at Sixty*, ed. J. Neusner (Leiden: Brill, 1975) 218–48; S.J.D. Cohen, Masada: Literary Tradition, Archaeological Remains and the Credibility of Josephus, *JJS* 33 (1982), 385–405.
2. C. Roth, *The Dead Sea Scrolls* (New York: Schocken, 1965; 2nd ed. of *The Historical Background of the Dead Sea Scrolls* [Oxford: Blackwell, 1958]); idem, The Zealots and Qumran: The Basic Issue, *RQ* 2 (1959–60) 81–4; idem, A Final Clarification Regarding the Dead Sea Sect, *RQ* 5 (1964) 81–7.
3. Yadin, *Fortress*, 172–4.
4. G. Vermes, *The Dead Sea Scrolls. Qumran in Perspective*[2] (London: SCM, 1982) 124.
5. The discovery of Qumran or Qumran-type writings among the Masada finds invalidates the assumption that not one member of the Qumran community escaped when the Romans conquered their settlement in 68 CE, as was claimed by J. Jeremias, *Die theologische Bedeutung der Funde am Toten Meer* (Göttingen: Vandenhoeck & Ruprecht, 1962) 10: "denn wenn auch nur ein einziger von ihnen entronnen wäre, hätten die Höhlen ihr Geheimnis nicht bis auf unsere Tage wahren können."

understanding of the variegated composition of the population on Masada. In this context, attention should be drawn to the excavators' explanation of the extensive renovation carried out in the complex of the large Western Palace, which "clearly testifies to occupation either by a group of military commanders (perhaps without their families), an important family, or a coherent community such as the group of Essenes who might have joined the Zealots in their life on Masada."[6] The threat of the impending debacle brought them together in the desert fortress which offered refuge to all. In the face of the imminent final attack of the Roman army, the barriers between the various socio-religious groups broke down to a certain extent: members of the mainstream community, Zealots, Sicarii, adherents of the 'Community of the Renewed Covenant', and Samaritans hoped to find safety on Masada.

6.   *Masada* III, 634.

THE BEN SIRA SCROLL FROM MASADA

Introduction, Emendations and Commentary

YIGAEL YADIN

The Hebrew University of Jerusalem

Notes on the Reading

ELISHA QIMRON

Ben-Gurion University of the Negev

Bibliography

FLORENTINO GARCÍA MARTÍNEZ

Qumrân Instituut, University of Groningen

This is a revised edition of
Y. Yadin, *The Ben Sira Scroll from Masada*, Jerusalem, 1965
first published and presented on the occasion of the opening of the Shrine of the Book
Jerusalem, April 20, 1965

Contents

INTRODUCTION

On April 8, 1964, we discovered, in one of the casemates of the eastern wall of Masada, Scroll fragments containing chapters 39, 27–43, 30 of the *Wisdom of Ben Sira* (*Ecclesiasticus*) in the original Hebrew version.

Owing to the signal importance of this discovery for the study of the original version of *Ben Sira*, I have acceded to the requests of several scholars engaged in research in this field and herewith make available all the fragments of the Scroll that have been discovered. Of course, this preliminary survey does not pretend to exhaust all the problems involved. Its chief aim is to place as quickly as possible before scholars concerned the full version, accompanied by photographs, and a preliminary deciphering as well as the annotations I have been able to formulate in the short time at my disposal.* In this way I hope that the final publication of the Masada discoveries will ultimately benefit. For we shall then be able to make the Ben Sira Scroll the subject of a more thorough study, and — what is more important — to improve and amend it in the light of the criticism, remarks and suggestions prompted by this preliminary publication, emanating from scholars better qualified to discuss the numerous and complicated problems involved.

Let it be pointed out at the very outset of this survey that the version of *Ben Sira* discovered at Masada — which is the most ancient of all extant MSS. (whether of the Hebrew original or in translation) — unmistakably confirms the main conclusions reached by a considerable number of scholars, that the MSS. discovered in the Cairo Genizah basically represent the original Hebrew version. At the same time, the Masada scroll confirms the findings of those scholars who maintained that the Genizah versions abound in corruptions partly due to copyists' errors and partly representing later developments, though still comparatively early, of the original version. Though the immediate importance of the discovery derives from the light it sheds on this basic problem, its chief contribution — for those who never cast doubt on the authenticity of the Genizah MSS. — lies precisely in the way it enables us, for the first time, to clarify the relationship of the various Genizah MSS. both to each other, and to the original consulted by the Greek and Syriac translators.

Before discussing the text of the Scroll itself, we shall devote a short chapter to its description and dating.

General

The Scroll fragments were found folded and crushed, near the northern wall of casemate 1109, lying

---

* The short time at my disposal for the preparation of this study for the press has caused some difficulties, in addition to those emanating from the nature of the subject. I am therefore more than ever thankful to my friend J. Aviram who — with the assistance of Mr. M. Broshi (Curator of the Shrine of the Book) — took great trouble in seeing this publication through. Special thanks are due to Mr. A. Newman for the English translation, which he prepared in a short time from the draft of the original Hebrew. I am grateful to Mr. R. Grafman for reading the proofs and for the technical editing of the English version and supervision of the printing. Messrs. R. Eshel and D. Rokach read the proofs of the Hebrew and Greek respectively.

Last, but not least, I am indebted to my colleague Prof. I. L. Seeligmann for reading the Hebrew draft of this study and making several valuable suggestions. Some of these, which were relevant to the limited scope of the present study, have been inserted in the Commentary, with due acknowledgement.

A Fragment of the Scroll as Found

close to the floor and under the debris covering this and other casemates.[1] Casemate 1109 is situated in the eastern portion of the wall, not far from the gate of the 'Snake Path'; in it were found objects characteristic of the period of the First Revolt, including a Hebrew ostrakon.

A total of 26 leather fragments were discovered: two of them quite large (11×18 and 16×23 cm.), four medium-sized (average 6×7 cm.) and the remainder mere shreds of a size varying between 2×5 and 1×1 cm. In most cases the medium- and small-sized fragments could be joined to the two larger fragments, but there are a number of cases where no direct joint can be found between the shreds and the other fragments because of the rotted state of the Scroll.

The Scroll fragments were badly damaged owing to the damp, which was responsible for the shrinkage of various portions of the leather and the covering of the script by a dark film which in most cases renders the text invisible to the naked eye. The photographs reproduced here were executed in infra red.[2] In addition, there are unmistakable traces, in some places, of decomposition as a result of the activity of vermin. Since the fragments form a continuous series of chapters (see below), it may be concluded that this piece of the Scroll had been torn from the main body and thrown onto the floor of the chamber at a time when the other pieces were perhaps thrown outside, and were thus lost. A similar phenomenon — which can perhaps be attributed to the Roman garrison — has been noted in other casemates, where similar discoveries of torn Scroll fragments were made.[3]

Owing to the shrinkage of the leather it was not possible to piece together the various fragments and straighten them out in accordance with their original state. In Pl. 8, I have reproduced the fragments as they now fit together, showing their dis-

torted character very clearly. This situation is particularly evident in the lower portion of the Scroll. What is more, this has precluded fitting in some of the lower portions of the columns exactly beneath the corresponding upper parts (see particularly Pl. 8, Page IV, bottom), In Pls. 1–4; 5–7, an attempt has been made to straighten them out by separating one page from the next in the photographs, but this did not always achieve the desired result.

The portions of Scroll discovered belong to two sheets of which the common seam had been sewn together in the manner normally found in Scrolls. The seam is found between Pages V and VI (see Pl. 8).

Description and Mode of Writing

The original height of the Scroll — about 17 cm. — can be deduced from some portions where both the top and bottom margins have survived. The preserved length of the Scroll is some 39 cm.

The Scroll is written in columns separated by narrow margins. These spaces are not equal, for though the copyist followed vertical lines (see below) the verses themselves are uneven in length and on the left side of a column protrude into the margin. On the basis of the margin to the right of Page VI (the first column of the second sheet), we may estimate the margin space to which the copyist had intended to adhere to be about 7 mm. This can also be noticed between Pages I and II, where the copyist succeeded in making the lines of Page I more or less uniform in length. A wider margin is found on the left of Page V, the last column on the first sheet, as in other Scrolls.[4] The copyist ruled his lines with a stylus and depended the letters from these. He similarly ruled a vertical line down the right side of each column (see particularly the left margin of Page V and the right of Page VI). We can also detect the method of ruling: First the copyist inked guide-dots in the margin for ruling the horizontal lines. Moreover, at the top of the right margin of Page VI, there are intermediary lines which the copyist ruled before starting to write, to determine the space needed between each line, ensuring that the bottom of final letters and the top of a *lamed* would not touch in successive

---

[1] Regarding the excavations of the first season at Masada, see Y. Yadin: *IEJ* 15 (1965), pp. 1–120 (= *IEJ*). On the character of the casemate wall and the finds discovered therein (including the various Scrolls), see *IEJ*, p. 69 ff.; for casemate 1109, its character and contents, see particularly, *IEJ*, pp. 96 f.

[2] The Scroll was opened by Prof. G. Bieberkraut, and the infra red photographs were taken by his wife, Helene Bieberkraut.

[3] See *IEJ*, the discussion of casemate 1039, pp. 79 f.

[4] See Y. Yadin: *The Message of the Scrolls*, London, 1957, p. 79.

lines. The lines (as is evident from the dots) were 6 mm. apart. The letters are not uniform in size; sometimes the top lines of a column are in larger script, the size progressively decreasing down the column. At any rate, the script may be termed tiny: the height of the average letters is about 2–3 mm.

Each verse of the text is given a separate line, and each line is divided into hemistichs.[5] Each page is thus composed of a right-hand column (*Col. A*) and a left-hand one (*Col. B*), the space between varying according to the length of the right-hand hemistich. The same arrangement is true of MSS. B and E from the Cairo Genizah, and of the two small fragments discovered at Qumran (see below). The poetic books of the Bible were transcribed in a similar fashion, as is shown by the fragments of *Psalms* discovered at Masada.[6] This is further indication of the special reverence given the *Book of Ben Sira*.

All in all, portions of 13 columns belonging to seven pages have been preserved. Each page contains 25 lines, a fact deducible from the pages preserved almost intact, and one of considerable assistance in deciphering the fragments and assigning them to their proper places. It was possible, almost without exception, to place the fragments correctly, on the basis of the calculation of 25 lines to a column, at the same time checking them with the corresponding verses in Cairo MS. B and the Greek version (see below).

Chapter Divisions, etc.

As a rule there are no indications of chapters. In one place (Page VII, before *l.* 24), the scribe left a blank line to indicate a new chapter,[7] as in Cairo MS. B, where a similar practice is adopted before chapter 38 and before 38, 24 (start of Section 7 in Segal); 42, 9; 42, 15; 51, 13. On the other hand, there are some marginal symbols (probably, but not certainly, written by the same copyist) also indicating beginnings of chapters and paragraphs.

The most frequent symbol is ד: on Page II, *l.* 8 (40, 18), to indicate the paragraph where the opening word of the end hemistich: ומשניהם, is repeated; on the same page, *l.* 24, indicating the paragraph on the subject of Death (41, 1); on Page III, *l.* 18, marking the paragraph beginning: מסר בשת שמעו בנים (41, 14); on Page IV, *l.* 16, to mark the paragraph on the Daughter: בת לאב מטמון שקר (42, 9 — and see also above, on MS. B). The above cases prove beyond a doubt that the symbol in question is an indication of a new chapter or paragraph, for that is where it invariably occurs, in reference to the context. It may be assumed that the copyist resorted to the same sign elsewhere, but margins have not been preserved in many of the spots where we would expect to see it, and we have no means of knowing whether it actually existed.[8]

Another symbol appears once at the top of Page V, the first line of which introduces a description of the mighty acts of God (42, 15). The sign is similar to the Greek letter ψ. Perhaps the sign connotes the content of this poetic portion which constitutes a psalm of praise to God, similar to the Biblical psalms ($= \psi[\alpha\lambda\mu\acute{o}\varsigma]$?). At any rate, the symbol here too coincides with the beginning of a chapter.

At the top of the left margin of this page occurs the only marginal note which perhaps serves as a kind of heading (see the Commentary, *ad loc*).

Copyist's Errors

The copyist was expert in his work and his script is particularly beautiful in the lines where the letters are small (see e.g. Pages VI–VII). In some places the copyist made mistakes but corrected himself. When a letter was forgotten, he inserted it above the line in the appropriate place (see Page III, *ll.* 16 and 25). In another place (Page VI, *l.* 19) he added the last letter underneath the line and forgot to correct the mistake (see the Notes, *ad loc*). He acted similarly when he omitted a whole word or a group of letters (Pages III, *l.* 2; VI, *ll.* 18 and 19). When he wrote a wrong letter or word he scratched out the mistake and inserted the correction above the erasure (Page III, *l.* 2) or he penned in the new letter over the erasure (Page V, *l.* 7 — where he began to write: ליון, instead of: עליון; traces of

---

[5] With the exception of one instance (Page V, *ll.* 14–15) where on account of the length of the first hemistich the scribe penned the second one beneath, on a new line. See the Commentary, *ad loc*.

[6] See *IEJ*, pp. 103 f.

[7] Regarding this mode of indicating chapters in the Scrolls, see Y. Yadin: *The Scroll of the War of the Sons of Light against the Sons of Darkness*, Oxford, 1962, p. 248.

[8] Similar signs indicating chapters and paragraphs are to be found in *The Manual of Discipline*.

the erased *lamed* can easily be detected between the lines, above the *'ayin*). In two places he tried to correct mistakes by altering the form of the previous letter in ink (Pages III, *l.* 25; IV, *l.* 16).

In a few instances the copyist did not notice his mistakes (see the Notes and Commentary to Pages II, *l.* 7; III, *l.* 1). The most serious case — which is of particular relevance to the development of MSS. corruptions — occurs on Page VII, before *l.* 8, where he omitted a whole verse (44, 3). This was because the opening letter of the line (*resh*) was identical with that at the beginning of the previous verse (see the Notes, and Commentary, *ad loc.*). Despite these errors the copyist still was an expert at his task.

Script and Date

Archaeologically speaking, the *terminus ad quem* of the scroll can be confidently fixed as 73 C.E., the year of the fall of Masada.[9] This alone makes the Scroll the earliest *Ben Sira* MS. extant (see below). But the date of this copy can also be fixed by paleographic data.[10]

The script may be defined as middle or late Hasmonean.[11] At any rate, it is unmistakably pre-Herodian[12] and it lies between the script of *Isaiah A* and the *Manual of Discipline*, on the one hand, and that of the Herodian script, which is well-represented by the other Scrolls from Cave 1, on the other. According to the script charts by Cross, it may be inserted between the example reproduced

in his fig. 2: 2 (125–100 B.C.E.) and that reproduced in his fig. 2: 3 (50–25 B.C.E.).[13] Up to a point, our script is similar to that of *Isaiah B* (though apparently the script of our Scroll is earlier), the date of which has been defined by Avigad as follows: 'It is intermediate in its forms between the preceding "Hasmonean" group (according to him, *Isaiah A* and the *Manual of Discipline* which he dates around the end of the 2nd century [Y.Y.]) and the following "Herodian" group.'[14]

A study of the script of the Scroll (reproduced on page 13 of the Hebrew section) — together with a study of the photographs — provides the following general characteristics:

Alef is small; its left leg is short and sometimes slightly bowed, not reaching the base-line of the right leg. The top of the left leg approaches the upper extremity of the diagonal stroke, which constitutes a certain development of the Hasmonean script; but it has not yet attained the Herodian form.

Bet is wider than in earlier scripts; the base stroke descends to the left and is executed in a separate stroke from left to right, and thus slightly crosses the downstroke.

Gimel is somewhat similar to the Herodian type. The left leg begins at the middle, or nearly so, of the right leg, and sometimes even lower than this. The left leg is sometimes slightly bowed. The top of the right leg occasionally displays a slight thickening, but not yet a true head.

Dalet is narrow; the top-line is executed by a stroke from left to right, beginning in an exaggerated tick, then descending slightly to the right.

He closely resembles the type beginning to appear in *Isaiah B*.

Waw has a triangular head resembling that of the *yod*, but its leg is longer.

Zayin is a simple downstroke, slightly bowed, without a head.

---

[9] Regarding the archaeological problems involved in the chronology of Masada, see *IEJ*, pp. 115 ff.

[10] For basic paleographical studies of Hebrew scripts of the Second Temple period, and the Scrolls in particular, see F.M. Cross, Jr.: The Development of the Jewish Script, apud G.E. Wright (ed.): *The Bible and the Ancient Near East* (Essays in Honor of William Foxwell Albright), New York, 1961, pp. 133 ff.; and N. Avigad: The Paleography of the Dead Sea Scrolls and Related Documents, in *Scripta Hierosolymitana* IV (1958) (The E. L. Sukenik Memorial Volume, C. Rabin and Y. Yadin eds.), pp. 56ff.

[11] Prof. Cross, who was kind enough to examine the photographs of the Scroll, does not hesitate in fixing the date between 100 and 75 B.C.E. At any rate, the first half of the first century B.C.E. seems quite safe to me. Prof. Avigad, too, reached the same conclusion, after examining the photographs.

[12] In the archaeological sense of the term 'Herodian', i.e. between 30 B.C.E. and 70 C.E.

[13] Cross: *op. cit.* (above, n. 10), p. 139.

[14] Avigad: *op. cit.* (above, n. 10), p. 73, as well as p. 75, col. IX of the chart.

Ḥet is narrow; the crossbar is slightly bowed and is executed in one stroke together with the left leg. The legs are straight.

Ṭet has a left arm projecting slightly upwards.

Yod has a large head and a short leg.

Kaf is narrow; the base-stroke descends slightly to the left. The final *kaf* still has a narrow, bowed head. The downstroke is of medium length, sometimes straight and other times bowed.

Lamed has an elongated top thickening at the end; the bottom tick is very small.

Mem has a base-line descending to the left. The left leg is short; the top-line resembles that of the *bet*; the left downstroke of the final *mem* sometimes turns upward and then straightens out. Occasionally the stroke slightly penetrates the top-line.

Nun has an almost nonexistant head. As a rule the letter is of medium size, but occasionally the copyist impulsively pens an unusually large letter. The final *nun* is usually still quite small.

Samekh is often open at the lower left, in contrast to the Herodian form, where it is completely closed.

'Ayin is particularly small and rounded.

Pe is narrow; its base-line descends to the left. The head is thickened. The final letter has a rounded head and a bowed downstroke. Sometimes the copyist resorts to an earlier form where the top does not curve down back to the right.

Ṣade has a slightly bent in and thickened right arm; the downstroke is hardly thickened at the top. The final form is bowed slightly at the bottom.

Qof is frequently small with a short tail; sometimes the cross-stroke of the head does not meet the tail and is particularly short.

Resh is occasionally very narrow.

Shin is of two kinds, which actually belong to the same type, as is reproduced on page 13 of the Hebrew section.

Taw is relatively small; the angle of the left leg is reminiscent of the *nun*.

The Text

Since this is the earliest MS. extant of an important part of *Ben Sira*, and the date of its copying, at any rate, falls within the range of a century or two of its original composition,[15] the chief contribution of the Scroll lies in its revelation of the original Hebrew version. We can also draw interesting conclusions regarding the reliability of the translations that have come down to us. Before dealing directly with this problem, even within the purview of a preliminary study like this, we must preface a brief survey of the present state of knowledge of this text and the problems involved. Till 1896, no Hebrew text of the book was known (with the exception of a number of isolated citations scattered in Talmudic and medieval literature); the sole sources for our knowledge of the text were the various surviving translations. The most important of them was, and still is, the Greek translation made by Ben Sira's Grandson in Egypt in the 38th year of the reign of Ptolemy Euergetes (evidently Euergetes II, surnamed Physcon), i.e. 132 B.C.E.[16] This translation, which appears in all the well-known uncial codices of the Septuagint, was made one or

---

[15] Today most scholars agree that *Ben Sira* was composed in the first third of the second century B.C.E. For the various arguments for this date, see the following works, which have aided me greatly in various matters:

G.H. Box & W.O.E. Oesterley: The Book of Sirach, pp. 268ff. (= 'Box & Oesterley'), apud R.H. Charles (ed.): *The Apocrypha and Pseudepigrapha* I (Apocrypha), Oxford, 1963 (= 'Charles').

I. Lévi: *L'Ecclésiastique* I, Paris, 1898, Chaps. XXXIX, 15–XLIX, 11 (= 'Lévi').

M.H. Segal: *The Complete Book of Ben Sira*, Jerusalem, 1958 (Hebrew) (= 'Segal').

R. Smend: *Die Weisheit des Jesus Sirach*, Berlin, 1906 (= 'Smend').

N. Peters: *Ecclesiasticus...*, Frieburg im Breisgau, 1902 (= 'Peters').

Facsimiles of the Fragments hitherto recovered of the Book of Ecclesiasticus in Hebrew, Oxford-Cambridge, 1901 (= 'Facsimile').

A.E. Cowley & A. Neubauer: *Ecclesiasticus*, Oxford, 1897, Chaps. XXXIX, 15–XLIX, 11 (= 'Cowley-Neubauer').

V. Ryssel: Die Sprüche Jesus, des Sohnes Sirachs, apud E. Kautzsch: *Die Apokryphen und Pseudepigraphen* I, Tübingen, 1921, pp. 230ff. (= 'Ryssel').

[16] Or circa 116 B.C.E., if Wilcken's theory is accepted — U. Wilcken: *Archiv für papyrusforschung und verwandte Gebiete* III, Leipzig, 1906, pp. 320–321. (I should like to thank my colleague I.L. Seeligmann for this reference.)

two generations at most before the Masada Scroll was copied. In addition to the Grandson's translation, there is one, among others, which reflects a recension of the Grandson's translation—which has largely been preserved in a number of Greek minuscule MSS., the most famous being known as 248.

The difficulty that faced scholars in understanding *Ben Sira* — not to speak of its restoration — from the Greek version sprang from the fact that even before the discovery of the Hebrew MSS. it transpired that the Greek translations could not always be relied upon.

The extant Greek versions abound, first of all, in many copyists' corruptions. Moreover — and this militates even more formidably against evaluating the version used by the translator — it has been conclusively shown that in many cases the Grandson failed to understand the Hebrew, and in others had difficulty in translating. There are also grounds for suspecting that, in more than a few instances, the version used by him was not completely 'pure' in spite of the fact that not more than several decades had elapsed between it and the initial composition of the book. But despite all these limitations, the Greek translation constitutes, to this day, the major basis for study of *Ben Sira*. This is due to the fact (which even now we shall have occasion to refer to) that we still lack a complete Hebrew version of all the chapters of the book, as they have survived in this translation. Another translation of note is the Syriac, known as the *Peshitta*. Most scholars today agree that this translation was made chiefly from a Hebrew source — of course at a much later period than the Grandson's effort — though the translator was helped, and often even influenced, by the Greek translation. Our Scroll enables us to prove, in a number of cases, the Syriac translator's independence of the Greek. This MS., too, is full of both 'original' and copyists' corruptions; in many places there are more lacunae than text.

A sensational development in the study of *Ben Sira* took place on May 13, 1896, when Prof. Solomon Schechter identified, amongst the bundles of MSS. brought from Palestine and Egypt by Mmes. Lewis and Gibson, a single leaf of *Ben Sira* containing chapters 39, 15–40, 8.[17] The dis-

covery of this single leaf led immediately to the identification of an additional nine leaves in the Bodleian at Oxford (chapters 40, 9–49, 11). All ten leaves were immediately published by Cowley and Neubauer (1897). Thus it transpired that the chapters preserved in the Masada Scroll figure among the chapters of the Hebrew original first studied and published. These discoveries led Schechter to have brought to Cambridge a significant part of the Cairo Synagogue Genizah (which had been the source of the preceding discoveries). He discovered additional leaves of this MS., which he designated MS. B, as well as leaves of other *Ben Sira* MSS. Subsequently, further leaves of both MS. B and other MSS. were discovered by scholars in different collections, all originating in the Cairo Genizah. Lately, Prof. Schirmann has announced fresh discoveries of additional leaves, including two of the same MS. B.[18] Five different MSS. are extant, respectively termed A, B, C, D and E. Since the chapters discovered at Masada figure only in MS. B, which incidentally is the largest and most beautifully executed, and not in the others, we shall confine ourselves to this MS. Before we do so, however, we must point out that to this list of Hebrew MSS. must be added two minor fragments discovered in Cave 2 at Qumran,[19] containing three whole words and traces of several additional ones which can be fitted into Chapter 9 of *Ben Sira*. The later chapter has survived, to date, only in MS. A. These fragments, which seem to be of slightly more recent date[20] than the Masada Scroll, were evidently written in column hemistichs, as well.

---

[17] By strange coincidence, the fragments found at Masada also begin at chapter 39.

[18] See H. Schirmann: A New Leaf from the Hebrew Book of Ben Sira, *Tarbiz* 27 (1958), pp. 440ff. (Hebrew); idem: Additional Leaves from the Book of Ben Sira, *ibid.* 29 (1960), pp. 125ff. (Hebrew). On the first leaf and the problems of the original text of Ben Sira, see also N.H. Tur-Sinai: A New Leaf for the Clarification of the Hebrew Book of Ben Sira, *Leshonenu* 22 (1958), pp. 213ff. (Hebrew).

[19] M. Baillet, J. T. Milik & R. de Vaux: Les 'Petites Grottes' de Qumran, Oxford, 1962 (= *DJD* III), pp. 75 ff; pl. XV. For these fragments, see also M.H. Segal: Ben-Sira in Qumran, *Tarbiz* 33 (1964), pp. 243ff. (Hebrew).

[20] The editors have dated it in the second half of the first century B.C.E. — *DJD* III, p. 75.

MS. B

This MS. was penned by an expert copyist, and, like the Masada Scroll (and MS. E), was arranged in hemistichs in double columns. It is of interest mainly in the abundant marginal corrections and *variae lectiones*, most of which are the work of its original copyist and the rest by another hand, or perhaps even two. Initial study of MS. B revealed that only rarely could the marginal notes be attributed to corrections or scribal errors, made by the copyist or other scribes. On the contrary, it can usually be argued that what we have here is an attempt to introduce, into the margin, variants from other MSS. available to the copyist and the other readers. A comparison of MS. B (= B*text*) and its marginal glosses (= B*marg*) both to the translations and to other Genizah MSS., where corresponding chapters had been preserved, furthered the critical study of the original Hebrew text of *Ben Sira*. Scholars engaged in these painstaking studies[21] were not able to reach absolutely definite conclusions and did not always agree among themselves, chiefly because it was evident that the MSS. from which the Genizah MSS. had been transcribed (including the marginal notes) were already partly corrupt in the Middle Ages.[22] For instance, the text sometimes agreed with the Greek translations but the marginal reading with the Syriac, even though on the whole the marginal reading agreed with the Greek. Sometimes, of course, there was no common ground between any of the versions. Moreover, where a comparison could be made, the marginal variant agreed with MS. D. A number of scholars, Lévi and Peters, in particular, accept (as we shall see further with a certain degree of justification) in many cases the superiority of the primary source of the marginal readings over the text. Others, however, including Smend, regarded it as slightly corrupt and detected a recension that tended to introduce Aramaisms or more 'vulgar' phraseology. These conclusions even led a number of scholars (again especially Lévi and Peters) to the conclusion that both text and marginal readings derive from a common archetypal text which itself

had become corrupt,[23] since the same errors and divergencies are found in both versions. Of course, our survey by no means exhausts all the views and problems involved, but it is sufficient to indicate the many difficulties faced by the investigator of this subject. Moreover, we must not forget to mention that, from the very moment of their discovery, there were a number of scholars who questioned the validity of the contention that the various Genizah MSS. represent — with of course certain corruptions and accretions — the Hebrew original. Prof. Margoliouth went further, prompted by isolated marginal glosses in Persian, and maintained that the Genizah text is from a medieval Persian translation which was based partly on the Greek and partly on the Syriac.[24] Margoliouth was not alone in this approach, and even today a number of modern scholars of note still doubt the autheticity of the Genizah version, maintaining it to be a translation made in the Middle Ages from the Syriac or the Greek.[25]

We have now succeeded in obtaining a portion of a Hebrew text dating from the Second Temple period, close to the generation of Ben Sira's Grandson. With its help a number of problems can be unequivocally solved and additional light thrown on others.

First of all, as we have noted earlier, one significant conclusion unmistakably emerges even from the most cursory study: the text of the scroll unquestionably confirms that B*text*[26] and the glosses of B*marg basically* represent the original Hebrew version! In other words, subsequent research must concentrate even now (and particularly now) on the detailed problems involved in the purification of the text — as it has survived in the Genizah MSS. — from the accretions, duplicatory readings,

---

[21] See particularly Lévi, Smend and Peters.

[22] The various Genizah MSS. are dated between the 11th (or perhaps the end of the 10th) and the 12th centuries C.E.

[23] Regarding duplicatory readings being introduced into the text, see also Tur-Sinai: *op. cit.* (above, n. 18).

[24] See particularly Box & Oesterley.

[25] For literature on this, see A.A. Di Lella: Authenticity of the Geniza Fragments of Sirach, *Biblica*, XLIV (1963), pp. 171. For an extremist opinion on this matter, see most recently H.L. Ginsberg: *JBL* LXXIV (1955), pp. 93ff.

[26] Further on we shall devote a special section to MS. B. As has been noted already, the chapters surviving in the Scroll are found only in MS. B. On the other hand, most of what has been said applied also to many of the problems involved in the other MSS.

glosses and corruptions. This has been done in the past with great success by the notable scholars who devoted themselves to study of *Ben Sira*.[27] They now have new and primary material available which will facilitate additional progress towards a long desired goal.

Within the framework of this preliminary survey I naturally cannot subject these problems to detailed treatment, especially as this would require complete mastery of the techniques of textual and linguistic criticism.

Before we proceed to a comparative analysis of the text with other versions, we must deal with one basic phenomenon of importance: the relative *defectiva* spelling employed by the text. A considerable weight of scholarly opinion has tended for some time to the view that the original texts were written *defectiva*, since this was the only way of accounting for some of the variations between MS. B and the Greek translation (the authors of which must evidently have read the consonants in the Hebrew original with a different vocalisation, a procedure hardly feasible had the text been *plena*), and particularly the corruptions and misunderstandings in the Greek (and Syriac) version itself. An obvious and instructive example of this can be detected in our Scroll (Page IV, *l.* 11; 42, 5c): צלע, where the Grandson read consonants as forming the word: צֶלַע, the true reading being: צֹלֵעַ (see the Commentary, *ad loc*).

Another feature to be noted at this preliminary stage is the style of handwriting and spelling. Textual critics have been quick to spot corruptions prompted by copyists' (and even translators') errors, where they confused similar letters, as ב and כ, ה and ח, י and ו, etc. The earlier text now available enables us to distinguish a further type of error of much earlier vintage, prompted by the misreading of ligatures. An error of this type which hitherto could not be detected occurs here on Page VI, *l.* 13 (43, 19): When the copyist transcribed from the text serving as the model for B*text*, the word: כסנה, altered to read: כספיר! A study of the photographs indicates how such a mistake could arise when the letters in question are partly joined to each other (see the Notes, *ad loc.*).

We shall begin our examination by comparing the text of the Scroll with that of B*marg*. The results of this examination are tabulated in the Hebrew section (on pp. 7–8 and 9). Table 1 presents cases where the Scroll and B*marg* agree, but diverge from B*text*. Table 2, on the other hand, presents cases where the reading in the Scroll and in B*text* is identical, but diverges from that of B*marg*.

The full implications of the conclusions emerging from Table 1, as in the two others, become clear only after a study of the detailed Commentary of the second part of this survey. But a number of basic findings become apparent even at this stage. First of all, the fact stands out that the Scroll and B*marg* versions agree in these instances with that used by the Greek translator. In some of these cases the Syriac, too, conforms to our text (see the Commentary), but there are cases where the Syriac agrees, on the contrary, with B*text* (נוצר מחמס, etc.). This phenomenon is reflected not only in the obvious instances where B*text* is corrupt, or where a few lines of the text are missing (Pages VI, *ll.* 9–10; VII, *l.* 22) or misplaced, but also in the basic meaning of a number of verses (such as: – נצר חמס נוצר מחמס; יתר–יין; ועל משפט–ועל מצדיק;ובת–ובית; מופיע בצאתו–מביע בצרתו; לשון–לשאן;וממנו–וזמני etc.). Some variants, however, are not fundamental and occasionally arise merely from misreading, misunderstanding or mistakes in copying (ונוקש–ינקש; חיל–מחול; הוי–חיים; יד–זר etc.). Other variants testify to basic differences of approach deliberately introduced into the text. A striking example of this is the role of the sun and moon in the determining of the appointed seasons, when in B*text* an unmistakable attempt was made to equate the sun with the moon (by writing: בם, instead of: לו, as in the Scroll (Page V, *l.* 24; B*marg*: בו). We may perhaps assume that here the text consulted by the scribe of B*text* belonged to the Dead Sea Sect (see the Commentary, *ad loc.*).[28] We may perhaps in-

---

27 See above, n. 15.

28 If this were true, it could be concluded that the Masada Scroll did *not* belong to the same Sect, thus disposing of the contention of the editors of the Qumran Scrolls that the very fact that MS. B is written in hemistichs indicates that it had been transcribed from a Qumran Scroll — *DJD* III, p. 75 and n. 1 there. For objections to this argument, see also Segal: *op. cit.* (above, n. 19).

TABLE 1

Cases of Scroll and B[marg.] agreement, in contrast to B[text]

B*text*	Scroll and B*marg.*	Chapter		Line Page
לרעה	לזרה (לזרא)	27 39	לט לז	1 I
מחול	חיל	13 40	מ יו	3 II
עם עם שאתו	עם שאתו	14	יז	4 II
נוצר מחמס	נצר חמס	15	יח	5 II
סלע	צר (צור)	15	יח	5 II
יין	יתר (יותר)	18	כא	8 II
סוד	יסור	29c	לה	22 II
כמו אש	כאש	30	לו	23 II
חיים	הוי	1 41	מא א	24 II
ינקש	ונוקש	2c	ד	2 III
סרב	אפס המראה (המרה)	2c	ד	2 III
חכמה	חמדה	12	יו	14 III
ימי מספר	מספר ימים	13	יז	15 III
ואוצר מוסתר	ורשימה (וסימה) מסותרת	14b	יח	16 III
אל זנות	על פחז	17	כב	20 III
יושב על	ושר על	17	כב	20 III
מחובר	משותף	18c	כד	22 III
וממקום	ממקום	18c	כד	22 III
על זר	על יד	18c	כד	22 III
חרפה	חסד	22c	ל	3 IV
ועל מצדיק	ועל משפט	2 42	מב ב	7 IV
חובר	שותף	3	ג	8 IV
ולקח	שואה (ושואה)	7	ח	13 IV
ושב וישיש ונוטל עצה בזנות	ושב כושל (ו)עונה בזנות	8	ט	14 IV
מטמנת	מטמון	9	יא	16 IV
מטוב	טוב	14	כ	25 IV
ובית	ובת	14	כ	25 IV
אשה	חרפה	14	כ	25 IV
רצונו	מעשיו	15c	כב	2 V
מביע בצרתו	מופיע בצאתו	2 43	מג ב	18 V
מצוק	מוצק	4	ד	20 V
לשאון	לשון	4c	ה	21 V
גדיל	גדול	5	ו	22 V
בם	לו (בו)	7	ח	24 V
וזמני	וממנו	7	ח	24 V
בחדשו	כשמו	8	ט	25 V
ואורו מזהיר	עד ומשריק (ועדי)	9	יא	2 VI
נאדרה	נהדרה	11	יג	4 VI
למען	למענו	14	יו	7 VI

* Where blank, the word or words are not given in B[text].

Table 1 (continued)

Btext	Scroll and Bmarg.	Chapter	Line Page
יחול	יחיל	מג יח 43 17	9 VI
	ובכחו; הרים	יח 17	9 VI
	תחריף תימן	יט 16b	10 VI
זלעפות צפון	עלעול	יט 17b	10 VI
ברשף	כרשף	כ 17c	11 VI
דרתו	רדתו	כ 17c	11 VI
ישכון	ישפך	כב 19	13 VI
אבותינו	את אבותינו	מד א 44 1	6 VII
חוק	קו	ז 5	11 VII
בדרם	בדרם נכבדו	ט 7	13 VII
	חכמתם תשנה עדה	יח 15	22 VII
	ותהלתם יספר קהל	יח 15	22 VII
לעת	בעת	כ 17	24 VII

clude in this category, too, the 'error' (Page II, *l.* 22) found in Btext where: סוד מעים, is written instead of: יסור מעים; this can perhaps be attributed to the frequency of the term: סוד, in the writings of the Sect.

But the most interesting variants between MS. B and our Scroll relate precisely to those instances where Bmarg has Aramaisms or words with synonymous implications to those in Btext. Hitherto, scholars have agreed that these are of later origin, introduced to 'modernise' the style. Now, our Scroll proves the very opposite to be true. It stands to reason that, on the contrary, Btext (in these places) tried to Hebraise Aramaic words, to explain difficult or somewhat obscure words and phrases, by the use of more common terms or Biblical idioms, etc. The following examples clearly indicate this: שימה (סימה)[29] in the Scroll and Bmarg — as against:

שותף – חובר; כאש – כמו אש; צר – סלע; אוצר, in Btext; על פחז – אל זנות; משריק – מזהיר; שואה – לקח; etc. In concluding our discussion of Table 1, it should be noted that most of the Bmarg glosses are the work of the actual copyist of Btext. In a number of cases (e.g.: יסור; אפס המראה; מטמון), however, they are by another hand. For other findings that emerge from this table, see below, in the detailed Commentary to each verse.

Had Table 1 accounted for all the data emerging from a comparison of Bmarg and the Scroll, we could quite easily and simply have concluded that Bmarg is closer to the original than is Btext. But in actuality the matter is not so simple, as emerges from Table 2, indicating that, in a considerable number of instances, the text of the Scroll corresponds to that of Btext and *not* to Bmarg; it is also evident that the Greek translator had before him the Scroll and Btext version! In other words, in those instances where the Scroll and Bmarg agree, but diverge from Btext, or where the Scroll agrees with Btext and diverges from Bmarg, the Scroll conforms to the Hebrew version consulted by Ben Sira's Grandson. This fact is underlined by Table 3 (illustrating the cases where the Scroll *diverges* from both Btext and Bmarg), which we shall discuss further on. However, this conclusion is also not completely without its difficulties. For instance, in at least one interesting case, in Table 2 (Page III,

---

[29] The use of *śin* in the Scroll, instead of the *samekh* of Bmarg (and Btext), is consistent and testifies to the antiquity of the Scroll; at any rate, we can learn from this that there is no need to resort to Tur-Sinai's explanation (*op. cit.* [above, n. 18], p. 223) of verse 38, 4, in Btext, where the reading is: תרופות, instead of Bmarg: שמים. Tur-Sinai's observation that the reading: שמים, must be regarded as an error of the copyist, who found here the creation of heaven and earth, is superfluous. On the other hand, the substitution of: תרופות, for: שמים, fits in with the character of Btext, as is seen below.

TABLE 2

Cases of Scroll and B^text agreement, in contrast to B^marg.

B*marg.*	Scroll and B*text*	Chapter	Line Page
רעה	כלה	מ יג 10 40	23 I
בן	נין	מא ח 5 41	6 III
מולידו	תולידו	יב 9	10 III
לקללתה	לקללה	יג 9b—11	11 III
מאונם אל אונם	מאפס אל אפס	יד 10	12 III
בן	כן	יד 10	12 III
טוב	טובת	יז 13	15 III
מאדון	מאיש	יט 15	17 III
משפטו	משפטי	כ 16	18 III
ונגיד	תגור	כד 18c	22 III
מיהשע	ומהשיב (מהשב)	כו 19d	24 III
התחרישו	החריש (מחריש)	כז 20	25 III
דבר	דברי	ל 22c	3 IV
על	כל	לא 1 42	4 IV
אל	על	מב א 1c	6 IV
אל	על	ב 2	7 IV
חשבון	מקנה	ה 4b	10 IV
מוסר	ממחיר	ה 4b	10 IV
תחשוב	מספר (תספור)	ח 7	13 IV
תזכר	זכר	יח 12	23 IV
מטוב	מטיב	כ 14	25 IV
לקח	לקחו	כג 16	2 V
להחזיק	להתחזק	כה 17c	5 V
עשה	עשהו	מג ו 5 43	22 V
עליון	אדני (ייי)	ו 5	22 V
עת עת (עד עת)	עתות	ז 6	23 V
והיא	הוא	ט 8	25 V
מערץ	מרצף	י 8c	1 VI
כמרומי	במרומי	יא 9	2 VI
ישון	ישח	יב 10	3 VI
עושה	עשיה	יג 11	4 VI
בכבודו	בכבודה	יד 12	5 VI
ויד לא	ויד אל	יד 12	5 VI
זיקים	זיקות	יה 13	6 VI
מקוה	מקור (מקורו)	כג 14	14 VI
ענן	ענן טל	כו 22	17 VI
אוצר	איים	כז 23	18 VI
חלק להם עליון	חלק עליון	מד ב 2 44	7 VII
במס׳	בספרתם	ו 4c	10 VII

l. 6 = 41, 5), it is the Greek which agrees with B*marg* (בן), in contrast to the Scroll and B*text* (נין). Noteworthy in this context is the fact that the B*marg* gloss here is the work of another scribe and not of the B*text* copyist. This constitutes a further proof that the MS. used by the Grandson was already corrupt in a number of places.

A study of Table 2 clearly indicates that in the cases discussed the text of the Scroll and B*text* is to be preferred over that of B*marg* (see the Commentary). A certain portion of the variants in B*marg* arise from simple copyists' errors (תולידו–מולידו; תגור–ונגיד; כל–על; מטיב–מטוב; במרומי–כמרומי; ישח–ישון; ויד אל–ויד לא; כן–בן; משפטי–משפטו; מקור–מקוה etc.). Others represent attempts to provide a gloss or paraphrase (מקנה–חשבון; ממחיר–מוסר; ספר–חשב; חלק עליון–חלק להם עליון; מאפס–מאונם etc.; see also additional examples in the Notes). The foregoing would seem to indicate that the B*marg* glosses cannot be reckoned as having been taken from a single MS., or at least that this MS. (which generally remained faithful to the original text) had been subject to corruptions, misinterpretations and attempts to provide a gloss and a simpler paraphrase.

But the most instructive contribution of the text of our Scroll to the determining of the characters of the Genizah MSS. and the Greek and Syriac versions emerges from Table 3. There we have tabulated all the cases (about 90) where the Scroll diverges from both B*text* and B*marg*. We shall preface our analysis of this table, too, by outlining a number of general findings. First, here, too, it can be proved that the Scroll agrees with the Greek in a considerable number[30] of the instances cited. This phenomenon is noticeable not only in the text itself (e.g. Pages II, *ll.* 3, 6, 8, 23; III, *ll.* 1, 5, 6, 7, 24; IV, *ll.* 4, 8, 12, 21; V, *li.* 3, 4, 6, 18, 20; VI, *ll.* 12, 13, 14, 18; VII, *l.* 20), but also in many instances where whole verses or portions of them are missing in the Genizah MSS. (Pages II, *l.* 2; IV, *ll.* 2, 11; V, *ll.* 7, 12; VII, *l.* 19). To this must be added a number of instances where, it can be demonstrated,

the text consulted by the Grandson was similar to that of the Scroll, but had been misread by him. In some cases the Syriac agrees with the Scroll, but much less frequently than we have noted in connection with the Greek (cf., e.g., Pages II, *ll.* 3, 6, 23; III, *ll.* 6, 7; IV, *l.* 21; V, *l.* 1; VI, *l.* 18). On the other hand, a few cases may be noted where the Syriac and the Scroll agree, but both diverge from the Greek (e.g. Page V, *l.* 16), a further indication that the Syriac was not dependent on the Greek. But as a rule it can be shown that here, too, the Syriac is often badly corrupted and full of lacunae. Though the agreement between the Greek and Scroll texts is the most striking feature of the instances collated in Table 3, the situation is reversed in some isolated cases. One such exception is Page III, *l.* 19 (41, 16b), where the Greek conforms to MS. B: לשמר, instead of: לבוש; another interesting example is to be found in Page V, *l.* 13 (42, 23), where the Greek (as in MS. B) read: נשמע, instead of: נשמר. There is here an instructive example — there are quite a few more like it — (see the Commentary for details) of an early error arising from the mishearing of a dictated text. The most significant example, from the point of view of the evolution of the MSS., is 44, 16 (see end, Page VII), from which it emerges that both in the Hebrew version employed by the Greek translator and in MS. B there occurred here a verse on Enoch which is not found in the Scroll. We may conclude from this (see the Commentary, *ad loc.*, on this point), that there already existed, during the Grandson's lifetime, another version which attempted to 'improve' Ben Sira on this point.

Another important feature to be noted is the fact that *l.* 22 of Page IV (42, 11e) occurs in both the Scroll and MS. B, but is missing in the Greek. We may similarly note that, in a number of cases, the verse order in the Scroll corresponds to that of B*text* and/or B*marg*, in contrast to the faulty order of the Greek. This is the fault of the Greek copyists and not of the text drawn on by the Grandson. On the other hand, in many cases the verse order of the Scroll conforms to that of the Greek, but diverges from that of the Genizah MSS.

Some instances where the Greek diverges from the text of our Scroll reflect error on the part of the translator (who drew on a text similar to ours).

[30] This number may be much larger, since in many instances where the variants are pure synonyms, it is impossible to reconstruct the exact Hebrew text drawn on by the Grandson, e.g.: כח–חיל; מטמין–מצפין; סס–עש; שאין–אשר אין etc.

TABLE 3

Cases of Scroll divergence from both B^{text} and B^{marg}.

B*marg.*	B*text*	Scroll	Chapter	Line Page
	[כל מש]	כל מש] [	12 40	מ יה	2 II
חיל מחיל	מחיל אל חיל	חיל מעול	13	יו	3 II
	כקרדמות	כקרמית	16	יט	6 II
	גפת	גפות	16	יט	6 II
מטר נדעכה	מטר נדעכו	חצר נדעך	16	יט	6 II
	וחסד לעולם לא ימוט	חסד כעד לא תכרת	17	כ	7 II
חיי יותר שכל	חיי יין ושכר	חיי יתר שכר	18	כא	8 II
	שם	ושאר	19c	כג	10 II
	ממסתולל	מפני חצף	28	לג	20 II
לאיש עז נפשות	לאיש עוז נפש	בפי עז נפש	30	לו	23 II
כאש בוערת	תבער כמו אש	כאש תבער	30	לו	23 II
	חיל	כח	1d 41	מא ב	25 II
	האח למות כי	הע (= הרע?) למות מה	2	ג	1 III
	לאיש אונים	לאין אונים (= אונים)	2	ג	1 III
	זכר כי ראשונים ואחרונים עמך	זכר קדמון ואחרון עמך	3	ה	3 III
	זה חלק	זה קץ	4	ו	4 III
	לאלף שנים מאה ועשר	לעשר מאה ואלף שנים	4c	ז	5 III
דבת ערים	דבר רעים	תולדות רעים	5	ח	6 III
	ממשלת רע	תאבד ממשלה	6	ט	7 III
	מצפין	מטמין	15	יט	17 III
	נאה לשמר	נאוה לבוש	16b	כא	19 III
	על שקר	על קשר	18	כג	21 III
פי רעיך	אפי רעך	את פני שארך	21a	כו	24 III
מחשבות	מחשבית	מחשות	21b	כז	25 III
התחרישו	מהחריש	החריש	20	כז	25 III
	ומהתק...	ומתבונן	20b	כח	1 IV
		מהתעשק עם שפחה לך	22a	כט	2 IV
		ומהתקומם על יצעיה	22b	כט	2 IV
	ומאחרי מתת אל תנאץ	ומאחר מתת חרף	22d	ל	3 IV
על אור	כל סוד	כל דבר	1 42	לא	4 IV
	בוש	בויש	1c	לב	5 IV
ואדון	ואדון יארח	ודרך	3	מב ג	8 IV
	שחק	שחקי	4a	ד	9 IV
תמורת	תמהות	תמחי	5a	ד	9 IV
		[ ] ועבד רע וצלע מהלכת	5b–c	ו	11 IV
	ידים רפות תפתח	ידים רבות מפתח	6	ז	12 IV
מפקד יד תחשוב	תפקיד יד תספור	תפקיד מספר	7	ח	13 IV
ושואה ותתה	ומתת ולקח	שואה ומתת	7 42	מב ח	13 IV
	פן תגור	פן תמאס	9c–d	יב	17 IV

*   Where blank, the word or words are not given in B^{text}.

** Where blank, the word or words are not noted in B^{marg}.

Table 3 (continued)

Bmarg.	Btext	Scroll	Chapter		Line Page
פן תתפתה	פן תפותה	פן תחל	10a, c	יג	18 IV
ובכ׳ איש	ועל אישה		10a, c	יג	18 IV
(?)	וקללת	וקהלת	11c	יו	21 IV
	אל יהי אשנב	אל יהי	11e	יז	22 IV
	תתן	תבן	12	חי	23 IV
	עש	סס	13	יט	24 IV
ובת מחרפת (מחפרת) תביע חרפה	ובית מחרפת תביע אשה	ובת מפחדת מכול חרפה	14	כ	25 IV
	אזכר; ואספרה	אזכרה; ואשננה	15	כא	1 V
	אלהים	אדני	15c	כב	2 V
	זורחת; על כל מעשיו	זהרת; מלא מעשיו	16	כג	3 V
נפלאות גבורותיו	נפלאות ייי	כל נפלאותיו	17	כד	4 V
	ובכל מערומיהם	ובמערמיהם	18	כו	6 V
		כי ידע עליון וגו׳	18c—d	כז	7 V
כל שכל; חלף מנו	כל שכל; חלפו	שכל; אבדו	20	כט	9 V
		הלוא כל מעשיו וגו׳	22	לב	12 V
הכל נשמע	הכל ישמע	והכל נשמר	23	לג	13 V
	זה מזה	זה לעמת זה	24	לד	14 V
טוב	טובו	טיבם	25	לה	16 V
רקע על טהר	(כל הפסוק חסר)	ורקיע לטהר	מג א 43 1		17 V
מופיע בצאתו חמה	מביע בצרתו חמה	מופיע בצאתו נכסה	2	ב	18 V
מה נורא	מה נורא	כלי נורא	2	ב	18 V
	חרבו	חרב	3	ג	19 V
	מהם	מעשי	4	ד	20 V
גדול עליון	גדיל ייי	גדול אדני	5	ו	22 V
ירח ירח עת עת (עד עת) שבות	ירח ירח עתות שבות	ירח יאריח עתות	6	ז	23 V
בו מועד; וזמני חוק	בם מועד; וזמני חוק	לו מועד; וממנו חג	7	ח	24 V
תואר; והדר	תואר; והדר	תור; והוד	9	יא	2 VI
ועדי משריק	ואורו מזהיר	עד ומשריק	9	יא	2 VI
	אל	אדני	10	יב	3 VI
הוד	חוק	חוג	12	יד	5 VI
בקר	ברק	ברד	13	יה	6 VI
	ברא	פרע	14	יו	7 VI
יזעים	***	יניף	17	יח	9 VI
אימתו	***	אמרתו	16b	יט	10 VI
	יניף	יפרח	17c	כ	11 VI
לבנה; יהבה	לבנה; יגהה	לבנו; יהג	18	כא	12 VI
	יהמה	יתמיה	18	כא	12 VI
	ויציץ כספיר	ויצמח כסנה	19	כב	13 VI
וכרקב; מקוה	וכרקבו; מקורו	וכרגב; מקור	20	כג	14 VI
משובתו תשיק	מחשבתו תשיק	אמר[תו] תעמיק	23	כד	18 VI

*** B text damaged at this spot.

Table 3 (continued)

Bmarg.	Btext	Scroll	Chapter		Line Page
רבה	רבה	רהב	25 43	כט מג	20 VI
	יש עוד	יש אל (?)	30	לד	25 VI
	וגדלו	וגדלה	2 44	מד ב	7 VII
רודי; בגבורם	דורי; בגבורתם	(כל הפסוק חסר)	3	ג	— —
יועצים	היועצים	ויועצים	3c	ד	8 VII
	במחקרותם	במחקק[תם]	4	ה	9 VII
	אשר אין	שאין	9	יא	15 VII
	(כל הפסוק חסר)	בבריתם עמד זרעם וגו׳	12	יה	19 VII
	וצדקתם	וכבודם	13	יו	20 VII
(כמו במגילה)	(כל הפסוק חסר)	חכמתם תשנה עדה וגו׳	15	יח	22 VII
	חנוך נמצא תמים וגו׳		16	יט	— —

Now however, we can trace the manner in which many of the corruptions arose, e.g. on Page II, *l.* 7 (40, 17) we find the phrase: כעד לא תכרת; in MS. B the reading is: לעולם לא ימוט. It is clear that the mistake made in the Greek (which read: כעֵדן) and in the Syriac (which read: עֵדן) was a corruption of the Scroll text and not of the text represented by MS. B.

In the above cases, a comparison of the Scroll with Btext and/or Bmarg generally indicates the same features that we have noted above, in our discussion of Tables 1 and 2.

In some cases, mistakes of early and late copyists are embedded in the Genizah versions (Pages III, *l.* 1: קשר – שקר; לאין אונים – לאיש אונים; III, *l.* 21: רבות – רפות; IV, *l.* 9: תמחי – תמהות; IV, *l.* 12: ירח יאריח – ירח ירח; V, *l.* 23: מפתח – תפתח; VII, *l.* 9: במחקקתם – במחקרותם), including examples of mishearing, misunderstanding, dittography (Page IV, *l.* 13), etc. On the other hand, we are likewise confronted by instances where the versions consulted by the copyists of the Genizah MSS. already contained glosses, simple paraphrases of 'difficult' or 'Aramaic' words (Page IV, *ll.* 18, 23) or their Hebraisation. There are several cases where it is clear that the copyists endeavoured to soften or give a different meaning to the original text (see particularly Pages II, *l.* 8; III, *l.* 24; IV, *l.* 25; V, *ll.* 14, 18, 24; VI, *l.* 25); sometimes this operation expresses itself in what appears to be deliberate omission (Page IV, *l.* 2).

A study of Tables 1–3 does not exhaust all the problems involved in the relationship between the archetypal text of Bmarg and that of Btext, since the Scroll text often corresponds only *partially* with the Bmarg wording, and for the rest follows Btext. In conclusion, the following general findings may be noted:

a. In spite of many variants, the Scroll text is basically identical with that of the Genizah MSS.

b. Where the texts of Btext and Bmarg differ,[31] they represent two recensions which diverge from each other at a period prior to the date of the Genizah MSS. In both versions there already occur a considerable number of corruptions arising both from copyists' errors and from deliberate re-editing. As a rule, it would appear that Btext represents a more popular version, which may have been influenced in its final form by a version current among the Sect of the Dead Sea Scrolls.

c. The text used by the Grandson is the *closest* to that of the Scroll. A considerable portion of the variants found in the Greek can be attributed to the Grandson's own mistakes, and to later copyists. That certain corruptions already existed in the

---

[31] The attention we have given to variant readings should not lead the reader to imagine that we are dealing here with two basically different texts. On the contrary, the majority of verses agree in all the versions.

text used by the Grandson is borne out, too, by our Scroll.

d. The text of our Scroll (with the exception of the few mistakes and lacunae in it) is closest to — and is perhaps identical with — the original, constituting the archetype for a number of recensions whose final development can be traced in those consulted by the copyist of B*text* and the annotators of B*marg.*

e. Since the last chapters have not survived among the Masada Scroll fragments, we are unfortunately precluded from clarifying a number of very important problems connected with chapter 51.

But we must be thankful for what *has* survived. The efforts of the excavators do indeed bear out the words of Ben Sira, that: 'It is nigh to those who seek her and he who giveth his soul doth find her' (51, 26).

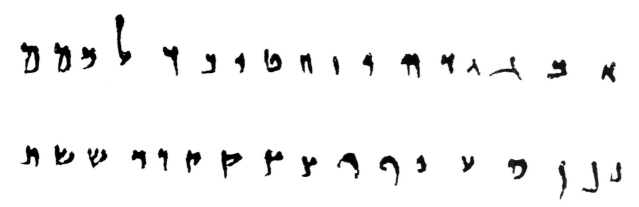

A representative alphabet of the Scroll (ca. 2:1).

THE TEXT OF THE SCROLL

The verses of the Scroll are reproduced below in their order, accompanied by two groups of notes: the *Notes* deal exclusively with paleographical problems involved in deciphering and correct reading; the *Commentary* deals with the comparison of variants and attempted restorations, etc. I have limited myself very often to cursory reference, since previous editors have already elucidated the meaning of the words and the intentions of Ben Sira in most of the instances where the Scroll conforms to B*text* or B*marg*. At the end of the Commentary, I give a restored text in both the original Hebrew and in English translation, which includes the portions not preserved in the Scroll fragments owing to its decayed state. In the English translation of the restored text, Mr. A. Newman generally followed Box & Oesterley (Charles ed.), although in several cases he has modified in accord with the new Masada text. This translation is merely intended to facilitate cor-relation between the existing Masada text and the restored text as based on the Cairo Genizah versions. For the exact meaning of my suggested interpretation, however, my actual Commentary must be consulted in each case. In the present section, I have attempted a restoration of only those lines which contain at least the slightest trace of a letter. I have not restored the text of the portions completely missing, since the Scroll gives not the slightest assistance in such reconstruction. The restoration has mainly been based on MS. B, though on rare occasions, when the text preserved would seem to indicate our version to be closer to the Greek or the Syriac, I have followed one of the latter. In all cases, however, I have indicated such insertions by square brackets. No attempt has been made to provide a vocalised text, since it is precisely in this form — *defectiva*, in most cases — that the state of the original text can be more clearly ascertained.

I,2–4/39,27–28c

I

(See Plate 1)

2	לֹפְכו [נֹ לזרה [	] [	]	27
3	יקו] יֵעֹ ים]	] [	]	28
4	יניחֹו הם]	] [	]	28c

Only the top left portion has survived of *Col. B*, as well as two words of *l. 23*.

1 Nothing has survived of this line but from the position of *l. 2*, which is even with *l. 2* of *Col. A* on Page II, we can safely assume that there was one line above this.

2 לֹפְכו [נֹ Reading undoubtedly correct. The lower left extremity of the *pe* is joined to the *kaf*. A slight trace of the *nun* is also visible.

3 ים, of הרים, is clearly visible.

4 הם.... The letter preceding the *he* cannot be deciphered with certainty.

2 לזרה Thus B*marg*: לזרא (see *Numbers* 11:20); Samaritan version: לזרה; B*text*: לרעה (cf. *Ben Sira* 37, 30).

3 Since only: ים..., has survived in B*text* too, it is impossible to decide on the basis of our Scroll between the various suggested restorations: הרים] (Cowley-Neubauer, Lévi, Segal), or: צור]ים (Smend). Cf. the Syriac: טורא. At any rate, the ending: ים..., agrees with B*text* and it is difficult to harmonise it with the Greek.

4 הם יניחֹו... This line is not preserved in B*text*, owing to a tear. Of the restorations, based on the Greek and Syriac versions (καὶ τὸν θυμὸν τοῦ ποιήσαντος αὐτοὺς κοπάσουσιν; ורוחא דמן דברא אינן מניחן) Lévi and Segal seem correct with regard to the last word: יניחו (Peters: ישביתו); for the word

I, 5–II, 1/39, 29–40, 11

5	‏[ראו‎	]	[	] 29
6	‏[עִׂים‎	]	[	] 30c
7	‏[וׄ‎	]	[	] 30
8	‏[הׄו (יו)‎	]	[	] 31
9	‏[יׄ‎	]	[	] 32
23	‏[וש כלה‎	]	[	] 10

5 ‏רׄאו‎.... Traces of the *resh* are discernible; the: ‏או‎, is clearly visible.

6 ‏עִׂים‎.... A tear separates the lower part of the final *mem* from the upper. The *yod* is squeezed tightly between the left end of the *'ayin* and the final *mem*.

7 The upper tip of the *waw* is visible.

8 Only the two last letters have been preserved: ‏הׄו‎, or: ‏יׄו‎, and it is difficult to decide which, though:

8 ‏הׄו‎... The upper left tip of the *he* is discernible, though it might well be that this is the tip of a *yod*. The *waw* is clearly discernible.

23 ‏וש כלה‎... These letters are found on a tiny fragment, the left side of which contains the beginning of *ll.* 22–24 of *Col. A* on Page II.

‏הו‎, is to be preferred. B*text*: ‏פיו‎; B*marg*: ‏פיהו‎.

9 The last letter (*yod*) is clearly discernible and fits in with the reading: ‏הנחתי‎, of MS. B.

before the last, Lévi and Peters proposed: ‏בוראם‎, but Segal's reading of: ‏עושהם‎, should be followed.

5 The last word has not been preserved in B*text*, owing to a tear. As the three last letters are clearly discernible in the Scroll: ‏ראו‎, Smend was right when he read: ‏נבראו‎ (Cowley-Neubauer, Lévi, Peters, Segal: ‏נוצרו‎). The Greek: ἔκτισται; the Syriac: ‏אתברי‎.

6 The last word has not been preserved in B*text*, owing to a tear. The ending: ‏עִׂים‎..., disposes of the proposals of Smend and Peters to read: ‏רשע‎, and lends support to the reading suggested by Lévi and Segal: ‏רעים‎, and perhaps: ‏רשעים‎. The Greek: ἀσεβεῖς; the Syriac: ‏לרשיעא‎.

7 Only the last letter (*waw*) has survived. It is of course difficult to restore the text on the basis of one letter, but this agrees with the last letter of the line in MS. B: ‏יפקדו‎.

23 ‏וש כלה‎... These letters undoubtedly belong to *Col. B* of this verse. It is unfortunate that the faded state of the Scroll precludes deciphering clearly (even with the aid of infra red photography) the letter before the *waw*, thus militating against deciding between the various possibilities. In B*text*, the text reads: ‏על רשע נבראה רעה / ובעבור תמוש כלה‎. B*marg* emends *Col. B* to read: ‏ובעבורו ת רעה‎. Cowley-Neubauer and Smend suggest the following emendation: ‏ועבורו לא תמוש רעה‎; Lévi: ‏תחוש‎; Peters: ‏תושם‎ and Segal: ‏תבוא‎. The *shin*, clearly discernible in the Scroll, disposes of the two latter possibilities. Of the others, Lévi's (‏תחוש‎) seems to me the most plausible, since neither the translations nor B*marg* bears traces of a negative word. Regarding: ‏תחוש‎, see my *The War of the Sons of Light and the Sons of Darkness*, notes to I, 12, on p. 261.

II

(See Plate 2)

1	[	]	[	‏כל מ]‎ 11

Page II is made up of a number of fragments: The upper portion of the right-hand fragment contains *Col. B* of Page I; the lower portion constitutes the lower right part of a large fragment containing Pages III and IV. Though some of the first and last lines of this page have been preserved, the middle section is missing.

1 The top margin above the beginning of the line indicates that this is the first line on the page.

1 ‏כל מ‎... Since the text of *Col. A* is identical in MS. B, in the Greek and in the Syriac, it can quite confidently be restored: ‏כל מ[ארץ אל ארץ ישוב]‎. Nothing has survived of *Col. B*. We are precluded therefore from deciding between the text of MS. B and the Syriac, on the one hand, and that of the Greek, on the other.

[171]

II,2–6/40,12–16

2	[ ]	[	כל מש[	12
3	ת[ ]	[	חיל מעול]	13
4	̇ם[ ]	[	עם שאתו כפ̇י]	14
5	[ ] עֹ̇ל [ ] צר]	[	נצר חמס לא יכ]	15
6	[ ] חצ̇ר נדעך		כקרמית עֹל גפות נחל	16

2 מש̇... Traces of the *shin* are clearly discernible.

3 חיל מעול̇ Only the slightest trace of the *lamed* has survived, but the identity of the letter is not in doubt, being indicated by both paleographic and contextual data (see Commentary). ת... The letter has been preserved in its entirety.

4 כפ̇י The reading is based on MS. B, and fits in with the existing traces of the letters. ̇ם... The slightest trace, which could fit a number of letters including final *mem*. This restoration conforms to the text of MS. B (see Commentary).

5 לא יכ (נ) The traces of the letter following the *yod* are compatible with either *kaf* or *nun*, and it is impossible to say which belongs here. עֹ̇ל has been preserved on the edge of a tiny shred, but examination through a magnifying glass indicates with certainty that the reading is: על. צר Reading definite.

6 כקרמית It is impossible to determine whether the reading is *yod* or *waw*, though I prefer *yod* (see Commentary). עֹל גפות נחל Reading definite. חצ̇ר נדעך The word: חצר, is divided by a tear. The *het* is clear and traces of the *ṣade* and the *resh* are visible. It is difficult to determine if there was a *yod* as well.

2 ...כל מש This line is missing in MS. B. Some scholars (including Peters and Segal) restore on the basis of the Greek: πᾶν δῶρον καὶ ἀδικία ἐξαλειφθήσεται, i.e.: כל שחד ועולה ישחת. The preservation of: מש, indicates that Ben Sira follows the structure of the previous verse here, too (...כל מארץ). Accordingly, if we follow the Greek, we should read: ...כל מש[חד]. Lévi proposed reading: כל משוחד, based on a variant in the Syriac: כל מחטאה (ומדעולא = כל מחטא ועול) instead of: כל מן דחטא ומדגל. On the basis of the Syriac, Smend proposed to emend the original text: שקר, instead of שחד. Since the letter after the *shin* has not been preserved, we cannot confirm the reading, though contextually this emendation sounds most plausible.

3 חיל מעול̇ Btext: מחול אל חול, has been recognised by most scholars as mutilated, influenced by 40, 11. The Bmarg correction (in the same copyist's hand): חיל מחיל, is not convincing and conforms neither to the Greek nor to the Syriac (χρήματα ἀδίκων; נכסא דשוקרא), but indicates that the second word began with a *mem*. Accordingly Lévi, Smend and Box & Oesterley (in the Charles ed.) proposed emending the original text to read: חיל מעול. The Scroll text bears out this emendation, and Bmarg: חיל מחיל, is a copyist's mutilation: מחיל, instead of: מעול. The last letter preserved at the end of Col. B (taw) fits in with the text of MS. B: קולֹ[ת].

4 ...עם שאתו כפ̇י The Scroll confirms the superiority of Bmarg: עם שאתו כפים, over Btext: עם שאתו כפים, which represents a case of dittography. The last letter preserved at the end of Col. B could be final *mem*, in conformity with the text of MS. B: [ית]ם.

5 נצר חמס The Scroll reading conforms with that of Bmarg, in contrast to Btext: נוצר מחמס. This reading is evidently closer to the Greek (ἔκγονα ἀσεβῶν) and even the Syriac (וחלפא לאנשא רשיעא). Unfortunately, we cannot determine, paleographically, whether the Scroll reading is: ...לא יכ, or: ...לא ינ (Btext: לא ינקה; Bmarg: לא יכה בו), but since the Scroll text agrees with that of Bmarg, in respect of the first clause, we feel justified in restoring the end clause according to Bmarg: על שן סלע Btext: עֹל [ ] צר .לא יכ[ה בו] Bmarg: עז שן צור. Since: עז, is a copyist's error (influenced by: שן), the Scroll reading agrees with that of Bmarg, and it is restored: על [שן] צר.

6 כקרמית The Scroll disqualifies Btext: כקר-דמות, and is in line with Cowley-Neubauer's initial emendation: קרומיות, followed by many others (כקרומית; כקרמות — and see the commentaries). The correct reading would seem to be: קרמית (see: קרמי דאגמא, *Erubin* 22a, and also Segal). גפות נחל MS. B: גפת נחל. It is unnecessary to emend to: שפת, as most editors; for: גף, in the sense of 'bank of a stream' (cf. Aramaic: גיף, and Syriac: גף), see *Makshirin* 1, 4: על גף הנהר (according to the Rav Hai version, as against the Printed editions: גב; and see Segal). Thus: גפה, is a synonym for: שפה.

[172]

7		וצדקה לעד תכן	חסד כעד לא תכרת	17
8	[	ומשניהם מוצא]	חיי יתר שכר ימתקו	18
9	[	ומשניהם מוצ]	ילד ו[ ]י[דו שם	19
10	[	]	ו]שאר [ ]	19c

7 כעד The upper traces of the *ʿayin* and the top left and lower right of the *dalet* are visible. לעד תכן The reading is beyond doubt, in spite of the faded character of some of the letters.

8 שכר The left-hand tip of the *śin*, most of the *kaf* and the upper part of the *resh* have been preserved. מוצא The מפני כל מטר Btext: חצר נדעך, emended in Bmarg to: לפני כל מטר. But most editors have already pointed out that: מטר, is out of place here. The Greek (χόρτου) and the Syriac (יורק) indicate something like: חציר (cf. *Job* 8:12: ולפני כל חציר ייבש). The Scroll confirms that the original text read: נדעכו (referring to: לפני כל] חציר (?) .נדעך Btext: כרדמות); Bmarg: נדעכה, perhaps influenced by: קרמית. The Scroll has perhaps been influenced by: חציר. The Bmarg reading would seem to be preferable.

7 חסד Similarly the Greek: χάρις, without: καί. MS. B: וחסד. כעד An unusual form. MS. B: לעולם. This 'difficult' reading would seem to be preferable; the Greek (παράδεισος) and Syriac (כעדנא) have been influenced by verse 27: יראת אלהים כעדן ברכה, but we can perhaps explain their 'mistake' if we assume that they used a text similar to the Scroll: כעד, which they emended to: כעדן (cf. *Isaiah* 51:3). לא תכרת MS. B: לא ימוט. The MS. B continuation: לעולם, is influenced by *Psalms* 15:5 and *Proverbs* 10:30. For the combination of: חסד, and: כרת, see *I Samuel* 20:15, as well as below, 41, 11. It is difficult to explain the employment of: תכרת, instead of: יכרת, except in terms of a copyist's error, influenced by the succeeding context and familiar biblical idioms (*Genesis* 41:36; *Proverbs* 23:18).

8 חיי יתר שכר The reading here enables us to clear up the quandary of the scribe of Btext in his rendering: חיי יין ושכר, and the attempted correction of Bmarg: חיי יותר שכל. The copyist of Btext read: שכר (influenced by 40, 20: יין ושכר יעליצו לב) and accordingly gave: יין, instead of: יתר, which can also be understood paleographically

traces of the letters fit this word, which is found in MS. B. Between *ll.* 7 and 8, on the right, we find the symbol ך, which evidently indicates a new paragraph (see the introduction and below, *l.* 24).

9 The reading is beyond doubt.

(see Facsimile). Bmarg gives the correct reading for the first word, but read: שכל, for: שכר. A number of editors (e.g. Smend) have noted that the Greek: ζωὴ αὐτάρκους ἐργάτου, hints at the combination of: יתר, and: שכר. The continuation of the verse: ומשניהם, demands: יתר *and* שכר, but it is interesting to note that the Greek, like the Scroll, gives the phrase without the *waw* conjunctive; the phrase as a whole resembles 10, 27: טוב עובד ויותר הון. At any rate, Segal's defence of the Btext reading is unwarranted. מוצא Insert here: מוצא [שימה], as in Bmarg: מוצא סימה (Btext: מוצא אוצר), since below, 41, 14b, the Scroll gives: ושימה מסותרת, as in Bmarg (וסימה מסותרת), instead of: ואוצר מוסתר, of Btext (see *ad loc.*).

9 Restored according to MS. B: ילד ו[עיר ו]ידו יעמ[שם; the Greek is more or less the same. The continuation of the verse in *Col. B* may be restored also according to MS. B: ומשניהם מוצא[חכמה]. This confirms the verse order in MS. B and the Syriac, which contrasts to that of the mutilated Greek.

10 שאר The only word that has been preserved, but of greatest importance. In MS. B, the word: שם, recurs, as in the previous verse. Smend deduced from the fact that the verse is missing in the Greek that it is not authentic, but is merely a duplication. Peters and others, however, maintained that the verse is authentic, the duplication of: שם, being explained as arising from the fact that the verse was inadvertently overlooked in the Greek translation. Others (e.g. Fuchs, and see also Charles) attempted to emend: שם, to: דשן, or the like. The Scroll thus represents the original text: שאר [שגר ונטע יפריחו], which best suits the context. For: שאר, see also below, Page III, *l.* 24 (41, 19d). This indicates that

[173]

II,11–23/40,27–30

11	[ ]	[ ]	27
17	[ ] [שׁנִיהֹם]	[ ]	28
18	ען] [מ עמה מה לבקש אין]	[ ]	
19	חפתה [ ] [כ]ל כל ועל	[ ]	26
20	טוב] [סף מפני חצף]	[ ]	26c
21	[מנות חיים]	[ ]	29
22	מעים יסור [יוד ש]	[ ] [מט]	29c
23	[ ] תבער כאש ו]	[בפי עז נפש ת]	30

11–16 These lines have not been preserved. The photographs seem to indicate a blank line after *l.* 10, though traces of a letter in *Col. B*, as well as a careful scrutiny, show that there was a verse here, now completely faded (see Commentary).

17 [   ]שׁנִיהֹם The traces fit this reading.

18 The reading of the end of the line is clear. The traces at the beginning exactly fit the proposed reading.

19 ...כל כל ועל This is written on a small shred which I have fitted into this place on the basis of context and the beginning of the verse in *Col. B* (see Commentary).

20 טוב On a small shred (see above, *l.* 19). סף.. Traces of the *samekh* can be clearly seen. The reading of the remaining letters is beyond doubt.

21 מנוֹת... The traces are clear.

22 ...מט The traces fit. It is difficult to decipher the traces of the preceding letters. יסור The tip of the *yod* can be seen above the tear.

23 ...בפי עז נפש ת On an odd shred. Reading definite. *Col. B*: The upper edge of the *waw* is visible above the tear.

the word: שם, in MS. B is an early copyist's error (thus also in the Syriac) under the influence of the previous verse. Prof. Seeligmann has pointed out to me that the exchange of: שם, for: שאר, may have been influenced by a misunderstanding of *II Samuel* 14: 7: שם ושארית. *Col. B* is restored from the reading in MS. B.

11–16 See the Notes. The number of verses corresponds to that of MS. B. This is indicated by the normal number of verses to a page (25); thus restored according to *l.* 17 (40, 26).

17 *Col. B* is restored according to MS. B: [ומ]~ שׁניהם [יראת אלהים].

18 מ[שׁ]ען There is a tear here in MS. B. The Scroll confirms the reading adopted by most editors (Bacher, Smend, Peters, Segal, etc.), in contrast to that of Cowley-Neubauer: מטמון]. For the use of: משען, in Ben Sira, see also 3, 31; 36, 29. The implications of: משען, in the latter עזר ומבצר ועמוד (משען) explain the Greek (βοήθειαν) and the Syriac (מעדרנא) translations of this verse.

19 וכן כל כבוד MS. B: ועל כל כ[בוד] חפתה etc. The Scroll text confirms the emendation proposed by most editors on the basis of the Greek (καὶ ὑπὲρ πᾶσαν) and the Syriac (ולעל מן כל).

20 The first part of *Col. B*: טוב נא[סף], restored on the basis of MS. B. מפני חצף MS. B: ממסתולל.

For: מסתולל, see the commentators. Its meaning is difficult, but the context calls for an expression connoting a beggar or someone making impudent demands, etc. So the Greek (ἢ ἐπαιτεῖν). פני חצף, fits in exactly with the context, i.e. someone making importunate demands, etc. See particularly Levy's dictionary to the *Targums*: ואחציפת אפהא (*Proverbs* 7:13); מחציף אפוי (*Proverbs* 21:29); and many more. See also the Syriac to 40, 30: חצפא (=impudent). For rabbinic usage (חצוף), see Ben Yehuda. Regarding Ben Sira's resorting to rabbinic idiom in various contexts, see particularly Segal, pp. 19ff.

21 *Col. B* is restored according to MS. B: אין] חייו ל[מנות חיים.

22 [   ]מט[   ] [   ] Restored on the basis of *Bmarg*: [מעגל נפשו] מט[עמי זבד] (see the commentaries). *Col. B*: יסור מעים So *Bmarg*: יסור מיעים (perhaps a copyist's error: מזעים) and in the Syriac: כאבא אנין דמעיא. *Btext*: סוד מעים — a corruption. Restored from MS. B: [לאי[שׁ יוד]ע] יסור מעים.

23 בפי עז נפש Thus the Greek (ἐν στόματι ἀναιδοῦς) and the Syriac (בפומה דחציפא). MS. B: לאיש עז נפש, a corruption influenced by: לאיש, in the previous verse, and the same applies to Bmarg: ...ת. לאיש עז נפשות Bmarg. ת[מתיק שאלה] Restored: ממתיק. *Col. B*: כאש תבער See *Psalms* 83:15. *Btext*: תבער כמו אש (*Psalms* 79:5; 89:47); *Bmarg*: כאש

II,24–III,3/41,1–3

1	[הו] [ל] [כרך]	
1c	[ ] שלׁו ומצׁליׄח בכל	

24	לאיש שקט על מכונתו
25	עוד בו כח לקבל תענוג

24 ...[ל] [הו] On the odd shred (see above). Above the line in the margin, the mark: ר. כרׄך... Only the lower parts have been preserved. The leg of the final *kaf* is clear.

The other traces fit the reading.

25 The traces are clear. This is the last line of the page; beneath is the lower margin.

בוערת (*Jeremiah* 20:9), which is closer to the Scroll reading. Restored according to MS. B: ובקרב[ו כאש תבער.

24 [הו] [ל] [ ] Restored according to B*marg*, the Greek and the Syriac: ז[כרך מר מה למות הוי.

B*text*: חיים למות מה מר זכרך. *Col. B* agrees with MS. B.

25 שלׁו [MS. B: שליו. Restored: שלו ומצליח [איש.

כח בכל. MS. B: חיל.

III
(See Plate 3)

1	[ ] [לאין אוינים (!) וחסר עצמה
2	אפס המרה ואבוד תקוה
3	זכר קדמון ואחרון עמך

2	הע למות מה טוב ח] [
2c	איש כשל ונוקש ב] [
3	אל תפחד ממות חקך

1 *Col. A* is on a small shred. This is the top line of the page; above is the margin. הׄע The traces of the right-hand letter fit *he*. My reading of *ḥet* at the end of the column is based on MS. B (see below). [אין] There is room for only one letter.

2 ונוקש Inserted between the lines after the copyist had erased a word after: כשל.

3 *Col. A* is preserved on three shreds, here pieced together.

1 A direct continuation of Page II. הׄע MS. B: האח; the Greek: ὦ (as above, 41, 1); the Syriac: או (see above, 41, 1; B*marg* there: הוי). It is difficult to imagine that we have here an expression of exclamation such as: הע! It therefore seems to me that this is a copyist's error: מה MS. B. הר[ע; כי; the Syriac: מא. Smend accordingly, and correctly, proposed the reading: ח...מה. Only the beginning of the word is preserved and it is impossible to decide between B*text* and B*marg*. It is seemingly: חקך (but see below, *l.* 3); Segal also read thus. [לאין אוינים (!) MS. B: לאיש אונים. The Scroll reading confirms Lévi's suggestion (on the basis of *Isaiah* 40:29: ולאין אונים עצמה ירבה), which was rejected by all other commentators. For a similar copyist's error, see *Ben Sira* 41, 4: איש; אין תוכחות תוכחות.

2 The Scroll agrees with one of the B*marg* readings. It is interesting to note that the copyist, by mistake, wrote another word (ומשל?; see one of the B*marg* readings), erased it and wrote over it: ונוקש. אפס המרה. איש כשל ונוקש ב[כל] Restored: MS. B: סרב; but B*marg* reads: אפס המראה, which is closer to the Scroll. The Greek (ἀπειθοῦντι) indicates an expression of rebellion and refusal; the Syriac, on the other hand, reads: חסיר ממונא (מזונא); as long as only B*marg* was available, it was possible to conjecture (Segal) that the original text was: אפס סבר (שבר), i.e. 'without hope', misunderstood by the translators. But the existence of: אפס המרה, 'devoid of sight', in the Scroll obliges us to assume that: המרה (המראה), is authentic and the Greek (as well as B*text*) read perhaps: המרה, connected with: מרי, 'rebellion' (cf. סורר ומרה, *Deuteronomy* 21:20; *Psalms* 78:8). The question is difficult and requires further study. ואבוד תקוה MS. B: ואבד תקוה.

3 חקך MS. B: חוקיך (cf. above, *l.* 1 — 41, 2). זכר קדמון ואחרון עמך MS. B: זכר כי ראשונים ואחרונים עמך

III,4–9/41,4–8

4	[עֶלְיוֹן]	[ ]	זֹה קֵץ כל] [זֹה	4
5	[ ]		לעשר מאה וֹאֹלֹף שנים	4c
6	שֹע]	[ ]	נין נמאס ת] [וֹת רעים	5
7	[תֹמִיֹ] [חרפה	[ ]	[ל תאבד ממשׁ] [זֹה	6
8	[גֹללו היו בוז	[ ]	יקב ילֹד [ ]	7
9	עֹזבי תורת עליון	[אנשי עוֹ] [ ]	8

⁴ As *l.* 3. זֹה Distinct traces. קֵץ The final *ṣade* is clearly preserved. Only the left edge of the *qof* is visible. זֹה... MS. B ends with: מאל, but the traces here do not permit such a restoration. The traces here are particularly suggestive of a *he* (see Commentary).

⁵ Pieced together from two fragments. וֹאֹלֹף The final *pe* is clearly discernible. The lower remains of the *lamed* and the right edge of the *alef* are similarly visible.

⁶ [וֹת ת] A tear after the *taw* obscures the next letter. The same applies to the letter before the *waw*, the traces of which could point to a *dalet*. שֹׁע... Inscribed on a tiny

fragment which I have pieced in here (see the next line).

⁷ זֹה] ...ל תאבד ממשׁ On a small fragment, fitted in here (see the Commentary). One can perhaps detect traces of the lower part of: תֹמי, in *Col. B.* חרפה On a small fragment pieced in here. The blank margin on the left side of the fragment fits only here (see the Commentary).

⁸ יקב ילֹד On a small fragment, pieced in here (see *l.* 7). *Col. B:* גֹללו... Reading definite.

⁹ אנשי עוֹ... On a separate fragment, fitted in here. (see *ll.* 7–8). עוֹ is discernible with difficulty. *Col. B:* Reading definite.

---

⁴ זֹה קֵץ כל] Cf. *Genesis* 6:13: ויאמר. MS. B: חלק אליהם לנח קֵץ כל בשר בא לפני. The Syriac gives a reading similar to the Scroll. *Col. A* is restored: זֹה קֵץ כל בשר מאל]ה. MS. B: מאל (see the Notes, above). *Col. B:* Restored according to MS. B: עליון] ומה תמאס בתורת].

⁵ לעשר מאה ואלף שנים Cf. the Greek: εἴτε δέκα εἴτε ἑκατὸν εἴτε χίλια ἔτη MS. B: לאלף שנים מאה ועשר.

⁶ נין Thus B*text*; the Syriac: זרעא; B*marg*: בן. וֹת רעים] [ת B*text*: דבר רעים; B*marg*: דבת רעים. Restored: ת]לד]וֹת רעים; and cf. the Syriac: תולדתא דחטיא (so according to MS. I; and see Smend) or: דעולא; Smend has already attempted to emend on the basis of the Greek: דור, instead of: דבר, in B*text*. *Col. B:* שֹׁע... Restored according to MS. B: ונכד אייל מגורי(?)ר]שע]; and cf. the Greek: παροικίαις ἀσεβῶν.

⁷ זֹה] ...ל תאבד ממשׁ B*text*: מבן עול ממשלת; B*marg*: מבן ערל ממשלת רע. The various editors have already noted that *Col. A* in MS. B is corrupt, and on the basis of the Greek (τέκνων ἁμαρτωλῶν ἀπολεῖται κληρονομία) and the Syriac (מן ברא עולא נאבד שולטנא) attempted to restore the original text. Lévi: ממשלה תרע; while Smend: ממשלה תקרע; Peters followed Lévi; while Segal: תאבד. Segal's suggestion agrees with the Scroll.

Thus restore: מבן עוֹל תאבד ממשלה. *Col. B:* חרפה [תֹמִיֹ] ... See the Notes, above. B*text* is mutilated (and only one word has survived: ...ז...זרע). Following the Greek (καὶ μετὰ τοῦ σπέρματος αὐτῶν ἐνδελεχιεῖ ὄνειδος) and partly the Syriac (ועם זרעיהו נעמר חוסרנא), the Scroll now enables us to restore the reading: ד]תמיֹ חרפה [ועם זרעו]. The Syriac indicates that several versions may have had: חסד, instead of: חרפה (see the Commentary to Page IV, *l.* 3 — 41, 22c, in connection with the interchanging of: חסד, and: חרפה), and mistakenly read: חסד.

⁸ יקב ילֹד ... Restored according to MS. B: אב רשע] יקב ילד. *Col. B:* גֹללו היו בוז ... Editors' attempts at restoration missed the mark — Smend: כי בגללו הוא חרפת עם; Lévi: כי בגללו יחרפון; Segal: כי בגללו יחרף; Peters: כי בגללו ינאץ.

⁹ אנשי עוֹ .. ... Mutilated in MS. B. Restorations on the basis of the Greek (οὐαὶ ὑμῖν ἄνδρες ἀσεβεῖς) and the Syriac (הי להון לאנשא עולא) as follows: Lévi: אוי לאנשים; Smend: אוי לכם אנשי עול; Peters: הוי לכם אנשי עולה; Segal: הוי לכם אנשי רשע. Traces of the ʿayin rule out the suggestions of Smend and Segal, and Peters' appears to be the most acceptable. *Col. B:* עזבי תורת עליון Mutilated in MS. B. Only Smend's reconstruction hits the mark, though the others came close: Lévi, Segal: אשר עזבתם תורת עליון; Peters: העוזבים תורת עליון.

[176]

10	ואם תולידו לאֹנחה	[ ] [ל] [ ]	9
11	ואם תמותו לקללה	[ ]ו לשמחת עֹלם	9b
12	כֹן חנף מתהו אל תהו	[ ]אפס אל אפס ישוב	10
13	[ ] שֹם חֹסד ללא יכרֹת	[הֹבֹל] [מֹ]	11
14	מאֹלפֹי [ ] חֹמדֹה (?)	פֹחֹ[ ] על שם כי הוא ילוך	12
15	וטובֹת [ ] אין מספר	[ ]ובת חׄ מספר ימים	13
16	מה תעלה בשתיהם	[כׄ]מה טמונה ושימה מסותרת	14b

10 ...ל... On a small fragment, pieced in here (see *ll.* 7–9). *Col. B*: לאֹנחה The copyist wrote: אנחה, and then inserted the *lamed* above the *alef*.

11 Traces of the letters clearly fit the reading. *Col. B*: Reading definite.

12 Reading definite.

13 From this point the Scroll has become distorted and is curved (see Plate 5 for its general appearance). On Pl. 3, I have joined the lower portion, shifting it somewhat after cutting the photograph. The next three lines of *Col. B* are

badly mutilated. *Col. A*: הֹבֹל The traces are discernible with difficulty. *Col. B*: Reading definite, though the lower parts of the letters are faded.

14 [פֹחֹ] On a distorted fragment, which curves upward. *Col. B*: The letters are very badly mutilated — a tentative reading (see the Commentary).

15 Reading definite. *Col. B*: Badly mutilated; traces are clearly discernible and certainly fit the proposed reading.

16 The word: בשתיהם, was incorrectly transcribed as: בתיהם, the *shin* being subsequently inserted above: בת.

10 Only a *lamed* has survived on a shred, but it is sufficient to reconstruct the line on the basis of B*marg*: [אם תפרו ע]ל[יד אסון]. *Col. B*: Thus B*text*; B*marg*: מולידו.

11 Restored on the basis of MS. B: [אם תכשלו] לשמחת עולם. *Col. B*: Thus B*text*; on the other hand, B*marg*: לקללתה. The verse order in the Scroll is also identical with that of MS. B. Part of the text has been omitted in the Greek.

12 [כל מ]אפס], etc. Thus B*text*, in contrast to B*marg*.

13 ....הֹבֹל It is difficult to decide between the reading of B*text*: הבל אדם, and that of B*marg*: הבל בני אדם, since the Scroll is badly mutilated at this spot. On the other hand, the space between the traces on the left of *Col. A* and the start of the line is too large to fit the reading of B*text*. I am therefore inclined to follow the reading of B*marg*. I can seemingly distinguish traces of a final *mem* at the end of the line, in which case it would fit the Greek, and the subject of the sentence in B*marg*: [בני] הבל אדם בגוית[ם]. *Col. B*: Thus MS. B, with one variation: ללא יכרת, instead of: לא יכרת; probably a copyist's error. Restored: [אך] שם חסד ל{לא יכרת}.

14 פֹח[ד] על שם כי הוא ילוך Thus MS. B. *Col. B* here is in a bad state of preservation. The traces are insufficient to enable us to decide between: אוצרות (B*text*), and: סימות (B*marg*). Guided by other

places (see below, *l.* 16—41, 14b), where B*marg* (סימה) and the Scroll (שימה) agree, but diverge from B*text* (אוצר), I am inclined to read here: שימות. חמדה See the Notes, above. The word: חמדה, better suits the context (see the commentators). The traces are insufficient to serve any definite reading. *Col. B* is thus restored: מאלפי [שימות] חמדה.

15 The Scroll reading fits partly that of B*text* and partly that of B*marg*, and it is easy to detect how the corruptions arose. [ט]ובת.. Thus B*text*, in contrast to: טוב, in B*marg*. מספר ימים Thus B*marg*, in contrast to: ימי מספר, in B*text*. In *Col. B*, too, the Scroll reads: וטובת, as in MS. B. *Col. B* is restored: וטובת [שם ימי] אין מספר. In *Col. A*, it is possible that the Greek drew on both the Scroll and B*marg* versions (מספר ימים): ἀριθμὸς ἡμερῶν.

16 וסימה מסותרת ושימה מסותרת Thus B*marg*, in contrast to B*text*: ואוצר מוסתר. The use of: שימה (סימה), instead of: אוצר, recurs a number of times in the Scroll and in B*marg*, in contradistinction to B*text*. This would lend force to the assumption that the Hebrew form in B*text* is not the original and not vice versa, as has hitherto been maintained. Additional weight is lent to this contention by the form: בשתיהם, in *Col. B*, preserved also in B*text*. תעלה Thus B*marg*, in contrast to: תועלה, in B*text* (cf. *Ben Sira* 30:23: ואין תעלה בקצפון).

III,17–22/41,15–18c

17	מאיש מצפן חכמתו	טוב איש מטמ] אולתו	15
18	16a [ ] ל]מו על משפטי	מוסר בשת שמעו בנים	14a
19	ולא כל הכלם נבחר	לא כל בשת נאוה לבוש	16b
20	מנשיא ושר על כחש	בוש מאב ואם על פחז	17
21	מעדה ועם] ל[ ] ש[ע	מאדון וגבר] על קשר	18
22	ממקום תגור ע] יד	משותף ורע על מעל	18c

17 Slightly damaged. Reading definite.

18 *Col. B*: The start of the column is mutilated, but the traces fit the proposed reading.

19 לבוש The lower part of the *bet* is mutilated.

20 כחש Reading definite.

21 ל[ ] The top of the *lamed* is visible. ש[ע] The left side of the *shin* has been preserved.

22 [ע] The right side of the *'ayin* has been preserved. יד is clearly written.

17 אולתו [מטמ]ן In Contrast to MS. B: מצפן. The Scroll reading is preferable, since it avoids resort to duplicating the word: מצפן. מ̇איש Thus B*text* (and the Greek), in contrast to: אדן, in B*marg*.

18 The verse order is as in MS. B, in contrast to that of the Greek, which is corrupt. *Col. A* agrees with MS. B. *Col. B* agrees with B*text*: משפטי (and thus in the Greek, which is as a rule mutilated here), in contrast to: משפטו, in B*marg*. *Col. B* is restored: [והכ]למו על משפטי.

19 נאוה The biblical form, instead of MS. B: נאה. A particularly interesting reading is found in the Scroll: נאוה לבוש, in contrast to: נאה לשמר, in MS. B, and the Greek: διαφυλάξαι. This same reading is also found in a selection of verses from *Ben Sira* among the Genizah fragments recently published by Schirmann (*Tarbiz* 29, 2, 1960, p. 132). The Scroll version fits the context: Not every apparent shame is to be ashamed of. Since the word: לשמר, occurs in all other versions, we may assume that these represent two early versions. *Col. B*: Thus MS. B.

20 The Scroll reading is identical with B*marg* and the Greek, in contrast to B*text*, which is partly a more popular version and partly a copyist's corruption. Instead of: על פחז (cf. *Genesis* 49:4), B*text* reads: אל זנות, whereas instead of: ושר על כחש, B*text* reads: יושב אל כחש. As mentioned, both the Scroll and B*marg* agree here with the Greek: (καὶ) ἀπὸ ἡγουμένου καὶ δυνάστου περὶ ψεύδους.

21 על קשר Instead of: על שקר (MS. B). The Greek (περὶ πλημμελείας) possibly hints at a reading similar to that of the Scroll, but see Smend regarding the use of this term in the Greek translation of *Ben Sira*, and in the LXX. At any rate, it seems to me that the Scroll reading is preferable, in keeping with the motif of 'master and mistress' (אדון וגברת). The Scroll supports the reading of MS. B: מאדון וגברת, in contrast to the Greek: ἀπὸ κριτοῦ καὶ ἄρχοντος (= מדיין וגביר), which is only a misreading or misunderstanding; this has already been noted by the various editors. *Col. B* is restored on the basis of MS. B: מעדה ועם [על] [פ]שע.

22 משותף ממקום Thus B*marg*. B*text*: מחובר. תגור Thus B*text* and the Greek (καὶ ἀπὸ τόπου οὗ παροικεῖς), in contrast to B*marg*: ממקום וגיד. ע[ל] יד Thus B*marg*. All the editors read in B*marg*: זד, but a study of the facsimile clearly indicates that the reading is: יד (and cf., e.g., in the handwriting of the B*marg* copyist, 42, 3: וישר, which is identical with the *yod* in: יד, here). B*text*: זר. There is little doubt that the reading of B*text* does not suit *Col. B* contextually, nor does it serve as a fitting parallel to: מעל, in *Col. A*. The Greek reading: περὶ κλοπῆς, does not correspond to: זר, but is indicative of theft or brigandage, etc. Since the reading of: יד, is definite, we must look for a suitable connotation. We do find a similar use in *Ben Sira*, both in the Scroll and in the Greek (cf. below, 42, 6). Similarly, the Scroll text enables us to see how corruptions arose in B*text* and in B*marg* (each in a different point). Segal's reservations regarding the reading of B*text* (תגור) and the Greek, thus are not justified.

III,23–IV,1/41,19b–21c

23	וממטה אציל על לחם	מהפֹר אלה וברית 19b
24	21a ומהשיב את פני שארך	ממנֹ[ ] מֹתת שאלה 19d
25	20 מֹשאל שלום החריֹש	מחשֹות מחלקת מֹנֹה 21b

23 מהפֹר Reading definite. וברית The copyist incorrectly transcribed: וברת, and inserted the missing *yod* afterwards, over רת.

24 מֹתת The top of the *mem* has been preserved.

25 The copyist made two mistakes and himself corrected each. He evidently began to write: מֹשאל (= start of *Col. B*), but afterwards inserted the *het* above: מֹש. He then un-

successfully tried to correct the *alef* (?). The letter after the *shin* is not *bet*, and resembles a thick *waw* superimposed over the erased *alef*. מחלקת Incorrectly transcribed: מחלת; afterwards corrected, the missing *qof* being inserted over the *taw*, since the top part of the *lamed* did not allow for its insertion above: לת. This is the last line on the page; the lower margin is largely preserved.

23 This verse was mistranslated in the Greek, and the fact that in B*text* the beginning is missing, owing to a tear, gave the editors much trouble. מהפֹר This is the very word sought after, as many editors had suspected on the basis of the Syriac (דמבטל), but hesitated to accept. Smend and Peters restored: משנות; Segal: משכח (see Segal, p. 281). The Greek reading is: ἀπὸ ἀληθείας, which may be a corruption of: ἀπὸ λήθης (Peters, Segal) — לשכוח, i.e. a free translation of: הפר. אלה Thus, too, restore B*text*; the Greek misunderstood the text, reading: אלה (θεοῦ), and so the Syriac: מוהבתא (a corruption of: מומתא, as most editors have already noted). וממטה Thus the Greek (καί); MS. B: מטה. על לחם Thus some of the Greek MSS.: ἐπ᾽ ἄρτοις. MS. B: אל לחם (= ἐπ᾽ ἄρτους, in most MSS.).

24 The verse order is the same as in MS. B. ממנֹ[ע] מֹתת שאלה Thus B*marg*. B*text* here is largely missing, owing to a tear. ומהשיב Close to B*text* and the Greek; B*marg* is corrupt: מיהשע. שארך Thus the Greek: συγγενοῦς. B*text*: רעך; B*marg*: רעיך. פני B*text*: אפי; B*marg*: פי.

25 The verse order is as in MS. B. מחשֹות See the Notes, above. In this instance, it is somewhat close to B*marg*: מחשֹ(ב)ות; B*text*: [ ]מהשֹ. Perhaps the reading should be: מחשות, from the root: חשה, i.e. in the sense of 'silencing' or 'withholding'. Regarding: חשה, in this sense, see *Ben Sira* 35, 20, and my *War of the Sons of Light...*, p. 108, n. 4. החריֹש Preferable to B*text*: מהחריש; or B*marg*: התחרישו.

IV
(See Plate 4)

1	20b ומהתבונן אל זרה	[מהביט אֹ] 21c

The lower portion of this page is on the one large fragment whilst the upper part is mostly on the other. The two parts could not be fitted exactly owing to shrinkage of the Scroll (see Pl. 8). On Pl. 4, I have cut the lower part from the larger fragment and have joined it with several other fragments in approximately the proper position. The same applies to the lower left-hand fragment, which I have cut from the other fragment and have thus straightened it out. A considerable amount of the lower portion of *Col. B* was damaged and much is missing.

1 This is the first line on the page, and is a direct continuation of the end of Page III. מהביט אֹ.... The lower part of the right leg of the *alef* is visible.

1 The first verse is badly mutilated in B*text*. It would seem also that the next two verses were telescoped into one. The verses in the Greek are similarly misplaced. The Scroll text clarifies these verses and their order, which have posed many problems to the editors. As is now evident, a further difficulty had been caused by the fact that *Col. A*

and *Col. B* both begin with words of similar content: מהביט, and: ומהתבונן. This, of course, is also reflected in the Greek, and thus has precluded the editors from a correct restoration. מהביטאֹ.... Now that we are able to compare the verses to the Greek, which is arranged in a different order, we can safely affirm that *Col. A* corresponds to: καὶ ἀπὸ κατα-

IV,2—9/41,22a—42,4a

2	ומהתקומם על יצעיה	22b	מהתעשק ע'] [חה לך	22a
3	ומאחר מתת חרף	22d	מאהב על דברי חסד	22c
4	ומחשף כל דבר עצה		משנות דבֹר תשמע	1
5	ומצא חן בעיני כל חי		וה]]ׄת בויש באמת	1c
6	ואל תשא פנים וחטא		[ ]ך על אלה אל תבוש	1e
7	ועל משפט להצדיק רשע		על תורת עליון וחק	2
8	ועל מחלקת נחלה ויש		על חשבון שותף ודרך	3
9	וׄעֹל תמחי איפה ואבן	5a	על שחקי מזנים ופלס	4a

2 חֹה̇ לך... Traces of: חה, are clearly discernible. The final *kaf* in: לך, is somewhat odd because the copyist 'squeezed' it to the right, into the *lamed* to avoid running over the νοήσεως γυναικὸς ὑπάνδρου (21c), i.e.: מהביט אל [אשת איש, etc. (cf. *Ben Sira* 9,9). Lévi, Smend: בעולה, or: בעולת בעל; while Segal: אשה בעולה. B*marg*: אשה. ומהתבונן אל זרה This parallels the Greek: ἀπὸ ὀράσεως γυναικὸς ἑταίρας (ἑτέρας) (20b), and this on the basis of *Ben Sira* 9, 3: אל תקרב אל אשה זרה, which has been rendered: μὴ ὑπάντα γυναικὶ ἑταιριζομένη. So also Smend, who, however, erred in connecting this with: מהביט, of *Col. A.* Other editors here were also wide of the mark.

2 מהתעשק, etc. Corresponding to: ἀπὸ περιεργείας παιδίσκης αὐτοῦ, already restored by Smend: מהתעשק (cf., following him, Segal: ומהתעסק). The rest of the verse is restored: עם שפ]חה לך. Others have already noted that the last clause, on the basis of the Greek, is not correct, and have proposed: שפחתך (see Segal). ומהתקומם על יצעיה Corresponding to: καὶ μὴ ἐπιστῆς ἐπὶ τὴν κοίτην αὐτῆς (22b). Smend was correct in his reconstruction of the beginning (in contrast to Lévi and Segal: ומהתקרב; their restoration of the last word was: משכבה). The Hebrew text now allows us to restore the correct verse order of the Greek, which is not as has hitherto been supposed (see Charles):

21c: καὶ ἀπὸ κατανοήσεως γυναικὸς ὑπάνδρου
20b: ἀπὸ ὀράσεως γυναικὸς ἑταίρας (ἑτέρας)
22e: ἀπὸ περιεργείας παιδίσκης (αὐτοῦ)
22b: καὶ μὴ ἐπιστῆς ἐπὶ τὴν κοίτην αὐτῆς.

3 דברי Thus in B*text*. חסד Thus in B*marg*. חרף Preferable to MS. B.: אל תנאץ. The editors have already noted that the infinitive is preferable (נאוץ).

4 Identical with MS. B and the Greek. *Col. B*:

end of the line, but there is no doubt as to the reading.

5 וׄהֹ] [ׄת The traces are clear.

9 וׄעֹל תמחי Reading definite.

דבר עצה The Greek: λόγων κρυφίων. MS. B: סוד עצה, evidently combining two variants: סוד, and: עצה, synonyms in the Dead Sea Scrolls (see Habermann's concordance, s.v.) connoting a closed, secret association. B*marg*: על אור, a gloss on: חסוף.

5 Thus in MS. B and the Greek. Note the form: בויש. MS. B: בוש; cf., e.g.: הבוישן, *Aboth* 2, 5, MS. Kaufmann (I thank my colleague Prof. Kutscher for this reference).

6 Thus in B*text*. B*marg*: אל, instead of: על.

7 Thus in B*text*. B*marg*: אל, instead of: על. *Col. B*: Thus in B*marg* and the Greek (καὶ περὶ κρίματος). B*text*, possibly a copyist's error: ועל מצדיק להצדיק רשע.

8 על חשבון שותף Thus in B*marg*, in contrast to: חובר, in B*text* (cf. above, Page III, *l.* 22—41, 18c). ודרך In B*text* a correction has been inserted between the lines: ואֹרח, a variant corresponding to: ודרך, connoting joining a fellow-traveller; the Greek: ὁδοιπόρων. ויש Thus in B*text*, in contrast to B*marg*: וישר.

9 על Thus also the Greek, without: καί; MS. B: ועל. שחקי In the plural (see *Col. B*). MS. B: שחק. The Greek (ἀκριβείας) understood this meaning (see Smend), and there is no reason to read: חק (Segal). מזנים — מאזנים (see below, Page VI, *l.* 2). *Col. B*: וׄעֹל תמחי B*text*: תמחות, a copyist's error, as is B*marg*: תמורת. Smend and others have already noted that the reading is a word from the root: מחה. The language of the Scroll indicates the existence of the word: תמחים (in plural; and cf. שחקי – שחקים, in *Col. A*), in the sense of dust wiped away from the scales. Cf.: החנוני מקנח מדותיו

[180]

10	] [ממחיר ממכר תגר	[ ]על מקנה בין רׄבׄ למׄ[ ]	4b
11	ועבד רע וצלע מהלכת	[ ]ה[	5b–c
12	ומקום ידים רבות מפתח	[ ]שׄת חותם[ ]	6
13	שׄ] [מׄתת הכל בכתב	על מׄ[ ] [תפקיד מספר	7
14	[ ]בׄ כׄושל ענה בזנות	על מׄ[ ] [ותה וכסיל	8

10 ...בין רׄבׄ למׄ Owing to the shrinkage of the Scroll, the letters have moved up. The traces visible beneath (= *he*) belong to the next line.

12 ...שׄת The letter to the right of the *taw* cannot possibly be *'ayin*. The most plausible conjecture is *shin*. See the Commentary.

פעמים בשבת וממחה משקלותיו פעם אחת בשבת ומקנח מאזנים על כל משקל ומשקל (*Baba Bathra* 5, 10; see also Peters and Segal).

10 Thus B*text*, and so restore: על מקנה בין רב [למ]עט. B*marg*: חשבן, instead of: מקנה, under influence of 42, 3. [ועל] ממחיר Thus B*text* (Cowley-Neubauer misread: ממחיו, as already noted by various editors). Most editors wish to emend B*text*: ממחיר, to: מחיר, but the Scroll confirms the B*text* reading. The sense here is 'to bargain' or 'to barter'. Similarly, the reading in the Greek should be: διαφόρου, instead of: ἀδιαφόρου (see also Smend) B*marg*: מוסר; see below regarding its relationship to the next line, missing in B*text*. ממכר תגר The Scroll reading confirms that of Lévi, Smend, Segal and others, in contrast to that of Cowley-Neubauer, who misread: עבד בגד!

11 Missing in MS. B. *Col. A* is restored according to the Greek (καὶ περὶ παιδείας τέκνων πολλῆς): [ועל מוסר בנים הרב]ה, and so most editors (who read: רב, instead of: הרבה). ועבד רע וצלע מהלכת This reading was undoubtedly that drawn on by the Greek, who misread: בצלע (πλευράν) instead of: וצלע, and: מהלכת (αἱμάξαι), instead of: מהלכֵת. For הלכת, cf. *The Manual of Discipline* III, 9: הכין פעמיו להלכת תמים. (I should like to thank Prof. Kutscher for this parallel.) From the view-point of history of the versions and translations, it is also interesting to compare the various attempts at restoration made by the editors on the basis of the Greek (καὶ οἰκέτῃ πονηρῷ πλευρὰν αἱμάξαι), which in part came very close to the combination of consonants in our text:

Lévi: ולעבד רע הכות צלע;
Peters: ועל הכות צלע לעבד רע;

13 ...על מׄ Because of the shrinkage the letters have been forced a little beneath the line: מׄתת ...שׄ Traces of the *shin* are clearly discernible. Only a bit of the *mem* is visible.

14 ...על מׄ בׄ כׄושל Reading definite. The *bet* is clear. The top of the *kaf* is slightly faded.

ועל הכות מתנים לעבד רע Segal. Another possibility in understanding this passage has been suggested by Prof. E. Urbach: וצלע מהלכת (= אשה), i.e. that the verse deals with sons, a bad slave and an evil wife, all at once.

על אשה רעה חותם B*text*: [ ]שׄת חותם **12** (after two dots, the scribe added: חכם). The marginal comment lengthwise on the MS. B leaf reads: על אשה רעה חותם (= ע אשה ר חותם) whereas B*marg* in the handwriting of the copyist of B*text* reads: טפשה, instead of: רעה. The Scroll has a clear *taw* before: חותם, and possibly even the left tip of a *shin*. Thus, possibly, restore: [על אשה רעה ת]שׄת. ומקום ידים רבות מפתח Thus חותם. *Col. B*: exactly restored by most editors, on the basis of the Greek (καὶ ὅπου χεῖρες πολλαὶ κλεῖσον); MS. B: ידים רפות תפתח, a copyist's error prompted by the frequency of the phrase: ידים רפות. מקום. ידים רבות, meaning a place where there are many thieves (cf. above, Page III, *l.* 22—41, 18c).

13 על מׄ[ ] [תפקיד מספר Restored: על [מ]קום, preferable to B*text*: תפקיד יד, perhaps a corruption of: תפקיד. B*marg*: מפקד יד, an attempt to correct the aforesaid corruption. מספר Thus B*text*. B*marg*: תחשב, which is certainly similar in meaning. [מׄ]תת [שׄ] B*marg*: ושואה ותתה. B*text*: ומתת ולקח. Restored according to B*marg*: ומתת ולקח, i.e. from the roots: נשא, and: נתן, connoting transacting of business (see the commentators).

14 על מׄ[ותה וכסיל Restored according to B*marg*: על מ[רדות פ]ותה וכסיל. The gap would seem to be too large for the word: מוסר (B*text*). *Col. B*: [שׄ]ב כׄושל ענה בזנות Thus B*marg* (though: וענה, instead of: ענה), and not as in B*text* (so also Segal).

IV,15–19/42,8c–10b

15	[ ] עֹ לפֹנֹי כל חֹי		והיית זהיר באמת	8c
16	[ ] יד נומה		[ ] שֹ [ ]שֹ [ ] לאב מטמון שק[ן	9
17	וּבֹיֹמֹיה פֹן תֹ[ ]הֹ		בנעוריה פן תמאס	9c–d
18	ועל אישֹה [ ] תשטהֹ		בבתוליה פן תחל	10a
19	[ ] צֹ[ ] ובעלֹ]		בית אבֹיֹהֹ פן תזריע	10b

15 עֹ לפֹני ... The space between the top of the *'ayin* and the *lamed* is too wide for: על פני.

16 Inscribed in the margin, at the beginning of the line, is the following mark: ך, indicating a new paragraph. It is difficult to make out the first word. The second letter is clearly a *shin*. In the first letter, attempts to correct it to a *bet* are discernible. Did the copyist write: אשה, instead of:

בת ... יד נומה ... Reading definite.

17 תמאס The copyist wrote: מאס, and then inserted the *taw* between: פן, and: מאס. וּבֹיֹמֹיה The lower edge of the *mem* is clearly visible. הֹ ... Reading not sure.

18 תשטהֹ The upper right edge of the *he* is clearly discernible.

19 ... צֹ ... Only the upper part of the *ṣade* is visible.

15 Thus MS. B. *Col. B*: Thus B*marg*, and thus restore: [ע לפני כל חי]. B*text*: [ואיש צנו]ע לפני כל חי. על פני.

16 In B*text* this line is preceded by a large space. The reading of the first word is uncertain; according to all the versions (including *Sanhedrin* 100b), this should be: בת. However, a *shin* is clearly evident, followed possibly by a *he*. The first letter, the present form of which is unclear, seemingly displays evidence of correction: *bet*(?). The copyist may have written: אשה, and then tried to correct it to: בת. I can suggest no truly satisfactory explanation. מטמון Thus B*marg*. B*text* (and *Sanhedrin* 100b): מטמנת. Various editors have already preferred the B*marg* reading. שׁקֹ[ ] Owing to a defect in the Scroll, it is impossible to decide between the reading of MS. B: שקר, and the attempts at restoration by the editors (שקד; on the basis of the Greek: ἀγρυπνία). The Talmudic version (שוא) would seem to support the reading of MS. B (for the whole verse, cf. *Ben Sira* 31, 1ff.). *Col. B*: [ ]יד נומה The end of the line is mutilated in MS. B and was restored by the editors on the basis of the translations. Peters, followed by Segal, guessed the true reading: נומה, in contrast to the others: שנה, or: שנתו. On the other hand, the clearly discernible letters: יד, confirm the reading of Cowley-Neubauer and agree with one of the Syriac versions (British Museum Codex 12138; see also Smend, p. 391): מפרדא, diverging from the restoration of the other editors: תפריע. *Col. B* is restored: [ודאגתה תפר]יד נומה. Prof. Seeligmann has pointed out the parallel: תפריעו (*Exodus*, 5, 4) which in the Samaritan version is: תפרידו.

17 The following lines are partly mutilated in

MS. B. A number of corrections have also been added here in a clumsy script, a source of perplexity to the editors. פן תמאס MS. B: פן תגור. The Scroll reading is obviously preferable (cf. also: ואשת נעורים כי תמאס — *Isaiah* 54:6). Perhaps this version was the one drawn on by the Greek (παρακμάσῃ) and the Syriac (תצטחא). Some have wanted to emend: תגור, to: תבגור, which would then bring it closer to our reading. וּבֹיֹמֹיה MS. B: ובבתוליה, which is misplaced (see below). Here, in contrast to: נעוריה, she is in her maturity, i.e. married (thus the Greek). It is difficult to restore the end of the sentence, since the traces of the last letter are vague. Perhaps restore according to B*marg*: תנשה, or: תשכח; the Greek read: תשנא.

18 בבתוליה פן תֵחֵל Thus the Greek: ἐν παρθενείᾳ μή ποτε βεβηλωθῇ (cf. also LXX, *Leviticus* 21, 4, 9). B*text*: תפותה; B*marg*: תתפתה. This is a more popular version and is similar to *Sanhedrin* 100b: בקטנותה שמא תתפתה. *Col. B*: ועל איש[ה] [פן] תשטהֹ The Scroll is close to B*marg* (as is the restored text by Smend; see also Segal), but is superior and is confirmed by the Greek: μετὰ ἀνδρὸς οὖσα μή ποτε παραβῇ.

19 בית אבֹיֹהֹ פן תזריע This corresponds to the Greek: καὶ ἐν τοῖς πατρικοῖς αὐτῆς ἔγκυος γένηται (10b). Smend and Peters came close to it in their restoration: בבית אביה פן תהרה. Segal: תזנה, out of context. For: תזריע (=תהרה), cf. *Leviticus* 12:2). *Col. B*: [ ]צֹ[ ] ובעל] This corresponds to the Greek: καὶ συνῳκηκυῖα μή ποτε στειρώσῃ (10d), and is restored: ובעל[ה פן תע]צֹ[ר]. B*text*: ובבית א[יש]ה [פן תע]צר. The verse order in the Scroll is the most plausible since it vividly un-

[182]

20	[ ] [ת]וֹ[ן]	[ ] [ ] עַׄל בַת חֹזֹק משמֹרׄ 11a-b
21	[ ]רׄ	דבת עיר וקהלת עם 11c
22	[ ] בׄ	מקום תגור אל יהי 11e
23	[ ]	לכל זכר אל תבן תאר 12
24	[ ] [שׁ]ה רעת [ה	כי מבגד יצא סס 13
25	ובת מפחדת מכול חרפֹה	טוב רע איש מטיב אשה 14

---

20 עַׄל The lower edge of the ʿayin is not quite at the beginning of the line, indicating that we must insert another short word before it.

derlines the correspondence and contrast between *Cols. A* and *B*. Thus, the verse order in the Greek should be as follows:

9c: ἐν νεότητι αὐτῆς μή ποτε παρακμάσῃ
9 : καὶ συνῳκηκυῖα μή ποτε μισηθῇ
10a: ἐν παρθενείᾳ μή ποτε βεβηλωθῇ
10c: μετὰ ἀνδρὸς οὖσα μή ποτε παραβῇ
10b: καὶ ἐν τοῖς πατρικοῖς αὐτῆς ἔγκυος γένηται
10d: καὶ συνῳκηκυῖα μή ποτε στειρώσῃ

and so already Smend and others.

20 [בני] עַׄל בת חֹזֹק משמֹרׄ Closer to B*marg* and the Syriac (ברי על ברתא אקים מטרתא), but: חזק, of the Scroll is superior and agrees with the Greek: στερέωσον. At any rate, in badly mutilated B*text*, the reading differs and perhaps partly resembles Smend's restoration: [בני על] בת עו[ל]ה [משמר] חזק (!). Smend emended: החזק, but since B*marg* corrected it to: החזק, and on the basis of the Scroll, the text is restored as above. *Col. B* is restored according to MS. B: [פ]ן ת[עשה לך שם סרה].

21 וקהלת עם B*text*: קללת עם. The Greek is similar: ἔκκλητον λαοῦ. *Col. B*: Only the *resh* has been preserved at the end of the column, which is restored: [והובישתך בעדת שער]. The Greek: ἐν πλήθει πολλῶν, a corruption of: πυλῶν (see the commentators).

22 Missing in the Greek. *Col. A* in the Scroll is incomprehensible and is restored according to B*text*: מקום תגור אל יהי (אשנב). The copyist presumably forgot to transcribe the last word. *Col. B*: Only the *bet* has been preserved at the end of the column, which is restored according to MS. B: [ובית מביט מבוא סבי]ב.

23 תבן MS. B: תתן. The Scroll reading must be understood from the root: בין, in the sense of 'exposing', 'showing', 'revealing' (cf. particularly,

21 *Col. B*: רׄ... The tip of the letter perhaps fits a *resh*.

22 אל יהי There is no trace of another word to the left of: יהי. See the Commentary. *Col. B*: בׄ... Reading definite.

Daniel 8:16: הבן להלז את המראה), i.e. the daughter should not expose her figure to any male — a presumably better reading than that of B*text*: תתן. Apparently the same consonants (תבן) were before the Greek translator when he rendered: ἔμβλεπε, and read: תביט, תתבונן; thus a great difficulty in the understanding of the Greek text is overcome (cf. also the commentators). *Col. B* has not survived and is restored on the basis of B*text*: [ובית נשים אל תסתויד]. B*marg*: תסתיד.

24 סס MS. B: עש (synonymous). The Syriac: ססא; the Greek: σής. *Col. B* is restored according to MS. B: [ומאש]ה רעת [א]שה.

25 טוב רע איש מטיב אשה The Scroll reading is similar to that of B*marg*. The additional *mem* before: טוב, at the beginning of the line in B*text* is a corruption. Though it is sometimes difficult to differentiate between *yod* and *waw* in the Scroll, the copyist here emphasized the *yod* in: מטיב, thus agreeing with B*text* and diverging from B*marg*: מטוב. A similar reading was drawn on by the Greek, though the latter misread slightly: κρείσσων πονηρία ἀνδρὸς ἢ ἀγαθοποιὸς γυνή. *Col. B*: This column is completely mutilated in MS. B. In the light of the Scroll: ובת מפחדת מכול חרפה, it is possible to understand the attempts at correction in B*marg*, which almost succeeded. Instead of: ובת, it reads: ובית, and instead of: מפחדת, it has: מחפרת. The end of the sentence: חרפה, has been preserved there. The word: תביע (MS. B), may be explained as a copyist's corruption of: מכול (see the photographs). The word: אשה, in B*text* crept in here from the end of the previous line. It may perhaps be presumed that the text drawn on by the Greek was similar, and that he gave a somewhat free rendering: καὶ γυνὴ καταισχύνουσα εἰς ὀνειδισμόν.

V, 1–5/42, 15–17c

V

(See Plate 5)

אזכרה נא מעׄ] [וזה חזיתי ואשננה	1	וזה חזיתי ואשננה	אזכרה נא מעשי אל · 15
	2	ופעל רצנו לקחו	באמר אדני מעשיו · 15c
	3	[ ]בׄוד אדני מלא מעשיו	שמש זהרת על כל נגלת[ ] · 16
	4	לספר כל נפלאתיו	לא השפיקו קדשי אל · 17
	5	להתחזק לפני כבודו	אמץ אדני צבׄאׄיו · 17c

Because of the shrinkage of the Scroll (see Pl. 8), I have cut the photograph between the two columns and have rejoined them to correct the spacing (see Pl. 5). This page is in effect made up of three fragments. The guide dots made by the copyist in the left margin, to aid in ruling the lines, are clearly discernible.

In the upper margin, above the start of *Col. A*, there is a trident-shaped sign on its side. The bend of its upper arm indicates the termination of the symbol, which thus has not been affected by the tear at the upper edge of the margin.

1 וזה The top of the *waw* can still be seen. The text in the left margin consists of three short lines in a different hand, slightly faded. Top: אזכרה נא; middle: Traces of the letters and the spacing would indicate the reading: [מעׄ]שׄי. Traces of lettering at the end of the line fit: וזה; below: חזיתי ואשננה. The reading would seem to rule out its being a variant, but would rather indicate a sort of heading or name to the whole paragraph, which one of the readers inserted (see the Commentary).

1 A new paragraph begins here, as is perhaps indicated by the symbol at the top of the right margin (see above, the Notes and the Introduction), as well as by the inscription — in a different hand — at the upper left corner of the margin. In MS. B there is a blank space one line wide just before this verse. אזכרה נא Thus, too, in the Scroll margin (cf. *Psalms* 77:12). MS. B: אזכר נא. ואשננה Thus, too, in the Scroll margin (cf. *Deuteronomy* 6:7). Perhaps this was the reading drawn on by the Greek (ἐκδιηγήσομαι) and the Syriac (מתנא). MS. B: ואספרה.

2 אדני See also below, *ll.* 3 and 5; cf. the Greek: κυρίου (also in verse 15). MS. B: אלהים. מעשיו Thus B*marg*, the Greek (τὰ ἔργα αὐτοῦ) and the Syriac (עבדוהי). B*text*: רצונו, a corruption which has crept in from *Col. B*. In the light of this, Peters' proposal to add: מעשיו (of B*marg*), after: רצונו, is pointless. לקחו Thus B*text*, in contrast to: לקח, in B*marg*. On the basis of the secondary hand in Sinaiticus (Sc), Smend emended: לחקו.

3 זהרת Thus the Greek: φωτίζων. MS. B: זורחת. (In 26, 16: זורחת; in the Greek, there: ἀνατέλλων.) אדני MS. B: יי (see above, *l.* 2).

2 ופעל The tip of the *waw* is visible.

3 [ ] נגלתׄ The reading is seemingly: נגלו, but this is an optical illusion: the Scroll is mutilated here and careful study through a magnifying glass reveals traces of script after the 'waw'. The 'waw' thus becomes the right leg of a *taw* (cf. other forms of *taw* on this page). *Col. B*: [כ]בׄוד The *kaf* has faded for the same reason as the *he* of: נגלתה (*l.* 3, above).

5 צבׄאׄיו The bottom of the letters: צב, can be made out.

מלא מעשיו Thus the version drawn on by the Greek: πλῆρες τὸ ἔργον αὐτοῦ; MS. B: על כל מעשיו.

קדשי אל MS. B: הספיקו. השפיקו MS. B thus; לספר כל נפלאתיו the Greek: ἁγίοις κύριος. Thus the Greek: ἐκδιηγήσασθαι πάντα τὰ θαυμάσια αὐτοῦ. B*text*: לספר נפלאות יי; B*marg*: לספר נפלאות גבורותיו.

5 אמץ The *defectiva* spelling of the Scroll precludes any decision between B*text*: אימץ, and B*marg*: אומץ. אדני MS. B: אלהים; the Greek: κύριος (see the Notes, above). צבׄאׄיו Thus MS. B, and certainly correct. The Greek misread: אדני צבאות — κύριος ὁ παντοκράτωρ. להתחזק Thus B*text* and the Greek (but the latter added at the end of the column: τὸ πᾶν), in contrast to B*marg*: להחזיק.

The last three verses (16–17c) contain expressions and idioms characteristic of the Dead Sea Scrolls, as a whole, and the *Thanksgiving Scroll*, in particular. See the index in my *The War of the Sons of Light...*, s.v., and in particular, p. 314, where I have compared the language of the Scrolls with the aforementioned verses of *Ben Sira*. See, also, Habermann's concordance.

6	ובמערמיהם יתבונן		תהום ולב חקר	18
7	[ ]יביט אתיות עולם		[ ]כי ידע עליון דעֹ	18c
8	[ ]מֹגלה חקר נֹסֹתרות	[	מחוה חליפֹות]	19
9	ולֹ[ ] אֹבֹ[ ]וֹ כל דבֹר		לא נעדר ממֹנֹו שכֹל	20
10	אחד הֹ[ ] אֹ[ ]]ולם	[	גבורת חכֹמֹ]	21
11	ולֹ[ ]]ולֹ מבין	[	לא נאסף]	21c
12	עד ניצוץ וחזות מראה	[	]הלוא כל מעשיו נחמֹד]	22

7 עליון Above the *ʿayin* there can be seen the tip of a *lamed* which was erased by the scribe when he wrote it by mistake, instead of *ʿayin*.

8 [מֹגלה חקר נֹסֹתרות] The line has been mutilated by a tear between the fragments, passing directly through it. The traces are clear.

9 ולֹ[ ] אֹבֹ[ ]וֹ So it should read, it seems to me (see the Commentary). דבֹר The *bet* is slightly faded.

10–11 Reading definite.

12 [ ]נחמֹד The reading would seem to be: נחמד, since to the left of the *dalet* no further traces of script can be seen; this fact may be accounted for by the tear in the Scroll, which cuts away most of the upper tip of the *dalet*, i.e. the *yod* was at the top edge of the tear, as was the final *mem*. ניצוץ The traces are clear.

6 *Col. A* agrees with MS. B. *Col. B*: ובמערמיהם MS. B: ובכל מערומיהם. The: כל, is omitted in the Greek, as well.

7 This verse is missing in MS. B. We have here for the first time its original Hebrew version. From the point of view of study of ancient texts, and restorations made on the basis of translations available, it is interesting to see how the editors have come close to our text, on the basis of the Greek:

Lévi: כי יודע עליון כל מדע / ומביט אל אותיות עולם;
Peters: כי ידע יהוה כל דעת / ויביט אל אותות לעולם;
Segal: כי יודע יײ כל דעת / ואותות עולם יביט.

The verse in the Scroll is restored: כי ידע עליון דעֹ[ת] / [ו]יביט אתיות עולם.

8 *Col. A* is restored on the basis of B*marg* and the Greek: מחוה חליפות [ונהיות]. B*text*: נהיות. For: נהיות, in the Dead Sea Scrolls, see my *The War of the Sons of Light...*, p. 340. *Col. B*: Agrees with MS. B: [ו]מגלה חקר נסתרות.

9 *Col. A* is similar to MS. B, but without: כל. *Col. B*: B*text*: ולא חלפו; B*marg*: ולא חלף מנו, perhaps under the influence of the previous verse. אֹבֹ[ד]וֹ According to the traces in the Scroll; from the point of view of the verb structure, it is similar to the reading of B*text*.

10 גבורת Thus evidently B*text* (slightly mutilated), as B*marg* corrected to: גבורות; since the spelling in the Scroll is *defectiva*, it is not decisive in the matter, and perhaps it should be pointed:

גבורת. Cf. the Greek: τὰ μεγαλεῖα. According to MS. B, restored: גבורת חכמֹ[תו תכן] (see the commentaries). *Col. B*: According to B*text*, restored: אחד הֹ[ו]לֹא [מעֹ]ולם.

11 לא נאסף All the editors have restored B*text*: לא נוסף, on the basis of the Greek: οὔτε προσετέθη. But the Scroll reading is evidently correct (see the dictionaries: אסף – יסף). According to MS. B, restored: לא נאסף [ולא נאצל]. *Col. B*: Restored according to MS. B: ול[א צריך/צרך לכ]ול מבין.

12 Missing in MS. B. Here we have for the first time the original Hebrew text. On the basis of the Greek (ὡς πάντα τὰ ἔργα αὐτοῦ ἐπιθυμητά), *Col. A* has been restored by Lévi (Segal following), almost exactly coinciding with the Scroll text: כל מעשיו נחמדים. In actuality, they could not have have been more exact, since: הלוא, is corrupt in the surviving MSS. The editors restored *Col. B* on the basis of the main Greek text: καὶ ὡς σπινθῆρός ἐστιν θεωρῆσαι. Most editors correctly restored the words: ניצוץ, and: מראה; but: καὶ ὡς, led them to: וכניצוץ (Peters and Segal). However, in the light of the Scroll text, the Greek preserved in the group of miniscule MSS. (248 and its cognates), and several uncial MSS., is preferable: ἕως (= עד) This indicates that: ὡς is a corruption.

From this point on, the verse order in MS. B is somewhat disturbed, as will be discussed below.

[185]

V,13–18/42,23–43,2

13	] [כׄל צרך הכל נשׁמׄר	הכל חי ועׂוׄ] [דׄ לעד	23
14	[ ] לעמת זה	[כלם]	42
15		[ ] ולא עשה מֹהֹם	24
16	] [מי ישבע להבׄיט הודׄם	זה על זה חלף טובם	25
17	עׂצׄם שמים מֹ] [רׄוׄ	תאר מרום ורקיע לטהר	1
18	כלי נורא מעשׂיׄ] [ליון	שמש מופיע בצאתו נכסה	2

14 כלם The tear between the two fragments intersects the final *mem*.

16 ישבע The copyist wrote: ישמע, but corrected himself. הודם The remains of the final *mem* can clearly be made

13 הכל חי Thus the Greek: πάντα ταῦτα ζῇ, and thus adjudged Smend; MS. B: [מד]הוא חי ועׂוׄ לעד. So apparently ran B*text*, since B*marg* emended to: וקים. Smend also correctly assumed the same; cf. the Greek: καὶ μένει εἰς τὸν αἰῶνα. *Col. B*: In B*text*, verse 25a crept in here by mistake (a number of lines of verse 23 have been pushed forward; see below). The proper order has been preserved in B*marg*. Restored: [ולכל צורך.]ול]כל צרך. B*text*: צורך; B*marg*: לכל צרוך. MS. B: הכל; but והכל נשמר. the Greek: καὶ πάντα. B*text*: ישמע; B*marg*: נשמע. The reading of the Scroll is unquestionably preferable; B*marg* comes close to it. Since the reading in the Greek is: ὑπακούει, it may be assumed that the corruption: נשמע – נשמר, is of early origin, and perhaps arose from a mishearing.

14-15 [ ] כלם In MS. B, v. 25a has crept into *Col. A* here by mistake, where the reading is: כלם שונים זה מזה, but on the basis of the Greek (πάντα δισσὰ ἕν κατέναντι τοῦ ἑνός) and in particular the Syriac (וכלהון תרין תרין חד לקובל חד), as well as *Col. B* (see below), restore: [שנים] כלם [שנים. The rest of the line was too long and did not allow *Col. B* to be written on the same line. The copyist therefore left a space at the end of the line, but it should be read as a continuation of the foregoing: זה לעמת זה זה (cf. *Ecclesiastes* 7:14); see especially Lévi, who guessed almost right; see also *Ben Sira* 36, 15: [זה] כולם שנים שנים זה לעומת זה. *Col. B*: Owing to lack of space, this was written on a new line beneath *Col. A*, and is restored on the basis of MS. B, the Syriac and the Greek: ולא עשה מהם [שוא]. This mode of transcribing the verse may have been the cause of the confusion in B*text*.

16 זה על זה חלף טובם This hemistich, in

out at the lower right and the upper left.

17 עׂצׄם, etc. The tear between the fragments intersects the line, but most of the letters have not been affected.

18 [ליון] מעשׂיׄ On the left side the Scroll has shrunk.

B*text*, appears earlier. B*text*: טובו; B*marg*: טוב; the Greek: τὰ ἀγαθά. Nevertheless, it seems that the Scroll reading should be followed, in view of the reading: הודם, in *Col. B. Col. B*: [ומי ישבע] להביט הודם This hemistich in B*text* appears earlier; there it is mutilated, and the first word incorrectly reads: וימי. B*marg*, the Greek and the Syriac indicate that: ומי, should be followed. הודם This is certainly the correct reading; the text evidently used by the Greek translator was the same, though it was read: הודו (δόξαν αὐτοῦ), influenced by *Col. A*. The Syriac: איקרהון. Restored by several of the editors (see, e.g., Segal): תואר (according to B*marg*), certainly incorrect, the word having crept in from the beginning of the next line.

17 תאר מרום ורקיע לטהר Missing in B*text* and the Syriac, but added in B*marg*: תואר מרום רקע על טהר. The Scroll reading is undoubtedly correct (cf. *Exodus* 24:10 and LXX, *ad loc.*). The Greek (στερέωμα καθαριότητος) also indicates no need for: על, as has been noted by the editors. *Col. B*: עׂצׄם שמים מֹ[ביע הד]רׄוׄ B*marg*: נהרה; I have restored it according to Bacher, the Greek (δόξης) and as indicated by the traces. The word: מביע, in the next line in B*text* may have slipped from here. [On the basis of the Greek, I think that the author wrote: הדרו (active participle) מַרְאֶה, and that the Grandson, not understanding, interpreted it as an abstract noun — I.L. Seeligmann].

18 שמש מופיע בצאתו נכסה B*text*: מביע בצרתו חמה, certainly corrupt. B*marg* is closer to the Scroll: שמש מופיע בצאתו חמה. Particularly interesting is the word: נכסה, in the Scroll. In my view it should be traced to the root: כסה (cf. in particular *Psalms* 81:4, where it implies the time

V, 19–24 / 43, 3–7

3	בהצהירו ירֹ] [ח תבל	ולפני חרב מי יתכל] [ל	19
4	] [וֹרֹ] [פֿוח מעֹשי מוצק	של] [מֹש] [	20
4c	לשון מאור ת] [מור נושבת	[ ]	21
5	כֹי גדול אדנֹי עשהו	ודב] [	22
6	וגמֹ] [רח יאריח עתות	מ] [	23
7	לו מֹוֹ] [ד וממנו חג	[ ]	24

19 [ל](יתכל) The lower parts of the letters are faded.
20 פֿוח[ ] [וֹרֹ] The traces are clear. [מֹש..] There do not seem to be any traces of script after the *shin*, but this can be ascribed to the general deterioration of the Scroll here, resulting in the fading, too, of the lower part of

the end of the previous line.
21 Most of *Col. B* is missing on the page from here on.
22 ודב... Clearly preserved till the tear.
23 מ... Clearly preserved till the tear.

at which the moon is full; see the dictionaries). Possibly the intention is that the sun is full of light immediately at its rise (cf. *Habakkuk* 3:3). The B*text* reading (חמה) may reflect a more popular version. At any rate, the Scroll reading solves the perplexities of the various editors. *Col. B*: כלי נורא מעשֹי עֹ]ליון MS. B: מה נורא מעשי ייי, corrupt. The Scroll agrees with the Greek (σκεῦος) and the Syriac (מאנא). They also read: עליון — ʽΥψίστου; דמרימא. For the spelling: מעשֹי – מעשה, see among others, the Dead Sea Scrolls, and below.
19 בהצהירו ירֹ]תי[ח תבל Thus MS. B (cf. *Job* 24:11; 41:23). *Col. B*: ולפני Thus the Greek (καὶ ἐναντίον) and the Syriac (וקדם). MS. B: לפני. חרב In MS. B, the Greek and the Syriac: חרבו. יתכל]כֹ]ל Restored according to MS. B (see the Notes, above).
20 נ]פֿוח [כ]וֹרֹ] Thus MS. B. מעֹשי Thus the Greek (ἔργοις). The Syriac: כעבדא; the word: מעשֹי, possibly here means: מעשה (see above). MS. B: מהם, corrupt. מוצק Thus B*marg*. B*text*: מצוק. *Col. B*: שלֹ[וח ש]מֹש Restored according to B*marg*. B*text*: שולח שמש. The end is restored according to B*marg*: יסיק הרים; B*text*: ידליק.
21 לשון מאור ת]גֹמור נושבת Thus B*marg*. B*text*: לשאן. *Col. B*: Restored according to MS. B: [ומנורה תכוה עין].
22 כֹי Thus MS. B. The word is missing in the Greek and the Syriac. גדול Thus B*text*, the Greek (μέγας) and the Syriac (רב). B*marg*: גדיל, a corruption. אדנֹי Thus B*text*: ייי, the Greek (κύριος) and the Syriac (מרנא). B*marg*: עליון. עשהו Thus B*text* (עושהו), the Greek (ὁ ποιήσας αὐτόν) and the Syriac (דעבדה); B*marg*: עשה. *Col. B*: Restored ac-

cording to B*text*: [ודב]ריו ינצח אבירייו. B*marg*: נצה (thus, and not the opposite, as Segal read). For the problem of this hemistich, see the commentators. In the light of the Scroll reading of the next hemistich (יארח), it is assumed that the Greek (πορείαν) and the Syriac (הלכתה) have been influenced by the next verse.
23 וגמֹ [יֹ]רח יאריח עתות Here the original Hebrew text has been preserved, according to which we may understand the reading of B*text*, the variants in the several versions and the difficulties of the commentators. B*text*: וגם ירח ירח עתות שבות, is close, and it is obvious that the word: שבות, is an accretion influenced by: ירח ירח, and should be omitted. The Scroll reading confirms Schechter's view, regarding the second: ירח, in B*text*, as a verb, which he compared to: تاريخ. We may now affirm that the B*text* reading is a corruption of: יאריח (in the sense of 'will guide', 'will prescribe the seasons'; and see the dictionaries). Here Ben Sira resorts to a play of words similar to that in the next hemistich. [Ziegler reads: ἵστησιν, on the basis of the Syriac: קאם, and a late MS. (631). If his reading is correct (as it seems to be), then the reading: εἰς στάσιν (248), is a most delightful corruption!, which later gave rise to: ἐν πᾶσιν — I.L. Seeligmann (however, see Charles—Y.Y.).] *Col. B*: Restored according to MS. B: מ]משלת קץ ואות עולם.
24 לו מֹוֹ]עֹ[ד וממנו חג This original Hebrew text is of great importance. It is close to B*marg*: בו מועד וזמני חוק (instead of: חג, perhaps a mishearing). The moon is also the subject in the Greek (ἀπὸ σελήνης σημεῖον ἑορτῆς) and the Syriac (מן סהרא). B*text*: בם, on the other hand, presupposes

V,25–VI,2/43,8–9

25   [   ]   [חׄדש כשמו הוא מתׄ]   8

25 Traces of the letters are visible.

that the subject is still both luminaries. Both the continuation of the verse in *Col. B* and the next verse indicate that Ben Sira is still speaking of the moon. In the light of this, we may assume that B*text* here is perhaps influenced by the *Ben Sira* recension originating with the Dead Sea Sect, where a deliberate attempt was made to introduce the sun as a factor in determining the seasons (see the Introduction). For this group of verses in general, cf. *The Manual of Discipline* X, 2–3: באופיע מאורות, etc. *Col. B*: It is difficult to decide on the restoration. MS. B: וחפץ ע[ה] בתקופתו, has been restored variously, chiefly: ע[ש]ה, but this diverges from the Greek and the Syriac which read, approximately, that the light of the moon wanes as it runs its course. Perhaps we should read: וחפץ ע[ת]ה. This seems cor-

rect to me, in the light of a fresh examination of the Facsimile. The restoration: בתקופתו, best fits the continuation in the next verse.

25 חׄדש כשמו הוא מתׄ[חדש] The closest reading to the Scroll is that of B*marg*: חדש כשמו והוא מתחדש, in contrast to B*text*: חדש בחדשו הוא מתחדש, which is certainly corrupt. The Greek testifies in the main to a reading similar to that of the Scroll, but the translator had difficulties in rendering the play on words, which can be understood only in the Hebrew: μὴν κατὰ τὸ ὄνομα αὐτῆς ἐστιν. The Syriac is similar: ירחא איך שמה איתוהי (cf. *The Manual of Discipline* X, 4). *Col. B*: Restored according to B*text* [מה נורא בהשתנותו]. The Greek and the Syriac are similar. B*marg*: בתשובתו.

VI
(See Plate 6)

1   [מ] [צׄףׄ]   כלי צבא נבלי מרום   8c

2   [עד ומשריק במרו]   תור שמים והוד כוכב   9

The entire page has been preserved on the left sheet of the largest fragment. The bottom part has shrunk considerably, the lines progressively getting shorter down the page. Traces of ruling of the lines are clearly visible in the upper margin. It should be noted that the copyist ruled the lines from the top of the page. Furthermore, intermediary lines can be made out, indicating the maximum height of the *lamed*.

1 מ] [צׄףׄ The lower parts of: צף, have been preserved.

2 במרו... Only the lower parts of: רן, have been preserved.

1 כלי צבא נבלי מרום Thus exactly MS. B, invalidating all the proposed emendations (Smend: נכלי; גיבורי; Peters: נפילי). כלי The Greek rendering is in the singular (σκεῦος), the Syriac following (מאנא). נבלי מרום See *Job* 38:37: נבלי שמים. The Greek and the Syriac omitted this difficult word. *Col. B*: מ] [צׄףׄ Thus B*text*. B*marg*: מערץ. Restored according to MS. B: מ[ר]צף [רקיע מזהירתו].

2 תור שמים MS. B: תואר שמים. We may assume that: תור, in the Scroll, meaning: תואר, is a phonetic spelling (see also below, *l.* 12). But it should be noted that in 42, 12 (see above, Page IV, *l.* 23), the copyist of the Scroll wrote: תאר. The reading of the Syriac (צכתא) indicates perhaps that he read:

תור, i.e. 'an ornament', on the basis of *Song of Songs* 1:10–11 (and see my article in: *The Military History of Palestine*, Tel Aviv, 1964, p. 340, n. 16 [Hebrew], and see *Col. B*, below). והוד MS. B: והדר; the Greek: δόξα. It would seem that the Scroll reading should be adopted. כוכב Thus MS. B and in the Syriac (דכוכבא). The Greek read: כוכבים (ἄστρων), but the Scroll text confirms that the whole verse refers to the moon. *Col. B*: עד ומשריק B*marg*: ועדי משריק; thus the Greek: κόσμος φωτίζων. B*text*: ואורו. The Scroll text apparently gives us a verbal connotation to: עד, meaning adorns and sparkles (cf. also above, Page V, *l.* 12: עד ניצוץ). ומשריק Thus B*marg*. In B*text*: מזהיר (see the

3	ולׂא ישח באשמרתם	בדבר אדני יעמד חק	10
4	[כי מאׄד נהדר]	ראה קשת וברך עשיה	11
5	[ ]יד אל נטׂתׂה בגב]	חׂוׂג [ ] בכבודה	12
6	ותנצח זיקות משפט	גערתו] הׄ ברד[	13
7	ויעף עבים כעׄיׄט	למענו פרע אוצר	14
8	ותגדע אבני ברד	גבורתו חזק ענן	15

³ ולׂא Reading definite.

⁴ מאׄד The *alef* has been damaged by vermin. [נהדר] Traces at the end of the line are discernible but cannot be deciphered with certainty (see the Commentary).

⁵ חׂוׂג Reading definite. יׂד[ ] The first letter has been

lost; the reading of the other letters is definite.

⁶ הׄ[ ] The tip of the *he* is visible, to the left of the gap.

⁷ כעׄיׄט Reading definite.

⁸ אׂבׂני The traces fit this reading.

Introduction). For: משריק, see also Th. Nöldeke, *Bemerkungen zum hebräischen Ben Sīrā*, *ZAW* 20 (1900), p. 86 (I thank Prof. Seeligmann for this reference). [במרוׄ] Restored according to MS. B: במרו]מי אל].

³ בדבר אדני יעמד חק Agrees with MS. B: בדבר אל יעמד חק. The Greek, and the Syriac following, is slightly different: ἐν λόγοις ἁγίου στήσονται κατὰ κρίμα (=בדברי קדוש יעמדו כחק). In the Scroll and MS. B, the moon continues to be the subject of the verse. *Col. B*: ולׂא ישח באשמרתם Thus in B*text*, i.e. the moon. B*marg*: ולא ישן באש־מרותם. For this terminology, cf. *The Manual of Discipline* X, 2.

⁴ ראה קשת וברך עשיה Thus exactly B*text*, and in effect in the Greek (τὸν ποιήσαντα αὐτό). B*marg*: עושה. *Col. B*: כי Thus MS. B. The Greek omitted the word. [נהדרה בכבוד] Thus B*marg*. B*text*: נאדרה. Lévi's and Peters' suggestion to read: בהוד, in B*text* does not sound plausible to me after a fresh examination of the Facsimile. The reading of Cowley-Neubauer and Smend: בכבוד, seems correct.

⁵ חׂוׂג B*text*: חוק; B*marg*: הוד, but the editors have already noted that it should read: חוג. Cf. also the Greek: ἐγύρωσεν. For the variants between the Scroll and B*text*, cf. *Proverbs* 8:27: בחקו חוג; and *Job* 26:10: חק חג (see also Lévi). Restored according to B*text*: [חוג הקיפה בכבודה]. B*marg*: בכבודו. *Col. B*: ויד אל נטתה בגב]ורה] Thus Smend has restored B*text*. The Scroll invalidates the proposals of Peters, Box & Oesterley and Segal: בגׄ]אׄן]. The Greek omitted the word altogether.

⁶ גערתו]הׄ ברד[Thus B*marg*, but the

Greek has: προστάγματι αὐτοῦ (see Smend). B*text*: גבורתו. הׄ[תתו] Thus MS. B. ברד B*text*: ברק; B*marg*: בקר. The Greek evidently also read as in the Scroll: χιόνα (= snow, hail; see the commentators). In spite of this, the B*text* reading seems preferable. The copyist of the Scroll perhaps erred under the influence of verse 15 (see below, *l.* 8). *Col. B*: ותנצח זיקות משפט Segal, following the Greek: משפטו; the others: במשפט. The Scroll reading is preferable. B*text*: ותנצח זיקות [משפט]. B*marg*, in the hand of B*text*: ותנצח זיקים; B*marg*, in a secondary hand: ותזנח יקום בם — both corruptions.

⁷ למענו Thus B*marg* and the Greek (διὰ τοῦτο). B*text*: פרע למען. MS. B: ברא, but the Scroll reading is preferable. Cf. the Greek: ἠνεῴχθησαν [and see LXX, *Psalms* 119:131 and *Proverbs* 31:26 — I.L. Seeligmann]. *Col. B*: B*text* is damaged. On the basis of the Greek (καὶ ἐξέπτησαν νεφέλαι ὡς πετεινά), Peters and Segal restored: עבים כרשף; Lévi: ענן כרשף; Smend: עבים כצפורים. We have here the original Hebrew reading. Cf. *Isaiah* 18:6 — לעיט הרים (= LXX: τοῖς πετεινοῖς τοῦ οὐρανοῦ).

⁸ גבורתו חזק ענן MS. B is damaged. It possibly should be: תחזק, there being a haplographical corruption (?) [I.L. Seeligmann]. The editors restored it almost right, on the basis of the Greek (ἐν μεγαλείῳ αὐτοῦ ἴσχυσεν νεφέλας). *Col. B*: ותגדע אבני ברד The Greek: καὶ διεθρύβησαν λίθοι χαλάζης, according to which the editors restored: ויפץ אבני (Lévi, Peters); וישברו אבני ברד (Smend); ויתפוצצו אבני ברד אלגביש (Segal). The Scroll version is undoubtedly correct, in the light of: גבורתו, in *Col. A*.

VI,9–13/43,17–19

9	ובכחו יניף הרים		קול רעמו יחיל ארצו	17
10	עלעול סופה וסערה	17b	אמרתו תחריף תימן	16b
11	וכארבה ישכן רדתו		כרשף יפרח שלגו	17
12	וממטרו יתמיה לבב		תור לבנו יהג עינים	18
13	ויצמח כסנה צצים		כפור כמלח ישפך [ ]	19

9 יחיל Both *yods* are clear.

10 אמרתו The reading: אימתו, is out of the question. The bottom of the *mem* can clearly be made out, to the left of the *alef* (see the Commentary).

11 רדתו The copyist clearly differentiates between *resh*

and *dalet*.

12 וממטרו With difficulty, this may be read: ובמטרו.

13 כפור [   ] The traces fit the reading. At any rate, at the start of the line there is a space to accommodate a short word (see the Commentary).

9 קול רעמו יחיל ארצו Thus B*marg*. B*text*: יחול. The Greek: φωνὴ βροντῆς αὐτοῦ ὠνείδισεν γῆν (=ארץ). [ὠνείδισεν cannot be considered a translation of: יחיל (=ὠδίνησεν!), though it is possible that it renders: תחריף, in *l.* 10 (misunderstanding), for which I can see no absolute parallel in the Greek — I.L. Seeligmann.] For: ὠδίνησεν, see Charles. *Col. B*: ובכחו יניף הרים In B*text* the second hemistich of the next verse crept in here by mistake (see below). B*marg*: ובכחו יזעים הרים. The verses are misplaced further down in B*text* and some are missing. The verse order is similarly confused in several Greek MSS. The order in the Scroll agrees with that of B*marg* and one group of Greek MSS. (23, 106, 157, 248, 253, etc.; see Charles, and Peters).

10 אמרתו תחריף תימן Missing in B*text*. B*marg*: אימתו תחרף תימן. The Greek: ἐν θελήματι αὐτοῦ πνεύσεται νότος, and seemingly read: אמרתו, as the editors have proposed. *Col. B* (17b): עלעול סופה וסערה Exactly as in B*marg*. B*text*, misplaced above in the second hemistich, 43, 17: זלעפות צפון סופה וסערה. The Greek: καὶ καταιγὶς βορέου καὶ συστροφὴ πνεύματος (=סופת-סערה). The original might have been: עלעול צפון סופה וסערה (see Smend).

11 כרשף The Greek: ὡς πετεινά (and see above, on: עיט); B*text*: ברשף, a corruption. יפרח Meaning: מעופף; MS. B: יניף. See the commentators on the Greek: καθιπτάμενα πάσσει. *Col. B*: וכארבה ישכן רדתו Thus exactly B*marg* and the Greek: ἡ κατάβασις αὐτῆς. B*text*: דרתו, a corruption.

12 תור MS. B: תואר; the Greek: κάλλος (for the spelling, see above, *l.* 2). לבנו MS. B: לבנה (=לבנה). Thus also the Greek (λευκότητος αὐτῆς).

and *dalet*.

יהג Close to B*marg*: יהגה. B*text*: יגהה. Perhaps to be explained as related to: הגה ('to divert', i.e. the whiteness of the snow diverts the eyes, which cannot bear to look at it; in effect, 'dazzles'). Cf. *Proverbs* 25:4–5, as well as *II Samuel* 20:12–13 (and see Smend). The Greek reads: ἐκθαυμάσει (something like "will puzzle") paralleling the phrase in *Col. B* (see below). *Col. B*: וממטרו יתמיה לבב The Greek: ἐκστήσεται καρδία; MS. B: יהמה לבב. The verbs were exchanged in the Greek.

13 [וגם] כפור כמלח ישפך Thus B*marg* and the Greek (χέει), which added: ἐπὶ γῆς (=על ארץ). B*text*: ישכן, a corruption influenced by 43, 17 (see above, *l.* 11). *Col. B*: ויצמח כסנה צצים MS. B: ויציץ כספיר ציצים. We have here an interesting development: a study of the photographs demonstrates how easy it was for the copyist to misread: כספיר. In contrast to MS. B, the Greek gives: καὶ παγεῖσα γίνεται σκολόπων ἄκρα. Assuming that: παγεῖσα (i.e. 'when congealed'), is an explanation added by the translator (see the editors), he translated the text in front of him: καὶ γίνεται, which could definitely be taken to correspond to: יצמח. The word: ἄκρα, represents: ציצים, and we are left with: σκόλοψ which implies 'a thorn'. In the light of the Scroll text, we may gauge that he either read: סנה (= 'a thorny shrub'), or he misread: כסכה. A study of the photographs likewise shows it easy to make this mistake as well (see LXX, *Numbers* 33:35 — לשכים בעיניכם — σκολόπεις ἐν τοῖς ὀφθαλμοῖς). Most editors, of course, tried to restore the Greek text from the reading: כספיר, and therefore proposed: כסופי קוצים, or: כסירי קוצים (Lévi); צנינים, instead of: צצים (Peters and Smend); כסופי צנינים (Segal).

[190]

VI,14–19/43,20–24

14	וכרגב יקפיא מקור		[	]וֹן יֵשִׁיֹב	20
17	[	]	[	]ף עֹנָן טֹ[	22
18	[	]אֹיים	[	אמר] תעֹמיק רֹ[	23
19	לשמע אזנינו נשמתם		[	קֹצֹ [ ]פֹ[ ]ם יֹ[	24

¹⁴]וֹן יֵשִׁיֹב[ ] The traces fit the reading. It is impossible to decide between: ישיב, and: ישוב (see the Commentary).

^{15–16} These lines are entirely missing, owing to a tear.

¹⁷ ...ף עֹנָן טֹ. Traces of the final *pe* are clearly discernible at the top of a small fragment pieced in here (see the Commentary). עֹנָן The traces coincide with the form of this word in *l.* 8, above (see the Commentary).

¹⁸ A part of this line is found on a shred which I have fitted here (see above, *l.* 17). The copyist made a number of errors in this line and the next, and has corrected them by inserting letters and words between the lines. ...אמר Clearly visible. Immediately after: יק רֹ. Above the: יק, a *mem* can

be clearly made out, preceeded by faint traces. The first letter resembles *taw* (see the Commentary). Col. B: אֹיים The upper right tip of the *alef* is visible.

¹⁹ קֹצֹ ..פ.י. ם... On the same shred as above (see above, *ll.* 17–18). The final *mem* can clearly be seen. Above the line, the copyist added a word, the traces of which best fit: ..פ.י.. The *pe* is particularly clear. קֹצֹ The traces of the *ṣade* are clearly discernible. The *qof* is doubtful, but the traces more closely resemble *qof* than *resh*. לשמע On another shred fitted here (see also *l.* 20, below). נשמתם The copyist wrote: נשמת, but added the final *mem* beneath the *taw* (see the Commentary).

¹⁴ Restored according to MS. B:]ציגת רוח צפ]ון ישיב. It is difficult to determine from the traces whether the reading is: ישוב (=πνεύσει). *Col. B*: וכרגב MS. B: כרקב, a reading which has given rise to extreme difficulty (see the commentators). There is no doubt that we have here the correct reading (cf. *Job* 21:33; 38:38). In the light of our text, we may assume that a similar or identical version was drawn on by the Greek: καὶ παγήσεται κρύσταλ-λος ἀφ' ὕδατος. מקור Preferable to: מקורו, of B*text* or: מקוה, of B*marg*, influenced by: מקוה, in the next verse.

^{15–16} Nothing has survived of these lines.

¹⁷ The traces (see the Notes, above) fit mainly the reading of B*text*: מרפא כל מער]ף ענן טל]. The B*marg* reading transposes the word: טל, to *Col. B*. If I have pieced the small shred in here correctly, the Scroll text is similar to that of B*text*. But the traces are too scanty to restore the other parts of the verse with any degree of certainty (see the commentators).

¹⁸ If the fragment has been correctly placed (see the Notes, above), as seems to me, we may be able to restore the text of this hemistich successfully. B*text*: מחשבתו תשיק רבה. B*marg*: תשובתו; the Greek: λογισμῷ αὐτοῦ ἐκόπασεν ἄβυσσον, on which basis Peters emended to: השקיע. It seems to

me that we should join here the *mem* (medial!) added above the line to: יק, to form: מיק.... We may thus restore: יעמיק, or: תעמיק (see below). אמר.. Since before the *mem* (see above), traces resembling *taw* are discernible, I should read: אמרתו, on the assumption that the scribe inserted the *taw*, too, above the line (for: אמרתו, see above, *l.* 10). In this event, we can restore the hemistich: אמר]תו תע]מיק רבה. Though this proposal appeals to me, I must admit that the fragment is too small, and it is difficult to reach any definite conclusions on account of the copyist's errors. *Col. B*: On the basis of MS. B, restored: איים [בתהום ויט]. Thus the Greek: νήσους (and not as in a number of MSS.: 'Ιησοῦς). B*marg*: ויט בתהום אוצר.

¹⁹ The traces occur on the fragment containing the remains of *ll.* 17–18 (see above). Here, too, the copyist erred and inserted: [פ[ס]רו]יק, above the line. ..קֹצֹ MS. B: קצהו; but the Greek (τὸν κίνδυνον αὐτῆς) has led some editors to propose restoring: צרתו. The traces on the fragment would seem to support the reading of MS. B. Restored according to MS. B: [יורדי הי]ם י[ס]פ[רו] קצ]הו]. *Col. B*: Restored on the basis of MS. B and the Greek: לשמ]ע אזנינו נשתמם]. The copyist incorrectly transcribed: נשמת, later inserting the *mem* under the line.

VI,20–VII,7/43,25–44,2

20	[גְּבוּרֹת רֹהֹב	]וֹ[	[	] 25
24	[תֹו (יֹו)	]	[	] 29
25	[שֹׁ אל	]	[	] 30

20 ...וֹ On the same shred as *l.* 19, above. The first letter resembles *waw* or *yod.* The next may be *mem* (see the Commentary). גְּבוּרֹת רֹהֹב Reading definite, with the help of a magnifying glass (see the Commentary).

21–23 These lines have been mutilated.

24 תֹו The place of these two letters is necessarily here because of the placing of the shred bearing part of Page VII, *l.* 24 (see below). It is difficult to determine whether the first letter is *yod* or *taw;* the latter would seem the more plausible (see the Commentary).

25 שֹׁ אל... On a shred fitted here. A part of the lower margin also fits here.

20 *Col. A* has not survived. Restored according to MS. B: [שם פלאות תמהי מעשיו]. *Col. B:* Restored: [מין כל חי ו]גבורת רהב, and thus correctly restored Peters, on the basis of the Greek: κητῶν (see *Job* 26:12), MS. B: רבה. The lower right portion of the page has not survived.

24 B*text* reads at the end of the hemistich: דבריו, but there is no doubt that the reading of B*marg* should be adopted: גבורתו; and thus in the Greek:

ἡ δυναστεία αὐτοῦ. The whole verse is thus restored: [נורא אדני מאד מאד ונפלאת גבור]תו (see above, the Notes, and cf. the commentators).

25 *Col. A* is missing. *Col. B:* If the fragment has been correctly placed (see the Notes, above), we should restore here: [בכל תוכלו כי י]שׁ אל (cf., e.g., *Psalms* 58:12), instead of the reading of MS. B: כי יש עוד, which has given rise to many difficulties. The Greek reads: ὑπερέξει γὰρ καὶ ἔτι.

VII

(See Plate 7)

| 6 | [| את אב] | חסד [ ]אֹנֹ[[ ] | 1 |
| 7 | [| וגדלה מי] | רב כבוד חלֹק עליון | 2 |

This page has been preserved on the left side of the largest fragment. It has shrunk considerably, the lines progressively growing shorter down the page (Pl. 8). On Pl. 7, the page appears after my having cut the photograph and remounting it, in order to correct the distortion. In the lower right corner I have placed a small, odd shred (see below, *l.* 24).

1–5 The upper part of the page has been eaten away, including these lines.

6 Calculation of the number of verses and the space above this line enable us to determine that the copyist had left one

blank line (see the Commentary). ...אֹנֹ The lower tips of the letters can be seen.

7 חלֹק Reading definite.

1–5 These lines are missing, due to the large tear running diagonally through the upper left of the left sheet (see also the Notes, above).

6 This is the first verse of the 'Praise of the Fathers of Old'. Calculation of the number of lines, comparing with Page VI (see Pl. 8, and the Notes, above), indicates that there was one blank line before this. On the other hand, it is impossible to determine whether there was a heading similar to that appearing in B*text:* שבח אבות עולם, or in the Greek: πατέρων ὕμνος (missing in MSS. 23, 106 and 253). It should be noted that this heading is missing also in the Syriac. *Col. A:* Restored according to MS. B:

[אהללה נא אנ]שׁי חסד. The Scroll text does not permit a decision between the MS. B reading (אהללה נא) and the Greek (αἰνέσωμεν δή), i.e. whether singular or plural. חסד This word is of importance in the Scroll (cf. the expressions: בני חסד, ;אביוני חסד in the *Thanksgiving Scroll* V, 23; VII, 20). The Greek: ἄνδρας ἐνδόξους; the Syriac: אנשא דטבותא. *Col. B:* ...את אב Fitting in with the beginning of the hemistich in B*marg:* את אבו]תינו [בדורותם. B*text,* without: את. The Greek adds: καί (*waw*). As a rule, all the versions agree.

7 רב כבוד חלק עליון Thus B*text.* B*marg* adds: להם, after: חלק. The version drawn on by the

VII,8–9/44,3c–4

8	[וחז כל בנב]	ויועצים בתבונתם 3c
9	[ורזנים במחקק]	שרי גוי במזמתם 4

8 וחזי Though the scribe distinguished between the *zayin* and the *yod*, they are still easily confused (see the Commentary).

Greek agrees with the Scroll reading and B*text*: πολλὴν δόξαν ἔκτισεν ὁ κύριος. A number of MSS. (e.g., 248) add: ἐν αὐτοῖς. There is no need to restore: יהוה (Peters), since we have already seen above that: עליון, in the Scroll is often rendered by: ὁ κύριος, in the Greek. The Syriac reads slightly differently: סגי איקרא נפלוג (= נחלק) להון. This is evidence that the Scroll reading is the original *Col. B*: וגדלה מי... The Scroll reading confirms that: וגדלו, in MS. B should be pointed: וְגִדְלוּ, as Smend and Peters have done (cf. above, Page, VI, *l*. 12: לבנה = לבנו), and not: וְגִדְלוֹ, as Segal has. The word: גדל, parallels: רב כבוד, in *Col. A*. Cf. the Greek: τὴν μεγαλωσύνην αὐτοῦ. The Syriac translator, too, understood: גדל, but attributed it to the Fathers: רבותהון. For the גדל, of God, see *The War of the Sons of Light* I, 8: יאיר רום גודלו; and especially p. 259 in my publication of that Scroll. Restored after to MS. B: וגדלה מי]מות עולם].

(44, 3). The Scroll omits 43, 3a–b, of MS. B and the Greek: דורי ארץ במלכותם / ואנשי שם בגבורתם. B*marg*: רודי... בגבורם. This verse is missing from the Syriac as well, but this is no criterion, since a number of other verses are also missing from it. The copyist of the Scroll probably omitted this verse by mistake, as is seemingly borne out by: ויועצים, at the beginning of the next verse.

8 ויועצים B*text*: היועצים; B*marg*: יועצים. The Greek omits both the *he* and the *waw*. At any rate, it may be concluded from here that the Scroll inadvertently omitted the previous verse, since the reading: ויועצים, is logical only if the copyist had that verse before him. **בתבונתם** Thus MS. B and the Greek (ἐν συνέσει αὐτῶν). *Col. B*: וחזי כל Thus MS. B: וחזי כל. The spelling in the Scroll (a study of the photographs indicates how easy it was to misread: וחזו) explains how the Greek, and the Syriac following, mistook it for a word from the root: חזה. The Greek: ἀπηγγελκότες; the Syriac: וחזיו (= וחזו). The last word may be restored according to MS. B: [ואתם]בנב. Cf. the Greek and

9 במזמתם Reading definite. The copyist evidently added the *bet* afterwards, and thus made it as small as possible, to fit into the remaining space. The same goes for the *zayin*.

the Syriac. It is interesting to note that a similar mistake in reading has caused modern editors to read in the *Damascus Covenant*: וחזה, instead of: וחזי. See Y. Yadin: *IEJ* 6 (1956), p. 158.

9 שרי גוי Thus the Greek: ἡγούμενοι λαοῦ, in contrast to MS. B: שרי גוים. The Scroll reading and the Greek, referring to the princes of Israel, is preferable. **במזמתם** Thus MS. B. In the Greek: ἐν διαβουλίοις (= במזמת). *Col. B*: ורזנים במ- MS. B: ורזנים במחקרותם. חקק.. It seems to me that the Scroll reading is undoubtedly the original (cf., especially, *Proverbs* 8:15 — ורזנים יחוקקו צדק). Moreover, it is probable that a similar text was drawn on by the Greek, but that it was not properly understood, and that the passage became corrupt in the course of time, till the second half of the next verse ultimately dropped out. The editors were very hard put to find a satisfactory explanation of the Greek (καὶ συνέσει γραμματείας λαοῦ; see also the variants in a group of MSS.: καὶ ἐν γραμματείαις γραμματεῖς; and see Charles). All connected: γραμματείας, with the: רוזנים, but as a result were faced with a sentence the structure of which baffled interpretation. In *Ben Sira* 10, 5, we have: ולפני מחוקק ישית הודו; and in the Greek: καὶ προσώπῳ γραμματέως ἐπιθήσει δόξαν αὐτοῦ. Furthermore, the LXX version should be compared with the one cited above from *Proverbs*: καὶ οἱ δυνάσται γράφουσιν δικαιοσύνην. Accordingly: συνέσει, may probably be attributed to a copyist's error (influenced by the existence of the same word in the previous verse), the original reading probably having been: δυνάσται. If we restore the Scroll version (following the structure of the other verses here and paralleling: במזמתם) to: [במחקק]תם, we can explain not only the corruption in MS. B, but also the Greek: λαοῦ, which read (a mishearing influenced by *Col. A*, above): במחקקת עם, precisely as happened in 45, 22 where the original text was: בארצם (mutilated in MS. B; the Syriac: בארעהון), but the Greek: ἐν γῇ λαοῦ (see the commentators,

VII,10–17/44,4c–10

10	[	ומשלים במֹ]	חכמי שיח בספרתם	4c
11	[	ונשאי מש]	חקרי מזמור על קו	5
12	[	ושקֹ]	אנשי חיל וסמכי כח	6
13	[	]	כל אלה בדרם נכבדו	7
14	[	לה]	יש מהם הניחו שֹם	8
15	[	]	ויש מהם שאין לו זכר	9
16	[	וֹ]	כאשר לא היו היו	9c
17	[	וצֹ]	אולם אלה אנשי חסד	10

11 חקרי A part of the *qof* is mutilated.
12 ...ושק The tip of the *qof* is clearly visible.
14 שֹם The right tip of the final *mem* is mutilated. ...לה The letters are clear.

16 *Col. B*: ...וֹ The lower edge of the letter is visible.
17 ...וצֹ The upper tip of the right leg of the *ṣade* is visible.

ad loc.). In this case: ἐν γραμματείαις, is to be preferred.

10 בספרתם Thus B*text*. B*marg*: במסׄ׳. Lévi conjectured that the reading here was: במסרם, as may also be concluded from the Greek: ἐν παιδείᾳ αὐτῶν. Again there is no doubt that the Scroll reading (and B*text*) is preferable. *Col. B*: ...ומשלים במֹ. The second word, somewhat faded in MS. B, has been read by the editors: במשמרותם; not only is this reading difficult contextually (see the quandary of the commentators), but also a study of the Facsimile indicates that the reading may be incorrect. It seems to me, after a detailed examination, that B*text* reads: במשמחותם, and thus we shall also read here: במֹ]שמחותם. If we accept the interpretation of most commentators that: מושלים, are speakers of proverbs (paralleling *Col. A*), the sense will then be: speakers of proverbs — at the festive gatherings where they recite their wise sayings. This proposed reading may also explain the occurrence of the *ḥet* in the Syriac: בתשבחתהן, i.e. that translator read: בתשבחותם. At any rate, owing to the tear, the Scroll reading does not provide us with sufficient grounds for determining the correct reading, and all that that has been said here remains conjecture.

11 על קו Thus read Cowley-Neubauer in B*marg*, and the Scroll reading would seem to bear them out. The other editors read: חקו. B*text*: על חוק. According to the Scroll, therefore, the reading should be: על קו, i.e. 'according to rule'. *Col. B*: ונשאי Thus a number of Greek MSS. (with: καὶ). The Syriac: ואמרי. Restored according to MS. B

and the translations: ונשאי מש]ל בכתב. The Syriac: בכתבא; the Greek: ἐν γραφῇ.

12 וסמכי כח MS. B: וסומכי כח. According to the spelling of the Scroll, it is impossible to decide between the view of most editors who read, basing on the Greek and the Syriac: וסמוכי כח, and those who accept the reading of B*text* (Segal). *Col. B*: Restored according to MS. B: ושקֹ[טים על מכונתם, and thus approximately the Greek (εἰρηνεύοντες ἐν παροικίαις αὐτῶν) and the Syriac (ושליו על תוקנהין).

13 כל אלה בדרם נכבדו Thus exactly B*marg* (B*text* omits: נכבדו), in the Greek and the Syriac. B*text*: בדורם. *Col. B*: Missing owing to the tear. Restored according to B*marg*, the Greek and the Syriac: ובימיהם תפארתם].

14 Thus MS. B, the Greek and the Syriac. *Col. B*: לה]... Restored according to B*marg*: להשתעות [בנחלתם. B*text*: להשתעונות. A preferable reading might be: בתהלתם, as in the Greek and the Syriac.

15 שאין לו זכר MS. B: אשר אין לו זכר. At any rate, the Scroll reading agrees with that of MS. B, and diverges from the Greek and the Syriac: (דלית להם להון דוכרנא). *Col.* B: Restored according to MS. B: וישבתו כאשר שבתו].

16 Thus MS. B and the Greek. The line is missing in the Syriac. *Col.* B: Restored according to MS. B and the Greek: ובניהם מאחריהם].

17 אולם MS. B: ואולם; the Greek may have read the same. The rest of the column agrees with MS. B and the Greek. *Col. B*: וצֹ.... Thus confirming the Greek: ὧν αἱ δικαιοσύναι (248 + αὐτῶν) οὐκ ἐπελήσθησαν (see Peters and Charles). The

VII,18–22/44,11–15

18	ונח] [	אם זרעם נאמן טובם	11
19	וצאצאיהֹם] [	בבריתם עמד זרעם	12
20	[וכבודם לא ימחֹ]	וֹעֹד עולם יעמד זרעם	13
21	ושמם חי לדור ודור	וגֹ] [ֹם בשלום נאספה	14
22	ותהלתם יספר קהל	הֹ עדה [ ]	15

20 וֹעֹד The traces fit the reading. ימֹחֹ. The lower tip of the right leg of the ḥet can be made out.

21 ֹם...וגֹ. The letters: וג, have been pushed slightly to the right because of the shrinkage of the Scroll. The traces are faintly discernible. ודור The right leg of the resh almost joins the leg of the waw.

22 ...הֹ עדה It is difficult to determine whether the traces before: עדה, are he or ʿayin; only context can decide (see the Commentary).

23 A blank line indicating a new paragraph. It seems, on the right, as if the space is larger, but this is due to the distortion of the Scroll (see especially, Pl. 8).

Syriac: טיבותהון לא תגמר .MS. B: ותקותם (see also below, the Commentary to *l.* 20). Since the Greek read: וצדקותם, and the Syriac: וצדקתם, the original was probably, as usual: וצדקתם, which can be understood in both singular and plural. The former is to be preferred. Restored: וצֹדקתם לא תכרת].

18 אם A copyist's error, instead of: עם, as in MS. B. The rest agrees with MS. B and the Syriac (ועם זרעהון קים טובהון). In the Greek: ἀγαθή, at the end of the column, has crept into the next column (see the commentators). *Col. B*: ונח,,, Restored according to MS. B (Cowley-Neubauer), the Syriac and the Greek: ונחֹלתם לבני בניהם]. In MS. B, the reading: ונחלתם לב, has been preserved, while the Syriac has: ושורשם) = ועקרהון (לבני בניהון. The Greek is similar to the Hebrew, and its corrupted text may be restored: κληρονομία αὐτῶν τοῖς ἐκγόνοις αὐτῶν (for: ἀγαθή, at the beginning here, see above; for the Greek text, see Lévi and Charles).

19 Missing in MS. B. We have here the original Hebrew text. According to the Greek (ἐν ταῖς διαθήκαις [70 + αὐτῶν] ἔστη σπέρμα αὐτῶν), the various editors restored the text almost exactly as the Scroll: בבריתם יעמד זרעם. In the singular. The Syriac: ובקימתהון. *Col. B*: וצאצאיהֹם On the basis of the Greek (τέκνα αὐτῶν) some editors have restored: ובניהם (see, e.g., Segal, following others). The Scroll reading confirms, on the other hand, the reading of the first part of the hemistich in the Syriac: ובני בניהון. Restored: וצאצאיהם [בעבורם], according to the Greek (δι' αὐτούς). The Syriac erred and read approximately: בעבודם (עבדא טבא).

20 וֹעֹד MS. B: עד; and the Greek: ἕως. The Syriac: ועדמא, as in the Scroll. זרעם MS. B: זכרם,

and thus the Syriac (דוכריהון). The Greek repeats: σπέρμα, twice as in the Scroll. *Col. B*: וכבודם MS. B: וצדקתם (see above, *l.* 17). The Greek (ἡ δόξα αὐτῶν) and the Syriac (ואיקרהון) agree with the Scroll. לא ימֹחֹ[ה] MS. B is mutilated. The Scroll reading almost conforms with Smend's reading, basing on: וצדקתם (followed by Segal): לא] תמח[ה, on the basis of the Greek (οὐκ ἐξαλειφθήσεται) and the Syriac (נתטעא).

21 וגֹ] ֹם בשלום נאספה Btext and Bmarg are both mutilated. Smend's restoration follows exactly the Scroll reading (without the waw at the beginning of the hemistich), on the basis of: τὸ σῶμα αὐτῶν. The proposal of Lévi, Peters, Box & Oesterley and Segal, which relies on the Syriac (פגריהון בשלמא אתכנשו) and on several Greek MSS. (τὰ σώματα αὐτῶν) which read: גויתם בשלום נאספו (Levi: פגריהם), should be abandoned. *Col. B*: Btext and Bmarg are both mutilated: ל....ודור. Correctly restored thus by Peters, according to the Greek (καὶ τὸ ὄνομα αὐτῶν ζῇ εἰς γενεάς) and the Syriac (ושמהון חי מן דר לדר). Segal followed Lévi: יחיה.... Smend: ושמם חי לדור דור.

22 הֹ עדה [ ] Missing in Btext, though it was added in Bmarg. *Col. A* is restored: חכמתם] תשנ[ה עדה. In the Greek: λαοί. [The Grandson is an ardent Septuagintist in changing national Jewish expressions into universalisms — I.L. Seeligmann.] This verse occurs also in 39, 10 (perhaps this was the reason for its omission here), and there the Greek rendered it: ἔθνη. Cowley-Neubauer read in Bmarg: תשמע, instead of: תשנה, but according also to the Greek (διηγήσονται) and the Syriac (see 39, 10: נתנין), the reading should be: תשנה, as adopted

VII,24–25/44,17–17c

| 24 | [| ב] | נוח צדיק נמצא תמים | 17 |
| 25 | [|] | [| ב] 17c |

²⁴ נוח צדיק On a small fragment joined in here. On the right traces of two letters of *l.* 24 of Page VI have been preserved (see above, the Notes, *ad loc.*).

²⁵ According to the number of verses, there should have been another line of script on this page. In actual fact, on the

edge of the small fragment illegible traces may be discerned. If the second fragment is correctly placed (see the Notes, Page VI, *l.* 25), we have here the start of the first letter, which may have been *bet* (see the Commentary).

by most editors, and thus, evidently, in the Scroll (see the Notes above). *Col. B*: Thus the addition in B*marg*; cf. also the translations: עמא; ἐκκλησία.

²⁴ In the line at the top of the large fragment, only the words: נמצא תמים ב..., have been preserved; fortunately, a small fragment of the Scroll has survived, which I have succeeded in placing to the right of the foregoing, on which is written: נוח צדיק (see the Notes, above). *Col. B*: Restored according to B*marg*, the Greek (ἐν καιρῷ) and the Syriac (בדמנא): ב]עת כלה היה תחליף]. B*text*: לעת. Had this small fragment not survived, we might have fallen into a trap and attributed: נמצא תמים, to Enoch (!) (see below). The Scroll reading now enables us to solve a problem in the structure of this chapter of *Ben Sira*, as well as to explain the difficulties involved in the variants hitherto extant. In B*text*, verse 16 has been preserved, transcribed in one line in the following wording: חנוך נמצא תמים והתהלך עם ייי וילקח אות דעת לדור דור. Thus, not only has this resulted in a verse made up of three parts (see Segal's arrangement), but also in duplicating the phrase: נמצא תמים, which, in the verse appearing in its place, refers to Noah. Moreover, these two words do not occur in the Greek translation. The Scroll now clearly indicates that Ben Sira began his listing of the 'Fathers of Old' with Noah, and not with Enoch. Thus, we can now understand why Enoch is referred to, seemingly again, in 49, 14, in the concluding verses. G. Bickell (*Zeitschrift für katholische Theologie*, 1882, pp. 326 ff.) has already argued that verse 16 of the Greek should be struck out, since it is misplaced; for Ben Sira deals with Enoch only later, in 49, 14, especially as the Syriac also omitted it. His view was not accepted, though several editors (Schlatter, Smend) erased: וילקח, and the corresponding Greek phrase (καὶ μετετέθη), since this subject is dealt with in 49, 14. Segal would not agree

even to this erasure. The Scroll now proves conclusively that Bickell was basically right in his arguments. We may now assume that at an early period an attempt had been made to artificially expunge a portion of Ben Sira's observations on Enoch in the concluding verses, and to insert them in their chronological order, i.e. before Noah. Thus, we may assume that a part of verse 16 was originally in chapter 49. Since the last third of verse 16 (i.e.: אות דעת לדור דור) occurs in the Greek (ὑπόδειγμα μετανοίας ταῖς γενεαῖς), and as it contains no repetition of what is said in chapter 49, we may assume that it is authentic. Moreover, the subject of Enoch's 'walking' with God is of fundamental importance, as is twice emphasised in *Genesis* (5:22 and 24). It is therefore difficult to imagine that Ben Sira would fail to refer to it (the 'walking' is not mentioned in chapter 49). We must therefore conclude that the theme concerned is embedded in verse 16 (Ἐνὼχ εὐηρέστησεν Κυρίῳ), where the translator resorts to the same word used by the LXX. B*text* after the omission of the first part has: והתהלך עם ייי. In the light of the above, we restore the verses and their order in chapter 49 as follows:

49, 14: מעט נוצר על הארץ כחנוך
44, 16: אות דעת לדור דור
44, 16: והתהלך עם אדני
49, 20: וגם הוא נלקח פנים.

Cf. also *Genesis* 5:24: ויתהלך חנוך את האלהים ואיננו. כי לקח אתו אלהים. In the Greek:

49, 14a: οὐδὲ εἷς ἐκτίσθη οἷος Ἐνὼχ τοιοῦτος ἐπὶ τῆς γῆς
44, 16b: ὑπόδειγμα μετανοίας ταῖς γενεαῖς
44, 16a: καὶ εὐηρέστησεν Κυρίῳ
49, 14b: καὶ γὰρ αὐτὸς ἀνελήμφθη ἀπὸ τῆς γῆς

²⁵ Only the tip of the first letter has been preserved in *Col. A*, and a few traces, extremely mutilated owing to a tear. Restored: ב]עבורו היה שארית] (but see the Notes, above).

PLATE 1

I

1	[	] [			
2	[פ֯כו [נ֯] לזרה	] [	לט לז 39 27		
3	[י֯קו [יע֯ם	] [	28c לח		
4	הם יני֯חו]	] [	28 לט		
5	ר֯או]	] [	29 מ		
6	עים]	] [	30c מא		
7	ו]	] [	30 מב		
8	הו (יו)]	] [	31 מג		
9	י֯]	] [	32 מד		
10	[	] [			
11	[	] [			
12	[	] [			
13	[	] [			
14	[	] [			
15	[	] [			
16	[	] [			
17	[	] [			
18	[	] [			
19	[	] [			
20	[	] [			
21	[	] [			
22	[	] [			
23	וש כלה]	] [	מ יג 40 10		
24	[	] [			
25	[	] [			

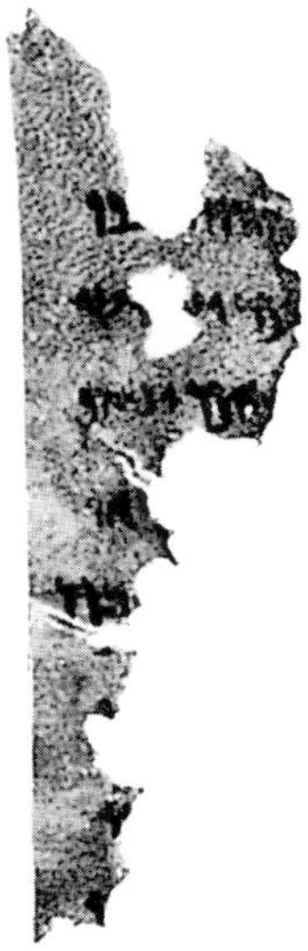

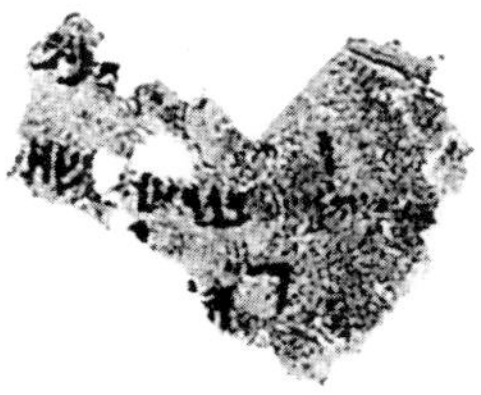

PLATE 2

#			ref
1	[ ]	[כל מ]	מ יד 40 11
2	[ ]	[כל מש]	יה 12
3	ת[ ]	[חיל מעול]	יו 13
4	ם[ ]	[עם שאתו כפי]	יז 14
5	צר [ ] על] [ ]	[נצר חמס לא יכ]	יח 15
6	חצר נדעך [ ]	כקרמית על גפות נחל	יט 16
7	וצדקה לעד תכן	חסד כעד לא תכרת	כ 17
8	ומשניהם מוצא] [	ר חיי יתר שכר ימתקו	כא 18
9	ומשניהם מוצ]	ילד ו] [ידו שם	כב 19
10	[ ]	ו שאר] [	כג 19c
11	[ ]	[ ]	
12	[ ]	[ ]	
13	[ ]	[ ]	
14	[ ]	[ ]	
15	[ ]	[ ]	
16	[ ]	[ ]	
17	[שניהם] [ ]	[ ]	ל 26
18	[ען] [אין לבקש עמה מ] [ ]	[ ]	לא 26 c
19	ועל כל כ] [חפתה	[ ]	לב 27
20	טוב] [סף מפני חצף	[ ]	לג 28
21	[מנות חיים]	[ ]	לד 29
22	[ש יוד] [יסור מעים	[מט] [ ]	לה 29c
23	]ו כאש תבער [ ]	בפי עז נפש ת] [	לו 30
24	לאיש שקט על מכונתו	ר הו] [ל] [כרך]	מא א 41 1
25	עוד בו כח לקבל תענוג	] [שלו ומצליח בכל	ב 1c

PLATE 3

III

[ ]אין אוינים (!) וחסר עצמה	1	הֹע למות מה טוב חֹ[	מא ג 41 2
אפס המרה ואבוד תקוה	2	איש כשל ונוקש ב[	ד 2c
זכר קדמון ואחרון עמך	3	אל תפחד ממות חֹקך	ה 3
[ ]עֹלֹיֹוֹן[	4	זה קץ כל [ ]הֹ[	ו 4
[ ]	5	לעשר מאה ואֹלֹף שנים	ז 4c
[ ]שֹע	6	נין נמאס ת[ ]וֹת רעים	ח 5
[ ]תֹמֹיֹ[ ]חֹרפה	7	]ל תאבד ממש[ ]הֹ	ט 6
[ ]גֹללו היו בוז	8	]יקב ילד[	י 7
עזבי תורת עליון	9	]אנשי עֹוֹ[ ]	יא 8
ואם תולידו לאֹנחה	10	]לֹ[ ]	יב 9
ואם תמותו לקללה	11	]ו לשמחת עֹלם[	יג 9b
כֹן חנף מתהו אל תהו	12	]אפס אל אפס ישוב	יד 10
[ ]שם חֹסֹד ללא יכרֹת	13	]הֹבֹל[ ]הֹ[	יה 11
מאֹלֹפֹי[ ]חֹמֹדֹה (?)[	14	פֹהֹ[ ]על שם כי הוא ילוך	יו 12
אין מספר[ ]וטובֹת[	15	]וֹבת חֹ מספר ימים	יז 13
מה תעלה בשתיהם	16	]כֹמֹה טמונה ושימה מסותרת	יח 14b
מאיש מֹצפן חכמתו	17	טוב איש מטמֹ[ ]אולתו	יט 15
16a]לֹמֹו על משפטי	18	מוסר בשת שמעו בנים	כ 14a
ולֹא כל הכלם נבחר	19	לא כל בשת נאוה לבוש	כא 16b
מנשיא ושר על כֹחֹש	20	בוש מאב ואם על פחז	כב 17
מעדה ועם[ ]לֹ[ ]שֹע	21	מאדון וגברֹ[ ]על קשר	כג 18
ממקום תגור עֹ[ ]יד	22	משותף ורע על מעל	כד 18c
וממטֹה אציל על לחם	23	מהפֹר אלה וברית	כה 19b
21a ומהשיב את פני שארך	24	ממֹנֹ[ ]מֹתת שאלה	כו 19d
20 מֹשאל שלום החריש	25	מחשות מחלקת מֹנֹה	כז 21b

[201]

PLATE 4

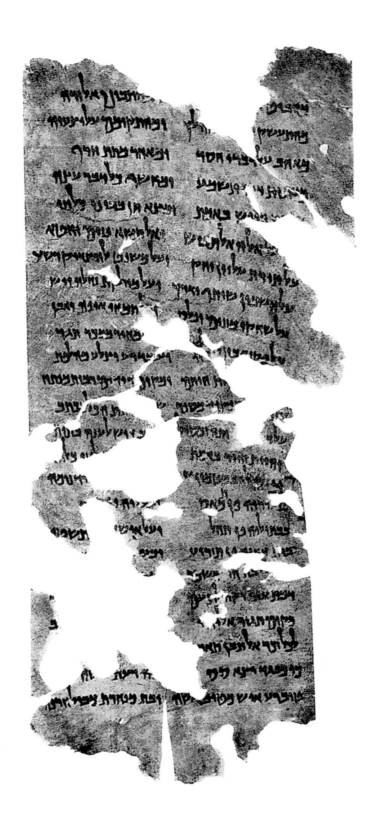

מא כח 41	21c	מהביט א[	

מהביט א[

כט 22a מהתעשק עֹ[ ]הֹה לך

ל 22c מאהב על דברי חסד

לא 42 1 משנות דבֹר תשמע

לב 1c וֹהֹ]ֹת בויש באמת

מב א 1e]ך על אלה אל תבוש

ב 2 על תורת עליון וחק

ג 3 על חשבון שותף ודרך

ד 4a על שחקי מזנים ופלס

ה 4b על מקנֹה בין רֹב למֹ[ ]

ו 5b–c [ ]ה

ז 6 [ ]שֹת חותם

ח 7 עֹל מֹ[ ]תֹפקיד מספר

ט 8 על מֹ[ ]ותה וכסיל

י 8c והיית זהיר באמת

יא 9 ר]שֹ[ ]לאב מטמון שֹק[ ]

יב 9c–d בנעוריה פן תמאס

יג 10a בבתוליה פן תחל

יד 10b בית אביֹה פן תזריע

יה 11a–b]עֹל בֹת חזק משמֹר[ ]

יו 11c דבת עיר וקהלת עם

יז 11e מקום תגור אל יהי

יח 12 לכל זכר אל תבן תאר

יט 13 כי מבגד יצא סס

כ 14 טוב רע איש מטיב אשה

---

1 20b ומהתבונן אל זרה

2 22b ומהתקומם על יצעיה

3 22d ומאחר מתת חרף

4 ומחשף כל דבר עצה

5 ומצא חן בעיני כל חי

6 ואל תשא פנים וחטא

7 ועל משפט להצדיק רשע

8 ועל מחלקת נחלה ויש

9 5a וֹעֹל תמחי איפה ואבן

10 [ ]מֹמחיר ממכר תגר

11 ועבד רע וצלע מהלכת

12 ומקום ידים רבות מפתח

13 ש] מֹתת הכל בכתב

14 [ ]בֹ כֹושל ענה בזנות

15 [ ]עֹ לפֹנֹי כל חֹי

16 [ ]יד נומה

17 ובֹימֹיה פֹן תֹ[ ]הֹ

18 ועל אישֹה [ ] תשטה

19 ובעל[ ]צֹ[ ]

20 [ ]ֹן תֹ[ ]

21 [ ]רֹ

22 [ ]בֹ

23 [ ]

24 [ ]ה רעת]שֹה

25 ובת מפחדת מכול חרפֹה

PLATE 5

מב כא · 15 42 · אזכרה נא מעשי אל
כב · 15c · באמר אדני מעשיו
כג · 16 · שמש זהרת על כל נגלת] [
כד · 17 · לא השפיקו קדשי אל
כה · 17c · אמץ אדני צבאיו
כו · 18 · תהום ולב חקר
כז · 18c · כי ידע עליון דע] [
כח · 19 · מחוה חליפות] [
כט · 20 · לא נעדר ממנו שכל
ל · 21 · גבורת חכמ] [
לא · 21c · לא נאסף] [
לב · 22 · הלוא כל מעשיו נחמד] [
לג · 23 · הכל חי ועו] [ד לעד
לד · 24 · כלם] [
לד · 24 · ולא עשה מהם] [
לה · 25 · זה על זה חלף טובם
מג א · 1 43 · תאר מרום ורקיע לטהר
ב · 2 · שמש מופיע בצאתו נכסה
ג · 3 · בהצהירו יר] [ח תבל
ד · 4 · [ ]ור [ ]פוח מעשי מוצק
ה · 4c · לשון מאור ת] [מור נושבת
ו · 5 · כי גדול אדני עשהו
ז · 6 · וגם] [רח יאריח עתות
ח · 7 · לו מו] [ד וממנו חג
ט · 8 · חדש כשמו הוא מת] [

---

1 · [אזכרה נא / מע] [וזה / חזיתי ואשננה] · וזה חזיתי ואשננה
2 · ופעל רצנו לקחו
3 · [ ]בוד אדני מלא מעשיו
4 · לספר כל נפלאתיו
5 · להתחזק לפני כבודו
6 · ובמערמיהם יתבונן
7 · [ ]יביט אתיות עולם
8 · [ ]מגלה חקר נסתרות
9 · ול] [אב] [ו] כל דבר
10 · אחד ה] [א] [ ]ולם
11 · ול] [ ]ול מבין
12 · עד ניצוץ וחזות מראה
13 · [ ]כל צרך הכל נשמר
14 · לעמת זה [ ]
15 ·
16 · [ ]מי ישבע להביט הודם
17 · עצם שמים מ] [ ]רו
18 · כלי נורא מעשי] [ליון
19 · ולפני חרב מי יתכל] [ל
20 · של] [[מש] [ ]
21 · [ ]
22 · ודב] [
23 · מ] [
24 · [ ]
25 · [ ]

PLATE 6

מג י	8c43	כלי צבא נבלי מרום	מ] [צֿף] [	1
יא	9	תור שמים והוד כוכב	עד ומשריק במרו[ו] [	2
יב	10	בדבר אדני יעמד חק	ולא ישח באשמרתם	3
יג	11	ראה קשת וברך עשיה	כי מאֹד נהדר[[	4
יד	12	חוֹג [ ] בכבודה	[ ]יד אל נטֿה בגב[[	5
יה	13	גערתו [ ]ֿה ברד	ותנצח זיקות משפט	6
יו	14	למענו פרע אוצר	ויעֿף עבים כעֿיט	7
יז	15	גבורתו חזק ענן	ותגדע אבֿני ברד	8
יח	17	קוֹל רעמו יחיל ארצו	ובכחו יניֿף הרים	9
יט	16b	אמֿרֿתֿו תחריֿף תימן	17b עלעול סופה וסערה	10
כ	17c	כרשֿף יפרח שלגו	וכארבה ישכן רדתו	11
כא	18	תור לבנו יהג עינים	וממטרו יתמיה לבב	12
כב	19	[ ] כֿפֿור כמלח ישפֿך	ויצמח כסנה צצים	13
כג	20	[ ]ֿון יֿשׁיֿב	וכרגב יקפיא מקור	14
				15
				16
כו	22	[ֿף ֿעֿנֿן ֿט] [ ]	[ ]	17
כז	23	אמֿר] [תֿעֿמיק רֿ] [	[ ]אֿים	18
כח	24	[ם יֿ] [ֿף] [קֿצֿ] [	[לשמע אזנינו נשמתֿם	19
כט	25	[ ] [וֿ] [ ]	גֿבֿורֿת רהֿב [	20
		[ ] [ ]	[	21
		[ ] [ ]	[	22
		[ ] [ ]	[	23
לג	29	[ ] [ ]	תֿו (יו)[	24
לד	30	[ ] [	שׁ אל[	25

PLATE 7

#				
1			[ ]	[ ]
2			[ ]	[ ]
3			[ ]	[ ]
4			[ ]	[ ]
5			[ ]	[ ]
6	מד א	44 1	[ ] אֵנ[ ] חסד [	את אב]
7	ב	2	רב כבוד חלק עליון	[וגדלה מי]
8	ד	3c	ויועצים בתבונתם	[וחזי כל בנב]
9	ה	4	שרי גוי בֿמזמֿתֿם	[ורוזֿנים במחקק]
10	ו	4c	חכמי שיח בספרתם	[ומשלים בֿמֿ]
11	ז	5	חקרי מזמור על קו	[ונשאי מש]
12	ח	6	אנשי חיל וסמכי כח	[ושקׄ]
13	ט	7	כל אלה בדרם נכבדו	[ ]
14	י	8	יש מהם הניחו שֿם	[לה]
15	יא	9	ויש מהם שאין לו זכר	[ ]
16	יב	9c	כאשר לא היו היו	[וׄ]
17	יג	10	אולם אלה אנשי חסד	[וצׄ]
18	יד	11	אם זרעם נאמן טובם	[ונחׄ]
19	יה	12	בבריתם עמד זרעם	[וצאצאיהֿםֿ]
20	יו	13	וֹעֿד עולם יעמד זרעם	וכבודם לא ימחׄ [ ]
21	יז	14	וגׄ[ ]ֿם בשלום נאספה	ושמם חי לדור ודורׄ
22	יח	15	[ ]ֿה עדה	ותהלתם יספׄר קהל
23				
24	כ	17	נוח צדיק נֿמצא תמים	[בׄ]
25	כא	17c	[בֹ]	[ ]

PLATE 8

The Fragments of the Scroll Pieced Together

THE RESTORED TEXT

I

#		
1	[ ]	[ ]
2	[כל אלה לטובים ייטיבו] 39 27 לט לז	[כן לרעים] לזרה נ[ה]פכו
3	[יש רוחות למשפט נבראו] 28 לח	[ובאפם הר]ים יע[ת]יקו
4	[ובעת כלה חילם ישפכו] 28c לט	[ורוח עוש]הם יניחו
5	[אש וברד רע ודבר] 29 מ	[גם אלה למשפט נב]ראו
6	[חית שן עקרב ופתן] 30 מא	[וחרב נקמות להחרים רש]עים
7	[כל (גם) אלה לצורכם נבראו (נבחרו)] 30c מב	[והמה באוצר (באוצרו) ולעת (לעת) יפקד]ו
8	[בצותו אותם ישישו] 31 מג	[ובחקם לא ימרו פ]יו (פיהו)
9	[על כן מראש התיצבתי] 32 מד	[והתבוננתי ובכתב הנחת]י
10	[ ]	[ ]
11	[ ]	[ ]
12	[ ]	[ ]
13	[ ]	[ ]
14	[ ]	[ ]
15	[ ]	[ ]
16	[ ]	[ ]
17	[ ]	[ ]
18	[ ]	[ ]
19	[ ]	[ ]
20	[ ]	[ ]
21	[ ]	[ ]
22	[ ]	[ ]
23	[על רשע נבראה רעה] 40 10 מ יג	[ובעבורו תח]וש כלה
24	[ ]	[ ]
25	[ ]	[ ]

TRANSLATION OF THE RESTORED TEXT

Page I

[1]

39, 27   **2**   [All these prove good to the good]
         [So for the evil] they are turned to loathing

     28   **3**   [There are winds created for judgement]
         [And in their fury] remove mountains

   28c   **4**   [And in the season of destruction they pour out their force]
         And appease [the spirit of] their [Maker]

     29   **5**   [Fire and hail, misfortune and pestilence]
         [These also for judgement are] created

     30   **6**   [Beasts of prey, scorpion and viper]
         [And an avenging sword to exterminate the wic]ked

   30c   **7**   [All these (too) are created (chosen) for their uses]
         [And are in the (his) treasure-house when] they [are required]

     31   **8**   [When He giveth them command they rejoice]
         [And in their prescribed tasks disobey not] his [behest]

     32   **9**   [Therefore from the beginning I was assured]
         [And when I considered it] I [set it down in writing]

[10–22]

40, 10   **23**   [For the wicked evil is created]
         [And on his account] destruction has[teneth]

[24–25]

II

1	[ואשר (ויש׳) ממרום אל מרום]		כל מ[ארץ אל ארץ ישוב]	40 11	מ יד
2	[ואמונה לעולם תעמד]		כל מש[קר (משוחד) ועולה ימחה]	12	יה
3	[וכאפיק אדיר בחזיז קולו]ת		חיל מעול [כנחל איתן]	13	יו
4	[כי פתאם לנצח ית]ם		עם שאתו כפי[ם נגולו]	14	יז
5	[ושורש חנף] על [שן] צר		נצר חמס לא יכ[ה בו]	15	יח
6	[לפני כל] חצר נדעך		כקרמית על גפות נחל	16	יט
7	וצדקה לעד תכן		חסד כעד לא תכרת	17	כ
8	ומשניהם מוצא [שימה]		חיי יתר שכר ימתקו	18	כא
9	ומשניהם מוצ[א חכמה]		ילד ו[עיר יעמ]ידו שם	19	כב
10	[ומשניהם אשה נחשקת]		[שגר ונטע יפריחו] שאר	19c	כג
11	[ ]	[ ]			
12	[ ]	[ ]			
13	[ ]	[ ]			
14	[ ]	[ ]			
15	[ ]	[ ]			
16	[ ]	[ ]			
17	[ומ]שניהם [יראת אלהים]		[חיל וכח יגילו לב]	26	ל
18	[ו]אין לבקש עמה מ[ש]ען		[אין ביראת אדני מחסור]	26c	לא
19	ועל כל כ[בוד] חפתה		[יראת אלהים כעדן ברכה]	27	לב
20	טוב [נא]סף מפני חצף		[בני חיי מתן אל תחי]	28	לג
21	[אין חייו ל]מנות חיים		[איש משגיח על שלחן זר]	29	לד
22	[לאי]ש יודע יסור מעים		[מעגל נפשו] מט[עמי זבד]	29c	לה
23	[ובקרב]ו כאש תבער		בפי עז נפש ת[מתיק שאלה]	30	לו
24	לאיש שקט על מכונתו		הו[י] ל[מות מה מר ז]כרך	41 1	מא א
25	עוד בו כח לקבל תענוג		[איש] שלו ומצליח בכל	1c	ב

Page II

40, 11 **1**   All (things) from the [earth to the earth return]
          [And what is from on high (returneth) on high]

    12 **2**   All that is of f[alsehood (bribe) and unjust is destroyed]
          [But what is true abideth for ever]

    13 **3**   Wealth from iniquity [is like a mighty torrent]
          [And like a water-course mighty in a thunderstor]m

    14 **4**   With its onrush rocks [are rolled away]
          [Even so, suddenly it cometh to an end for eve]r

    15 **5**   A branch sprung from violence shall not take root
          [For an impious root] is on the [point] of a crag

    16 **6**   Like reed-stalks on the banks of a stream
          Which are consumed [before any] grass

    17 **7**   Kindness, like eternity, shall never be cut off
          And righteousness shall be established for ever

    18 **8**   A life of luxury (and) remuneration is sweet
          But better than both he that findeth [a treasure]

    19 **9**   A child and [city est]ablish a name
          But better than both he that findeth [wisdom]

  19c **10**   [Young cattle and planting maketh] a kinsman [to flourish]
          [But better than both is a woman beloved]

[11–16]

    26 **17**   [Wealth and strength rejoice the heart]
          [And better than] both [the fear of God]

  26c **18**   [In the fear of the Lord there is no want]
          And with it there is no need to seek support

    27 **19**   [The fear of God is a very Eden of blessing]
          And its canopy over all that is glo[rious]

    28 **20**   [My son, live not a beggar's life]
          Better is one dead than importunate

    29 **21**   [A man that looketh to a stranger's table]
          [His life is not] to be reckoned as a life

  29c **22**   [A pollution of his soul are the] dai[nties presented]
          [To a m]an of understand[ing] inward torture

    30 **23**   In the mouth of a bold man [begging is sweet]
          [But inward]ly it burneth as a fire

41, 1 **24**   Oh to [Death! How bitter is the re]membrance of thee
          To him that liveth at peace in his habitation

    1c **25**   [(To) him] that is at ease and prospereth in all
          And still hath strength to enjoy luxury

III

#	(left column)		(right column)	ref	ref
1	[ל]אין אוינים וחסר עצמה		ה(ר)ע למות מה טוב ח[קך]	2 41	מא ג
2	אפס המר(א)ה ואבוד תקוה		איש כשל ונוקש ב[כל]	2c	ד
3	זכר קדמון ואחרון עמך		אל תפחד ממות חקך	3	ה
4	[ומה תמאס בתורת] עליו[ן]		זה קץ כל [בשר מאל]ה	4	ו
5	[אין (איש) תוכחות (חיים) בשאול]		לעשר מאה ואלף שנים	4c	ז
6	[ונכד אויל מגור(י) ר]שע		נין נמאס ת[לד]ות רעים	5	ח
7	[ועם זרעו] תמי[ד] חרפה		[מבן עו]ל תאבד ממש[ל]ה	6	ט
8	[כי ב]גללו היו בוז		[אב רשע] יקב ילד	7	י
9	עזבי תורת עליון		[אוי לכם] אנשי עו[לה]	8	יא
10	ואם תולידו לאנחה		[אם תפרו ע]ל [יד(י) אסון]	9	יב
11	ואם תמותו לקללה		[אם תכשל]ו לשמחת עלם	9b	יג
12	כן חנף מתהו אל תהו		[כל מ]אפס אל אפס ישוב	10	יד
13	[אך] שם חסד {ל}לא יכרת		הבל [בני אדם בגוית]ם	11	יה
14	מאלפי [שימות] חמדה (?)		פח[ד] על שם כי הוא ילוך	12	יו
15	וטובת [שם ימי] אין מספר		[ט]ובת חי מספר ימים	13	יז
16	מה תעלה בשתיהם		[ח]כמה טמונה ושימה מסותרת	14b	יה
17	מאיש מצפן חכמתו		טוב איש מטמ[ן] אולתו	15	יט
18	[והכ]למו על משפטי 16a		מוסר בשת שמעו בנים	14a	כ
19	ולא כל הכלם נבחר		לא כל בשת נאוה לבוש	16b	כא
20	מנשיא ושר על כחש		בוש מאב ואם על פחז	17	כב
21	מעדה ועם [ע]ל [פ]שע		מאדון וגבר[ת] על קשר	18	כג
22	ממקום תגור ע[ל] יד		משותף ורע על מעל	18c	כד
23	וממטה אציל על לחם		מהפר אלה וברית	19b	כה
24	ומהשיב את פני שארך 21a		ממנ[ע] מתת שאלה	19d	כו
25	משאל שלום החריש 20		מחשות מחלקת מנה	21b	כז

Page III

41, 2	**1**	Hail to Death, how welcome is thy de[cree]	
		[To] him that hath no might and that lacketh strength	
2c	**2**	That stumbleth and trippeth at [every thing]	
		Devoid of sight and hope-lorn	
3	**3**	Fear not Death, thy destiny	
		Remember, former and latter (share it) with thee	
4	**4**	This is the span of all [flesh from Go]d	
		[And how canst thou withstand the decree of the Most] Hig[h(?)]	
4c	**5**	Be it for ten, a hundred or a thousand years	
		[In Sheol there are no reproaches concerning life]	
5	**6**	An abominable offspring is the [gene]ration of sinners	
		[And a godless sprout is in the dwellings of the w]icked	
6	**7**	[From the son of the unrighteou]s shall domi[n]ion be wrenched away	
		[And with his seed] alway[s] contempt	
7	**8**	[A wicked father] a child doth curse	
		[For on] his account they suffer reproach	
8	**9**	[Woe unto you] men of iniqui[ty]	
		Forsakers of the Law of the Most High	
9	**10**	[If ye be fruitful — b]y [dint of mischief]	
		And if ye bear children — for sighing	
9b	**11**	[If ye stumble] — for everlasting joy	
		And if ye die — for a curse	
10	**12**	[All that is of] naught returneth to naught	
		So the godless — from nothingness to nothingness	
11	**13**	Vain [are men in] their [bodies]	
		[But] a good name shall not be cut off	
12	**14**	Fea[r] for name, for that will accompany thee	
		More than thousands of precious [treasures]	
13	**15**	[The go]od things of life last for numbered days	
		But the goodness of [name] hath days without number	
14b	**16**	Hidden [wi]sdom and concealed treasure	
		What is the use of either?	
15	**17**	Better the man who hid[eth] his folly	
		Than a man who hideth his wisdom	
14a	**18**	Hear, O children, instruction concerning shame	
		[And be aba]shed according to my judgement	
16b	**19**	For not every kind of shame is shameful	
		Nor is every kind of abashment approved	
17	**20**	Be ashamed of a father and mother of wantonness	
		Of a prince and ruler of lies	
18	**21**	Of a master and mistr[ess] of intrigue	
		Of an assembly and a people [o]f [trans]gression	
18c	**22**	Of a partner and friend of treachery	
		Of a place where thou sojournest o[f] sleight of hand	
19b	**23**	Of breaking an oath or covenant	
		Of stretching out the elbow at bread	
19d	**24**	Of withholding the granting of a request	
		21a	And of turning away the face of thy kinsman
21b	**25**	Of stopping the dividing of a portion	
		20	Of being silent towards him that greeteth

IV

מא כח 41 21c	מהביט א[ל אשת איש]	20b	ומהתבונן אל זרה	1
כט 22a	מהתעשק [עם שפ]חה לך	22b	ומהתקומם על יצעיה	2
ל 22c	מאהב על דברי חסד	22d	ומאחר מתת חרף	3
לא 42 1	משנות דבר תשמע		ומחשף כל דבר עצה	4
לב 1c	וה[י]ית בויש באמת		ומצא חן בעיני כל חי	5
מב א 1e	[א]ך על אלה אל תבוש		ואל תשא פנים וחטא	6
ב 2	על תורת עליון וחק		ועל משפט להצדיק רשע	7
ג 3	על חשבון שותף ודרך		ועל מחלקת נחלה ויש	8
ד 4a	על שחקי מזנים ופלס	5a	ועל תמחי איפה ואבן	9
ה 4b	על מקנה בין רב למ[עט]		[ועל] ממחיר ממכר תגר	10
ו 5b-c	[ועל מוסר בנים הרב]ה		ועבד רע וצלע מהלכת	11
ז 6	[על אשה רעה ת]שת חותם		ומקום ידים רבות מפתח	12
ח 7	על מ[קום] תפקיד מספר		ש[וא]ה ו[מתת הכל בכתב	13
ט 8	על מ[רדות פ]ותה וכסיל		[ש]ב כושל ענה בזנות	14
י 8c	והיית זהיר באמת		[ואיש צנו]ע לפני כל חי	15
יא 9	[בת?] לאב מטמון שק[ר]		[ודאגתה תפר]יד נומה	16
יב 9c-d	בנעוריה פן תמאס		ובימיה פן ת[נש]ה	17
יג 10a	בבתוליה פן תֵחָל		ועל אישה [פן] תשטה	18
יד 10b	בית אביה פן תזריע		ובעֵל[ה פן תע[צ]ר]	19
יה 11a-b	[בני] על בת חזק משמר		[פ]ן ת[עשה לך שם סרה]	20
יו 11c	דבת עיר וקהלת עם		[והובישתך בעדת שע[ר]	21
יז 11e	מקום תגור על יהי (אשנב)		[ובית מביט מבוא סבי]ב	22
יח 12	לכל זכר אל תבן תאר		[ובית נשים על תסתויד (תסתיד)]	23
יט 13	כי מבגד יצא סס		[ומאש]ה רעת [א]שה	24
כ 14	טוב רע איש מטיב אשה		ובת מפחדת מכול חרפה	25

Page IV

41, 21c **1** Of looking up[on a woman that hath a husband]
        20b   And of gazing upon a strange (woman)

22a **2** Of dallying wi[th a mai]d of thine
        22b   And of violating her bed

22c **3** Of reproachful words to a friend
        22d   And of reviling after giving a gift

42, 1 **4** Of repeating a word thou hast heard
        And of laying bare any piece of secret counsel

1c **5** So shalt thou [be] truly shamefast
        And find favour in the sight of all living

1e **6** [Bu]t of these things be not ashamed
        And respect no persons and sin

2 **7** Of the Law of the Most High and the statute
        And when justice (demands) to justify the wicked

3 **8** Of reckoning with a partner and a fellow-traveller
        And of the division of an inheritance and property

4a **9** Of the small dust of the scales and balance
        5a   And of the polishing of measure and weight

4b **10** Of buying, whether much or li[ttle]
        [Of] bargaining in traffick with a merchant

5b-c **11** [And of frequen]t [correction of children]
        And a bad servant who feigns limping

6 **12** [And on an evil wife, of] putting a seal
        And where many hands are — a key

7 **13** Upon the pl[ace] of a deposit a mark
        And all [tran]sactions be in writing

8 **14** Of the (correction) of the re[bellion of the] simple and foolish
        Of the tottering gray [beard] occupied with whoredom

8c **15** So shalt thou be truly well-advised
        [And a man (truly) modes]t before all living

9 **16** [A daughter] is to her father a deceptive treasure
        [And the care of her dis]pelleth slumber

9c-d **17** In her youth lest she be disfavoured
        And in her heyday lest she be [forgotten]

10a **18** In her virginity lest she be defiled
        And by her husband [lest] she prove unfaithful

10b **19** In her father's house lest she become pregnant
        And at her husband's [lest she become barren]

11a-b **20** [My son] over a daughter strictly watch
        [Le]st she [make thee a name of evil odour]

11c **21** A byword in the city and the assembly of the people
        [And shame thee in the assembly of the ga]te

11e **22** Where she lodgeth let there be no [window]
        [Or spot overlooking the entrance round ab]out

12 **23** Let her not reveal her beauty to any male
        [And in the house of women let her not converse]

13 **24** For from the garment issueth the moth
        [And from a woma]n a wo[man's] wickedness

14 **25** Better the wickedness of a man than the goodness of a woman
        And a daughter who dreadeth any disgrace

V

#				
1	וזה חזיתי ואשננה	אזכרה נא מעשי אל	15 42	מב כא
2	ופעל רצנו לקחו	באמר אדני מעשיו	15c	כב
3	[וכ]בוד אדני מלא מעשיו	שמש זהרת על כל נגלת[ה]	16	כג
4	לספר כל נפלאתיו	לא השפיקו קדשי אל	17	כד
5	להתחזק לפני כבודו	אמץ אדני צבאיו	17c	כה
6	ובמערמיהם יתבונן	תהום ולב חקר	18	כו
7	[ו]יביט אתיות עולם	כי ידע עליון דע[ת]	18c	כז
8	[ו]מגלה חקר נסתרות	מחוה חליפות [ונהיות]	19	כח
9	ול[א] אב[ד]ו כל דבר	לא נעדר ממנו שכל	20	כט
10	אחד ה[ו]א [מע]ולם	גבורת חכמ[תו תכן]	21	ל
11	ול[א צריך (צרך) לכ]ול מבין	לא נאסף [ולא נאצל]	21c	לא
12	עד ניצוץ וחזות מראה	הלוא כל מעשיו נחמד[ים]	22	לב
13	[ול]כל צרך הכל נשמר	הכל חי ועו[מ]ד לעד	23a	לג
14—15	ולא עשה מהם [שוא]	כלם [שנים שנים זה] לעמת זה	24	לד
16	[ו]מי ישבע להביט הודם	זה על זה חלף טובם	25	לה
17	עצם שמים מ[ביע הד]רו	תאר מרום ורקיע לטהר	1 43	מג א
18	כלי נורא מעשי [ע]ליון	שמש מופיע בצאתו נכסה	2	ב
19	ולפני חרב מי יתכל[כ]ל	בהצהירו יר[תי]ח תבל	3	ג
20	של[וח ש]מ[ש] [יסיק הרים]	[כ]ור [נ]פוח מעשי מוצק	4	ד
21	[ומנורה תכוה עין]	לשון מאור ת[ג]מור נושבת	4c	ה
22	ודב[ריו ינצח אביר'ו]	כי גדול אדני עשהו	5	ו
23	מ[משלת קץ ואות עולם]	וגם [י]רח יאריח עתות	6	ז
24	[וחפץ עתה בתקופתו]	לו מו[ע]ד וממנו חג	7	ח
25	[מה נורא בהשתנותו]	חדש כשמו הוא מת[חדש]	8	ט

Page V

42, 15	**1**	I will now make mention of the works of God And what I have seen shall I repeat
15c	**2**	By the word of God — His works And His doctrine — an act of His grace
16	**3**	The shining sun over all is revealed [And the gl]ory of the Lord doth fill His works
17	**4**	God's holy ones have not the power To recount all His wonders
17c	**5**	God hath strengthened His hosts To endure before His glory
18	**6**	He searcheth out the deep and the heart And their secrets He surveyeth
18c	**7**	For the Most High possesseth know[ledge] [And] seeth what cometh to eternity
19	**8**	He declared bygones [and what is to be] And revealeth the deepest secrets
20	**9**	Knowledge is not lacking to Him And n[o] matter is lo[s]t upon Him
21	**10**	The might of [His] wisdom [is established] [From ev]erlasting H[e is] One
21c	**11**	Nothing can be added [and nothing taken away] And He [needeth n]one to give counsel
22	**12**	All His works are lovely (Even) unto a spark and a fleeting vision
23a	**13**	All liveth and abi[deth] for ever [And] all is kept for every need
24	**14/15**	All of them [are twos], one against the other And he hath not made any of them [in vain]
25	**16**	One with other exchangeth their (respective) good [And] who can be sated with beholding their majesty?
43, 1	**17**	The beauty of the (heavenly) height and the pure firmament The firm heaven m[anifesteth its m]ajesty
2	**18**	The sun when he goeth forth shineth to the full An awe-inspiring mechanism, the work of the Most High
3	**19**	At noontide he bringeth the world to bo[ili]ng heat And before scorching heat who can maintain himself
4	**20**	Like a glowing furnace of solid cast The su[n's] dar[t setteth the mountains ablaze]
4c	**21**	A tongue of flame con[su]meth the inhabited (world) [And with its fire the eye is scorched]
5	**22**	For great is the Lord that made him And [His] wor[ds ?]
6	**23**	Moreover, the moon prescribeth seasons A r[ule of period and for an everlasting sign]
7	**24**	His the appointed season and from him feast [?]
8	**25**	New moon as its name (betokens) rene[weth] [How awe-inspiring is it in its changing!]

VI

מ[ר]צף [רקיע מזהירתו]	1	כלי צבא נבלי מרום	8c 43	מג י
עד ומשריק במרו[מי אל]	2	תור (תואר) שמים והוד כוכב	9	יא
ולא ישה באשמרתם	3	בדבר אדני יעמד חק	10	יב
כי מאד נהדר[ה בכבוד]	4	ראה קשת וברך עשיה	11	יג
[ו]יד אל נטתה בגב[ורה]	5	חוג [הקיפה] בכבודה	12	יד
ותנצח זיקות משפט	6	גערתו [תתו]ה ברד	13	יה
ויעף עבים כעיט	7	למענו פרע אוצר	14	יו
ותגדע אבני ברד	8	גבורתו חזק ענן	15	יז
ובכחו יניף הרים	9	קול רעמו יחיל ארצו	17	יח
עלעול סופה וסערה	10	אמרתו תחריף תימן	16b	יט
וכארבה ישכן רדתו	11	כרשף יפרח שלגו	17c	כ
וממטרו יתמיה לבב	12	תור (תואר) לבנו יהג עינים	18	כא
ויצמח כסנה צצים	13	[וגם] כפור כמלח ישפך	19	כב
וכרגב יקפיא מקור	14	[צינת רוח צפ]ון ישיב (ישוב)	20	כג
[ ]	15	[ ]		
[ ]	16	[ ]		
[פורע לדשן שרב (רטב)]	17	[מרפא כל מער]ף ענן ט[ל]	22	כו
[ויט בתהום] איים	18	אמר[תו?] תעמיק ר[בה]	23	כז
לשמע אזנינו נשתמם	19	[יורדי הי]ם י[ס]פ[רו] קצ[הו]	24	כח
ו[מין כל חי ו]גבורת רהב	20	[שם פלאות תמהי מעשיו]	25	כט
[ ]	21	[ ]		
[ ]	22	[ ]		
[ ]	23	[ ]		
[ונפלאת גבור]תו	24	[נורא אדני מאד מאד]	29	לג
[בכל תוכלו כי י]ש אל	25	[מגדלי אדני חרימו קול]	30	לד

Page VI

43, 8c **1** A vessel of the host of heavenly clouds
It pa[v]eth [the firmament with its shining]

9 **2** The beauty of heaven and the glory of a star
Adorns the hei[ghts of God] and sparkles therein

10 **3** By the word of the Lord it takes its prescribed place
And it does not fade at their (morning) watch

11 **4** Behold the rainbow and bless its Maker
For exceeding majestic [is it in glory]

12 **5** The heavenly vault [it encompasseth] with its glory
[And] the hand of God hath spread it out in mi[ght]

13 **6** His rebuke [marketh] out the hail
And maketh brilliant the flashes of judgement

14 **7** On His account He hath let loose a treasure-house
And He maketh the clouds to fly vulture-like

15 **8** His might maketh strong the cloud
And breaketh down the hailstones

17 **9** The voice of His thunder maketh His earth to be in anguish
And by His strength He shaketh mountains

16b **10** At His word the south wind bloweth keen
17b Whirlwind, hurricane and tempest

17c **11** Like flocks of birds He letteth flow His snow
And like settling locusts is the falling down thereof

18 **12** The beauty of its whiteness dazzleth the eyes
And the heart marvelleth at the raining thereof

19 **13** [And also] the hoar-frost He poureth out like salt
And produceth thorn-like blooms

20 **14** [The icy blast of the no]rth wind He causeth to blow
And He congealeth the source like a clod

[15–16]

22 **17** A healing for all such is the disti[llation of the cloud of d]ew
[Hastening to bring refreshment after heat]

23 **18** [His] word penetrateth the m[ighty] deep
[He hath stretched out] islands [in the ocean]

24 **19** [They that go down to the s]ea t[e]l[l of its] extent
When our ears hear we are astonished

25 **20** [Therein are marvels, the most wondrous of His works]
And [all kinds of living things and the] mights of Rahab

48

[21–23]

29 **24** [Terrible is the Lord exceedingly]
[And wonderful] His [mighty acts]

30 **25** [Ye that magnify the Lord, lift up your voices]
[As much as ye can, for] God is!

[223]

VII

#				
1	[ ]	[ ]		
2	[ ]	[ ]		
3	[ ]	[ ]		
4	[ ]	[ ]		
5	[ ]	[ ]		
6	את אב[ותינו בדורותם]	[אהללה נא] אנ[שי] חסד	44 1	מד א
7	וגדלה מי[מות עולם]	רב כבוד חלק עליון	2	ב
	(ואנשי שם בגבורתם)	(רודי (דורי) ארץ במלכותם)	3	ג
8	וחזי כל בנב[ואתם]	ויועצים בתבונתם	3c	ד
9	ורוזנים במחקק[תם]	שרי גוי במזמתם	4	ה
10	ומשלים במ[שמחותם]	חכמי שיח בספרתם	4c	ו
11	ונשאי מש[ל בכתב]	חקרי מזמור על קו	5	ז
12	ושק[טים על מכונתם]	אנשי חיל וסמכי כח	6	ח
13	[ובימיהם תפארתם]	כל אלה בדרם נכבדו	7	ט
14	לה[שתעות בנחלתם]	יש מהם הניחו שם	8	י
15	[וישבתו כאשר שבתו]	ויש מהם שאין לו זכר	9	יא
16	ו[בניהם מאחריהם]	כאשר לא היו היו	9c	יב
17	וצ[דקתם לא תכרת]	אולם אלה אנשי חסד	10	יג
18	ונח[לתם לבני בניהם]	עם זרעם נאמן טובם	11	יד
19	וצאצאיהם [בעבורם]	בבריתם עמד זרעם	12	יה
20	וכבודם לא ימח[ה]	ועד עולם יעמד זרעם	13	יו
21	ושמם חי לדור ודור	וג[ויית]ם בשלום נאספה	14	יז
22	ותהלתם יספר קהל	[חכמתם תשנ]ה עדה	15	יח
23				
24	ב[עת כלה היה תחליף]	נוח צדיק נמצא תמים	17	כ
25	[ובבריתו חדל מבול]	ב[עבורו היה שארית]	17c	כא

Page VII

44, 1   **6**   [Let me now hymn the praises of] me᷄[n of] piety
                  [Our] fathers [in their generations]

    2   **7**   Great honour did the Most High allot
                  And His greatness from the d[ays of old]

    3   [(Men) who wielded dominion over the earth in their royalty]
                  [And men of renown in their might]

   3c **8**   And counsellors in their discernment
                  And all-seeing in [their] prophe[cy]

    4   **9**   Princes of the nation in their statesmanship
                  And leaders in [their] decre[es]

   4c **10** Clever of speech in their (scribal) instruction
                  And speakers of wise sayings at [their] fes[tivities]

    5 **11** Devisers of psalms according to rule
                  And authors of prov[erbs in books]

    6 **12** Men of resource and supported with strength
                  And living at eas[e in their dwelling-places]

    7 **13** All these were honoured in their generation
                  [And in their days had glory]

    8 **14** Some of them there are who have left a name
                  [That men might tell of it in their inheritance]

    9 **15** And some of them there are who have no memorial
                  [So that there was an end of them when they came to their end]

   9c **16** They were as though they had not been
                  And [their children after them]

   10 **17** Nevertheless these were men of piety
                  And their good[ness shall not be cut off]

   11 **18** With their seed their goodness remaineth sure
                  And [their] inheri[tance to their children's children]

   12 **19** In their covenant their seed abideth
                  And their children's children [for their sakes]

   13 **20** And for ever their seed abideth
                  And their glory shall not be erase[d]

   14 **21** And their b[od]y is buried in peace
                  But their name liveth unto all generations

   15 **22/23** The assembly [recount]eth [their wisdom]
                  And their praise the congregation relateth

   17 **24** Noah the righteous was found blameless
                  In [the season of destruction he became the continuator]

  17c **25** For [his sake there was a remnant]
                  [And by reason of the covenant with him the flood ceased]

Notes on the Reading

Elisha Qimron

Even though the editor had parallel versions, deciphering and reconstructing the Ben Sira Scroll was not easy at all. The scroll is fragmentary and dark, and some of the surface was eaten by worms. Moreover, its text differs considerably from those of the other versions. Yadin overcame the major problems in a short time and produced an excellent annotated edition that has not yet been replaced; his text has been used with only several minor changes in subsequent comprehensive editions of Ben Sira. His research is still the cornerstone for the study of the original text of this work. Those responsible for the publication of the final report of the Masada excavations decided that this edition could appear in the final report, yet they requested that I prepare a list of improved readings. These are presented here. The list includes several new readings, which I discovered in the course of reexamination of the scroll, and alternative readings proposed by others: Milik, *Biblica* 47:425–426 (1966); Skehan, *JBL* 85:260–262 (1966); Baumgarten, *JQR* 58:323–327 (1967–68); Strugnell, *Eretz-Israel* 9:109–119 (1969).

Occasionally, I have added linguistic comments necessary to justify a given suggested reading. I made use of computer imaging carried out in the facilities of the Israel Antiquities Authority. I also used infra-red photographs and occasionally checked the original scroll. I am indebted to several individuals who assisted me: Mrs. Zilla Sagiv and Dr. Dan Blumberg provided willing assistance in use of the imaging equipment; Prof. Menachem Kister provided illuminating comments; Dr. Adolfo Roitman let me use the photographs found in the Shrine of the Book.

Here is the list of emendations arranged according to the order of the scroll:

I 6	= 39:30	— ‏[ ]וֹעים‎, read ‏[ ]וֹבֹם‎ as proposed by Strugnell and others.
II 6	= 40:16	— ‏חצֹר‎, read: ‏חצוֹיוֹר‎ as suggested by Strugnell.
II 7–8	= 40:17–18	— The reading of each of the first hemistiches is uncertain. The uncertain letter is marked with diacritical dots: ‏חסד כֹעֹד לֹא תכרת‎ and ‏חיי יתֹר שֹכֹר ימתקוֹ‎.
II 18	= 40:26	— ‏אֹיֹן לֹבֹקֹש‎, read: ‏אֹיֹן לבקש עמה משען‎.

II 20 = 40:28 — ‏טוב]נא[סֹף מפני חצף‎, Strugnell reads ‏]טוֹ]ב[נא[סֹף מֹמֹחֹצף‎ (the additional dots are mine). His reading better fits the traces, but before the first *mem* there are ink traces filling up the space between it and the preceding word. Linguistically, this reading is preferable: the use of a participle would match the preceding participle ‏]נא[סֹף‎ better than the awkward phrase ‏פני חצף‎. If this reading is correct, Ben-Sira tells us that death is better than life depending on sustenance from others

(see the first hemistich). This accords with the following saying: איש
משגיח על שלחן זר אין חייו למנות חיים. The verb חצף has a range of
meanings similar to those of the verb חזק which also mean hold,
sustain'. The reading מסתולל found in the Geniza manuscript is a
biblical hapax legomenon Exod 9:17 (עודך מסתולל בעמי) and some
commentators interpreted it as 'hold' in agreement with the continuation לבלתי שלחם (see Fin, האוצר, p. 232). Note the discussion of
יסתוללל/יתבוללל 19 below. However, Menachem Kister prefers
Yadin's reading, which can be interpreted according to the Syriac
(see his forthcoming article in T. Muraoka and J.F. Elwolde [eds.]
*Proceedings of the Second Symposium on the Hebrew of the Dead
Sea Scrolls and Ben Sira.*

III 13 = 41:11 — ואן שם חסד ללא יכרת. The preposition ל in ללא is redundant and Yadin
suggests to delete it in agreement with the Geniza version. In my
view, this *lamed* is part of the preceding word, as there is a space
between it and the second *lamed*. Nevertheless, I have thus far been
unable to propose a meaningful reading to the traces of the word
preceding לא. Obviously, the reading of the Scroll differs from that
of the Geniza manuscript. The reading of the first hemistich is also
problematic and uninstructive.

III 14 = 41:12 — פחדו על שם. Read according to Strugnell ופחד על שם.

III 16 = 41:14 — מסותרת. The word is in fact written defectively, i.e. מסתרת.

III 22 = 41:18 — ממקום תגור עולן יד. I read ממקום תגור עולניד with traces of a narrow letter
before יד. The original text is still unclear.

III 25 = 41:20 — read ומשאל שלום החריש with conjunctive waw before the first word.

IV 5 = 42:1 — בויש (the *beth* is also damaged). Some authorities proposed בייש
(or ביוש). I think that Yadin s reading should be preferred on the
basis of orthographical and linguistic considerations. As for the
orthography, the use of two *yod*s to represent consonantal *yod* was
very exceptional in that period. The linguistic considerations for
my preference will be given in a forthcoming article.

IV 11 = 42:5 — ועבד רע וצלע מהלכת. Strugnell reads: מהלמת instead of מהלכת. A close
examination of both the computer imaging and the infra-red photograph insures this reading beyond any doubt. This passage has been
interpreted by Menachem Kister (in the forthcoming article mentioned above II 20) as saying that a lazy slave deserves beatings.
There is no telling whether מהלמת is a singular *מַהֲלֻמֶת or a plural
מַהֲלֻמֹת (cf. Prov 18:6, 19:29). The orthography would better fit the
former.

IV 12 = 42:6 — על אשה רעה תושת חותם. The lacuna is too narrow for this restoration and perfectly fits the restoration ‫ועל אשה טפ]שת חותם‬. This restoration is favored by the comparison to other versions of Ben-Sira: the Geniza manuscript B reads ‫על אשה רעה חותם‬ with a gloss ‫טפשה‬ referring to ‫רעה‬. From the linguistic point of view, the form ‫טְפֶּשֶׁת‬ should be preferred over ‫טְפְּשָׁה‬. The former occurs in Mishnaic Hebrew (though in post Tannaitic literature) and in medieval Hebrew texts, while the latter occurs only in later and less reliable sources (see Y. Avineri, ‫היכל המשקלים‬, 446). The feminine ending ‫ת‬ is typical of participles and adjectives, particularly to adjective of the *qittel* pattern. In this pattern, I was able to find only one early (?) and reliable (?) form terminated with ‫יה‬: ‫שְׁכֵּלָה(ן‬in a Babylonian manuscript of Song of Songs (see Y. Yeivin ‫מסורת הלשון העברית המשתקפת בניקוד הבבלי‬, p. 961). Therefore, the aforementioned form ‫טפשה‬ in the Geniza manuscript should be explained away as a scribal error. Or perhaps it is an editor's misreading for ‫טפשת‬? (Dr. Efrat Habas-Rubin has kindly checked the original manuscript in the Bodleian Library at Oxford. In her view, the final letter looks like a ‫ה‬, but she was not entirely certain).

IV 13 = 42:7 — ‫על מ]קום תפקיד מספר / שו]אה ומתת הכל בכתב‬. The lacuna is too narrow for the restoration made in the second hemistich. Before ‫תת‬ I can see the bottommost part of a *waw*. I therefore propose the reading ‫שואה ותת[‬ or ‫שואת ותת[‬ For a thorough discussion of this passage, see Menachem Kister in *Lĕsonenu* 47 [1983]: 138). Finally, I would add that the word ‫תפקיד‬ in the first hemistich is a verbal noun rather than a finite verb paralleling the infinitive forms ‫שאת‬ and ‫תת‬. It means 'deposition', namely: 'wherever there is goods' deposition a booking should be kept' (On ‫תפקיד‬ 'deposition' in Aramaic, see Jastrow's dictionary s.v. ‫פלט‬).

IV 17 = 42:9 — ‫ובי]מיה פן תֹ[ת] ‫הֹ[‬. The reading is unclear and the original text of this passage can hardly be established. Strugnell suggests reading ‫ובֹעֹלֹיה‬ which is materially more likely. If we take ‫עוּלֶיהָ‬ as 'her youth' it will agree with the citation found in *b. Sanhedrin* 100b ‫שמא בקטנותה תתפתה‬. Yet what seems to be required here is an expression of time different than ‫בנעוריה‬ of the preceding hemistich.

IV 22 = 42:11 — ‫מקום תגור אל יהי‬. Yadin notes that "there is no trace of another word to the left of ‫יהי‬" and that "the copyist presumably forgot to transcribe the last word". He correctly restored ‫אשנב‬ according to the Geniza manuscript B. Examination of the original scroll proves that nothing was ever written after ‫יהי‬. In another article, I intend to discuss a similar omission in the Dead Sea Scrolls and in the Geniza manuscripts of the Damascus Covenant.

IV 25 = 42:14 — טוב רע איש מטיב אשה/ ובת מפחדת מכול חרפה. The reading מטיב has rightly been rejected. The word טיב is non-existent in early Hebrew. The Geniza version טיב should be reexamined; if the *yod* is clear, it should be deemed a scribal error for *waw*.

Both Baumgarten and Strugnell suspect the reading מכול on orthographical and paleographical grounds (the word כל is written defectively throughout the scroll, and the second letter is ב rather than כ). They assume that the original text was ובת מפחדת מבן לחרפה 'and a daughter is more worrisome than a son with regards to shame'.

V 1 = 42:15 — In the marginal addition, I suggest restoring מעש[ו] or מעש[יו], (or less probable מעש[י אל). A pronominal suffix referring to God is required, while the restoration מעש[י makes no sense.

V 7 = 42:18 — כי ידע עליון כל דעות/. Strugnell reads: כי ידע עליון דע[ות]/[ו]מביט אתיות עולם. This last reading is preferable materially and is supported by the versions.

V 9 = 42:20 — לא נעדר מפניו שכל/. Strugnell proposed/לא נעדר ממנו שכל/[ו]ל[א] א[ב]ד[ו] כל דבר ול[א] ע[ב]רו כל דבר. The traces fit his reading. The verb ע[ב]רו is a synonym of חלפו found in the Geniza manuscript.

V 11 = 42:21 — [ו]ל[כ]ול מבין. Strugnell s alternative reading ל[כ]ל fits both the traces and the orthography of the scroll.

V 13 = 42:23 — הכל חי ועמ'ד לעד/[ו]ב[כ]ל צרך והכל נשמר. Read הכל חי וע[ו]מ]ד לעד/[ו]ב[כ]ל צרך הכל נשמר.

V 18 = 43:2 — כלי נורא מעשי [על]יון. The examination of the original manuscript indicates that the last letter of מעשי is not a *yod* but rather a *he* eaten by worms.

V 19 = 43:3 — ולפני חרב מי יתכל[כ]ל. The last five letters have been eaten by worms. The reading יתכל[כ]ל follows the Geniza version with the meaning 'sustain' which perfectly fits the context. The traces however hardly support this reading. Skehan proposed (though hesitantly) to read יתכ[ו]לל, namely a *hitpolel* of the root כול with the same meaning. Evidently, the third letter looks like *kaf* and there is no space between the two *lameds*. Yet the second letter has a curve typical of *samekh*. Is it possible to read יסת[ו]לל? For the suitable meaning, see my discussion of II 20.

VI 1 = 43:8 — מ[ו]ר[צף [רקיע מזהירתו]. Read as proposed by Strugnell: [רקיע מזהירתו].

VI 4 = 43:11 — כי מאד נהדר[ה בכבוד]. The second letter in the second word looks like a *waw*, which is obviously narrower than *alef*. The form מוד reflects a

pronunciation such as *mōd* or *môd* (with extra-long vowel) known
from the Dead Sea Scrolls.

VI 18–19 = 43:22–24 — Milik noted that the little fragment was misplaced and
misread.

One should read:

[על כל מ]עֹמד מִׄים יקרׄוׄים]

[יבול הרי]ם חֹרֹב יש]יק]

VII 8 = 44:3 — וייעצים בתבונתם. The correct reading is either וייעצים (Strugnell) or
rather יועצים (as in the other versions).

VII 18 = 44:11 — עם זרעם נאמן טובם. The scroll has אם which is obviously a phonetic
error for עם. This should be corrected in the Note on the Reading
and not in the transcription.

VII 20 = 44:13 — ועד עולם יעמד זרעם. The first word is עד (without *waw*) as Strugnell
notes.

Ben Sira: A Bibliography of Studies, 1965–1997

FLORENTINO GARCÍA MARTÍNEZ

Qumrân Instituut — University of Groningen

This bibliography is based on the card system of the Qumrân Instituut of the University of Groningen and covers only the studies published since 1965, the year of Yadin's publication of the fragments from Masada. This year is generally taken as a watershed in the study of the book of Ben Sira, because, together with Yadin's edition, it also saw the publication of a truly critical edition of the Greek text by Joseph Ziegler.

For a listing of the numerous studies published between the edition of the Geniza fragments and 1965, as for older studies on Ben Sira, the reader is directed to the bibliography prepeared by Franz Böhmisch, "Bibliographie zu Jesus Sirach, Version 3.," which is electronically available on:

http://www.ktf.uni-passau.de/mitarbeiter/boehmisch/BenSira.Bibliographie.html

The present bibliography follows the conventions and abbreviations of the *Journal of Biblical Literature*: "Instruction for Contributors," *JBL* 117 (1998) 555–79. The entries are alphabetically arranged by authors names; several entries of the same author are also alphabetically arranged according to the first words; entries of a single author which begin with identical words, are arranged chronologically. This bibliography does not cover book reviews, unless they appeared as review articles.

Adinolfi, Marco, "Il medico in Sir 38,1–15," *Anton* 62 (1987) 172–83.

Alonso Schökel, Luis, *A Manual of Hebrew Poetics* (Roma: Editrice Pontificio Istituto Biblico, 1988).

Alonso Schökel, Luis, "Notas exegéticas al Eclesiástico (Ben Sira)," *EstBib* 53 (1995) 433–48.

Alonso Schökel, Luis, "Notas exegéticas al Eclesiástico (Ben Sira)," *EstBib* 54 (1996) 299–312.

Alonso Schökel, Luis, *Proverbios y Eclesiástico* (Los Libros Sagrados VIII,1; Madrid: Ediciones Cristiandad, 1968).

Alonso Schökel, Luis, *Sprache Gottes und der Menschen: Literarische und Sprachpsychologische Behandlungen zur Heiligen Schrift* (Düsseldorf, 1968)

Alonso Schökel, Luis, "The Vision of Man in Sirach 16.24–17:14," in J. Gammie *et al.* (eds.), *Israelite Wisdom. Theological and Literary Essays in Honor of Samuel Terrien* (Missoula: Scholars Press, 1978) 235–45.

Anderson, G. A. and S.M. Olyan, *Priesthood and Cult in Ancient Israel* (JSOTSup 125: Sheffield: Sheffield Academic Press, 1991)

Anoz, J., "La muerte en el Ben Sira," *Mayéutica* 5 (1979) 7–13.

Arduini, M.L., "Il tema 'vir' et 'mulier' nell' esegesi patristica e medievale di Eccli., XLII, 14: A proposito di un' interpretazione di Ruperto di Deutz," *Aevum* 54 (1980) 315–30.

Arduini, M.L., "Il tema 'vir' et 'mulier' nell' esegesi patristica e medievale di Eccli., XLII, 14: A proposito di un' interpretazione di Ruperto di Deutz," *Aevum* 55 (1981) 246–61.

Argall, Randal Allen, *1 Enoch and Sirach: A Comparative Literary and Conceptual Analysis of the Themes* of *Revelation, Creation and Judgement*, Diss. University of Iowa, 1992.

Argall, Randal Allen, *1 Enoch and Sirach. A Comparative Literary and Conceptual Analysis of the Themes of Revelation, Creation and Judgement* (SBL Early Judaism and its Literature 8; Atlanta: Scholars Press, 1995).

Argall, Randal Allen, "Reflections on 1 Enoch and Sirach: A Comparative Literary and Conceptual Analysis of the Themes of Revelation, Creation and Judgement," in *SBL 1995 Seminar Papers*, 337–51.

Baars, W., "On a Latin Fragment of Sirach," *VT* 15 (1965) 280–81.

Backhaus, F.J., "Qohelet und Sirach," *BN* 69 (1993) 32–55.

Bailey, K.E., "Women in Ben Sirach and in the New Testament," in R.A. Coughenour (ed.), *For Me to Live. Essays in Honor of James Leon Kelso* (Cleveland: Dillon, 1972) 56–73.

Baldauf, Borghild, *Arme und Armut im Buch Ben Sira. Eine philologisch-exegetische Untersuchung*, Diss. Salzburg, 1983.

Bar Ilan, Meir, *Polemics between Sages and Priests towards the End of the Second Commonwealth*, Diss. Bar-Ilan University 1982 [Hebrew].

Barker, Margaret, "The Other Books," in S. Bigeer (ed.), *Creating the Old Testament.* (Oxford: Blackwell. 1989) 319–44.

Barthélemy, Dominique and Otto Rickenbacher, *Konkordanz zum hebräischen Sirach mit syrisch-hebräischem Index.* (Freiburg-Göttingen: Biblischen Instituts der Universität Freiburg, Vandenhoeck & Ruprecht, 1973).

Barré, Michel (ed.), *Wisdom, You are My Sister: Studies in Honor of Roland E. Murphy, O. Carm., on the Occasion of his Eightieth Birthday* (CBQMS 29; Washington: The Catholic Biblical Association of America, 1997).

Baudry, G.H., "La théorie du 'penchant mauvais' et la doctrine du 'péché originel'," *Bulletin de littérature ecclésiastique* 95 (1994) 271–301.

Baumgarten, J.M., "Some Notes on the Ben Sira Scroll from Masada," *JQR* 59 (1967/68) 323–27.

Beauchamp, Paul, "Sur deux mots de l'Ecclesiastique (Si 3,27b)," in J. Doré and C. Théobald (eds.), *Penser la foi. Recherches en téologie aujourdhui. Mélanges offerts à Joseph Moingt* (Paris: Cerf, 1993) 15–25.

Beavin, E.L., "Ecclesiasticus or the Wisdom of Jesus the Son of Sirach," in C.M. Laymon (ed.), *The Interpreter's One-Volume Commentary on the Bible* (Nashville: Abingdon, 1971) 550–76.

Becker, J., *Gottesfurcht im Alten Testament* (AnBib 22; Roma: Editrice Pontificio Istituto Biblico, 1965).

Beckwith, Roger, "The Evidence of Greek Ecclesiasticus," in *The Old Testament Canon of the New Testament Church and its Background in Early Judaism* (London: SPCK, 1985) 110–11.

Beentjes, Pancratius C., "A Closer Look at the Newly Discovered Sixth Hebrew Manuscript (Ms. F) of Ben Sira," *EstBib* 51 (1993) 171–86.

Beentjes, Pancratius C., "Ben Sira 5, 1: A Literary and Rhetorical Analysis, "in E.G. Schrijver *et al.*, (eds.), *The Literary Analysis of Hebrew Texts* (Publications of the Juda Palache Institute 7; Amsterdam, 1992) 45–59.

Beentjes, Pancratius C., "Ben Sira 36,26d According to Ms. C: A New Proposal," *EstBib* 52 (1994) 535–39.

Beentjes, Pancratius C., "De getallenspreuk en zijn reikwijdte: Een pleidooi voor de literaire eenheid van Jesus Sirach 26:28–27:10," *Bijdragen* 43 (1982) 383–89.

Beentjes, Pancratius C., "De stammen van Israel herstellen. Het portret van Elia bij Jesus Sirach," *Amsterdamse Cahiers voor Exegese en Bijbelse Theologie* 5 (1984) 147–55.

Beentjes, Pancratius C., "De verhalen van het begin terug(ge)lezen: Jesus Sirach en Genesis 1–3," in C. Verdegaal and W. Weren (eds.), *Stromen uit Eden. Genesis 1–11 in Bijbel, joodse exegese en moderne literatuur* (Boxtel: Katholieke Bijbelstichting, 1992) 98–110.

Beentjes, Pancratius C., "De wijsheid van Jezus Sirach," in E. Eynikel (ed.), *Wie wijsheid zoek, vindt het leven. De wijsheidsliteratuur van het Oude Testament* (Leuven: Acco, 1991) 135–59.

Beentjes, Pancratius C., "'Ein Mensch ohne Freund ist wie eine linke Hand ohne die Rechte': Prolegomena zur Kommentierung des Freundschaftperikope Sir 6, 5–17," in F.V. Reiterer (ed.), *Freundschaft bei Ben Sira*, 1–18.

Beentjes, Pancratius C., "Full Wisdom is Fear of the Lord." Ben Sira 19,20–20,31: Context, Composition and Concept," *EstBib* 47 (1989) 27–45.

Beentjes, Pancratius C., "Hermeneutics in the Book of Ben Sira. Some observations on the Hebrew Ms. C," *EstBib* 46 (1988) 45–60.

Beentjes, Pancratius C., "Hezekiah and Isaiah: A Study on Ben Sira 48, 15–25," in A. S. van der Woude (ed.), *New Avenues in the Study of the Old Testament* (OTS 25; Leiden : Brill, 1989) 77–88.

Beentjes, Pancratius C., "How can a jug be friends with a kettle? A note on the Structure of Ben Sira Chapter 13," *BZ* 36 (1992) 87–93.

Beentjes, Pancratius C., "In de marge van manuscript B: kanttekeningen bij de hebreuwse tekst van Sirach 30:12e," *Bijdragen* 48 (1987) 132–38.

Beentjes, Pancratius C., "Inverted Quotations in the Bible: A Neglected Stylistic Pattern "[Sir 46:19] *Bib* 63 (1982) 506–23.

Beentjes, Pancratius C., *Jesus, de zoon van Sirach* (Cahiers voor levensverdieping 14; Averbode, 1982).

Beentjes, Pancratius C., "Jesus Sirach 7:1–17. Kanttekeningen bij de structuur en de tekst van een verwaarloosde passage," *Bijdragen* 41 (1980) 251–59.

Beentjes, Pancratius C., "Jesus Sirach 38:1–15. Problemen rondom een symbol," *Bijdragen* 41 (1980) 260–65.

Beentjes, Pancratius C., *Jesus Sirach en Tenach, Een onderzoek naar en clasificatie van parallelen, met bijzondere aandacht voor hun functie in Sirach 46,6–26,* (Nieuwegein, 1981).

Beentjes, Pancratius C., "Profetie bij Jesus Sirach," in B. Becking *et al.* (eds.), *Door het oog van de profeten* (Utrechtse Theol. R. 8: Utrecht, 1989) 23–30.

Beentjes, Pancratius C., "Reading the Hebrew Ben Sira Manuscripts Synoptically: A New Hypothesis," in P.C. Beentjes (ed.), *The Book of Ben Sira in Modern Research*, 95–111.

Beentjes, Pancratius C., "Recent Publications on the Wisdom of Jesus ben Sira (Ecclesiasticus)," *Bijdragen* 43 (1982) 188–98.

Beentjes, Pancratius C., "Relations between Ben Sira and the Book of Isaiah," in J. Vermeylen (ed.), *The Book of Isaiah. Le Livre d'Isaie* (BETL 81; Leuven: Peeters, 1989) 155–59.

Beentjes, Pancratius C., "Sirach 22:22–23:6 in zijn context," *Bijdragen* 39 (1978) 144–51.

Beentjes, Pancratius C., "Some Misplaced Words in the Hebrew Manuscript C. of the Book of Ben Sira," *Bib* 67 (1986) 397–401.

Beentjes, Pancratius C., "Sweet is his Memory, Like Honey to the Palate: King Josiah in Ben Sira 59,1–4," *BZ* 34 (1990) 262–66.

Beentjes, Pancratius C., "The Book of Ben Sira in Hebrew. Preliminary Remarks toward a New Text Edition and Synopsis," in *Actes du Troisième Colloque International Bible et Informatique: Interpretation, Herméneutique, Compétence Informatique* (Paris-Gen ve, 1992) 471–84.

Beentjes, Pancratius C., *The Book of Ben Sira in Hebrew. A Text Edition of all Extant Hebrew Manuscripts and a Synopsis of all Parallel Hebrew Ben Sira Texts* (VTSup 68; Leiden: Brill 1997).

Beentijes, Pancratius C. (ed.), *The Book of Ben Sira in Modern Research* (Berlin: De Gruyter 1997).

Beentjes, Pancratius C., "'The Countries Marvelled at You': King Solomon in Ben Sira 47:12–22," *Bijdragen* 45 (1984) 6–14.

Beentjes, Pancratius C., "The Praise of the Famous and its Prolog," *Bijdragen* 45 (1984) 374–83.

Begg, C., "Ben-Sirach's No-Mention of Ezra," *BN* 42 (1988) 14–18.

Ben-Hayyim, Z. (ed.), *The Book of Ben Sira. Text, Concordance and an Analysis of the Vocabulary* (The Historical Dictionary of the Hebrew Language; Jerusalem: Keter, 1973) [Hebrew].

Berger, Klaus, *Die Gesetzesauslegung Jesu. Ihr historischer Hintergrund im Judentum und im Alten Testament.* Teil I (WMANT 40; Neukirchen: Neukirchener Verlag, 1972).

Beyer, Klaus, "Woran erkennt man, daß ein griechischer Text aus dem Hebräischen oder Aramäischen übersetzt ist?," in M. Macuch *et al.* (eds), *Studia semitica, necnon iranica Rudolpho Macuch septuagenario ab amicis et discipulis dedicata* (Wiesbaden: Harrassowitz, 1989) 21–32.

Bickerman(n), Elias Joseph, "Scribes and Sages," in *The Jews in the Greek Age* (Cambridge, Massachusetts: Harvard University Press, 1988) 161–76.

Blockmuehl, Markus N.A., *Revelation and Mystery in Ancient Judaism and Pauline Christianity* (WUNT 36; Tübingen: Mohr, 1990) 57–68.

Blomqvist, J., "Textual and Interpretational Problems in Sirach," *Eranos* 83 (1985) 33–43.

Boccaccini, Gabrielle, "La Sapienza dello Pseudo-Aristea," in A. Vivian (ed.), *Biblische und judaistische Studien. Festschrift für Paolo Sacchi* (Judentum und Umwelt 29; Frankfurt am Main: Peter Lang, 1990) 143–76.

Boccaccini, Gabrielle, "Origine del male, libertà dell'uomo e retribuzione nella Sapienza di Ben Sira," *Henoch* 8 (1986) 1–37.

Boccaccini, Gabrielle, *Middle Judaism. Jewish Thought 300 BCE to 200 BCE* (Minneapolis: Fortress, 1991) 77–125.

Boccaccio, P. and Berardi, G., *Ecclesiasticus. Textus hebraeus secundum fragmenta reperta* (Rome: Biblical Institute Press, 1976).

Boer, P.A.H. de, "עולם יעמד זרעם Sir 44,12a," in *Hebräische Wortforschung. FS W. Baumgartner* (VTSup 16; Leiden: Brill, 1967) 25–29.

Bogaert, P.M., "Septante, 37. Sagesse de Sirach," *DBSup* XII/Fasc. 68 (Paris: Letouzey & An , 1988) 628–630.

Bohlen, Reinhold, *Die Ehrung der Eltern bei Ben Sira. Studien zur Motivation eines familienethischen Grundwertes in frühhellenistischer Zeit* (Trierer

Theologische Studien 51; Trier: Paulinus, 1991).

Böhmisch, F., "Die Textformen des Sirachbuches und ihre Zielgruppen," *Protokole zur Bibel* 6 (1997) 87–122.

Bonora, Antonio, "Il binomio Sapienza-Torah nell'ermeneutica e nella genesi dei testi sapienziali (Gb 28; Pro 8; Sir 1,14; Sap 9), in *Sapienza e Torah. Atti della XXIX Settimana Biblica* (Bologna: Dehoniane 1987) 31–48.

Born, A. van den, *Wijsheid van Jesus Sirach (Ecclesiasticus) uit de grondtekst vertaalt en uitgelegd* (De boeken van het Oude Testament 8,5; Roermond: Roemen & Zn, 1968).

Bosson, Nathalie, "Un palimpseste du Musée Copte du Caire," *Le Muséon* 104 (1991) 5–37.

Botha, P.J., "The Ideology of Shame in the Wisdom of Ben Sira: Ecclesiasticus 41:14–42:8," *Old Testament Essays* 9 (1996) 350–71.

Botha, P.J., "Through the Figure of a Woman Many Have Perished: Ben Sira's View of Women," *Old Testament Essays* 9 (1996) 20–34.

Breid, F., *Die Struktur der Gesellschaft im Buch Ben Sirach*, Diss., Graz, 1971.

Broekhoven, Harold van, "A New Social Model for Discerning Wisdom: The Case of Sirach and Pseudo-Solomon," in Paul V.M. Flesher (ed.), *New Perspectives on Ancient Judaism. Vol. Five. Society and Literature in Analysis* (Lanham-New York-London, 1990) 3–46.

Broekhoven, Harold van., *Wisdom and World: The Functions of Wisdom Imagery in Sirach, Pseudo-Solomon and Colossians*, Diss. Boston University, 1988.

Bronznick, N.N., "An Unrecognized Denotation of the Verb HSR in Ben Sira and Rabbinic Hebrew," *HAR* 9 (1985) 91–105.

Bryce, G., "'Better' Proverbs: An Historical and Structural Study," in *SBL 1972 Seminar Papers*. Vol. 2 (Missoula: Scholars Press, 1972) 343–54.

Bühlmann, Walter, *Gott in einer kritischen Welt? Ein Schlüssel zu den Spätschriften des Alten Testaments* (Luzern-Stuttgart, 1991).

Burton, Keith Wayne, *Sirach and the Judaic Doctrine of Creation*, Diss. University of Glasgow, 1987.

Busto Saiz, Jos R. "Macarismos desarrollados: un tipo de poema sapiencial," in N. Fernández Marcos *et al.* (eds.), *Simposio Bíblico Español* (Madrid: Editorial de la Universidad Complutense, 1984) 345–56.

Busto Saiz, José R., "Sabiduría y Torá en Jesús Ben Sira," *EstBib* 52 (1994) 228–39.

Caird, G.B., "Ben Sira and the Dating of the Septua-

gint," *Bulletin of the International Organisation for Septuagint and Cognate Studies* 7 (1974) 21–22.

Caird, G.B., "Ben Sira and the Dating of the Septuagint," in E.A. Livingstone (ed.), *Studia Evangelica VII* (TU 126; Berlin, de Gruyter, 1982) 95–100.

Calduch Benages, Núria, "Ben Sira y el Canon de las Escrituras," *Gregorianum* 78 (1997) 359–70.

Calduch Benages, Núria, "Ben Sira 2 y el Nuevo Testamento," *EstBíb* 53 (1995) 305–16.

Calduch Benages, Núria, "Elementos de inculturación helenistica en el libro de Ben Sira: los viajes," *EstBib* 54 (1996), 289–98.

Calduch Benages, Núria, "Elements d'inculturació hellenista en el llibre de Ben Sira: els viatges," in A. Borrel, A. de la Fuente, A. Puic (eds.), *La Bíblia i el Mediterrani. Actes del Congrés de Barcelona 18–22 de setembre de 1995*, Volum II (Barcelona: Associació Bíblica de Catalunya, 1997) 113–21.

Calduch Benages, Núria, *En el crisol de la prueba. Estudio exegetico de Sir 2*, Diss. Pontifical Biblical Institute, Rome 1995.

Calduch Benages, Núria, *En el crisol de la prueba. Estudio exegético de Sir 2* (ABE 32: Estella: Verbo Divino, 1997).

Calduch Benages, Núria, "La Sabiduría y la prueba en Sir 4,11–19," *EstBib* 49 (1991) 25–48.

Calduch Benages, Núria, "Traducir — Interpretar: La versión siríaca de Sirácida 1," *EstBib* 55 (1997) 313–40.

Calduch Benages, Núria, "Trial Motif in the Book of Ben Sira with Special Reference to Sir 2,1–6," in P.C. Beentjes (ed.), *The Book of Ben Sira in Modern Research*, 135–51.

Camp. Claudia V., "Honor and Shame in Ben Sira: Anthropological and Theological Reflections," in P.C. Beentjes (ed.), *The Book of Ben Sira in Modern Research*, 171–87.

Camp, Claudia V., "Honor, Shame, and the Hermeneutics of Ben Sira's MS C," in M. Barré (ed.), *Wisdom, You Are My Sister*, 157–71.

Camp, Claudia V., "Understanding a Patriarchy: Women in Second Century Jerusalem Through the Eyes of Ben Sira," in Amy-Jill Levin (ed.), *Women Like This. New Perspectives on Jewish Women in the Greco-Roman World* (SBL Early Judaism and its Literature 1; Atlanta: Scholars Press, 1991) 1–39.

Caquot, André, "Ben Sira et le messianisme," *Sem* 16 (1966) 43–68.

Caquot, André, "Le Siracide a-t-il parlé d'une 'espèce' humaine?," *RHPR* 62 (1982) 225–30.

Carmignac, Jean, "L'infinitif absolu chez Ben Sira et à Qumran," *RevQ* 12 (1985–1987) 251–61.

Celniker, Michael, "Lo sviluppo della sapienza (chokhmà) nell'Antico Testamento e negli apocrufi (Sapienza di Ben Sira e Sapienza di Salomone)," *Annuario di Studi Ebraici* 11 (1988) 15–28.

Ceresko, Hope W., "The Liberative Strategy of Ben Sira: The Sage as Prophet," *BibBh* 22 (1996) 210–31.

Ceresko, Hope W., "The Liberative Strategy of Ben Sira: The Sage as Prophet," *Toronto Journal of Theology* 13 (1997) 169–85.

Chester, Andrew, "Citing the Old Testament," in D.A. Carson and H.G.M. Williamson (eds.), *It is Written: Scripture Citing Scripture. Essays in Honour of Barnabas Lindars*, (Cambridge University Press, Cambridge, 1988) 141–69.

Chmiel, Jerzy, "Centenary of the Discovery of the Hebrew Manuscripts of the Book of Ben Sira in the Cairo Geniza," in E. Szweg (ed.), *Swiatla prawdy bozej*. FS. Lech Stachowiak (Lódz, 1996) 15–19 [Polish].

Cohen Stuart, G.H., *The Struggle in Man between Good and Evil: An Inquiry into the Origin of the Rabbinic Concept of Yeser Harac* (Kampen: Kok, 1984).

Collins, John J., "Ben Sira in His Hellenistic Context," in *Jewish Wisdom in the Hellenistic Age*, 23–41.

Collins, John J., "Ben Sira's Ethics," in *Jewish Wisdom in the Hellenistic Age*, 62–79.

Collins, John J., *Jewish Wisdom in the Hellenistic Age* (The Old Testament Library; Louisville: Westminster John Knox, 1997).

Collins, John J., *Seers, Sybils and Sages in Hellenistic-Roman Judaism* (JSJSup 54; Leiden: Brill, 1997).

Collins, John J., "The History and Destiny of Israel," in *Jewish Wisdom in the Hellenistic Age*, 97–111.

Collins, John J., "The Origin of Evil in Apocalyptic Literature and the Dead Sea Scrolls," in J.A. Emerton (ed.), *Congress Volume: Paris* (VTSup 61; Leiden: Brill 1995) 25–38.

Collins, John J., "The Problem of Evil and the Justice of God,", in *Jewish Wisdom in the Hellenistic Age*, 80–96.

Collins, John J., "The Root of Immortality: Death in the Context of Jewish Wisdom," *HTR* 71 (1978) 177–92.

Collins, John J., The Root of Immortality: Death in the Context of Jewish Wisdom," in *Seers, Sibyls and Sages*, 351–67.

Collins, John J., "Wisdom and the Law," in *Jewish Wisdom in the Hellenistic Age*, 42–61.

Collins, John J., "Wisdom, Apocalypticism and the Dead Sea Scrolls," in *Seers, Sibyls and Sages*, 369–83.

Conzelmann, H., "The Mother of Wisdom," [Sir 24,3s] in J. McConkey Robinson (ed.), *The Future of Our Religious Past. Essays in Honour of Rudolf Bultman* (New York, 1971) 230–243.

Corley, Jeremy, "Caution, Fidelity, and the Fear of God: Ben Sira's Teaching on Friendship in Sir 6:5–17," *EstBib* 54 (1996) 313–26.

Corley, Jeremy, "Rediscovering Sirach," *ScrB* 27 (1997) 2–7.

Couroyer, Bernard, "Un égyptianisme dans Ben Sira iv,11," *RB* 82 (1975) 206–217.

Cox, D., "צדקה and מישפט: The Concept of Righteousness in Later Wisdom," *SBFLA* 27 (1977) 33–50.

Cox, D., *Proverbs, with an Introduction to Sapiental Books* (Old Testament Message 17; Wilmington, 1982).

Crenshaw, J., *Old Testament Wisdom. An Introduction*, (Atlanta: Knox, 1981).

Crenshaw, J., *Studies in Ancient Israelite Wisdom* (New York: KTAV, 1976).

Crenshaw, James L., "The Primacy of Listening in Ben Sira's Pedagogy," in M. Barré (ed.), *Wisdom, You Are My Sister*, 172–87.

Crenshaw, James L., "The Problem of Theodicy in Sirach: On Human Bondage," *JBL* 94 (1975) 47–64.

Crenshaw, James L., "Wisdom," in J.H. Hayes (ed.), *Old Testament Form Criticism* (San Antonio, 1974) 225–64.

Crenshaw, James L., "Wisdom and the Sage: On knowing and not knowing," in *World Congress of Jewish Studies, Jerusalem 1994*, 137–44.

Crenshaw, James L., "Wisdom in the OT," in *IDBSup.*, (Nashville: Abingdon, 1976) 952–56.

Crepaldi, M.G., "Il tempo nei libri sapienziali," *Studia Patavina* 29 (1982) 25–47.

Critchlow, J., *Exegetical and Topical Studies in the Greek Ecclesiasticus*, Diss. Manchester University, 1978.

Crüsemann, F. *Studien zur Formgeschichte von Hymnus und Danklied in Israel* (WMANT 32; Neukirchen-Vluyn: Neukirchener Verlag, 1969).

Da S. Marco, E., "Lo Pseudo-Aristea e il Siracida (Ecclo 50) sulla cittadella e il tempio di Gerusalemme," *Atti del V convegno Biblico-Francescano Roma 1969* (Assisi, 1971) 193–207.

Daube, David, "Example and precept; from Sirach to R. Ishmael," in G.F. Hawthorne with O. Betz (eds.), *Tradition and Interpretation in the New Testament. Essays in Honor of E.Earle Ellis* (Michigan-Tübingen: Eerdmans-Mohr, 1987) 16–21.

Davies, Philip R., "Scenes from the Early History of Judaism," in D. Vikander Edelman (ed.), *The Triumph of Elohim. From Yahwisms to Judaisms*

(Grand Rapids: Eerdmans 1995) 145–82.

Dawes, Stephen B., "'Anawâ' in Translation and Tradition," *VT* 41 (1991) 38–48.

Delcor, Mathias, "Ecclesiasticus or Sirach," in W.D. Davies and L. Finkelstein (eds.), *The Cambridge History of Judaism*, Vol. 2 (Cambridge: Cambridge University Press, 1989) 415–22.

Delcor, Mathias, "Le Texte hébreu du cantique de Siracide 51,13 et ss. et les anciennes versions," *Textus* 6 (1968) 27–47.

Delsman, Wilhelmus C., "Oudhebreeuwse bespiegelingen van Jezus Sirach," in K.R. Veenhof (ed.), *Schrijven verleden. Documenten uit het oude Nabij Oosten vertaald en toegelicht* (Leiden-Zutphen: Ex Oriente Lux-Terra, 1983) 361–66.

Derousseaux, L., *La Crainte de Dieu dans l'Ancien Testament* (LD 63; Paris: Cerf, 1970).

Desecar, Alejandro J., "La necedad en Sirac 23,12–15," *SBFLA* 20 (1970) 264–72.

Desecar, Alejandro J., "'Sapiente' e 'stolto' in Eccli 27,11–13," *BeO* 16 (1974) 193–98.

Desecar, Alejandro J., *La sabiduría y la necedad en Sirac 21–22* (Presenza 3; Rome: Edizioni Francescane, 1970).

Deutsch, Celia, "The Sirach 51 Acrostic: Confession and Exhortation," *ZAW* 94 (1982) 400–09.

Di Lella, Alexander A., "Conservative and Progresive Theology: Sirach and Wisdom," in J.L. Crenshaw (ed.), *Israelite Wisdom*, 401–16.

Di Lella, Alexander A., *Ecclesiasticus* (NCE 5; New York: McGraw-Hill. 1967), 33–34.

Di Lella, Alexander A., "Fear of the Lord and Belief and Hope in the Lord amid Trials: Sirach 2:1–16," in M. Barré (ed.), *Wisdom, You are My Sister*, 188–204.

Di Lella, Alexander A., "Fear of the Lord as Wisdom: Ben Sira 1, 11–30," in P.C. Beentjes (ed.), *The Book of Ben Sira in Modern Research*, 113–33.

Di Lella, Alexander A., "Sirach," in R. Brown (ed.), *The New Jerome Biblical Commentary*, 496–509.

Di Lella, Alexander A., "Sirach 10:19–11:6: Textual Criticism, Poetic Analysis, and Exegesis," in C.L. Meyers and M. O'Conner (eds.), *The Word of the Lord Shall Go Forth. Essays in Honor of David Noel Freedman in Celebration of His Sixtieth Birthday* (Winona Lake: Eisenbrauns, 1982) 157–64.

Di Lella, Alexander A., "Sirac 51:1–12: Poetic Structure and Analysis of Ben Sira's Psalm," *CBQ* 48 (1986) 395–407.

Di Lella, Alexander A., *The Hebrew Text of Sirach. A textcritical and historical study* (Studies in Classical Literature 1; The Hague: Mouton, 1966).

Di Lella, Alexander A., "The Meaning of Wisdom in Ben Sira" in Leo G. Perdue, Bernard Brandon Scott, William Johnston Wiseman (eds.), *In Search of Wisdom. Essays in Memory of John G. Gammie* (Louisville: Westminster John Knox, 1993) 139–48.

Di Lella, Alexander A., "The Newly Discovered Sixth Manuscript of Ben Sira from the Cairo Geniza," *Bib* 69 (1988) 226–38.

Di Lella, Alexander A., "The Poetry of Ben Sira," *ErIsr* 16 (1982) 26*–33*.

Di Lella, Alexander A., "The Problem of Retribution in the Wisdom Literature," in *Rediscovery of Scripture: Biblical Theology Today. Report of the 46th Annual Meeting of the Franciscan Educational Conference* (Burlington, 1967) 109–27.

Di Lella, Alexander A., "The Search of Wisdom in Ben Sira," in J.C. Knight (ed.), *The Psalms and Other Studies on the Old Testament* (Nashotah, Wisconsin: Nashotah House Seminary, 1990) 185–96.

Di Lella, Alexander A., "The Wisdom of Ben Sira: Resources and Recent Research," *Biblical Studies* 4 (1996) 161–81.

Di Lella, Alexander A., "Use and Abuse of the Tongue: Ben Sira 5,9–6,1," in A.A. Diesel *et al.* (eds.), *'Jedes Ding hat seine Zeit...' Studien zur israelitischen altorientalischen Weisheit: Diethelm Michel zum 65. Geburtstag* (BZAW 241; Berlin: de Gruyter, 1996) 33–48.

Di Lella, Alexander A., "Wisdom of Ben Sira," in David Noel Freedman (ed.), *The Anchor Bible Dictionary*. Vol. 6 (New York: Doubleday, 1992) 931–45.

Di Lella, Alexander A., "Wisdom in Ben Sira," *TBT* 35 (1997) 136–40.

Di Lella, Alexander A., "Women in the Wisdom of Ben Sira and the Book of Judith: A Study in Contrasts and Reversals," in J.A. Emerton (ed.), *Congress Volume, Paris 1992* (VTSup 61; Leiden: Brill, 1995) 39–52.

Diebner, B.J., "Mein Grossvater Jesus," *DBAT* 16 (1982) 1–37.

Dogniez, Cécile, "Siracide," in *Bibliography of the Septuagint. Bibliographie de la Septante 1970–1993* (VTSup 60; Brill: Leiden 1995) 230–41.

Dommershausen, W., "Zum Vergeltungsdenken des Ben Sira," in H. Gese and H.P. Rüger (eds.), *Wort und Geschichte* (AOAT 18; Kevelaer: Neukirchen-Vluyn, 1973) 37–43.

Doré, D., *Qohélet et le Siracide ou l'Ecclésiaste et l'Ecclésiastique* (Cahiers Évangile 91; Paris: Cerf, 1995).

Dorival, G.; Barl, M.; Munnich, O., *La Bible Grecque*

des Septante. Du judaisme hellénistique au christian-isme ancien (Paris: Cerf-Éditions du CNRS, 1988).

Duesberg, H., "La Dignité de l'homme: Siracide 16,24–17,14," *BVC* 82 (1968) 15–21.

Duesberg, H., "Le médecin, un sage (Ecclesiastique 38, 1–15)," *BVC* 38 (1961) 43–48.

Duesberg, H., *Les Scribes inspirés: Introduction aux livres sapientiaux de la Bible.* 2. vols. (Paris, 1966).

Duesberg, H., and I. Fransen, *Ecclesiastico* (La Sacra Bibbia; Turin-Rome: Marietti, 1966).

Duhaime, Jean, "El elogio de los Padres de Ben Sira y el Cántico de Moisés (Sir 44–50 y Dt 32)," *EstBib* 35 (1976) 223–29.

Egger-Wenzel, Renate, "Der Gebrauch von תמים bei Ijob und Ben Sira: Ein Vergleich zweier Weisheits-bücher," in F.V. Reiterer (ed.), *Freundschaft bei Ben Sira*, 203–38.

Elwolde, John F., "Developments in Hebrew Vocabu-lary between Bible and Mishnah," in T. Muraoka and J. Elwolde (eds.), *The Hebrew of the Dead Sea Scrolls and Ben Sira*, 17–55.

Engberg-Pedersen, Troel, "Erfaring og åbenbaring I Siraks Bog," in T. Engber-Pedersen and Niels Peter Lemche (eds.), *Tradition og nybrud. Jødendommen I hellenistisk tid* (København: Museum Tusculanum, 1990) 93–122.

Fahey, Michael A., *Cyprian and the Bible. A Study in third-Century Exegesis*, Diss. Tübingen, 1971.

Fassberg, S.E., "On the Syntax of Independent Clauses in Ben Sira," in T. Muraoka and John F. Elwolde (eds.), *The Hebrew of the Dead Sea Scrolls and Ben Sira*, 56–71.

Faure, Patrick, "Comme un fleuve que irrigue: Ben Sira 24,30–34, I. Critique textuelle," *RB* 102 (1995) 5–27.

Faure, Patrick, "La Sagesse et le Sage. Ben Sira 24,30–34. II. Exégèse," *RB* 103 (1996) 348–70.

Fensham, "Widow, Orphan and the Poor," in Frederick E. Greenspahn (ed.), *Essential Papers on Israel and the Ancient Near East* (New York-London, 1991) 176–92.

Fernández Marcos, Natalio, "Interpretaciones helenís-ticas del pasado de Israel," *Cuadernos de Filología Clásica* 8 (1975) 157–86.

Fischer, Heribert (ed.), *Expositio libri exodi sermones et lectiones super ecclesiastici Cap. 24. Expositio libri sapientiae, expositio cantici canticorum Cap 1,6. Hrsg. und übersetzt von Heribert Fischer* (Stuttgart, 1992).

Fleischer, Ezra, "Additional Fragments of the 'Rhymed

Ben Sira'", in M. Cogan *at al.* (ed.), *Tehilla le-Moshe. Biblical and Judaic Studies in Honor of Moshe Grennberg* (Winona Lake: Eisenbrauns, 1997) 205*–218*.

Foulkes, Pamela A., "'To Expound Discipline or Judge-ment': The Portrait of the Scribe in Ben Sira," *Pacifica: Australian Theological Studies* 7 (1994) 75–84.

Fournier-Bidoz, Alain, "L'Arbre et la demeure: Sira-cide XXIV 10–17," *VT* 34 (1984) 1–10.

Fox, Douglas E., "Ben Sira on OT Canon Again: The Date of Daniel," *WThJ* 49 (1987) 335–50.

Fraenkel, Pierre, "Le débat entre Martin Chemnitz et Robert Bellarmin sur les livres deutérocanoniques et la place du Siracide," in J.-D. Kaestli et O. Wermel-inger (eds.), *Le Canon de l'Ancien Testament. Sa formation et son histoire* (Geneva, 1984) 283–312.

Frank, R. M., *The Wisdom of Jesus Ben Sirach (Sinai ar. 155 IXth/Xth cent.) edited with an Arabic-Greek word index* (CSCO.A 30; Louvain: Peeters, 1974).

Frankemölle, Hubert, "Zum Thema des Jakobusbriefes im Kontext der Rezeption von Sir 2,1–18 und 15, 11–20," *BN* 48 (1989) 21–49.

Fransen, I., "Les oeuvres de Dieu (Sir 42,1–50,20)," *BVC* 81 (1968) 26–35.

Frost, Stanley Brice, "Who Were the Heroes? An Exer-cise in Bitestamentary Exegesis, with Christological Implications," in L.D. Hurst and N.T. Wright (eds.), *The Glory of Christ in the New Testament. Studies in Christology. In Memory of G.B. Caird* (Oxford, 1987) 165–72.

Gammie, John G. (ed.), *Israelite Wisdom: Theological and Literary Essays in Honour of Samuel Terrien* (Missoula: Scholars Press, 1978).

Gammie, John G., "The Sage in Sirach," in Leo G. Perdue and J.G. Gammie (eds.) *The Sage in Israel and the Ancient Near East* (Winona Lake: Eisen-brauns, 1990) 355–72.

Garibay Kintana, A.M., *Proverbios de Salomón y Sabi-duría de Jesús ben Sirak* (Mexico: Porrúa, 1966).

Gilbert, Maurice, "Ben Sira et la femme," *RTL* 7 (1976) 426–42.

Gilbert, Maurice, "Grégoire de Nazianze et le Sira-cide," in *Mémorial Dom Jean Gribomont* (1920–1986), 307–314.

Gilbert, Maurice, "Comment lire les écrits sapientiaux de l'Ancien Testament," in M. Gilbert *et al.* (eds.), *Morale et Ancien Testament* (Lex Spiritus Vitae 1; Louvain: Université Catholique de Louvain, 1976) 131–75.

Gilbert, Maurice, *Introduction au livre de Ben Sira ou*

Siracide ou Ecclésiastique (Roma: Editrice Pontificio Istituto Biblico, 1989).

Gilbert, Maurice, "Jérôme et l'oeuvre de Ben Sira," *Le Muséon* 100 (1987) 109–20.

Gilbert, Maurice, "Jesus Sirach," in: *RAC* 17, 1995, 878–906.

Gilbert, Maurice, "La prière des sages d'Israel," in H. Limet and J. Ries (eds.), *L'experience de la prière dans les grandes religions* (Homo Religiosus 5; Centre d'Histoire des Religions: Louvain, 1998) 227–43.

Gilbert, Maurice (ed.), *La Sagesse de l'Ancien Testament* (BETL 51: Leuven: Duculot, 1979.

Gilbert, Maurice, "La Sagesse personnifiée dans les textes de l'Ancien Testament," *Cahiers Évangile* 32 (1980) 5–35.

Gilbert, Maurice, "La Sapienza si offre come nutrimento (Sir 24,19–22)," *Parola, Spirito e Vita*, 7 (1983) 51–60.

Gilbert, Maurice, "La sequela della Sapienza: Lettura di Sir 6," *Parola, Spirito e Vita*, 2 (1980) 53–70.

Gilbert, Maurice, "L'action de grâce de Ben Sira (Si 51,1–12)," in R. Kuntzmann (ed.), *Ce Dieu qui vient: Mélanges offerts à Bernard Renaud* (LD 159; Paris: Cerf, 1995) 232–42.

Gilbert, Maurice, "L'Ecclésiastique. Quel texte? Quelle autorité?," *RB* 94 (1987) 233–50.

Gilbert, Maurice, "L'éloge de la Sagesse (Siracide 24)," *RTL* 5 (1974) 326–48.

Gilbert, Maurice, "Lecture mariale et ecclésiale de Siracide 24,10 (15)," *Marianum* 47 (1985) 536–42.

Gilbert, Maurice, "Siracide," in *DBSup* XII, Fasc. 71 (Paris: Letouzey & Ané, 1996) 1389–1437.

Gilbert, Maurice, "Spirito, sapienza e legge secondo Ben Sira e il libro della Sapienza," *Parola, Spirito e Vita* 4 (1981) 65–73.

Gilbert, Maurice, "The Book of Ben Sira: Implications for Jewish and Christian Traditions," in S. Talmon (ed.), *Jewish Civilization in the Hellenistic-Roman Period* (JSPSup 10; Sheffield: Sheffield Academic Press,1991) 81–91.

Gilbert, Maurice, "Wisdom Literature," in M.E. Stone (ed.), *Jewish Writings of the Second Temple Period. Apocrypha, Pseudepigrapha, Qumran Sectarian Writings, Philo, Josephus* (CRINT 2/II; Assen-Philadelphia: Van Gorcum-Fortress, 1984) 283–324.

Gilbert, Maurice, "Wisdom of the Poor: Ben Sira 10,19–11,6," in P.C. Beentjes (ed.), *The Book of Ben Sira in Modern Research*, 153–69.

Glasson, T. Francis, "Colossians 1.18,15 and Sirach 24," *JBL* 86 (1967) 214–16.

Goan, Seán, "Creation in Ben Sira," *Miltown Studies* 36 (1995) 75–85.

Gordis, Robert, "The Social Background of Wisdom Literature," in *Poets, Prophets, and Sages. Essays in Biblical Interpretation* (Bloomington-London, 1971) 160–97.

Greenfield, Jonas C., "Ben Sira 42,9–10 and its Talmudic Paraphrase," in Ph. R. Davies and Richard T. White (eds.), *A Tribute to Geza Vermes: Essays on Jewish and Christian Literature and History* (JSTOTSup 100; Sheffield: JSOT Press, 1990) 167–73.

Hadot, J., *Penchant mauvais et volonté libre dans La Sagesse de Ben Sira (L'Ecclésiastique)* (Bruxelles: Presses Universitaires de Bruxelles, 1970.

Hahn, F., "Einige notwendige Bemerkungen zu zwei Texteditionen," *VuF* 36 (1991) 22–34.

Hamp, V., *Weisheit und Gottesfurcht: Aufsätze zur alttestamentlichen Einleitung, Exegese und Theologie*, edited by G. Schmuttermayer (St. Ottilien, 1990).

Harrington, Daniel J., "Sage Advice about Friendship," *The Bible Today* 32 (1994) 79–83.

Harrington, Daniel J., "Sirach Research Since 1965: Progress and Questions," in John C. Reeves & John Kampen (eds.), *Pursuing the Text: studies in honor of Ben Zion Wacholder on the occasion of his seventieth birthday* (JSOTSup 184; Sheffield: Sheffield Academic Press, 1994) 164–76.

Harrington, Daniel J., "The Wisdom of the Scribe According to Ben Sira," in John J. Collins and G.W.E. Nickelburg (eds.), *Ideal Figures in Ancient Judaism: Profiles and Paradigms* (Chico: Scholars Press, 1980) 181–88.

Harrington, Daniel J., "Two Early Jewish Approaches to Wisdom: Sirach and Qumran Sapiential Work A," in *SBL* 1996 Seminar Papers, 123–32.

Harrington, Daniel J., "Two Early Jewish Approaches to Wisdom: Sirach and Qumran Sapiential Work A.," *JSP* 16 (1997) 25–38.

Harrington, Daniel J., *Wisdom Texts from Qumran* (The Literature of the Dead Sea Scrolls; London: Routledge 1996).

Hartman, L.F., "Sirach in Hebrew and Greek," *CBQ* 23 (1961) 443–451.

Hartom, A., "Ben Sira," in הספרים החצונים (Tel-Aviv: Yavne 1969) [Hebrew].

Harvey, J.D., "Toward a Degree of Order in Ben Sira's Book," *ZAW* 105 (1993) 52–62.

Haspecker, J., *Gottesfurcht bei Jesus Sirah. Ihre religiöse Struktur und ihre literarische und doktrinäre Bedeutung* (AnBib 30; Rome: Editrice Pontificio Istituto Biblico 1967).

Hauer, Christian H. "Water in the Mountain?," *PEQ* 101 (1969) 44–45.

Hayward, C.T.R., "Sacrifice and World Order: Some Observations on Ben Sira's Attitude to The Temple Service," in S.W. Sykes (ed.), *Sacrifice and Redemption. Durham Essays in Theology* (Cambridge, 1991) 22–34.

Hayward, C.T.R., *The Jewish Temple. A Non-Biblical Sourcebook* (London: Routledge, 1996).

Hayward, C.T.R., "The New Jerusalem in the Wisdom of Jesus Ben Sira," *JSOT* 6 (1992) 123–38.

Hayward, C.T.R., "The Wisdom of Jesus Ben Sira in Hebrew," in *The Jewish Temple*, 38–72.

Hayward, C.T.R., "The Wisdom of Jesus Ben Sira in Greek," in *The Jewish Temple*, 73–84.

Hengel, Martin, "Die Septuaginta als von den Christen beanspruchte Schriftensammlung bei Justin und den Vätern vor Origenes," in J.D.G. Dunn (ed.), *Jews and Christians. The Parting of the Ways* (WUNT 66; Tübingen: Mohr, 1992) 39–84.

Hengel, Martin, "Die Septuaginta als "christliche Schriftensammlung" und das Problem ihres Kanons," in W. Pannenberg and Th. Schneider (eds.), *Verbindliches Zeugnis I. Kanon — Schrift — Tradition* (Freiburg-Göttingen, 1992) 34–127.

Hengel, Martin, *Juden, Griechen und Barbaren. Aspekte der Hellenisierung des Judentums in vorchristlicher Zeit* (SBS 76; Stuttgart, 1976).

Hengel, Martin, *Judentum und Hellenismus. Studien zu ihrer Begegnung unter besonderer Berücksichtigung Palästinas bis zur Mitte des 2. Jh.s v. Chr.*, (WUNT 10; Tübingen: Mohr, 1973²).

Hengel, Martin, "Schriftauslegung" und "Schriftwerdung" in der Zeit des Zweiten Tempels," in M. Hengel and H. Löhr (eds.), *Schriftauslegung im antiken Judentum und im Urchristentum* (WUNT 73; Tübingen: Mohr, 1994) 1–71.

Hildesheim, R., *Bis daß ein Prophete aufstand wie Feur: Untersuchungen zum Prophetenverständnis des Ben Sira in Sir 48,1–49,16* (Trier theologische Studien; Trier: Paulinus, 1996).

Himmelfarb, M. "The Temple and the Garden of Eden in Ezekiel, the Book of Watchers, and the Wisdom of Ben Sira," in J. Scott and P. Simpson-Housley (eds.), *Sacred Places and Profane Spaces: Essays in the Geographics of Judaism, Christianity, and Islam* (New York: Greenwood Press, 1991) 63–78.

Höffken, P., "Warum schwieg Jesus Sirach über Esra?," *ZAW* 87 (1975) 184–201.

Hogan, Larry P., *Healing in the Second Temple Period* (NTOA 21; Freiburg-Göttingen: Universitätsverlag-Vandenhoeck & Ruprecht, 1992) 38–448.

Hoglund, K. G., "The Fool and the Wise in Dialogue," in *The Listening Heart. Essays in Wisdom and the Psalms in Honour of Roland E. Murphy* (Sheffield: JSOT Press, 1987).

Hopkins, Simon, *A Miscellany of Literary Pieces from the Cambridge Genizah Collections. A Catalogue and Selection of Texts in the Taylor-Schechter Collection, Old Series, Box A 45* (Cambridge: Cambridge University Press, 1978).

Horbury, William, "Jewish Inscriptions and Jewish Literature in Egypt, with Special Reference to Ecclesiasticus," in J.W. van Henten and P.W. van der Horst, *Studies in Early Jewish Epigraphy* (AGJU 21; Brill: Leiden, 1994) 9–43.

Irwyn, William H., "Fear of God, the Analogy of Friendship and Ben Sira's Theodicy," *Bib* 76 (1995) 551–59.

Iwry, Samuel, "A New Designation for the Luminaries in Ben Sira and the Manual of Discipline (1QS), [Sir 43,5]" *BASOR* 200 (1970) 41–47.

Jacob, Édmond, "Sagesse et religion chez Ben Sira," in *Sagesse et religion. Colloque de Strasbourg (octobre 1976)* (*Bibliothéque des Centres d'Éudes Supérieures Spécialisés*. Travaux du Centre d'Études Supérieures spécialisé d'Histoire des Religions de Strasbourg, Paris 1979) 83–98.

Jacob, Édmond, "Wisdom and Religion in Sirach," in J.G. Gammie, *et al.* (eds.), *Israelite Wisdom. Theological and Literary Essays in Honor of Samuel Terrien* (New York, 1978) 247–60.

Janssen, H. Laudin, *Das Gottesvolk und seine Geschichte. Geschichtbild und Selbstverständnis im palästinensischen Schriftum von Jesus Sirach bis Jehuda ha-Nasi* (Neukirchen-Vluyn: Neukirchener Verlag, 1971).

Jervell, J. *Imago Dei. Gen 1,26f in Spätjudentum, in der Gnosis un in den paulischen Briefen* (FRALANT 76; Göttingen: Vandenhoeck & Ruprecht, 1960).

Jolley, Marc Alan, *The Function of Torah in Sirach* (*Wisdom Literature*), Diss. Southern Baptist Theological Seminary, 1993.

Jongeling, B., "Un passage difficile dans le Siracide de Masada (col. IV, 22a = Sir. 42,11e)," in W.C. Deelsman *et al.* (eds.), *Von Kanaan bis Kerala* (AOAT 211; Neukirchener Verlag: Kevelaer; Neukirchen-Vluyn 1982), 303–310.

Kadari, M.Z., The Syntax of כי in the Language of Ben Sira," in T. Muraoka and John Elwolde (eds.), *The Hebrew of the Dead Sea Scrolls and of Ben Sira*, 87–91.

Kaiser, Otto, "Gottesgewißheit und Weltbewußtsein in der frühhellenistischen Weisheit," in Otto Kaiser, *Der Mensch unter dem Schicksal. Studien zur Geschichte, Theologie und Gegenwartsbedeutung der Weisheit* (BZAW 161; Berlin: de Gruyter, 1985) 122–34.

Kaiser, Otto, "Judentum und Hellenismus. Ein Beitrag zur Frage nach dem hellenistischen Einfluss auf Kohelet und Jesus Sirach," in Otto Kaiser, *Der Mensch unter dem Schicksal*, 135–53.

Kaiser, Otto, "Was ein Freund nicht tun darf: Eine Auslegung von Sir 27,16–21," in F.V. Reiterer (ed.), *Freundschaft bei Ben Sira*, 107–22.

Kearns, C., "Ecclesiasticus, or the Wisdom of Jesus the son of Sirach," in R.C. Fuller; L. Johston, C. Kearns (eds.), *A New Catholic Commentary on Holy Scripture* (New York: Nelson, 1969) 541–62.

Kieweler, Hans-Volker, "Abraham und der Preis der Väter bei Ben Sira," in *Schaut Abraham an, euren Vater. FS G. Sauer* (Amt und Gemeinde 37; 1986) 70–72.

Kieweler, Hans-Volker, *Ben Sira zwischen Judentum und Hellenismus. Eine kritische Auseinandersetzung mit Th. Middendorp* (Beiträge zur Erforschung des Alten Testaments und des Antiken Judentums 30; Frankfurt am Main: Peter Lang, 1992).

Kieweler, Hans-Volker, "Freundschaft und böse Nachrede: Exegetische Anmerkungen zu Sir 19,6–19," in F.V. Reiterer (ed.), *Freundschaft bei Ben Sira*, 61–85.

Kister, Menahem, "A Contribution to the Interpretation of Ben Sira," *Tarbiz* 59 (1989–1990) 303–378 [Hebrew].

Kister, Menahem, "Additions to the Article 'In the Margins of the Book of Ben Sira'," *Leshonenu* 53 (1988–1989) 36–53 [Hebrew].

Kister, Menahem, "In the Margins of the Book of Ben Sira," *Leshonenu* 47 (1982–1983) 125–146, [Hebrew].

Kister, Menahem, "On a New Fragment of the Damascus Document," *JQR* 84 (1993–94) 249–51.

Kister, Menahem, "On the Language of the Book of Ben Sira," *Leshonenu* 54 (1991) 69–80 [Hebrew].

Klinzing, Georg, *Die Umdeutung des Kultus in der Qumrangemeinde und im Neuen Testament* (SUNT 7; Göttingen: Vandenhoeck & Ruprecht, 1971).

Köbert, Raimund, "Ode Salomons 20,6 und Sir 33,31," *Bib* 58 (1977) 529–30.

Koch, E., Die "'Himmlische Philosophia des heiligen Geistes'. Zur Bedeutung alttestamentlicher Spruchweisheit im Lutertum des 16. und 17. Jahrhunderts," *TLZ* 115 (1990) 705–19.

Kogut, Simcha, "The Biblical Phrase יש/אין לאל יד: On the Development of a Mistake," *Tarbiz* 57 (1987–88) 435–44 [Hebrew].

Kondracki, A. *La* צדקה *che espia I pecatti. Studio esegetico di Sir 3,1–4,10*. Diss. Pontifical Biblical Institute, Rome 1996.

Koole, J.L., "Die Bibel des Ben-Sira, *OTS* 14 (1965) 374–96.

Kraft, Robert A., "Philo (Josephus, Sirach and Wisdom of Solomon) on Enoch," in *SBL Seminar Papers 1978*. Vol. 1 (Chico: Scholars Press, 1978) 253–57.

Kraft, Thomas, "Justicia y Liturgia: La maravillosa síntesis del Sirácida," *RevTL* 30 (1996) 307–18.

Krammer, Ingrid, "Scham in Zusammenhang mit Freundschaft," in F.V. Reiterer (ed.), *Freundschaft bei Ben Sira*, 171–201.

Krinetzki, G., *Das Reden und Schweigen nach Sir 20* (Passau, 1984).

Krinetzki, G., "Die Sprüche bei das Reden und Schweigen in Sir 20 in traditionsgeschichtlicher Sicht," in R. Beer *et al.* (eds.), *Diener in Eurer Mitte. FS für Bischof Dr. Antonius Hofmann* (Passau, 1984) 64–81.

Krinetzki, Günther, "Die Freundschaftsperikope Sir 6, 5–17 in traditionsgeschichtlicher Sicht," *BZ* 23 (1979) 212–33.

Kuchler, Max, *Frühjüdische Weisheitstraditionen* (OBO 26: Göttingen: Vandenhoeck & Ruprecht, 1979).

Kuntzmann, Raymond, (ed.), *Ce Dieu qui vient: M langes offerts à Bernard Renaud* (LD 159; Paris: Cerf, 1995).

Kurz, Williams S., "The Intertextual Use of Sirach 48:1–16 in Plotting Luke-Acts," in C.A. Evans; W.R. Stegner (eds.), *The Gospels and the Scriptures of Israel* (JSNTSup 104; Sheffield: Sheffield Academic Press, 1994).

Lamparter, H. *Das Buch Jesus Sirach* (Die Botschaft des Alten Testaments 25.1; Stuttgart: Calwer, 1972).

Lamparter, H., *Die Apocryphe, 1. Das Buch Jesus Sirach* (Stuttgart: Calwer, 1972).

Lang, B., *Anweisungen gegen die Torheit: Sprichwörter, Jesus Sirach* (SKKAT 19; Stuttgart, 1973).

Leanza, Sandro, "Eccl. 12,1–7: L'interpretazione escatologica dei Padri e degli esegeti medievali," *Augustinianum* 18 (1989) 191–207.

Lebram, J.C.H., "Jerusalem, Wohnsitz der Weisheit [Sirach 24]," in M.J. Vermaseren (ed.), *Studies in Hellenistic Religions* (EPRO 78; Leiden: Brill, 1979) 103–28.

Lee, T.R., *Studies in the Form of Sirach 44–50* (SBLDS 75; Atlanta: Scholars Press, 1986).

Lehmann, Manfred R., "11QPsa and Ben Sira," *RevQ* 11 (1983) 239–51.

Lehmann, Manfred R., "Ben Sira and the Dead Sea Scrolls," *Tarbiz* 39 (1969/70) 232–47 [Hebrew].

Lehmann, Manfred R., "Jewish Wisdom Formulae: Ben Sira, the Dead Sea Scrolls, and Pirke Avot," in *World Congress of Jewish Studies, Jerusalem 1994*, 159–62.

Lévêque, Jean, *Job et son Dieu. Essai d'exégese et de théologie biblique* (EB; Paris: Gabalda, 1970).

Lévêque, Jean, "Le Portrait d'Élie dans l'Éloge des Pères (Si 48, 1–11)," in R. Kuntzmann (ed.), *Ce Dieu qui vient: Mélanges offerts à Bernard Renaud* (LD 159; Paris: Cerf ,1995), 215–29.

Levison, John R., *Portraits of Adam in Early Judaism from Sirach to 2 Baruch* (JSPSup 1; Sheffield: JSOT Press ,1988).

Levison, Kack, "Is Eve to Blame? A Contextual Analysis of Sirach 25:24," *CBQ* 47 (1995) 617–23.

Lichtheim, Miriam, *Late Egyptian Wisdom Literature in the International Context. A Study of Demotic Instructions* (OBO 52; Freiburg-Göttingen: Universitäts Verlag-Vandenhoeck & Ruprecht, 1983).

Lim, Timothy, "Nevertheless These Were Men of Piety (Ben Sira XLIV 10," *VT* 38 (1988) 338–41.

Lips, Hermann von, *Weisheitliche Traditionen im Neuen Testament* (WMANT 64; Neukirchen-Vluyn, 1990).

Liesen, Jan, *Full of Praise. An Exegetical Study of Sir 39,12–35*. Diss., Pontifical Biblical Institute, Rome 1997.

Lohfink, N., *Lobgesänge der Armen. Studien zum Magnificat, den Hodajot von Qumran und einigen späten Psalmen*. Mit einem Anhang: Hodajot-Bibliographie 1948–1989 von U. Dahmen (SBS 143; Stuttgart, 1990).

Löhr, Martin, *Bildung aus dem Glauben: Beiträge zum Verständnis der Lehrreden des Buches Jesus Sirach*, Diss. Bonn, 1975.

Lowe, A.D., "Some Correct Renderings in Ancient Biblical Versions," in R.Y. Ebied and M.J.L. Young (eds.), *Oriental Studies Presented to Benedik Isserlin by Friends and Colleagues on the Occasion of his Sixtieth Birthday* (Leiden: Brill, 1980) 24–38.

Luciani, Ferdinando, "La funzione profetica di Enoch (Sir. 44,16b secondo la versione greca)," *RivB* 39 (1982) 215–24.

Luciani, Ferdinando, "La giustizia di Enoch in Sir. 44, 16b secondo la versione greca," *BeO* 23 (1981) 185–92.

Luhrmann, Dieter, "Henoch und die Metanoia," *ZNW* 66 (1975) 103–16.

Lys, D., "L'Être et le Temps. Communication de Qohéleth," in M. Gilbert (ed.), *La sagesse dans l'Ancien Testament* (BETL 51: Leuven/Gembloux, University Press/Duculot, 1979) 249–58.

Mack, Burton L., *Logos und Sophia: Untersuchungen zur Weisheitstheologie im hellenistischen Judentum* (SUNT 10; Göttingen: Vandenhoeck & Ruprecht, 1973).

Mack, Burton L., "Sirach (Ecclesiasticus)," in B.W. Anderson (ed.), *The Books of the Bible*. II (1989) 65–86.

Mack, Burton L., *Wisdom and the Hebrew Epic. Ben Sira's hymn in praise of the Fathers* (Chicago Studies in the History of Judaism; Chicago: University of Chicago Press 1985).

Mack, Burton L. and Roland E. Murphy, "Wisdom Literature," in Robert A. Kraft and George W.E. Nickelsburg (eds.), *Early Post-Biblical Judaism and its Modern Interpreters* (The Bible and Its Modern Interpreters 2; Philadelphia-Atlanta: Fortress-Scholars Press, 1986) 371–410.

Mack, Burton L., "Annotations to Sirach," in W. Meeks et al. (eds.) *The Harper-Collins Study Bible* (New York: Harper-Collins, 1993) 1530–1616.

MacKenzie, Roderick A.F., "Ben Sira as Historian," in T.A. Dumme, J.-M. Laporte (eds.) *Trinification of the World. A Festschrift in Honor of F.E. Crowe* (Toronto, 1978) 313–27.

MacKenzie, Roderick A.F., *Sirach* (Old Testmaent Message 19: Wilmington, Glazier, 1983).

Maier, G., *Mensch und freier Wille. Nach den jüdischen Religionsparteien zwischen Ben Sira und Paulus* (WUNT 12: Tübingen: Mohr, 1971).

Malchow, B.V., "Social Justice in Wisdom Literature," *BTB* 12 (1982) 120–24.

Manfredi, S. "La Sapienza madre in Sir 24,18 (cod. 248)," in C. Militello (ed.), *Donna e ministero* (Rome, 1991) 444–51.

Marböck, Johannes, "Das Gebet um die Rettung Zions Sir 36,1–22 (G: 33, 1–13a; 36,16b-22) im Zusammenhang der Geschichtsschau Ben Siras," in J.B. Bauer and J. Marböck (eds.), *Memoria Jerusalem. Freundesgabe Franz Sauer* (Graz, 1977) 93–115.

Marböck, Johannes, "Die 'Geschichte Israels' als 'Bundesgeschichte' nach dem Sirachbuch," in E. Zenger (ed.), *Der Neue Bund im Alten. Studien zur Bundestheologie der beiden Testamente* (QD 146; Freiburg: Herder, 1993) 177–97.

Marböck, Johannes, "Gefährdung und Bewährung: Kontexte zur Freundschaftsperikope Sir 22,19-26," in F.V. Reiterer (ed.), *Freundschaft bei Ben Sira*, 87–106.

Marböck, Johannes, "Gesetz und Weisheit. Zum Ver-
tändnis des Gesetzes bei Jesus ben Sira," *BZ* 20
(1976) 1–21.

Marböck, Johannes, "Gottes Weisheit unter uns. Sir 24
als Beitrag zur biblischen Theologie," in *Verbum
caro factum est. FS. Wechbischof Dr. Alois Stöger zur
Vollendung seines 80 Lebensjahres* (St. Pölten, 1984)
55–65.

Marböck, Johannes, "Henoch-Adam-der Thronwagen:
Zu frühjüdischen pseudepigraphischen Traditionen
bei Ben Sira," *BZ* 25 (1981) 103–111.

Marböck, Johannes, "Jesus Sirach," in E. Zenger (ed.),
Einleitung in das Alte Testament (Kohlhammer Stu-
dienbücher Theologie, Band 1,1; Stuttgart: Kohlhammer, 1995).

Marböck, Johannes, "Macht und Mächtige im Buch
Jesus Sirach. Ein Beitrag zur politischen Ethik in der
Weisheitsliteratur des Alten Testaments," in O.
Komminich *et al.* (eds.), *Mit Realismus und Leidens-
chaft. Ethik im Dienst einer humanen Welt. Valentin
Zsifkovits zum 60. Geburtstag* (Graz-Budapest,
1993) 364–71.

Marböck, Johannes, "Sir 15,9f. — Ansätze zu einer
Theologie des Gotteslobes bei Jesus Sirach," in I.
Seybold (ed.), *Meqor hajjim. Festschrift für Georg
Molin zu seinem 75. Geburtstag.* (Graz, 1983) 267–
76.

Marböck, Johannes, "Sir 38,24–39,11: Der schriftge-
lehrte Weise. Ein Beitrag zu Gestalt und Werk Ben
Siras," in M. Gilbert (ed.), *La sagesse de l'Ancien
Testament*, 293–316.

Marböck, Johannes, "Sirachliteratur seit 1966. Ein
Überblick," *ThRv* 71 (1975) 178–84.

Marböck, Johannes, "Structure and Redaction History
of the Book of Ben Sira: Review and Prospects," in
P.C. Beentjes (ed.), *The Book of Ben Sira in Modern
Research*, 61–79.

Marböck, Johannes, "Sündevergebung bei Jesus Sirach:
Eine Notiz zur Theologie und Frömmigkeit der deu-
terokanonischen Schriften," *ZKT* 116 (1994) 480–
86.

Marböck, Johannes, *Weisheit im Wandel. Untersuchungen zur Weisheitstheologie bei Ben Sira* (BBB
37; Bonn: Peter Hanstein, 1971).

Martin, J.D., "Ben Sira — A Child of His Time," in
J.D. Martin and Ph.R. Davies (eds.), *A Word in
Season: Essays in Honor of William McKane* (JSOT
Sup 42; Sheffield: JSOT Press, 1986) 141–161.

Martin, James D., "Ben Sira's Hymn to the Fathers. A
messianic perspective," in A.S. van der Woude (ed.),
Crises and Perspectives. (OTS 24, Leiden: Brill,
1986) 107–23.

Martin Juarez, Miguel Angel, *La historia de Israel vista
por Ben Sira (Sir 44,16–49,16)*, Diss. Pontifical Biblical Institute, Rome, 1978.

Martin Juarez, Miguel Angel, "Sabiduría y ley en Jesús
Ben Sira," *Religión y Cultura* 25 (1979) 567–74.

Martone, C., "Il testo hebraico dell'Ecclesiastico: ori-
ginale o retroversione," *Renovatio* 25 (1990) 595–
601 [Annali di Storia dell'esegesi].

Martone, C., "Ben Sira Manuscripts from Qumran and
Masada," in P.C. Beentjes (ed.), *The Book of Ben
Sira in Modern Research*, 81–94.

*Materials for the Dictionary. Series I 200 B.C.E.–300
C.E.* (Microfiche Edition) (Jerusalem: The Academy
of the Hebrew Language — The Historical Dictionary of the Hebrew Language, 1988).

McEvoy, J., "The Sun as Res and Signum: Grosseteste's
Commentary on Ecclesiasticus ch. 43,vv. 1–5,"
RTAM 41 (1974) 38–91.

McHardy, W.D., "Cambridge Syriac Fragment XXVI
[Sir 13:1–13]," in, J.R. McKay and J.F. Miller (eds.),
Biblical Studies, FS W. Barclay (London, 1976).

McKeating, Henry, "Jesus ben Sira's Attitude to Woman," *ExpTim* 85 (1973–1974) 85–87.

McKenzie, J.L., "Reflections on Wisdom," *JBL* 86
(1967) 1–9.

McKenzie, R.A.F., "Ben Sira as Historian," in T.A.
Dunne — J.M. Laporte (ed.), *Trinification of the
World. A Festschrift in Honor of F.E. Crowe* (Tor-
onto, 1978) 313–327.

Mendels, D., *The Land of Israel as a Political Concept.
Recourse to History in Second Century B.C. Claims
to the Holy Land* (Tübingen: Mohr, 1987) 7–17.

Metzger, B.M. (ed.), *The Apocrypha of the Old Testament Revised Standard Version* (New York, 1977).

Michaud, Robert, *Ben Sira et le Judaïsme. La littérature de sagesse, histoire et théologie*, III (Collection
"Lire la Bible" 82; Paris, 1980).

Michaud, Robert, *Ben Sira et le judaisme: la littérature
de sagesse, histoire et theologie* (Paris: Cerf, 1988).

Middendorp, T., *Die Stellung Jesu ben Sira zwischen
Judentum und Hellenismus* (Leiden: Brill, 1973).

Milani, Marcello, "Pietà, moderazione e vitalit nel
rituale di lutto per il morto: Sir 38,16–23," *Studia
Patavina* 42 (1995) 197–213.

Milani, Marcello, *La correlazione tra morte e vita in
Ben Sira. Dimensione antropologica, cosmica e teolo-
gica dell'antitesi*, Diss. Pontifical Biblical Institute,
Rome 1995.

Milik, Jozef T., "Un fragment mal placé dans l'édition
du Siracide de Masada," *Bib* 47 (1966) 425–26.

Miller, Naomi F., "The Aspalathus Caper," *BASOR*
297 (1995) 55–60.

Minissale, Antonio, "A Descriptive Feature of the Greek Sirach: The Effect Instead of the Cause," in *IX Congress of the International Organization for Septuagint and Cognate Studies*, Cambridge 1995, 421–29.

Minissale, Antonio, *La versione greca del Siracide. Confronto con il testo ebraico alla luce dell'attivià midrascica e del metodo targumico* (Analecta Biblica 133; Rome: Editrice Pontificio Istituto Biblico, 1995).

Minissale, Antonio, "Il libro del Siracide: da epigono a protagonista," *Laós* 2 (1995) 3–19.

Minisalle, A., *Siracide* (*Ecclesiastico*): *Versione-introduzione-note* (Nuovissima Versione 23; Rome: Paoline, 1980).

Minisalle, A., *Siracide: le radici nella tradizione* (Leggere oggi la Bibbia 1/17; Brescia: Queriniana, 1988).

Moreno, A., "Jesús ben Sira. Un Judío en un tiempo de crisis," *Teología y Vida* 10 (1969) 24–42.

Morla Asensio, Víctor, "Dos notas filológicas: Jer 29,22 y Eclo 8,10b," *EstBib* 46 (1988) 249–52.

Morla Asensio, Víctor, "Sabiduria, culto y piedad en Ben Sira," *Scriptorium Victoriense* 40 (1993) 125–142.

Muffs, Yochanan, *Love & Joy. Law, Language and Religion in Ancient Israel.* (Cambridge: Harvard University Press, 1992) 165–193.

Muilenberg, J., "The Linguistic and Rhetorical Usages of the Particle כי in the Old Testament," *HUCA* 32 (1961) 135–160.

Mulder, M.J. (ed.), *Mikra, Text, Translation and Interpretation of the Hebrew Bible in Ancient Judaism and Early Christianity* (CRINT II/1; Assen-Philadelphia: Van Gorcum-Fortress, 1988).

Müller, Augustin R., "Eine neue Textaufgabe von Jesus Sirach," *BN* 89 (1997) 19–21.

Muraoka, Takamitsu, *Ben Sira, Apocrypha and Pseudepigrapha* II. (Tokyo: Japanese Institute of Biblical Studies, 1977) 67–207, 365–510 [Japanese].

Muraoka, Takamitsu, "Hebrew Philological Notes," *Annual of the Japanese Biblical Institute* 5 (1979) 88–104.

Muraoka, Takamitsu, "Sir 51, 13–30: An Erotic Hymn to Wisdom?," *JSJ* 10 (1979) 166–78.

Muraoka, Takamitsu, "Some Observations on Ben Sira," *Evangelical Theology* 8 (1977) 22–41 [Japanese].

Muraoka, Takamitsu and John F. Elwolde (eds.), *The Hebrew of the Dead Sea Scrolls and Ben Sira. Proceedings of a Symposium Held at Leiden University, 11–14 December 1985* (STDJ 26; Leiden: Brill, 1997).

Murphy, Roland Edmund, "Assumptions and Problems in Old Testament Wisdom Research," *CBQ* 29 (1967) 101–12.

Murphy, Roland Edmund, "Hebrew Wisdom," *JAOS* 101 (1981) 21–34.

Murphy, Roland Edmund, "Israel's Wisdom: A Biblical Model of Salvation," *Voies de Salut. Studia Missionalia* 30 (1981) 1–43.

Murphy, Roland Edmund, "The Personification of Wisdom," in J. Day *et al.* (eds.), *Wisdom in Ancient Israel. Essays in Honour of J.A. Emerton* (Cambridge: Cambridge University Press, 1995) 222–33.

Murphy, Roland Edmund, *The Tree of Life: An Exploration of Biblical Wisdom Literature* (New York: Doubleday, 1990).

Murphy, Roland Edmund, *The Tree of Life: An Exploration of Biblical Wisdom Literature* (Grand Rapids: Eerdmans, 1996).

Murphy, Roland Edmund, "What and Where is Wisdom?," *Currents in Theology and Mission* 4 (1977) 283–87.

Murphy, Roland Edmund, "Wisdom and Creation," *JBL* 104 (1985) 3–11.

Murphy, Roland Edmund, *Wisdom Literature and Psalms. Interpreting Biblical Texts* (Nashville, 1983).

Murphy, R. *Wisdom Literature, Job, Proverbs, Ruth, Canticles, Ecclesiastes, and Esther* (FOTL 13; Grand Rapids: Eerdmans, 1981).

Naerebout, F.G., *Ethics in the Second Century B.C. The concept of duty in the Wisdom of Ben Sira and Cicero's De Officiis*, Diss. Leiden University 1979.

Nebe, Gerhard-Wilhelm, "Sirach 42,5c," *ZAW* 82 (1970) 283–86.

Neilly, Raymond Roosevelt, *Human Achievement in the Wisdom Literature of Ancient Israel: The Gift of God as Attainment, Piety, of Simple Pleasure*, Diss. Drew University, 1994.

Nelis, Jan T., "Sir 38,15," in W.C. Delsman *et al.* (eds.) *Von Kanaan bis Kerala.* (AOAT 211; Neukirchener Verlag: Kevelaer, Neukirchen-Vlyn 1982) 173–84.

Nelson, Milward D., *The Syriac Version of Ben Sira Compared to the Greek and Hebrew Materials*, Diss. UCLA, Los Angeles, 1981.

Nelson, Milward D., *The Syriac Version of Ben Sira Compared to the Greek and Hebrew Materials* (SBLDS 107; Atlanta: Scholars Press 1988).

Niccacci, Alviero, "Siracide 6,19 e Giovanni 4,34–38," *BeO* 23 (1981) 149–53.

Nickels, P., "Wisdoms Table — Daily Bread," *TBT* 19 (1981) 168–72.

Nickelsburg, George W.E., *Jewish Literature between the Bible and the Mishnah: A Historical and Literary Introduction* (Philadelphia: Fortress, 1981) 59–69.

Nickelsburg, George W.E and Michael E. Stone, *Faith and Piety in Early Judaism. Texts and Documents* (Philadelphia: Fortress, 1983).

Nicola, A. de, "Quasi cypressus in monte Sion (Eccli 24,17b)," *BeO* 17 (1975) 269–77.

Niederwimmer, K., "LXX, Jes. Sirach 29,13–26a," in H. Loebenstein *et al.* (eds.), *Papyrus Erzherzog Reiner (P. Reiner Cent.). Festschrift zum 100–järigen Bestehen des Papyrussammlung der sterreichischen Nationalbibliothek* (Vienna, 1983) 271–73, pl. 48.

Nobile, M., "Il motivo della crescità delle acque in Ez 47,1–12 e Sir 24,30–31 e suoi sviluppi successivi," in *Sapienza e Torah. Atti della XXIX Settimana Biblica* (Bologna: Dehoniane 1987) 223–45.

Noorda, S. "Illness and Sin, Forgiving and Healing. The Connection of Medical Treatement and Religious Beliefs in Ben Sira 38, 1–15," in M.J. Vermaseren (ed.), *Studies in Hellenistic Relgions* (EPRO 78; Leiden: Brill, 1979) 214–24.

O'Callaghan, José, "Frammenti antologici dell'*Ecclesiaste*, del *Cantico dei Cantici*, e dell'*Ecclesiastico* (PPalau Rib. Inv. 225r)," in *Atti del XVII Congresso Internazionale di papirologia*, II (Napoli, 1984) 357–65, pl. I.

O'Fearghail, Fearghus, "Sir 50, 5–21: Yom Kippur or The Daily Whole-Offering?," *Bib* 59 (1978) 301–16.

Ogden, G., "The 'Better'-Proverb (tôb spruch): Rhetorical Criticism, and Qohelet," *JBL* 96 (1997) 489–050.

Ogushi, M., "Ist nur das Herz die Mitte des Menschen?," in F. Crüsemann (ed.), *'Was ist der Mensch...? Beiträge zur Anthropologie des Alten Testaments: Hans Walter Wolff zum 80. Geburtstag* (München: Kaiser, 1992) 42–47.

Okoye, John I., *Speech in Ben Sira with Special Reference to 5,9–6,1* (European University Studies Series 23, Theology 535; Frankfurt am Main: Peter Lang, 1995).

Olyan, Saul M., "Ben Sira's Relationship to the Priesthood," *HTR* 80 (1987) 261–86.

Orlinsky, Harry M., "Some Terms in the Prologue to Ben Sira and the Hebrew Canon," *JBL* 110 (1991) 483–90.

Orton, David, "Ben Sira and the Model Scribe," in *The Understanding Scribe. Matthew and the Apocalyptic Ideal* (JSNTSup 25; Sheffield: JSOT Press, 1989) 65–75.

Osty, E. et Trinquet, J., *Le Bible. Vol. 13. Le Livre de l'Ecclésiastique* (Lausanne: Rencontre, 1971).

Owens, R.J., "The Early Syriac Text of Ben Sira in the Demonstrations of Aphrahat," *JSS* 34 (1989) 39–75.

Patterson, R.K. Jr., *A Study of the Hebrew Text of Sirach 39:27–41:24*, Diss. Duke University 1967.

Pax, Elpidius Wolfgang, "Dialog und Selbstgespräch bei Sirach 27,3–10," *SBLFA* 20 (1970) 247–63.

Payne, Ph.B., "A Critical Note on Ecclesiasticus 44,21's Commentary on the Abrahamic Covenant," *JETS* 15 (1972) 186–187.

Peels, H. *De wraak van God. De betekenis van de wortel NQM en de functie van de NQM-teksten in het kader van de Oudtestamentische Godsopenbaring* (Zoetermeer: Boekencentrum, 1992).

Peursen, W.T. van, "Periphrastic Tenses in Ben Sira," in T. Muraoka and John Elwolde (eds.), *The Hebrew of the Dead Sea Scrolls and Ben Sira*, 158–73.

Penar, Tadeusz, *Northwest Semitic Philology and the Hebrew Fragments of Ben Sira* (BibOr 28; Roma: Editrice Pontificio Istituto Biblico, 1975).

Penar, Tadeusz, "Job 19,19 in the Light of Ben Sira 6,11," *Bib* 48 (1967) 293–95.

Penar, Tadeusz, "Three Philological Notes on the Hebrew Fragments of Ben Sira," *Bib* 57 (1976) 112–13.

Perdue., Leo G., "'I Covered the Earth Like a Mist': Cosmos and History in Ben Sira," in *Wisdom & Creation. The Theology of Wisdom Literature* (Nashville: Abingdon Press, 1994) 243–290.

Perdue, Leo G., *Wisdom and Cult* (SBLDL 30; Missoula: Scholars Press, 1977).

Peri, Israel, "Steinhaufen im Wadi (zu Sirach 21,8)," *ZAW* 102 (1990) 212–25.

Perrot, Charles, "Les sages et la sagesse dans le judaïsme ancien,", in J. Trublet (ed.), *La sagesse biblique de l'Ancien au Nouveau Testament* (LD 160; Paris: Cerf, 1995) 231–62.

Peterca, V., "Das Porträt Salomos bei Ben Sirach (47,12–22): ein Beitrag zu der Midraschexegese," in M. Augusin and K.D. Sdchunk (eds.), *Wünschet Jerusalem Frieden. IOSOT Congress, Jerusalem 1986*, (BEATAJ 13; Frankfurt am Main: Peter Lang, 1988) 457–63.

Petraglio, Renzo, *Il libro che contamina le mani. Ben Sira rilegge il libro e la storia d'Israele* (Theologia 4: Palermo: Edizioni Augustinus, 1993).

Petraglio, Renzo, "Le Siracide et l'Ancien Testament: relecture et tendances," *Apocrypha* 8 (1997) 287–301.

Phillips, David, "Musical Instruments in the Peshitta to

Chronicles and Contacts with the Peshitta to Ben Sira," *Le Muséon* 108 (1995) 49–67.

Philonenko, Marc, "Sur une interpolation essénisante dans le Siracide (16,15–16)," *Orientalia Suecana* 33 (1986) 317–21.

Pietersma, A., "The 'Lost' Folio of the Chester Beatty Ecclesiasticus," *VT* 25 (1975) 497–99.

Pilch, John J., "'Bent His Ribs while He is Young' (Sir 30:12): A Window on the Mediterranean World," *BTB* 23 (1993) 101–113.

Pomykala, Kenneth Edmund, "The Wisdom of Jesus Ben Sira," in *The Davidic Dynasty Tradition in Early Judaism: Its Background, Content, and Function*, Diss. Claremont Graduate School, 1992, 201–232.

Pomykala, Kenneth Edmund, "The Wisdom of Jesus Ben Sira," in *The Davidic Dynasty Tradition in Early Judaism: Its History and Significance for Messianism* (SBL Early Judaism and Its Literature 7; Atlanta: Scholars Press, 1995), 131–52.

Poulssen, N., "Het wijsheidsideaal van Jezus Sirach: Een impressie," *Ons Geestelijk Leve*, 54 (1977) 105–108.

Prato, Gian Luigi, "Classi lavorative e 'otium' sapientiale — Il significato theologico di una dicotomia sociale secondo Ben Sira (32,24–39,11)," in G. de Gennaro (ed.), *Lavoro e riposo nella Bibbia* (Studia Biblico Aquilano 7; Bologna: Dehomiane, 1987) 168–71.

Prato, Gian Luigi, *Il problema della teodicea in Ben Sira. Composizioni dei contrari e richiamo alle origine* (AnBib 65; Roma: Editrice Pontificio Istituto Biblico, 1975).

Prato, Gian Luigi, "La lumiére interprète de la sagesse dans la tradition textuelle de Ben Sira," in M. Gilbert (ed.), *La sagesse de l'Ancien Testament*, 317–346.

Prato, Gianl Luigi, "L'universo come ordine e come disordine," *RivB* 30 (1982) 51–77.

Preuß, Horst D., *Einführung in die alttestamentliche Weisheitsliteratur* (Stuttgart, 1987).

Priest, J., "Ben Sira 45,25 in the light of the Qumran Literature," *RevQ* 5 (1964–66) 111–118.

Prockter, Lewish J., "Alms and the Man: The Merits of Charity," *JNSL* 17 (1991) 69–80.

Prockter, Lewis J., "'His Yesterday and Yours Today' (Sir 38:22): Reflections on Ben Sira's View of Death," *Journal of Semitics* 2 (1990) 44–56.

Prockter, Lewis J., "Torah as a Fence against Apocalyptic Speculation: Ben Sira 3:17–24," in *World Union of Jewish Studies, Proceedings of the Tenth World Congress of Jewish Studies, Jerusalem, August 16–24, 1989*, Vol. 1 (Jerusalem, 1990) 245–52.

Puech, Émile., "4Q525 et les pericopes des Béatitudes en Ben Sira et Matthieu," *RB* 98 (1991) 80–106.

Puech, Émile, "Ben Sira 48:11 et la Résurrection," in H.W. Attridge, J.J. Collins, Th.H. Tobin (eds.), *Of Scribes and Scrolls: Studies on the Hebrew Bible, Intertestamental Judaism and Christian origins presented to John Strugnell* (College Theology Society Resources in Religion 5; Lanham, 1990) 81–90.

Puech, Émile, *La croyance des Esséniens en la vie future: Immortalité, résurrection, vie éternelle?* (Ebib 22; Paris: Gabalda 1993).

Puech, Émile, "Un hymne essénien en partie retrouvé et les Béatitudes: 1QH V12–VI18, [col. XIII–XIV7] et 4QBéat.," *RevQ* 13 (1988) 59–88.

Purvis, James D., "Ben Sira and the Foolish People of Shechem," *JNES* 24 (1965) 88–94.

Pury, A. de, "Sagesse et révélation dans l'Ancien Testament," *RTP* 27 (1977) 1–50.

Qimron, Elisha, "New Readings in Ben Sira" [31,10; 36,9; 38,10.16] *Tarbiz* 58 (1988–1989) 117 [Hebrew].

Rabinowitz, Isaac, "The Qumran Hebrew Original of Ben Sira's Concluding Acrostic of Wisdom," *HUCA* 42 (1971) 173–84.

Rad, G. von, "Die Weisheit des Jesus Sirach," *EvTh* 29 (1969) 113–33.

Rad, G. von, *Theologie des Alten Testaments*, Band II (München 1965⁴).

Rad, G. von, *Weisheit in Israel* (Neukirchen-Vluyn, 1970).

Rad, G. von, *Wisdom in Israel* (Nashville: Abingdon, 1972).

Raurell, Frederic, "Ecli 45,1–5: La 'doxa' de Moisès," *Revista Catalana de Teologia* 17 (1992) 1–42.

Raurell, Frederic, "Siràcida: 'Doxa Theou' vista per Moisès," in *'Doxa' en la Teologia i Antropologia dels LXX* (Collectània Sant Pacià 59; Barcelona: Facultat de Teologia de Catalunya-Herder, 1996) 201–43.

Reif, Stephan C., "The Discovery of the Cairo Genizah Fragments of Ben Sira: Scholars and Texts," in P.C. Beentjes (ed.), *The Book of Ben Sira in Modern Research*, 1–22.

Reiterer, Friedrich Vinzenz, "Das Verhältnis Ijobs und Ben Siras," in W.A.M. Beuken (ed.) *The Book of Job* (BETL 114; Peeters: Leuven, 1994) 405–29.

Reiterer, Friedrich Vinzenz, "Deutung und Wertung des Todes durch Ben Sira," in J. Zmijewski (ed.), *Die alttestamentliche Botschaft als Wegweisung, FS H. Reinelt* (Stuttgart, 1990) 203–36.

Reiterer, Friedrich Vinzenz, "Die Stellung Ben Siras

zur 'Arbeit'. Notizen zu einem kaum berücksichtig-
ten Thema sirazidischer Lehre," in *Ein Gott — Eine
Offenbarung. Beiträge zur biblischen Exegese, Theologie und Spiritualität, FS N. Füglister* (Würzburg,
1991) 257–89.

Reiterer, Fredrich Vinzenz (ed.), *Freundschaft bei Ben
Sira. Beiträge des Symposiuns zu Ben Sira, Salzburg
1995* (BZAW 244; Berlin: De Gruyter, 1996).

Reiterer, Friedrich Vinzenz, "Gelungene Freundschaft
als tragende Säule einer Gesellschaft: Exegetische
Untersuchungen van Sir 25,1–11," in *Freundschaft
bei Ben Sira*, 133–69.

Reiterer, Friedrich Vinzenz, "Markierte und nicht markierte direkte Objekte bei Ben Sira. Präliminaria zur
Untersuchung der Hebraizität Siras anhand der Ver-
ben mit ta-Verwendung," in W. Gross; H. Irsigler
and Th. Seidl (eds.), *Text, Methode und Grammatik.
Wolfgang Richter zum 65.Geburtstag* (St. Ottilien,
1991) 359–78.

Reiterer, Friedrich Vinzenz, "Review of Recent Re-
search on the Book of Ben Sira (1980–1996)," in
P.C. Beentjes (ed.), *The Book of Ben Sira in Recent
Research*, 23–60.

Reiterer, Friedrich Vinzenz, *'Urtext' und Übersetzungen: Sprachstudie ber Sir 44, 16–45,26 als Beitrag zur
Siraforschung* (ATS 12; St. Ottilien: EOS Verlag,
1980).

Rendorff, R., "Gechichtliches und weisheitliches Denk-
en im Alten Testament," in H. Donner *et al.* (eds.),
*Reiträge zur Alttestamentlichen Theologie. Festsch-
rift für Walter Zimmerli zim 70. Geburtstag* (Göttingen: Vandenhoeck & Ruperecht, 1977) 344–53.

Rickenbacher, O., *Nachträge zum 'griechisch-syrisch-
hebräischen Index zur Weisheit des Jesus Sirach von
Rudolf Smend'* (Werthenstein, 1970).

Rickenbacher, O., *Weisheitsperikopen bei Ben Sirach*
(OBO 1; Freiburg-Göttingen: Universitätsverlag-
Vandenhoeck & Ruprecht, 1973).

Rinaldi, Giovanni, "εκτισεν... κοινη nell' Ecclesiastico
(18.1), *BeO* 25 (1983) 115–16.

Rinaldi, G., "Onus meum leve: Osservazioni su Ecclesiastico 51 (v. 26, Volg. 34) e Matteo 11,25–30,"
BeO 9 (1967) 13–23.

Rivkin, Ellis, "Ben Sira — The Bridge between Aaron-
ide and Pharisaic Revolutions," *ErIsr* 12 (1975)
95*–103*.

Rizzi, Giovanni, "La versione greca del Siracide," *RivB*
45 (1997) 347–51.

Rofé, Alexander, "The Onset of Sects in Postexilic
Judaism: Neglected Evidence from the Septuagint,
Trito-Jesaja, Ben Sira, and Malachi," in H. C. Kee
and J. Neusner (eds.), *The Social World of Formative

Christianity and Judaism. Essays in Tribute to How-
ard Clark Kee* (Philadelphia, 1988) 39–49.

Rogers, Jessie F., "Wisdom and Creation in Sirach 24,"
JNSL 22 (1996) 141–56.

Romaniuk, Kazimierz, "Le traducteur grec du livre de
Jésus Ben Sira n'est-il pas l'auteur du livre de la
Sagesse?," *RivB* 15 (1967) 163–70.

Romero, Elena, "Versiones judeoespañolas del libro
hebreo medieval: Los relatos de Ben Sirá," in Tamar
Alexander *et al.* (eds.), *History and Creativity in the
Sephardi and Oriental Jewish Communities* (Jerusalem: Misgav Yerushalayim, 1994) 177–87.

Roth, Wolfgang, "On the Gnomic-Discursive Wisdom
of Jesus Ben Sirach," *Semeia* 17 (1980) 59–79.

Roth, Wolfgang, "Sirach: The First Graded Curricu-
lum," *TBT* 29 (1991) 298–302.

Roth, Wolfgang, "The Lord's Glory Fills Creation: A
Study of Sirach's Praise of God's Works (42:15–
50:24)," *Explor* 6 (1981) 85–95.

Roth, Wolfgang, "The Relation between the Fear of the
Lord and Wisdom," *Beth Mikra* 25 (1980) 150–62
[Hebrew].

Rowley, H.H., *The Origin and Significance of the Apocrypha* (London: SPCK, 1967).

Rüger, Hans Peter, "Le Siracide: un livre à la frontiére
du canon," in J.-D. Kaestli et O. Wermelinger (eds.),
*Le Canon de l'Ancien Testament. Sa formation et son
histoire* (Geneva, 1984) 47–69.

Rüger, Hans Peter, *Text und Textform im hebräischen
Sirach. Untersuchungen zur Textgeschichte und
Textkritik der hebräischen Sirachfragmente aus der
Kairoer Geniza* (BZAW 112; Berlin: De Gruyter,
1970).

Rüger, Hans Peter, "Zum Text von Sir 40,10 und Ex
10,21," *ZAW* 80 (1970) 103–09.

Sacchi, Paolo, *Storia del Secondo Tempio. Israele tra VI
secolo a.C. e I secolo d.C.* (Torino: Società Editrice
Internazionale, 1994).

Safrai, S. "Education and the Study of the Torah," in
The Jewish People in the First Century, 945–70.

Samaan, Kamil W., *Sept traductions arabes de Ben Sira*
(Europäische Hochschulschriften XXIII/492;
Frankfurt am Main: Peter Lang, 1994).

Sandelin, K.G., "Wisdom as nourisher in the Book of
Sirach," in *Wisdom as Nourisher: A Study of an Old
Testament Theme, its Developments within Early
Judaism and its Impact on Early Christianity* (Acta
Academicae Aboensis 65; Åbo, 1986) 27–53.

Sanders, Jack T., "A Hellenistic Egyptian Parallel to
Ben Sira," *JBL* 97 (1978) 257–58.

Sanders, Jack T., *Ben Sira and Demotic Wisdom* (SBL.MS 28: Chico: Scholars Press, 1983).

Sanders, Jack T., "Ben Sira's Ethics of Caution," *HUCA* 50 (1979) 73–106.

Sanders, Jack T., "On Ben Sira 24 and Wisdom's Mother Isis," *World Union of Jewish Studies. Proceedings of the Eight World Congress of Jewish Studies* (Jerusalem, 1982) 73–78.

Sanders, James A., *The Dead Sea Psalms Scroll* (Ithaca: Cornell University Press, 1967).

Sanders, James A., "The Sirach 51 Acrostic," in A. Caquot et M. Philonenko (eds.), *Hommages à André Dupont-Sommer* (Paris, 1971) 429–38.

Sanders, James A., *The Psalms Scroll of Qumran Cave 11 (11Qps^a)* (DJD IV; Oxford: Clarendon, 1965).

Saracino, Francesco, "La sapienza e la vita: Sir 4,11–19," *RivB* 29 (1981) 257–72.

Saracino, Francesco, "Risurrezione in Ben Sira?," *Henoch* 4 (1982) 185–203.

Sasson, Jack M., "Time to Begin," in M. Fishbane *et al.* (eds.), *Sha^carei Talmon. Studies in the Bible, Qumran, and the Ancient Near East Presented to Shemaryahu Talmon* (Winona Lake, IN, Eisenbrauns, 1992) 183–94.

Sauer, Georg, "Freundschaft nach Ben Sira 37,1–6," in F.V. Reiterer (ed.), *Freundschaft bei Ben Sira*, 123–31.

Sauer, Georg, *Jesus Sirach* (JSHRZ III/5; Gütersloh, Gerd Mohn, 1981) 481–644.

Sauer, Georg, "Weisheit und Torah in qumranischer Zeit," in B. Janowski (ed.), *Weisheit ausserhalb der kanonischen Weistheitsschriften* (Gütersloh: Kaiser, 1996) 107–27.

Savigni, Raffaele, "L'interpretazione dei libro sapienziali in Rabano Mauro: tradizione patristica e 'moderna tempora'," *Annali di Storia dell'Exegesi* 9 (1992) 557–87.

Sawyer, J.F.A., "Was Jeshua Ben Sira a Priest?," in *World Union of Jewish Studies, Proceedings of the Eighth World Congress of Jewish Studies, Jerusalem, August 16–21, 1981*, (Jerusalem, 1982) 65–71.

Scheiber, Alexander, "A New Leaf of the Fourth Manuscript of the Ben Sira from the Geniza," with 8 plates. *Magyar Könyvszemle* 98 (1982) 179–85.

Schiffman, Lawrence H., "The Dead Sea Scrolls and the Early History of the Jewish Liturgy," in L.I. Levine (ed.), *The Synagogue in Late Antiquity* (Philadelphia, 1986) 33–48.

Schiffman, Lawrence H., *Texts and Traditions. A Source Reader for the Study of Second Temple and Rabbinic Judaism* (New York: KTAV, 1998).

Schnabel, E.J., *Law and Wisdom from Ben Sira to Paul: A Traditional Historical Enquiry into the Relation of Law* (WUNT 2/16; Tübingen: Mohr, 1985).

Schrader, Lutz, *Leiden und Gerechtigkeit — Untersuchungen zu Theologie und Textgeschichte des Sirachbuches*, Diss. Kiel, 1993.

Schrader, Lutz, *Leiden und Gerechtigkeit. Studien zu Theologie und Textgeschichte des Sirachbuches* (BET 27; Frankfurt am Main: Peter Lang, 1994).

Schrader, Lutz, "Unzuverlässige Freundschaft und verläßliche Feindschaft. Überlegungen zu Sir 12,8–12," in F. Reiterer (ed.), *Freundschaft bei Ben Sira*, 19–59.

Schroer, Silvia, "Die Zweiggöttin in Palästina/Israel: Von der Mittelbronze II B-Zeit bis zu Jesus Sirach," in Max K chler; Christoph Uehlinger (eds.), *Jerusalem. Texte-Bilder-Steine* (NTOA 6; Freiburg-Göttingen: Univeritätsverlag-Vandenhoeck & Ruprecht, 1987) 201–25.

Schürer, Emil, *The History of the Jewish People in the Age of Jesus Christ. A New English Edition*. Revised and Edited by G. Vermes, F. Millar and M. Goodman, III/1 (Edinburgh, 1986) 198–212.

Schwantes, Milton, *Das Recht der Armen* (BET 4; Frankfurt am Main: Peter Lang, 1977).

Schwartz, Daniel R., "On Sacrifice by Gentiles in the Temple of Jerusalem," in *Studies in the Jewish Background of Christianity* (WUNT 60; Tübingen: Mohr, 1992) 102–16.

Scott, R.B.Y., *The Way of Wisdom in the Old Testament* (New York: Macmillan, 1971).

Scott, R.B.Y., "Wisdom; Wisdom Literature," *EncJud* 4, 1971, 557–63.

Segal, M.S. , "Ben Sira, Wisdom of," *EncJud*, 4, 1971, 550–53.

Segal, M.S., ספר בן-סירה השלם (Jerusalem, 1972³).

Sheppard, G.T., "Wisdom and Torah: The Interpretation of Deuteronomy Underlying Sirach 24:23," in G.A. Tuttle (ed.), *Biblical and Near Eastern Studies* (Grand Rapids: Eerdmans,1978) 166–76.

Sheppard, G.T., *Wisdom as a Hermeneutical Construct* (BZAW 151; Berlin: de Gruyter, 1980).

Silva, David A. de, "The Wisdom of Ben Sira: Honor, Shame, and the Maintenance of Values of a Minority Culture," *CBQ* 58 (1996) 433–55.

Skehan, Patrick W., "Didache 1:6 and Sirach 12:1," in *Studies in Israelite Poetry and Wisdom*, 124–26.

Skehan, PatrickW., "Ecclesiasticus," *IDBSup*, (Nashville: Abingdon, 1976) 250–51.

Skehan, Patrick W., "Sirach 30:12 and Related Texts," *CBQ* 36 (1974) 535–42.

Skehan, Patrick W., "Sirach 40,11–17," *CBQ* 30 (1968) 570–72.

Skehan, Patrick W., "Staves, and Nails, and Scribal Slips (Ben Sira 44:2–5)," *BASOR* 200 (1970) 66–71.

Skehan, Patrick W., "Structures in Poems on Wisdom: Proverbs 8 and Sirach 24," *CBQ* 41 (1979) 365–79.

Skehan, Patrick W., *Studies in Israelite Poetry and Wisdom* (CBQMS 1; Washington: Catholic Biblical Association of America, 1971).

Skehan, Patrick W., "The Acrostic Poem in Sirach 51:13–30," *HTR* 64 (1971) 387–400.

Skehan, Patrick W., "The Divine Name at Qumran, in the Massada Scroll, and in the Septuagint," *BIOSCS* 13 (1980) 14–44.

Skehan, Patrick W., "They shall not be found in parables (Sir 38:33)," *CBQ* 23 (1961) 40.

Skehan, Patrick W., "Tower of Death or Deadly Snare? (Sir 26:22)," in *Studies in Israelite Poetry and Wisdom*, 127.

Skehan, Patrick W. and Alexander A. Di Lella, *The Wisdom of Ben Sira* (AncB 39; New York: Doubleday, 1987).

Smith, Michael, *The Wisdom Literature, Psalms and Wisdom* (Scripture Discussion Commentary 6; London, 1972) 109–248.

Snaith, J.G., "Ben Sira's Supposed Love of Liturgy," *VT* 25 (1975) 167–74.

Snaith, John G., "Biblical Quotations in the Hebrew of Ecclesiasticus," *JTS* 18 (1967) 1–12.

Snaith, John G., "Ecclesiasticus: a tract for the times," in J. Day (ed.), *Wisdom in Ancient Israel*, 170–81.

Snaith, J.G., *Ecclesiasticus or the Wisdom of Jesus Son of Sirach* (The Cambridge Bible Commentary of the New English Bible; Cambridge, 1974).

Soden, W. von, "Einige Beobachtungen zur ungleichen Häufigkeit wichtiger Begriffe in den Büchern Sprüche und Jesus Sirach," M. Dietrich and O. Loretz (eds.), *Mesopotamia — Ugaritica — Biblica* (AOAT 232; Neukirchener Verlag; Neukirchen-Vluyn, 1993) 419–25.

Soggin, J.A., *Introduction to the Old Testament: From Its Origins to the Closing of the Alexandrian Canon*, Revised Edition. Tr. J. Bowden (OTL; Philadelphia: Fortress, 1980).

Söding, Thomas, "Nächstenliebe bei Jesus Sirach," *BZ* 42 (1998) 239–47.

Stadelmann, Helge, *Ben Sira als Schriftgelehrter: Eine Untersuchung zum Berufsbild des vor-Makkabäischen Sofer unter Berücksichtigung seines Verhältnisses zu Priester-Propheten und Weisheitslehretum* (WUNT 2/6; Tübingen: Mohr, 1981).

Steck, Odil H., "Das Problem theologischer Strömungen in nachexilischer Zeit," *EvT* 28 (1968) 445–58.

Steck, Odil H., "Zu Eigenart und Herkunft von Psalm 102," *ZAW* 102 (1990) 357–72.

Steck, Odil H., "Zukunft des einzelnen — Zukunft des Gottesvolkes. Beobachtungen zur Annäherung von weisheitlichen und eschatologischen Lebensperspektiven im Israel der hellenistischen Zeit," in W. Richter *et al.* (eds), *Text, Methode und Grammatik* (St. Ottilien, 1991) 595–606.

Steck, Odil H., "Externe Indizien aus dem hebräischen Sirachbuch," in *Der Abschluß der Prophetie im Alten Testament. Ein Versuch zur Frage der Vorgeschichte des Kanons* (Biblisch-Theologische Studien 17; Neukirchen-Vluyn: Neukirchener Verlag, 1991) 136–44.

Stendebach, Franz J., "Weisheitliche Mahnung zu mitmenschlichem Verhalten. Eine Auslegung zu Sir 4,1–10," in U. Bail and R. Jost (eds.), *Gott and den Rändern: Sozialgeschichtliche Perspektiven aus die Bibel* (Gütersloh: Kaiser, 1996) 83–90.

Stöger, A., "Der Arzt nach Jesus Sirach (38,1–15)," *Arzt und Christ* 11 (1965) 3–11.

Stone, Michael E., "Apocryphal Notes and Readings," *Israel Oriental Studies* 1 (1971) 123–31.

Stramare, Tarcisio, "Il Libro dell'Ecclesiastico nella Neo-Volgata," *RivB* 27 (1979) 219–26.

Stroete, G.T., "Van Henoch tot Simon. Israels geschiedenis in de 'Lof der vaderen' van Sirach 44,1–50,24," in R. A. Hulst (ed.), *Vruchten van de uithof. FS-B.A. Brongers* (Utrecht, 1974) 120–33.

Strothmann, Werner, "Jesus-Sirach-Zitate bei Afrahat, Ephraem und im Liber Graduum," in R. H. Fischer (ed.), *Studies in Early Christian Literature and Its Environment*, (Chicago, 1977) 144–55.

Strothmann, Werner, *Johannes von Mosul, Bar Sira, Syräische Texte: Überzetzung und vollständiges Wortverzeichnis* (Göttingen Orientforschungen 1. Syriaca 19; Wiesbaden: Harrassowitz, 1979).

Strothmann, Werner, *Wörterverzeichnis der apokryphen-deuterokanonistischen Schriften des alten Testaments in der Peshitta* (1988).

Strotmann, Angelika, *Mein Vater bist du! (Sir 51,10). Zur Bedeutung der Vaterschaft Gottes in kanonischen und nichtkanonischen frühjüdischen Schriften* (Frankfurter Theologische Studien 39; Frankfurt a. Main: Knecht, 1991).

Strugnell, John, "Notes and Queries on 'The Ben Sira Scroll from Masada'," *ErIsr* 9 (1969) 109–119.

Strugnell, John, "'Of Cabbages and Kings' — or Queens: Notes on Ben Sira 36:18–21," in W.F. Stinespring (ed.), *The Use of the Old Testament in the New and other Essays*, 204–209.

Swidler, L. *Women in Judaism. The Status of Women in Formative Judaism* (Metuchen: Scarecrow, 1976).

Tapia Alder, Ramón, "La Sabiduria de Ben Siraj," *Cuadernos Judaicos* 13 (1984) 66–72.

The Book of Sirach, Annotated Critical Translation from the Original Languages by the Studium Biblicum Franciscanum (Tokyo, 1980) [Japanese].

The Old Testament in Syriac According to the Peshitta Version, edited on behalf of the International Organisation for the Study of the Old Testament by the Peshitta Institut Leiden (Leiden: Brill, 1976).

Thiele, Walter (ed.), *Sirach (Ecclesiasticus)* (Vetus Latina. Die Reste der altlateinischen Bibel, 11/II, 1–6 Lieferung; Freiburg: Herder, 1987–1996).

Thiele, Walter, "Zum Titel des Sirachbuches in der lateinischen Überlieferung," in R. Gribson et P.M. Bogaert (eds.), *Recherches sur l'histoire de la Bible Latine* (Louvain, 1987) 43–49.

Thomas, D.W., "A Note on Ecclus 51:21a," *JTS* 20 (1969) 225–26.

Toloni, Giancarlo, "Il significato di yesurûn nei profeti e negli agiographi: TM e versioni greche," *BeO* 37 (1995) 65–93.

Tomes, R., "A Father's Anxieties (Sirach 42:9–11)," in G.J. Mellen (ed.) *Women in the Biblical Tradition* (Lewiston, NY, 1992) 71–91.

Tournay, Raymond J., "Polémique antisamaritaine et le feu du Tofet," *RB* 104 (1997) 354–67.

Trebolle Barrera, Julio, La Biblia Judía y la Biblia Cristiana (Estructuras y Procesos; Madrid: Trotta, 1993).

Trenchard, W.C., *Ben Sira's View of Woman: A Literary Analysis* (BJS 38; Chico: Scholars Press, 1982).

Tromp, N. *Primitive Conceptions of Death and the Nether World in the Old Testament* (BibOr 21; Rome: Editrice Pontificio Istituto Biblico, 1969).

Tromp, N., "Jesus Ben Sira en het offer: Proeve van een portret," *Bijdragen* 34 (1973) 250–66.

Trublet, J., "Constitution et clôture du canon hébraïque," in C. Théobald (ed.), *Le canon des Écritures* (Lectio Divina 140; Paris: Cerf, 1990) 77–187.

Vattioni, Francesco, *Ecclesiastico. Testo hebraico con apparato critico e versioni greca, latina e siriaca* (Testi 1; Napoli: Istituto Orientali di Napoli, 1968).

Vattioni, Francesco, "Il sacrificio dei fanciulli in Sir 34 (31)24," in F. Vattioni (ed.), *Atti della Settimana. Sangue e antropologia biblica nella patristica (Roma, 157–160., 23–28 novembre 1981)* (Rome, 1982).

Vattioni, Freancesco, "San Girolamo e l'Ecclesiastico," *Vetera Christianorum* 4 (1967) 131–49.

Vawter, B., *The Book of Sirach with a Commentary* (Pamphlet Bible Series 40–41; New York, 1962).

Vella, J., *Ecclesiástico. La Sagrada Escritura, Texto y commentario*, Antiguo Testamento V (BAC 312; Madrid: Biblioteca de Autores Cristianos, 1970) 3–218.

Veltri, Giuseppe, "Zur traditionsgeschichtlichen Entwicklung des Bewußtseins von einem Kanon: Die Yavneh-Frage," *JSJ* 21 (1990) 210–25.

Vian, Giovanni Maria, "Ancora sull'antologia esegetica dai Salmi del Laudiano greco 42," *Annali di Storia dell'Esegesi* 8 (1991) 589–97.

Vignolo, R., "'Che cos'è l'uomo, Signore?' III. Le riflessione del Siracide (18,7–11) e della Lettera agli Ebrei (2,5–18)," *Rivista del Clero Italiano* 77 (1996) 588–602.

Vinel, F. (ed.) *Grégoire de Nysse. Homélies sur l'Ecclésiastique*. Texte grec de l'édition P. Alexander. Introduction, traduction, notes et index par F. Vinel (Sources Chrétiennes 416; Paris: Cerf, 1996).

Vogt, Ernst, "Die Bankettschüssel und der Rat von Sir 31,14," *Bib* 48 (1967) 72–74.

Wahl, O., *Der Sirach-Test der Sacra Parallela* (Forschung zur Bibel 16; Würzburg, 1974).

Watson, Wilfrid, "Reclustering Hebrew *l·yd*," *Biblica* 58 (1977) 213–14.

Weber, Kathleen, "Wisdom False and True (Sir 19,20–30)," *Bib* 77 (1996) 330–48.

Weber, R.-B. Fischer (eds.), "Sirach seu Ecclesiasticus," in *Biblia Sacra iuxta vulgatam versionem. Editio tertia emendata*. Tomus II (Stuttgart: Deutsche Bibelgesellschaft, 1983) 1029–1095.

Weber, Thomas H., "Sirach," in R. Brown *et al.* (eds.), *The Jerome Bible Commentary* (Englewood: Prentice Hall, 1968) 541–55.

Weinfeld, Moshe, "Traces of Kedushat Yozer and Pesukey de Zimra in the Qumran Literature and in Ben-Sira," *Tarbiz* 45 (1975/6) 15–26 [Hebrew].

Westerman, C., *Roots of Wisdom* (Louisville: Westminster John Knox, 1995).

Whybray, R. *The Intellectual Tradition in the Old Testament* (BZAW 135) (De Gruyter: Berlin 1974.

Wieder, Arnold A., "Ben Sira and the Praises of Wine," *JQR* 61 (1970–71) 155–66.

Wilch, J., *Time and Event. An Exegetical Study of the Use of 'eth in the Old Testament in Comparison to Other Temporal Expressions in Clarification of the Concept of Time* (Leiden: Brill, 1969).

Winston, David S., "Freedom and Determinism in Greek Philosophy and Jewish Hellenistic Wisdom," *Studia Philonica* 2 (1973) 40–50.

Winston, David S., "Theodicy in Ben Sira and Stoic Philosophy," in R. Link-Salinger (ed.), *Of Scholars, Savants, and Their Texts* (New York: Lang, 1989) 239–49.

Winter, Michael M., *A Concordance to the Peshitta Version of Ben Sira* (Monographs of the Peshitta Institut Leiden 2; Leiden: Brill, 1976).

Winter, Michael. M., *Ben Sira in Syriac*, Diss. Fribourg 1975.

Winter, Michael M., "Ben Sira in Syriac. An Ebionite Translation?," in E.A. Livingstone (ed.), *Studia Patristica XVI. Papers Presented to the Seventh International Conference on Patristic Studies Held in Oxford 1975* (Oxford, 1984) 121–26.

Winter, Michael M., "The Origins of Ben Sira in Syriac (Part I)," *VT* 27 (1997) 237–53.

Winter, Michael M., "The Origins of Ben Sira in Syriac (Part II)," *VT* 27 (1997) 494–507.

Wischmeyer, Oda, *Die Kultur des Buches Jesus Sirach* (BZNW 77; Berlin: de Gruyter, 1995).

Wlosinski, M., "Implikacje teologiczne Syr 17,1–14," *Ruch Biblijny i Liturgiczny* 34 (1981) 163–73.

Wood, J., *Wisdom Literature* (Studies in Theology; London: Duckworth, 1967).

Wright, Benjamin G., "Ben Sira 43:11b — 'To What Does the Greek Correspond?'," *Textus* 13 (1986) 111–16.

Wright, Benjamin G., "'Fear the Lord and Honor the Priest': Ben Sira as Defender of the Jerusalem Priesthood," in P.C. Beentjes (ed.), *The Book of Ben Sira in Modern Research*, 189–222.

Wright, Benjamin G., *New Approaches to the Greek Vocabulary and Translation Technique in the Wisdom of Jesus Ben Sira*, Diss. University of Pennsylvania 1990.

Wright, Benjamin G., *No Small Difference. Sirach's Relationship to Its Hebrew Parent Text* (SCS 26; Atlanta: Scholars Press, 1989).

Wright, Benjamin G., "Putting the Puzzle Together: Some Suggestions Concerning the Social Location of the Wisdom of Ben Sira, in *SBL 1996 Seminar Papers*, 133–49.

Wright, Robert B. and R.R. Hann, "A New Fragment of the Greek Text of Sirach," *JBL* 94 (1975) 111–12.

Yadin, Y., "מגילת בן־סירה שנתגלתה במצדה," *ErIsr* 8 (1965) 1–45.

Yadin, Yigael, *The Ben Sira Scroll from Masada. With Introduction, Emmendations and Commentary* (Jerusalem: Israel Exploration Society, The Shrine of the Book, 1965).

Yifrach, Esther, "The Construct Infinitive in the Language of Ben Sira," *Leshonenu* 59 (1996) 275–94.

Zapella, Marco, "L'immagine di Israele in Sir 33 (36),1–19 secondo il ms. ebraico B e la tradizione manoscritta greca. Analisi letteraria e lessicale," *RivB* 42 (1994) 409–46.

Zappella, Marco, "Criteri antologici e questioni testuali del manoscritto ebraico C di Siracide," *RivB* 38 (1990) 273–300.

Zatelli, Ida, "Yir'at JHWH nella Bibbia, in Ben Sira e nei rotoli di Qumran: considerazioni sintattico-semantiche," *RivB* 36 (1988) 229–37.

Zeitlin, Solomon, "The Ben Sira Scroll from Masada," *JQR* 56 (1965/66) 185–90.

Zerbe, Gordon M., *Non-Retaliation in Early Jewish and New Testament Texts. Ethical Themes in Social Contexts* (JSPSup 13; Sheffield: Sheffield Academic Press, 1993) 39–44.

Ziegler, Joseph, *Sapientia Jesu Filii Sirach* (Septuaginta. Vetus Testamentum Graecum auctoritate Societatis Litterarum Gottingensis editum XII,2; Göttingen: Vandenhoeck & Ruprecht, 1965).

Ziegler, Joseph, *Sylloge. Gesammelte Aufsätze zur Septuaginta* (MSU 10; Göttingen: Vandenhoeck & Ruprecht, 1971).

Zincone, S., "Dio e la disiguaglianza sociale: l'esegesi crisostomiana di Agg. 2,8; Prov. 22,2; Sir. 11,14," *Augustinianum* 17 (1977) 209–19.